SERIAL KILLERS

SERIAL KILLERS

The Method and Madness of Monsters

PETER VRONSKY

BERKLEY BOOKS, NEW YORK

THE BERKLEY PUBLISHING GROUP
Published by the Penguin Group
Penguin Group (USA) Inc.
375 Hudson Street, New York, New York 10014, USA
Penguin Group (Canada), 90 Eglinton Avenue East, Suite 700, Toronto, Ontario M4P 2Y3, Canada
(a division of Pearson Penguin Canada Inc.)
Penguin Books Ltd., 80 Strand, London WC2R 0RL, England
Penguin Group Ireland, 25 St. Stephen's Green, Dublin 2, Ireland (a division of Penguin Books Ltd.)
Penguin Group (Australia), 250 Camberwell Road, Camberwell, Victoria 3124, Australia
(a division of Pearson Australia Group Pty. Ltd.)
Penguin Books India Pvt. Ltd., 11 Community Centre, Panchsheel Park, New Delhi—110 017, India
Penguin Group (NZ), 67 Apollo Drive, Rosedale, North Shore 0632, New Zealand
(a division of Pearson New Zealand Ltd.)
Penguin Books (South Africa) (Pty.) Ltd., 24 Sturdee Avenue, Rosebank, Johannesburg 2196,
South Africa

Penguin Books Ltd., Registered Offices: 80 Strand, London WC2R 0RL, England

This book is an original publication of The Berkley Publishing Group.

The publisher does not have any control over and does not assume any responsibility for author or third-party websites or their content.

Copyright © 2004 by Peter Vronsky.
Cover design by Jill Boltin.
Interior text design by Kristin del Rosario.

PRINTING HISTORY
Berkley trade paperback edition / October 2004

Library of Congress Cataloging-in-Publication Data

Vronsky, Peter.
        Serial killers : the method and madness of monsters / Peter Vronsky.
                p. cm.
        Includes bibliographical references and index.
        ISBN: 978-0-425-19640-3
            1. Serial murderers—Psychology. 2. Serial murders—Case studies. 3. Psychology,
        Pathological. I. Title.

        HV6515.V76 2004
        364.152'3'019—dc22

PRINTED IN THE UNITED STATES OF AMERICA

30   29   28   27

For my wife, Anna,
and
my daughters,
Quantel and Alisa

Contents

PART THREE ▪ **FIGHTING MONSTERS**

MY TWO SERIAL KILLERS

Serial killers know *they're invisible.*
—ROBERT D. KEPPEL, criminal investigator

I have a problem with women.
—RICHARD COTTINGHAM, The Times Square Torso Ripper

I am not a highly educated expert on serial killers. I was never an FBI profiler, a police officer, a criminologist, or a forensic psychologist. I did not write a college thesis about them and I never interviewed incarcerated serial killers or exchanged letters with any. I never bought their art or collected their memorabilia. In other words, I am probably a lot like you: a curious amateur. Other than reading about them and seeing them on TV, my only experience with serial killers is my two brief personal encounters with them before they were identified and captured. You might think *that* is what makes me different from you—but don't be too hasty in your conclusion.

In my travels I randomly bumped into two notorious "rippers": Richard Cottingham, the Times Square Torso Ripper, who was eventually linked to five torture dismemberment murders in New York and New Jersey, and Andrei Chikatilo, the Red Ripper, whom I briefly met in Russia just days before he committed the last three of his more than fifty cannibalistic murders of women, youths, and children. In both cases I did not know until much later whom it was I had encountered. My run-in with Cottingham was as dramatic as my meeting with Chikatilo was banal and forgettable.

I bumped into Richard Cottingham for about ten seconds one early Sunday morning in New York City in December 1979. I was working as a production assistant on a movie being shot in Toronto. My job was to fly out to New York every few days and personally deliver our exposed film for a special type of processing at a laboratory located near the Times Square area. It was a great gig: I would fly into New York in the morning and quickly drop off the film, and then I was on my own until it was ready for pick up the next day.

Usually I would be handed an airline ticket and an envelope of cash, and I was expected to arrange my own hotel and meals. Film crews routinely stayed at good business-class hotels—Sheraton, Hilton, and so on—and I'd be given enough cash to stay and eat in those kinds of places. Young, punkish, having backpacked to New York previously and slept on the floor of CBGB's on the Bowery and fed myself on cheese and wine by attending gallery openings, I couldn't care less about upscale accommodations. I was content to routinely book cheap tourist-class hotel rooms on my film deliveries. I would spend the cash I saved on clubbing, record albums, books, and electronics. But on one such trip I went too far.

An unforeseen technical delay at the lab forced me to stay an entire weekend in New York. In order to stretch out my expense cash for the extra unexpected nights, I decided to check into a really marginal hotel on the last day. Early on a Sunday morning, I walked over to a nondescript medium-sized hotel on West 42nd Street, about two blocks from the Hudson River near the collapsed husks of the West Side Highway. Offering bargain rates, the hotel was located near nothing—no convenient subway station, no tourist sites, no office buildings—in what was at that time a derelict neighborhood around Tenth Avenue deserving of its historical name, Hell's Kitchen. The hotel was even inconvenient for the junkies and hookers who hung out in *Taxi Driver* country a few blocks west on what was then called the forty-deuce—a sleazy stretch of West 42nd Street lined with porn shops, live sex shows, and knife stores that ran from Broadway and past the bus terminal toward Eighth and Ninth Avenues. The hotel had bargain rates but for the price it appeared to be clean and secure enough, and within quick walking distance of the film lab I would have to go to early the next morning.

I showed up without a reservation and was told that a room would be ready for me shortly if I would wait about half an hour, as people were checking out. I decided that in the meantime I would go up and wander around a few floors just to see how bad the place might really be. As I waited at the elevator, I was mildly annoyed to see that it had stopped for what seemed an eternity on the top floor. Finally the stalled elevator began to come down, and when the doors opened, presumably the jerk who had held the elevator on the upper floor got off. He almost walked over me like some kind of glassy-eyed zombie, looking right through me and brushing me aside as if I were not there. As he passed me by heading into the lobby he lightly bumped my leg with a bag or a suitcase or something. I never noticed what exactly he carried, nor could I today describe the feel of it against my leg. The only other thing I would later remember was that he seemed to glow with a thin sheen of perspiration and he had this really bad moplike haircut. He appeared to be in his midthirties with sandy-colored hair and looked like a junior pasty-faced office worker—which was precisely what he turned out to be later (although he was described by other witnesses as having an "olive" complexion). By the time the elevator doors closed behind me, I had forgotten all about him.

I took the elevator up and got off on one of the floors at random. I immediately noticed a faint but distinct odor of something burning, but I did not see any smoke and thought it was the natural smell of the hotel. As I walked around the halls I did not detect anything particularly nasty about the place, but I did notice the smell getting stronger, and now with an unmistakable underlying back-odor of burnt chicken feathers or hair. I did not know it at the time, but that was the smell of roasting human flesh.

In the corridor my eyes were drawn to several elusively small, dark, greasy slivers of sooty substances floating and circulating in the air like tiny black snowflakes. When I caught one, it stained my fingers black. As I moved along the hall it seemed to get lightly misty and the smell was now unquestionably that of a building fire—that kind of woody-paint burning smell. I heard all sorts of commotion and shouting in the stairwells and fire alarms began ringing. I quickly made my way down to the lobby, emerging just as the fire department was pulling up in the street outside. All this gave me a bad vibe about the place (to say the least) and I left almost immediately to seek out another hotel without a glance backward.

The next morning I read in the newspapers that firemen responding to flames in one of the rooms of the hotel had discovered the corpses of two murdered women laid out on twin beds that had been set on fire. A firefighter had dragged one of the women out of the smoky room into the hallway and attempted to give her mouth-to-mouth resuscitation only to discover that she had no head or hands. At first he thought it was a mannequin. A fifteen-year veteran of the NYFD, the firefighter said he nearly had to undergo trauma counseling afterwards: "I've never come across something like that. I hope I never do again."[1]

The victims' clothing was found folded in the bathtub in two neat stacks with their platform shoes on top of each pile. Except for blood on the mattresses, the hotel room was remarkably free of any bloodstains, fingerprints, or any other evidence. Whatever the killer used to dismember the bodies, he took it with him. In addition to the mutilation, the bodies showed signs of horrific torture—cigarette burns, beatings, and bite marks around the breasts.

At the time I never made the connection with the man I bumped into at the elevator. I did not even remember him. Somehow my wandering around the hotel in the black floating flakes, the fire alarm going off, and finding the fire engines outside all overwhelmed the minor memory of him. He came to me only later when Richard Cottingham was arrested and tried for the mutilation murders of young women, mostly prostitutes in New York and New Jersey, including the two victims at the hotel. Seeing his picture in the paper, I immediately recognized him: the bad haircut and pasty face.

Since then I always assumed that when he stepped by me in the elevator that Sunday morning, he must have been carrying the severed heads and hands with him. I could not imagine him taking the risk of leaving two headless corpses unattended in the hotel room to go out and dump the heads and hands and then return to set fire to the room. Whatever he had transported the heads in, it must have been what he brushed my leg with as he stepped by me in the elevator doors. (On the other hand, did he kill one woman and leave her body in the room, then go out to seek out another, or were they both alive together before he killed them? Cottingham never said.)

Richard Francis Cottingham, age thirty-four, I learned, was the recently separated father of three children and lived in suburban New Jersey. Neighbors typically described him as aloof and private but a doting father who always took his children out trick-or-treating on Halloween. The son of an insurance industry executive, a high school athlete but nonetheless a lonely boy, Richard had been steadily employed for the last sixteen years as a computer operator at Empire State Blue Cross–Blue Shield insurance company on Third Avenue in midtown Manhattan. He was a valued and dependable employee. Choosing the 3:00–11:00 P.M. shift, he would do his killing in the morning, after work at night, or on the weekends.

The heads and hands from the victims in the Times Square hotel were never found despite an extensive search by police of the river area nearby. One victim was identified through hospital X rays as Kuwaiti-born Deedah Godzari, a twenty-three-year-old prostitute from New Jersey and mother of a four-month baby. The other victim, estimated to be in her late teens, remains unidentified to this day.

Six months later, Cottingham killed and mutilated another New York prostitute, twenty-five-year-old Jean Mary Ann Reyner. She was found in the historic but declined Seville Hotel on 29th Street near Madison Avenue. This time he severed the victim's breasts and set them down side by side on the headboard of the bed before setting fire to the room.

Cottingham actually preferred to do his thing closer to home in New Jersey. He would either pick up his victims on the streets of Manhattan or meet them in bars. Either way, he would buy them drinks or dinner and slip a date rape–type drug into their glass. He then would maneuver or lure the semiconscious victims to his car and drive them across the river to New Jersey to cheap motels that lined the complex of highways there. He carried them in through motel back doors and then molested and tortured them in his room for extended periods of time. The lucky ones would later awake from the effects of the drug finding themselves raped and sodomized and covered with horrific wounds, dumped naked by a roadside or on the floor of a motel room with little memory of what had transpired. They were alive because Cottingham was a particular type of serial killer—an *anger-excitation* or *sadistic-lust* offender. Cottingham did not derive his pleasure from killing, but from torturing the victim. He couldn't care less whether the victim lived or died once he was finished with his torture—and if the victim did die during the attack before Cottingham was satisfied, he would continue abusing the corpse until satisfied. Once done, he would abandon the victim like "trash," and whether she was dead or alive was inconsequential to him. Some victims were lucky to survive, but others were not.

The body of nineteen-year-old Valerie Ann Street was found in a Hasbrouck Heights Quality Inn in New Jersey by housekeeping staff. A cleaning woman was attempting to vacuum the floor under the bed but something was jammed under it. Lifting up the mattress, she found a hideously disfigured corpse stuffed underneath the bed. The victim's hands were tightly handcuffed behind her back; she was covered in bite marks and was beaten across the shins. Valerie Street had died of asphyxiation and traces of adhesive tape were found on her mouth. Cottingham had carefully taken it away with him after killing the girl. He must have lost the key to the handcuffs, as he left them behind still restraining the victim—a fatal mistake, as police would lift his fingerprint from the inner ratchet of the cuffs.

One of the victims was not a prostitute. Twenty-six-year-old radiologist Mary Ann Carr had been found dumped by a chain-link fence near the parking lot of the same New Jersey motel two years previously. She had been cut about the chest and legs, beaten with a blunt instrument, and covered in bites and bruises. Her wrists showed marks from handcuffs and her mouth had traces of adhesive tape. She had been strangled and suffocated by the adhesive tape.

Cottingham was arrested on May 22, 1980, about six months after my encounter with him. He had picked up eighteen-year-old Leslie Ann O'Dell, who was soliciting on the corner of Lexington Avenue and 25th Street. She had arrived in New York on a bus from Washington State four days earlier and was quickly turned to street prostitution by bus station pimps. Cottingham bought her drinks and talked to her about his job and house in the suburbs until about 3:00 A.M. He then offered to take her to a bus terminal in New Jersey so that she could escape the pimps in New York. Leslie appreciatively accepted. After crossing the George Washington Bridge into New Jersey, he bought her a steak at an all-night diner. He was charming, generous, sympathetic, and helpful. At some point she agreed to have sex with him for $100. It was around dawn when they checked into the very same Hasbrouck Heights Quality Inn where he had left his last mutilated victim stuffed under the bed eighteen days earlier. Nobody recognized Cottingham.

After getting a room, Cottingham drove to the back of the motel and they went in through a rear entrance. Leaving the girl in the room alone, Cottingham returned to his car, telling her he wanted to move it to the front. He came back carrying a paper bag with whiskey and an attaché case. It was now nearly 5:00 A.M.

Cottingham offered to give the tired girl a massage and she gratefully rolled over onto her stomach. Straddling her back, he drew a knife from the attaché case and put it to her throat as he snapped a pair of handcuffs on her wrists. While Leslie attempted to persuade Cottingham that all that was unnecessary, he began torturing her, nearly biting off one of her nipples. She later testified that he said, "You have to take it. The other girls did, you have to take it too. You're a whore and you have to be punished."

The charges that would be listed in Cottingham's New Jersey indictment give us some idea of how the next four hours passed for O'Dell:

Kidnapping, attempted murder, aggravated assault, aggravated assault with deadly weapon, aggravated sexual assault while armed (rape), aggravated sexual assault while armed (sodomy), aggravated sexual assault while armed (fellatio), possession of a weapon; possession of controlled dangerous substances, Secobarbital and Amobarbital, or Tuinal, and possession of controlled dangerous substance, Diazepam or Valium.

Between bouts of rape, sodomy, forced oral sex, biting, beating, cutting with the knife, and whipping with a leather belt, Cottingham would pause to gently wipe down the face of his victim with a cool, damp washcloth. Then he would begin anew. O'Dell's muffled cries of pain became so loud that the motel staff, already spooked by the murder eighteen days earlier, called the police and then rushed to the room demanding that Cottingham open the door. Cottingham gathered up his torture implements and dashed out of the room but was apprehended by arriving police officers in the hallway.

That was the end of Cottingham. For his crimes in New Jersey, he received several terms ranging from sixty to ninety-five years, a term of twenty-five years to life, and another term to run consecutively of a minimum of thirty years. And then he was extradited to New York to stand trial for the "torso" homicides there. We won't be seeing Richard again.

Cottingham denied committing any of the murders to the bitter end, despite the fact that some of the victims' property was found in his home and his fingerprint was found on the handcuffs restraining one of the victims. The only thing Cottingham admitted was, "I have a problem with women."

My brief run-in with Cottingham was a hell of a story and I told it for a long time, long after had I met, but did not know it, yet another serial killer—one for the record books, the Ukrainian cannibal Andrei Chikatilo, who killed and mutilated an extraordinary fifty-three victims in the Soviet Union.

In 1990 I was making television documentaries, and in October of that year I found myself in Moscow making a film about the changes taking place there under Gorbachev. One day we came upon an extraordinary sight. A tent city with about five hundred people had been spontaneously erected on the front lawn of a hotel immediately behind the Red Square beneath the domes of St. Basil's Cathedral. The residents seemed to have come in from all parts of the country and were mostly aged pensioners protesting Stalinist abuses of the past. They had bizarre placards attached to their tents and shelters. Some pasted to their foreheads little slips of paper with protests with strange things written in broken archaic English, such as "Lenin is bonehead." Others held up placards with elaborately laid-out documents, letters, and photographs documenting their complaints. I waded into the crowd with my crew and started speaking with some of the people, seeking out possible interviews to film. It seemed that almost everybody there was somehow traumatized and mentally ill, and considering what had happened to them during the Stalin era, it was understandable.

At some point I spotted a small stand decorated with the white, blue, and red of the old Imperial Russian tricolor flag. In 1990 it was still a rare thing to see those colors in the USSR. It belonged to a gaunt man with graying hair and big glasses. His other features I cannot recall, other than his being closely shaved and dressed relatively well (for the USSR) in a mid-length jacket, clean shirt, and neatly knotted tie. He looked to be maybe in his late forties or early fifties and stood out with his neat dress and younger age when compared to the many raggedy-scruffy bearded Russian pensioners occupying the tent city around him. There was something refined about him—perhaps delicate or prissy. Next to him was a typical battered leather briefcase like those that almost every Soviet bureaucrat and office worker carried.

He introduced himself, but later I forgot his name and where he said he came from. At first he spoke quietly, calmly, and in a highly educated manner. The few phrases he attempted in English were well pronounced and grammatical. He reminded me of a librarian. He explained that he held several university degrees and was "not like" the rest of the rabble around him. As his story began to pour out, he gradually was overcome with emotion; his eyes welled up with tears and his glasses actually fogged up. But his story was so absurd that I would never forget it: He was here in Moscow, he told me, to see Gorbachev to complain that somebody was building an illegal garage and toilet beneath the windows of his son's apartment. *It was a conspiracy*, he wailed.

I had just interviewed an old woman a few rows away who had told me she was dying of cancer and fifty years earlier had been arrested and put in the gulag while her children were sent to a state institution. She had not seen them since and was desperate to find them before she died, but the authorities were not helping. This neatly dressed man's prissy complaints about some garage seemed to me petty and stupid in comparison—and worse: boring television. Searching for somebody else to interview, I drifted away from him as fast as I politely could, not even listening to the last few things he had to say, and quickly forgot all about him. That is how I missed filming an interview with Andrei Romanovich Chikatilo—the Red Ripper—"Citizen X"—three weeks before his capture—one of the most prolific serial killers in modern history.

While Cottingham I remembered, I forgot everything about Chikatilo other than the neatness of his dress and the banality of his complaint. I do not remember his eyes, other than the tears in them and the fogged veil of the lenses in his glasses; nothing of his face other than it was clean shaven. He remains but a softly spoken shadowy politeness in my memory—but in my nightmares, he stills comes to me as a monstrous geek with eyeless sockets spewing tears.

Within days of my brief conversation with him in Moscow, he would return to his home in Rostov in the Ukraine to kill his fifty-first known victim. Riding on a local train, he convinced a sixteen-year-old mentally handicapped boy to accompany him to his "cottage" with the promise that there were girls there. The two got off the train and Chikatilo walked the boy into a dense wood, where he suddenly forced him to the ground and ripped off his trousers. He tied the boy with a rope that he carried with him in his briefcase just for that kind of occasion and then rolled him over and removed the rest of his clothes. (Was it the same briefcase I saw that day in the tent city?) He molested him and then bit off the tip of the boy's tongue and stabbed him repeatedly in the head and stomach. Afterward he cut off the boy's genitals and threw them into the bushes. After dragging the body into some thick undergrowth he recovered the rope and wiped the blood off himself and his knife with the boy's clothes. He straightened out his own clothing (and was it the same shirt and tie I saw him in?) and then calmly returned to the nearby railway station and took the train home.

Ten days later at a different railway station, Chikatilo killed another sixteen-year-old boy, mutilating him in a similar fashion, his fifty-second victim. A week later, behind the same station where he killed the mentally handicapped youth, he murdered his fifty-third and final victim, a twenty-two-year-old woman. He cut off the tip of her tongue and both her nipples after mutilating her genitals. After he emerged from the bush with blood smeared on his face, he was washing up at a platform water tap when a police officer, on the lookout for a killer, briefly questioned Chikatilo and recorded his identification. He was allowed to continue on his way—the police officer later stated that he had no way of determining that the smear on Chikatilo's face was actually blood. Gorbachev's new rules strictly regulated police conduct toward citizens—everything was to be done by the book now. The police officer let Chikatilo go, but for the next few days he was put under surveillance. When the body of the female victim was eventually discovered near the station where he was questioned, Chikatilo was immediately picked up.

The following year I watched the Chikatilo trial on Russian television and saw photographs of him. Chikatilo had killed women, girls, boys, and youths indiscriminately, almost always luring them either to a killing shack he kept in a seedy part of town or to isolated fields or woods. He used his refined and educated persona to seduce his victims into trusting him. Often preying on the destitute, the mentally handicapped, the lost, and the young, he offered food, sex, shelter, or directions to entice his victims to accompany him to their deaths. Once he had his victims isolated, he would brutally attack and mutilate them using a "killing kit" of various knives and sharp instruments he carried with him in his briefcase.

By the time the trial began, Chikatilo's head was shaved and he appeared quite mad, howling at the courtroom spectators from within a specially built cage. But even seeing the earlier photographs of him in the press, I never recognized him from that day I met him in the Moscow tent city. I still occasionally told my Richard Cottingham story, never realizing what punchline lurked beyond it. It was only years later that I came across a transcript of Chikatilo's police interrogation in which he complained about the conspiratorial attempt to build a garage and toilet behind his son's apartment and his intention to meet with Gorbachev in Moscow. I was transfixed in horror—could it possibly be the same guy? It *had to be*—the story was just too eccentric, and even the Russian investigator remarked on Chikatilo's emotional peaks when he began to speak of the garage. Indeed, after some further research I uncovered an account of Chikatilo's visit to Moscow in October 1990 just before he committed his last three murders.[2]

I came to realize that in my life I had met not one, but *two* serial killers—unidentified and out there killing—and for the longest time I had not even known it. How many more could there be? And where the hell were they coming from?

I was puzzled by the conventional backgrounds of these two killers— both gainfully employed family men: Cottingham, a New York City computer operator with a house and three kids in the suburbs; and Chikatilo, a university-educated schoolteacher, father of two children, writer of political essays for Soviet publications, and, later, factory materials purchaser. These two were not grizzled glassy-eyed drifters or twitchy recluses—types we frequently associate with serial killers. They were ordinary.

Most of all, I was fascinated with their invisibility—their forgettability. Apparently they stalked and killed like evil transparent ghosts. Even when I had run into Cottingham, presumably carrying two severed heads and having just set fire to a hotel I was checking into, I would forget him within seconds of the encounter. Cottingham was so forgettable that after leaving behind a mutilated corpse under a motel bed, he checked back into the very *same* motel a mere eighteen days later, and nobody recognized him.

Of Chikatilo himself, I still have no memory—just that of his ridiculous story and fragmentary glimpses of the monster: glasses, the knot of his tie, a clean-shaven cheek, a briefcase lying in the grass by his feet—but of *him* . . . nothing. This invisibility let him kill fifty-three people and almost walk away untouched, with blood on his face, from a police officer looking for him. What manner of ghoulish monsters were these?

All of this led me to contemplate how Cottingham and Chikatilo came to exist—where had they sprung from and by what means and paths did they move about for me to so randomly stumble across these *two* homicidal monsters, roaming free in the wild among us?

In my attempt to map the primordial substance from which they rose, I came to write this book, and in a way, map my own substance as well. Was there something about me that led me to cross their paths? I learned that many victims of serial killers "facilitate" their own deaths by their choice of lifestyle or behavior—hitchhikers, runaways, street hookers. While not a victim, I perhaps facilitated my meeting with Cottingham by my choice of hotels near a hookers' stroll. I strayed into a serial killer's hunting grounds as a trespasser and got a bump from a monster.

While my Cottingham encounter in New York was one of those experiences that one can easily write off as coincidence, my second encounter with a serial killer made me wonder. I questioned the mathematical odds of running into *two* killers in that manner. One killer I could easily understand, but *two* made me ask, *how many more* might there be out there that I did not know about? I wondered what the odds were of walking by a serial killer without ever finding out about it—on the street, waiting in line for a burger, browsing for books in a true-crime section, or sitting next to one on a train or bus? I shuddered when I heard somebody explain that serial killers might be strangers—but only to you. They become very familiar with you if they pick you as their target—you are no stranger to them.

It seemed to me that millions of people move about their daily lives without meeting a serial killer—or at least, without *finding out* they had met one. Perhaps *that* is precisely what makes me different from you—that I have uncovered the transparent monsters who had tramped across my path—*my* serial killers—while you perhaps have not uncovered *yours*. I pray you never will.

PART ONE

A HISTORY OF MONSTERS

ONE

THE POSTMODERN AGE OF SERIAL HOMICIDE, 1970–2000:

The Silence of the "Less-Dead"

All creatures kill—there seems to be no exception.
But of the whole list man is the only one that kills for fun . . .
—MARK TWAIN

Every society gets the kind of criminal it deserves.
—ROBERT F. KENNEDY[3]

The Postmodern Serial Killer

He was a handsome, athletic, well-spoken young man. He was unfailingly polite and popular, and appeared caring and concerned to those in his proximity. He was educated, sophisticated, and well mannered, a graduate with a university degree in psychology. He had plenty of friends of different ages and romantic relationships with women. Many other women considered him their trusted friend and confidant. An elderly woman he befriended described him as a "lovable rascal." Another woman, a former police officer who would become America's leading true-crime writer and who coincidentally knew him, described him as having "old-world gallantry." He had worked as a suicide counselor at a phone-in crisis clinic and had been recently admitted into law school in Seattle. The state government hired him as a crime-control consultant and he even wrote a rape-prevention handbook for women. He was a hardworking volunteer for the Republican Party, an often-invited dinner guest, and a popular date, and was considered by his elders as somebody worth grooming for a possible future as state governor, perhaps even president. He was a necrophiliac who kidnapped, murdered, raped, and mutilated, in that order, twenty college-age women over a period of sixteen months. At one point he kept four of their heads in his apartment. He burned the head of another in his girlfriend's fireplace.[4] His name was Theodore "Ted" Bundy.

It is bitterly said that Bundy is our first "postmodern" serial killer. He came at the right time to be that—we would have first heard of him at the end of the 1970s. Back then, we the public did not use the term *serial killer,* nor had we such a concept in mind despite the fact that such a thing was on the increase and was being puzzled over by experts and police.

Yes, we knew that more people were being murdered. We had *felt* it since that Friday afternoon in November 1963 when JFK was assassinated in Dallas. Those of us who were children then remember how all the cartoon TV shows were preempted that afternoon and remained off the air until the next week. The only thing to see on the tube for the first three days were lots of shaken and frightened people. On the third day they put somebody on live TV and showed *him* being shot dead. Then they broadcast it over and over in replay. If Bert the Turtle warning us kids to "duck and cover" when the bomb fell hadn't gotten to us before, then after the Kennedy assassination the world definitely became spooky forever. The death of JFK defined for us the halfway point between Pearl Harbor and 9/11—when bad things stopped happening "over there" and began to occur "over here."

The statistics may prove something else, but that is when it really started to *feel* bad: in November 1963. It was precisely around that time, on the second day after the assassination, that the Boston Strangler was ushering in the new times by raping and killing his twelfth victim, a twenty-three-year-old Sunday school teacher. Twelve is a lot even by today's standards—academics studying serial homicide describe it as an "extreme" case: more than eight. (How did they come up with that number—why not seven or nine?)

Things would get worse quickly. The times that followed were hyper-violent. People were being killed everywhere: in their homes, in church, at work, in the streets, overseas at war, in rice paddies, on college campuses, in cotton-belt bayous, in shopping centers, in riots. It was confusing. It was coming to and from all over, and out of it would spring forth occasional monstrous episodes: In 1966 we heard that in Chicago some alcoholic drifter killed eight student nurses in one hot amphetamine-frenzied night of binding, strangling, and stabbing. Three weeks later a crazed college boy in Texas climbed a clock tower with a high-powered rifle and gunned down forty-five people, killing sixteen. Then Martin Luther King and Robert Kennedy were shot months apart, with more street riots in between. And when our boys came home from My Lai as baby killers and Sharon Tate was hacked to death by crazed hippies, we could not imagine it getting any worse. But then the 1970s had not crawled in on us yet.

The first big case of that decade to reach public notice occurred in May 1971. Again, even by today's standards, the number was huge; police dug up twenty-six bodies of transient agricultural workers in a California peach orchard. Juan Corona, a labor contractor and a father of four children, was charged with the murders. We did not get it: How can someone kill that many people and nobody noticed it? That they were killed over a prolonged period of time just did not compute. Nor was there much follow-up in the press—it looked like Corona was simply insane, and to boot, according to the press, some kind of closet-homosexual aberrant, while the victims were all transient agricultural workers and Mexicans hardly worth mourning over.

Likewise two years later, reports of Dean Corll's murder of twenty-seven transient male youths in Houston also quickly faded, for he was a "white-trash homo," and he was dead, as were his delinquent runaway victims— no trial, no story, nobody cared. The big wave was yet to come. A recent study of serial homicides in the United States between 1800 and 1995 discovered that 45 percent of known serial homicides would occur in the recent twenty-year period between 1975 and 1995.[5]

In 1976–1977, David Berkowitz was systematically shooting women in Queens, New York, and sending taunting letters à la Jack the Ripper, signed "Son of Sam," to the police and press. This time everybody noticed when college girls on the way home from school or on dates were being slaughtered. New York City was in a panic. When Berkowitz was captured we were surprised by how mild-mannered, soft, and pudgy the killer looked. Again, he seemed totally insane, claiming to receive orders from a black dog, and that was sufficient explanation for us.

The whole serial-sequential aspect of these murders somehow slipped by us. These crimes were perceived as inexplicable, sudden explosive acts of deranged monsters, a perception that was still rooted in the 1880s with our experiences of Jack the Ripper. From Jack the Ripper to the Boston Strangler, there were many cases in between, but rarely any attempts to grasp exactly what was going on. These homicides were perceived as isolated acts of animalistic depravity, sometimes called "lust murders," a symptom of the modern industrialized world, we thought.

It would be Ted Bundy who would define for us the new postmodern serial killer role model. His story first slowly trickled out in Colorado in 1977, when he was linked to seventeen homicides of young women, and then grew into a torrent everywhere after his two escapes and three subsequent murders in Florida. Many of his victims were "respectable" college students, and so was he. As Bundy's trial in Florida was televised live and the scope of his secret life began to be understood, the concept of a particular type of multiple murderer who kills serially began to take form in popular lore. Ann Rule's classic account of Bundy, *The Stranger Beside Me*, pioneered a whole new resurgence of true-crime literature. It introduced the general public to the concept of serial murder, even though the term never appeared in the text of her 1980 book.

Jack the Ripper was always imagined as an aristocrat with a top hat—the best of our society gone worst. The serial killers who followed were portrayed as depraved monsters—freaks of nature—outcasts and drifters whose demented criminal features should have given them away. But not Bundy—he was like so many of us: an attractive college student with typical ambitions who drove a cute Volkswagen bug. He was an updated and egalitarianized version of Jack the Ripper—a killer of superior social qualities attributed to all the young middle-class upwardly mobile professionals taking over America. In other words, unlike serial killers of the past, he was not one of "them" but one of "us."

After Bundy, the crimes of Corona, Corll, and the Son of Sam began to take on a different perspective, and when people backtracked, they learned that there had been more serial killings recently than we realized. Near where Bundy started murdering, shoe fetishist Jerry Brudos had killed four women in 1968–1969, cutting off their feet; in Michigan, John Norman Collins murdered seven young women between 1967 and 1969. And apparently there were others who entered guilty pleas, while some never went to trial by reason of insanity, so we never heard much about them. In Santa Cruz, California, John Frazier killed five people in 1970, while Edmund Kemper, also in Santa Cruz, killed eight women between 1972 and 1973; at about the same time, in Santa Cruz once again, Herbert Mullin killed thirteen people. That one California town contributed a huge body count all on its own.

Toward the end of the 1970s Kenneth Bianchi and Angelo Buono dumped their ten victims on Hollywood hillsides and Wayne Williams threw the last five of his twenty-two victims into the river in Atlanta, while Richard Cottingham cut the heads and hands off his and set their torsos on fire in fleabag hotels in New York City. By now everyone knew what this was. By then the FBI was on it, trying to figure it out by asking the killers themselves what *they* thought they were doing and why. From those interviews a new system of criminal profiling would emerge. In the meantime, more and more new reports kept coming in, faster and faster:

In Chicago, a middle-aged man was a successful construction contractor and a respected figure in his community. He led the annual Polish Constitution Day parade and in his spare time he volunteered to entertain sick children at local hospitals, dressed as "Pogo the Clown." He was a Democratic Party precinct captain and when the president's wife, Rosalynn Carter, was in Chicago on a community visit, he was one of her escorts. In his house, buried in a basement crawl space, police found the trussed-up corpses of twenty-eight boys and young men. John Wayne Gacy was convicted of killing thirty-three victims, despite his assertion that "clowns can get away with murder."

In rural Missouri, a man working for a friendly seventy-five-year-old farmer and his sweet sixty-nine-year-old white-haired wife discovered a skull while plowing a section of their fields. The worker reported his find to the police, and a subsequent search of the property revealed five male bodies, all shot in the head with a .22-caliber rifle. In the house, a notebook was found with lists of temporary employees hired at the farm, some of the names marked with a sinister X. Upstairs in the bedroom, the police discovered a patchwork quilt spread on the bed, made by the wife from pieces of cloth torn from the clothing of the victims buried in the fields out back. The couple, Ray and Fay Copeland, became the oldest convicts on death row in America.*

A Cincinnati hospital orderly, Donald Harvey, pleaded guilty to murdering thirty-four elderly patients by suffocating some with a pillow or plastic bags or by cutting off their oxygen supply. Others he killed with arsenic, rat poison, cyanide, colostomy cleaner, and adhesive remover. He ex-

---

* Ray recently died of natural causes in prison.

plained, "I felt that what I was doing was right. I was putting people out of their misery . . . I'm doing them a favor." After his sentencing in Ohio, Harvey was extradited to Kentucky, where he pleaded guilty to another nine homicides. Then he was returned to Ohio to stand trial for the murder of a neighbor. Eventually he confessed to a total of fifty-eight murders. Until Gary Ridgway's guilty plea in November 2003 for the forty-eight Green River murders of prostitutes, Harvey had the highest convicted victim count of any American serial killer.

WHO ARE THE SERIAL KILLERS?

Statistically speaking, identified serial killers usually turn out to be white males of above-average intelligence who begin killing in their twenties or thirties, although some have been as young as ten years old when they first killed. Carroll Edward Cole in the United States was ten when he deliberately drowned a boy, and would go on to commit nine more homicides in his adult life—of women. In England, Mary Bell murdered and mutilated two boys on separate occasions when she was only eleven, probably the youngest serial killer on record, if you accept the definition of serial murder as more than one murder on separate occasions. Jürgen Bartsch, who killed five boys in Germany between 1962 and 1966, was fifteen when he started to kill, as was Edmund Kemper in California, when he shot dead both his grandparents in 1963. In his adulthood, Kemper went on to kill six young women, his mother, and her best friend. Some serial killers can be as old as seventy-five, like farmer Ray Copeland, described earlier, who was sentenced to death with his wife in 1991 in Missouri for the five murders.

Sometimes serial killers work in teams of two and sometimes they consist of husband-and-wife or boyfriend-girlfriend couples. There are also several cases of cult group serial killers consisting of more than two people.

In the United States, serial killers are most often individual white males, although African Americans, Hispanics, Native Americans, and even an Eskimo have been convicted. The incidence of African American serial killers is currently increasing dramatically—from 10 percent of the total reported prior to 1975, to 21 percent currently.[6] Frequently, but not always, serial murder is intraracial—white killers murdering white victims, blacks killing blacks.

A recent study identified 399 serial killers in the United States between 1800 and 1995 who were responsible for a number of victims between 2,526 and 3,860.[7] Sixty-two females represented 16 percent of those serial killers, murdering between four hundred and six hundred victims. Seventy-five percent of known female serial killers have made their appearance since 1950. Of all the female killers, a third committed their crimes with an accomplice, frequently a male.[8]

Although victims of serial killers are often robbed, the most common driving force of serial murder is sexual control and dominance. Many victims are raped before or after being killed, while bondage, torture, dismemberment, and cannibalism are not uncommon features of a serial homicide. Other motives for serial murder have been financial profit; ritual, political, social, or moral imperatives (missionary murders); attention (mothers killing their children); and compassion (frequent in medical-type serial murders.)

A PRIMER ON THE NATURE OF SERIAL KILLERS AND THEIR VICTIMS

In many of these cases, the killer and the victim did not know each other or were strangers who had just recently met. Most of the victims were not murdered while being robbed, nor did they get into an argument or dispute with their killers—they had no personal or business dealings with their murderer. The victims were strangers who were all murdered to be murdered. A perverse pleasure derived from killing them was the primary motive for their deaths. A study of 326 U.S. male serial killers between 1800 and 1995 concluded that 87 percent had killed at least one stranger among their victims, and 70 percent killed *only* strangers.[9] In each of these cases, the killers carefully covered their tracks after the crime and maintained a normal-looking facade: farmer, doctor, businessman, harmless drifter, schoolteacher, law school student, deputy sheriff, office manager. After killing once, the killer rested for days, weeks, or months, then sought out a new victim and killed again and again.

Serial killers, although often described as "monsters," rarely appear to be creatures with blood dripping from their fangs or crazed psychopaths babbling satanic rituals. While a few are exactly like that, many appear at first glance to be healthy, normal, and even attractive people. And that is precisely the problem—with a serial killer a victim rarely gets beyond the first glance. Others are simply invisibly unmemorable and unnoticeable, until somebody notices them killing.

Policemen would tell you that most murderers, when they killed, did not know that they were going to kill. They killed in the heat of an argument, in a jealous rage, or sometimes accidentally while committing another crime. And cops would tell you that if you were going to be murdered, it was statistically likely that your killer was somebody you already knew—and knew well. Your husband or wife, a parent or your own child, a friend, lover, relative, or acquaintance was more likely to kill you than a stranger. Murder was an intimate occasion that usually unfolded between friends and lovers. Often, remorse and horror quickly overcame those who found themselves having just committed a murder. Many sat passively waiting at the crime scene for the police to arrive. Some tenderly covered or washed the body of the victim they had just murdered. They quietly surrendered to police and quickly confessed; most would never kill again whether they ended up in prison or not. While even today the majority of murders still take place between people who know each other, the proportion is becoming significantly smaller. One's chance of being murdered by a stranger has increased dramatically during the last three decades.

Serial killers deliberately and relentlessly hunt down their victims with the sole intention of coldly murdering them. The motive for a serial killer does not arise from factors in his* relationship with the victim—there usually is no relationship. The serial killer generally preys on strangers for a complex set of motives known only to him. The serial killer also prefers strangers because it makes him harder to catch and the anonymous fill-in-the-blank victim easier to torment and kill. At one time, serial murders were called "stranger-on-stranger" killings, but because there were sufficiently numerous exceptions to this (serial killers will also turn on those near them if necessary) other terms were applied: "motiveless homicides," "recreational killings," "thrill kills," and finally "serial murders."

Serial killers do everything in their power not to be caught by the police, so that they can remain free to kill again. While it can be argued that professional assassins, like Mafia hit men, also avoid being arrested by the

---

* Although there are female serial killers, the majority are males; therefore, I refer to them as *he* instead of *he/she* to facilitate the flow of text.

police and kill many victims, they ostensibly kill for money and their victims are individually targeted by the assassin's clients, not by the killer himself. Serial killers, however, murder for their own personal pleasure and carefully select their victims for their own reasons. Their killings are often highly sexual in nature and rarely offer any financial gain.

At one time serial killers were also called "mass murderers," but today the term is reserved only for individuals who suddenly go berserk and indiscriminately kill numerous victims during a single frenzied suicidal episode. Mass murderers are out of control and totally deranged and are quickly captured or shot dead by the police, or they commit suicide once their ammunition begins to run out. Serial killers, on the other hand, slip back to their normal state of life between their murders. They are controlled, are aware of what they are doing, and scrupulously avoid arrest. Some studiously read police investigative-technique manuals and familiarize themselves with all levels of police procedure. This, and the fact that serial killers so often prey on strangers, makes them very difficult to identify and capture. Moreover, about a third of serial killers are highly mobile and travel undetected thousands of miles a year, crossing different police jurisdictions during their killing, which further makes investigation difficult.

Experts argue over *how many* victims define a serial killer. Some, like the FBI, insist on a minimum of three victims. Most agree that serial homicide is when victims are killed on separate occasions with a "cooling-off" period between the murders. Others, and I am in that school, argue that two or more murders on separate occasions with a cooling-off period in between are sufficient to define a serial killer. (As far as I am concerned, one murder is freaky enough; anything more is horribly incomprehensible.)

How and why do serial murderers kill again and again? Serial killing is an *addiction,* some experts say. Simply explained, once they begin killing (and sometimes they kill the first time by accident), serial killers find themselves addicted to murder in an intense cycle that begins with homicidal sexual fantasies that in turn spark a desperate search for victims, leading to their brutal killing, followed by a period of cooling off and a return to normal daily routine—with all its unbearable stresses, disappointments, and hurts, which lead back to the reemerging need to start fantasizing about killing again. Once a killing cycle is triggered, it is rarely broken. The worst aspect of this is that murder fantasies are often the *only* thing the budding serial killer has that gives him comfort and solace. Once he crosses the line and actually realizes his fantasy and discovers that actual murder is not as satisfying as the fantasy, he is driven into the depths of depression and despair, from which rise even more intense homicidal fantasies driving him forward to kill again in an attempt to realize in the reality of murder the same satisfaction he derives in fantasy. With time, trapped in this addictive cycle, serial killers become more frenzied, and the frequency and violence of their murders escalate exponentially until they are either caught or "burn out"—reach a point where killing no longer satisfies them and they stop on their own accord if nothing else interrupts their killing career. (Which is why some unsolved serial murders seem to mysteriously cease without the offender ever being identified.) Others commit suicide, move on to commit other crimes, or turn themselves in to police.

A "Typical" Serial Killer: Gary Leon Ridgway, "The Green River Killer"

When fifty-four-year-old Gary Ridgway pleaded guilty in November 2003 to the murder of forty-eight prostitutes in Washington State in the 1980s, and as the result of his plea was spared the death penalty, the media lamented that there was nothing new to learn about serial killers from Ridgway.[10] Even though he now holds the record in the United States for killing the most victims—and perhaps for evading authorities the longest— Ridgway seems to have eluded the kind of frenzied press coverage that serial homicide cases frequently attract. Ridgway was so typical and his victims, as street prostitutes, held in such low esteem in society that even the remarkable number of deaths did not evoke more than mildly routine press coverage outside the Washington State area.

Indeed, Ridgway does represent everything typically known about serial killers. Born in 1949, he is the middle child of three sons who grew up in a working-class neighborhood south of Seattle. His mother was reportedly highly domineering over the sons and her husband. According to one of Ridgeway's former wives, she once broke a dinner plate over the father's head.[11]

As a child Ridgway was a slow learner, failed twice in school, committed acts of arson, suffocated a cat, and paid a little girl to allow him to molest her, and as a teenager he nearly stabbed to death a six-year-old boy for no apparent reason.

He was married three times. His first wife claims their marriage failed because his mother dominated him. She described him, however, as socially and sexually normal.

When arrested, Ridgway was steadily employed as a $21/hour truck painter at the same place he began working in after graduating high school thirty-two years earlier. His fellow workers remembered him as a gregarious and pleasant fellow worker and would socialize with him after work. Some of the women he supervised recalled that he was a patient instructor who never yelled at them.

He owned a $200,000 house, had a son, walked his dog, was friendly with his neighbors, went to church, held garage sales, sold Amway products, had friends, and read the Bible avidly, and for a while he proselytized door to door, calling on his neighbors to come closer to God. He also strangled at least forty-eight prostitutes, dumped them in wooded areas in what he called "clusters," and would return routinely to have sex with their decomposing corpses.

His second wife remembers him as a loner obsessed with anal and oral sex. Both his second and third wives recalled he used to like having sex outdoors. Only after his arrest did they realize that those locations were at or near those where some of his victims were dumped.

He killed most of his victims in a two-year span between 1982 and 1984. He carefully deposited cigarette butts and chewing gum belonging to others at the crime scenes and body dumps to mislead police. (He did not smoke or chew gum.) He trimmed the victims' fingernails in case there was evidence lodged under them. He dropped advertising leaflets around the body of one victim, hoping to mislead investigators, and transported the skeletal remains of two victims in the trunk of his car to another state while on a camping trip with his son. Ridgway confessed that he had placed a mound of sausage, trout, and a wine bottle on one victim's body, creating a "Last Supper" scenario in order to deliberately confuse the police. In police terminology, Ridgway's attempt to give a false meaning to the crime scenes is called *staging*.

Ridgway became a suspect in 1984 when police caught him soliciting prostitutes; his co-workers often kidded about it behind his back, calling him "Green River Gary" and joking that the initials of his name were the same as in Green River. As soon as he became a suspect, Ridgway appeared to almost cease committing murders—he confessed to one in 1986, one in 1988, and another in 1998. Police suspect, however, that he may have committed another twenty murders in other jurisdictions. Only advances in DNA technology led to Ridgway's arrest in 2001, nearly twenty years after most of the murders.

Ridgway explained to police that he chose to kill prostitutes because they would not be missed: "Prostitutes were the easiest. I went from having sex with them to just plain killing them . . . The young ones stood out more when they talked when they were dying."

According to his plea-bargain statement, "I picked prostitutes as my victims because I hate most prostitutes and I did not want to pay them for sex. I also picked prostitutes as victims because they were easy to pick up without being noticed. I knew they would not be reported missing right away, and might never be reported missing. I picked prostitutes because I thought I could kill as many of them as I wanted without getting caught."

By now Ridgway is almost indistinguishable from other serial prostitute killers. Just like Richard Cottingham, Ridgway was steadily employed and had a wife, a house, and children (just like fifty-year-old Robert Yates, who had five children, a wife, a house, and a mortgage. Like Ridgway, Yates quoted biblical scriptures as he murdered thirteen women in the Spokane region.) Although many of them were in failed relationships, the failures were often no more extraordinary than the typical divorce. Cottingham, for example, had separated from his wife, but had a relationship with a girlfriend until the day he was arrested. She described him as entirely "normal" even though he did take her several times to the same Quality Inn in New Jersey where he murdered two of his victims and was arrested torturing his last. William Lester Suff (thirteen prostitute murders) and Arthur Shawcross (eleven victims) were in long-term relationships when they committed their murders.

Ridgway represents truly everything we know about serial killers today—everything and nothing at the same time—because the answer to the main question of *why* continues to elude us.

The Serial Killer Epidemic: The Statistics of Murder

How many serial homicides take place? Almost every month somewhere in the world a new case of serial homicide is reported by the police, and except for Antarctica, no continent has been spared. From Alaska to New Zealand, from South Africa to China, cases of serial murder appear to be on the increase—slowly in the Third World, and alarmingly rapidly in the industrialized nations. Anybody could be a potential victim of a serial killer—absolutely anybody: man, woman, child, old, rich, poor, obscure, or famous—nothing makes one immune from being a potential victim, as the murder of Gianni Versace demonstrated. And should anybody suggest the obvious, there is even a case of a serial killer being killed by another serial killer! (In August 1970, Dean Corll, who murdered at least twenty-seven male youths, was killed by Elmer Wayne Henley, one of his partners in the murders.)

As noted earlier, while not all serial killings are stranger-on-stranger, many are. Serial murder statistics are buried somewhere within the rising rate of "motiveless" and stranger murders, which have been on a breathtakingly dramatic rise since the 1970s. The FBI reported that motiveless crimes accounted for 8.5 percent of all homicides in 1976; 17.8 percent in 1981; and 22.5 percent in 1986.[12] Serial murders were considered motiveless and fell into that category. (Today, serial murders, because of their sexual component, are often defined as felony-related.)

By 1995, when the aggregate numbers of homicides in the United States peaked, an extraordinary 55 percent of victims were slain by strangers *and persons unknown*—a total of 11,800 people![13] Before going further here, however, we should make one thing clear: "Strangers" means that the investigation determined definitively that the victim did not know the killer. This includes not only random victims of serial killers, but also, for example, store clerks shot dead by strangers in the course of a robbery. "Persons unknown" on the other hand, means precisely that—investigators simply did not know whether the victim knew the murderer; it does not necessarily mean that the perpetrator was a stranger—only that the relationship to the victim was not determined or not entered into a supplementary report upon which these statistics are based. There has been a tendency in the past, especially on the part of the media, to lump together "stranger" and "unknown" killings and issue alarmist reports that serial homicides by strangers are approaching 50 percent of all murders, without drawing attention to the ambiguity in the categories as explained here. Moreover, the FBI has done little to discourage that practice for its own political reasons, as we shall see further on.[14] However, the fact remains that serial murder victim totals fall into those two categories—stranger and unknown—and the proportions of these categories among total murder statistics continue to rise.

Throughout most of the 1990s, the murder rate in the United States (as opposed to aggregate numbers of murders) has been dramatically declining, with a drop from 9.8 per 100,000 citizens in 1991 to a record low of 4.1 by 2000.[15] But since 2001 the rate has begun to creep upward again, and this is without including the deaths on 9/11 incurred during the terrorist attacks that year. Moreover, the volume of homicides by persons unknown and strangers continued to climb steadily to a current rate of 57.7 percent of all murders in 2001.[16] Of that number, strangers perpetrated 13.1 percent, while in the remaining 44.6 percent of homicides the relationship between victim and offender was simply unknown. There are no precise figures as to how many of those homicides were committed by serial killers. This does not bode well when accompanied by the fact that in 2001, only 62.4 percent of homicides were cleared, a percentage that has been continually declining since 1961, when 94 percent of the 8,599 U.S. murders that year were routinely solved.[17] Today one's chances of getting away with a "perfect murder" are steadily creeping toward fifty-fifty.

How many unidentified serial killers are currently out there? Serial killers stop murdering because they move to a different jurisdiction, are arrested for some other crime, die, are killed, commit suicide, or simply grow old, mature, and become bored with or burned out on their fantasy by the process described previously. Many such unresolved serial murders seem to mysteriously cease on their own, such as the infamous Zodiac Killer, who killed between six and thirty-seven victims in San Francisco between 1968 and 1969; the Southside Slayer, who killed twelve black women in Los Angeles beginning in 1984; and the Black Doodler, who killed fourteen gay men in San Francisco nearly two decades ago. The Green River killings appeared to mysteriously cease in 1984 and remained unsolved until 2001.

Serial killers sometimes do burn out, and depending on the personality of the individual they either allow themselves to be captured, commit suicide, or cease killing on their own and quietly fade away back to where they came from. Some are arrested for other crimes after they stop killing and end up suddenly confessing, like Albert DeSalvo (the Boston Strangler) or Danny Rolling (the Gainesville Ripper). Obviously there is no known fixed number of victims before a serial killer stops: Edmund Kemper killed ten women before he ended his career by killing his mother and then surrendered quietly to the police. Henry Lee Lucas, on the other hand, *began* by killing his mother and went on killing for decades before he murdered the only person he said he truly loved—his thirteen-year-old common-law wife—who, at least according to Lucas, was his 360th victim. (Lucas's claim is highly contestable.)

Nothing, however, short of capture, will stop a serial killer if he is in his midcycle of murder. Arthur Shawcross first killed two children in upstate New York, was quickly arrested, and served fourteen years in prison before being released in 1987. He immediately began where he left off and killed eleven women in a twenty-one-month period in Rochester, New York, before being rearrested.

In New Jersey in 1958, Richard Biegenwald was arrested after committing his first murder and served seventeen years before being released in 1975. When he was rearrested in 1983, he had killed at least seven additional victims by then.

In Toronto, Canada, seventeen-year-old Peter Woodcock murdered two boys and a girl between September 1956 and January 1957. He was found not guilty by reason of insanity and confined in a psychiatric facility. He was treated for thirty-five years and was eventually groomed for gradual release back into society. On July 13, 1991, the now fifty-two-year-old Woodcock was given his first three-hour pass allowing him to leave the grounds of the psychiatric facility to go for a walk in town and buy a pizza to bring back to the hospital. Before he could make it off the hospital grounds, Woodcock battered, hacked and stabbed to death, then sodomized a fellow inmate in a bushy area on the facility's perimeter. Using his pass, he then walked two miles to a nearby police station and confessed to the crime.

Serial killing appears to be incurable: Time or prison does not relieve the need that serial killers feel for murder—only killing does.

• • •

It is impossible to get an accurate estimate of how many serial killers and victims there are. In 1987, the U.S. Department of Justice estimated that serial killers murdered between 1,000 and 2,500 people that year.[18] Other sources cited a number as high as 6,000 a year.[19] In the Green River region in Washington Gary Ridgway murdered forty-eight women by himself in a twenty-month period in 1982–1984.

Remarkably, nobody even knows precisely how many homicides in total take place annually in the United States, as there are all sorts of reporting discrepancies. It is believed that until the recent decline in murders, approximately 20,000 to 22,000 murders occurred every year in the United States, but some sources estimate that the number is as high as 40,000 due to variations in reporting procedures.[20] (By 2000 the number of murders declined to 15,586 but began to rise in 2001 to 15,980, not including the victims of 9/11—an increase of 2.5 percent. Preliminary statistics for 2002 indicate a further increase of 0.8 percent in the number of murders. This recent rate is distributed strangely across the United States: a decline of 4.8 percent in the Northeast but a rise of 5.2 percent in the West. Cities of more than a million inhabitants show a decline in murders of 4 percent, while towns of 50,000 to 100,000 show a dramatic 6.7 percent rise in homicides in 2002. Suburban counties reported an extraordinary 12.4 percent rise in homicides.[21])

These statistics do not include the number of people who appear to mysteriously disappear. An often-cited 1984 U.S. Department of Health report estimated that 1.8 million children vanished from home every year. Of those, 95 percent were listed as "runaways" and 90 percent of those returned home within fourteen days. That left 171,000 runaways simply unaccounted for! The other 5 percent of the missing were victims of abduction, of which 72,000 were abducted by parents in custody disputes. The remaining 18,000 children and adolescents simply vanished with no further explanation, according to the statistics.[22]

The fate of missing adults is even harder to determine—if anybody notices them missing in the first place. In 1971, when Juan Corona initiated the era of big-number serial murder, none of his twenty-six transient victims were reported missing until their graves were discovered. Five remain nameless to this day. Some of the victims for whose deaths Henry Lee Lucas was convicted remain unidentified. During his trial they would be named for articles of clothing they were wearing when their bodies were found. A young woman Lucas picked up hitchhiking in Oklahoma City was found dead in a culvert wearing only socks. She remained known to the police and the courts only by the name "Orange Socks." Richard Cottingham's teenage victim found in the Times Square hotel with her head severed remains unidentified. Some of the bodies dug up from under Gacy's house remain anonymous.

While serial murder is not a new phenomenon, its dramatic rise in incidence in the last three decades is. Eighty percent of all known male serial killers in the United States appeared between 1950 and 1995. Serial killers between 1975 and 1995 accounted for 45 percent of the total of both male and female killers in the United States between 1800 and 1995.[23] Between 1960 and 1990, confirmed serial homicides increased by 940 percent.[24] By early 1980, the rapid rise in serial murder was causing a panic that seized the nation. Most frightening were statistics that began to emerge from reliable sources that a huge number of children were being abducted by serial killers. Congress began to look into the issue, declaring that the nation was facing a "serial killer epidemic." Even Atlanta's Centers for Disease Control got into the controversy with its assessment of serial murders as an increasing cause of death in America.

In the 1990s there were all sorts of secondary stories related to serial killing. First was the movie *Silence of the Lambs,* which introduced into mass consciousness the idea of FBI profilers and the character of serial killer Hannibal Lecter. The controversies of Bret Easton Ellis's book *American Psycho,* the marketing of serial killer trading cards, AOL's closing of Sondra London's serial killer Web site, the market for artworks created by serial killers, and online auctions of their artifacts all contributed to a prevailing serial killer culture.

The 1990s marked a continuing wave of serial homicides heavily covered by the media. Television satellite trucks rushed to Gainesville, Florida, to cover practically live the five gruesome mutilations of college students in August 1990. In July 1991, an estimated 450 journalists covered the trial of Jeffrey Dahmer, who was charged with cannibalizing seventeen victims in Wisconsin and Ohio. The capture of serial bomber Ted Kaczynski—the

Unabomber—after twenty years of bombings dominated headlines in the mid-1990s, and media organizations paid $6,500 for the privilege of access to his subsequent trial. The murder of Italian fashion mogul Gianni Versace in Miami propelled the issue of serial spree homicide into the headlines in 1997. In 2001 there was the arrest of Gary Ridgway, the suspect in the Green River murders, which had remained unsolved for twenty years.

It just keeps coming and coming. In the autumn of 2002, the Beltway Sniper murders were covered on live television as they unfolded—another case of serial spree killing. In May 2003, police arrested a man suspected in a series of seven rape murders in Baton Rouge, Louisiana, and later that year police in Washington State announced the closing of the Green River Killer case with Gary Ridgway's guilty plea in an astonishing forty-eight murders. In February 2004, law enforcement in Arkansas and Mississippi joined agencies from Texas and Oklahoma to search for a killer who police say is a long-haul truck driver and preys on women around truck stops. The bodies of ten victims, many of them prostitutes, were dumped near a river, creek, or around bridges in four states between 1999 and 2004.[25]

As this book went to press in the spring of 2004, Kansas suddenly became the nation's serial murder hotspot. In Witchita, after a silence of twenty-five years an unidentified serial killer known as the "BTK Strangler" suddenly contacted authorities by mailing them identification of one of his previous victims and photographs of her corpse. The killer had murdered at least eight people between 1974 and 1986, including a family of four, while taunting police with letters and phone calls. He frequently entered the victims' homes, sometimes during the day, cutting their phone line before proceeding to torture and strangle them. He wrote in one letter [spelling as in original]:

> I can't stop it so the monster goes on, and hurt me as well as society. Society can be thankful that there are ways for people like me to relieve myself at time by day dreams of some victims being torture and being mine. It a big compicated game my friend of the monster play putting victims number down, follow them, checking up on them waiting in the dark, waiting, waiting . . . the pressure is great and sometimes he run the game to his liking. Maybe you can stop him. I can't. He has aready chosen his next victim

or victims. I don't who they are yet. The next day after I read the paper, I will know, but it to late. Good luck hunting. P.S. Since sex criminals do not change their M.O. or by nature cannot do so, I will not change mine. The code words for me will be . . . Bind them, toture them, kill them, B.T.K., you see he at it again. They will be on the next victim.

Then suddenly, in 1979, the BTK strangler broke off contact and except for the 1986 murder of Vickie Wegerle, which was not at first linked to him, he appeared to have stopped killing. By 1987, the special BTK task force was disbanded.

In January 2004, Kansas newspapers marked the thirtieth anniversary of the BTK killer's first murders—the strangulation of the Otero family. Six weeks later, police announced that photos of Vickie Wegerle's body taken by the killer had been mailed in to a Wichita paper. Police are now combing prison records in the hope that perhaps the BTK strangler has been incarcerated on other charges during the last two decades and can be identified.

Meanwhile, in Kansas City, police announced in April that they had charged a suspect in a series of twelve rape strangulation murders of women between 1977 and 1993. The accused is a forty-three-year-old married supervisor in a Kansas trash-collecting company who was linked by DNA traces to the victims: nine white and three black women ranging in age from fifteen to thirty-six. Eleven of the victims, according to police, were prostitutes, while the twelfth was a mentally ill woman known to wander the streets and accept rides from strangers.*

In Canada, police have spent $25 million so far investigating farmer Robert Pickton, who is suspected in the disappearances of some sixty Vancouver women, many of them down-on-their-luck street hookers and drug addicts. Investigators have been sifting the grounds of his pig farm for eighteen months, recovering the remains of twenty-two bodies and DNA traces linked to some of the missing women. Pickton is currently charged with fifteen counts of first-degree murder, but in January 2004, police announced that they discovered the remains of an additional nine women on the pig farm. Six of the nine were identified through DNA testing. Prose-

---

* Christine Vendel, "KC Man Charged with 12 Murders," *Kansas City Star,* April 19, 2004.

cutors informed the courts that they would be charging Pickton with additional counts of murder. His trial is scheduled to begin in 2005.[26]

In China, in April 2004, police dug up more bodies on the property of Huang Yong, the twenty-nine-year-old son of a pig farmer. He had already confessed to killing seventeen high school boys he lured from Internet cafes and video game centers. He tied his victims to a table, tortured them, strangled and dismembered them, because as Yong explained, he liked to "experience the sensation of killing." Yong had been executed in December, but relatives continued to search his property discovering additional bodies.

China has been recently plagued with cases of serial murder. Xu Ming, a twenty-six-year-old man in China's Hebei province, raped at least thirty-seven women between the ages of seventy-one and ninety-three. Older women were "easier to control," he told police. Yang Xinhai, China's worst serial killer to date, murdered sixty-five people and raped twenty-three women. In the southern city of Shenzhen, a couple murdered seventeen young job seekers. In Beijing, a taxi driver and his wife killed seven people, including four prostitutes whose bodies they chopped into pieces and partially ate. In Nanjing, a snack-shop owner who grew worried about competition put rat poison in a rival's products, killing thirty-eight people.

Back on the Pacific coast of the U.S., not far from where Gary Ridgway murdered forty-eight victims, David and Michelle Knotek—husband and wife—stand accused of the torture murders of at least four people at their idyllic white-picket-fence farmhouse decorated with smiley faces. At this writing they are awaiting trial. Meanwhile, farther south along the coast, in California, as Scott Peterson stands charged with the murder of his pregnant wife, Laci, his defense is hinting that he has been "framed" by a serial killer, the real perpetrator of her murder.

As I write here, you cannot turn on the TV without major network news magazine shows like *Dateline* or *20/20* running previously broadcast episodes or updated shows on some serial killer. Tune in to the Discovery Channel for the "science of catching serial killers." Go to the History Channel and you will find the "history of serial killers." PBS offers us "The Mind of a Serial Killer," while the Biography Channel . . . well, you guessed it. Only the Food Network seems to have resisted presenting serial killer cannibal recipes.

No wonder they call this the age of serial slaughter; we seem to live in a world truly plagued by an epidemic of crazy homicides that do not appear to be waning.

Behind the Making of the "Serial Killer Epidemic"

If I have been doing my job right as a popular writer so far, you should be breathlessly alarmed by this described sudden and steady three-decade onslaught of crazed serial killers threatening us in every corner of the world. The alarm you feel feeds sales of books, magazines, and commercial time on television. The historian in me, however, wants to know what *really* happened, even if the truth is more prosaic than the myth. This wave of serial murder is not as simple a story as a lot of true-crime literature, the government, and the media have been presenting it.

Yes, it *felt* as if an epidemic of serial murder were starting in the 1970s, just the way I described it, but first we need to acknowledge that the population had risen rapidly over the last half of the century. More people; more victims; more serial killers.

Second, in the earlier part of the century, television did not exist and newspapers were not linked by wire services and syndication deals to the extent they are today. Stories of serial murder often did not get reported beyond a local region, and therefore historians have a hard time identifying cases in the past with which comparisons can be made. By the 1960s, news reporting had become highly centralized by wire services, modern communication, and corporate amalgamation, and thus stories of serial murders, even in remote regions, were more likely to be broadly reported during the 1970s and 1980s, giving us this sense of a sudden epidemic of unprecedented serial killings. Reports of almost any multiple homicides anywhere would be big news and received national distribution on the wire services.

Finally, our "serial killer epidemic" can be attributed to the fact that many of the startling crime statistics in the early 1980s were issuing forth from the U.S. Department of Justice and anticrime lobbies and victim advocate groups. The FBI at precisely that time was lobbying the government for funding for new programs. The FBI had realized that some murders were not being recognized as having been committed by the same person because of jurisdictional disparities (a failure called "linkage blindness") and was calling for a massive database system to address this issue.

The FBI's Behavioral Sciences Unit (BSU) at Quantico, Virginia (of *Silence of the Lambs* fame), which was first formed for psychological studies of hostage takers, began to investigate the psychology and techniques of serial killers in an attempt to model their behavior into identifiable patterns. Between 1979 and 1983, agents from the BSU conducted intimate and detailed interviews in prisons with thirty-six convicted sex murderers, of whom twenty-nine were serial killers.[27] Everything was asked of them, from their earliest childhood recollections to the most horrifying details of their crimes and motives. The families, friends, and acquaintances of the killers were also extensively interviewed, as were their surviving victims. The BSU also made a detailed study of the 118 dead victims attributed to the killers in the study: their occupations, their lifestyles, vital statistics, where they encountered their killers, their autopsies, and the conditions in which their bodies were found. All that data served as the basis for the FBI's profiling system.

In order for the profiling system to be applied usefully to serial crimes in different parts of the United States, there needed to be some kind of formal, centralized organization and system of collecting very detailed crime data, storing it, and making it available for analysis. Big money would need to be allocated for that.

At the exact same time (1981–1983), three major committees on Capitol Hill were looking into the issue of increasing violence, linkage blindness, the kidnapping of children, child pornography, and serial killers: the Attorney General's Task Force on Violent Crime; the House Committee on Civil and Constitutional Rights; and Senator Specter's Juvenile Justice Subcommittee of the Judiciary Committee of the U.S. Senate.

The start of these hearings in 1981 was punctuated by several dramatic cases of child murders. In Atlanta, Wayne Williams was arrested for a series of murders of black male children and youths; in New York, Etan Patz vanished on his way to school; and in Florida, six-year-old Adam Walsh vanished in a mall when his mother left him alone for a moment. The boy's decapitated remains were found floating in a canal. An out-of-state car was linked to the crime but the perpetrator was never identified. There would later be some controversy that it might have been Ottis Elwood Toole, Henry Lee Lucas's partner (the two dubiously claimed killing a total of 360 victims as they roamed the highways). Adam was the son of John Walsh, who would become a vocal victims' and missing children's advocate and host of *America's Most Wanted*.

A year after his son's murder, the tragic figure of John Walsh testified before the Senate committee describing recent cases of serial murder and suggesting that missing children are in a large measure murdered by serial killers. The problem, Walsh said, was linkage blindness and the failure of law enforcement agencies to coordinate information and intelligence across multiple jurisdictions. Because of this weakness, young people were disappearing without a trace, until they might be found in a mass grave somewhere. Using the controversial Department of Health figure that 1.8 million children go missing every year, Walsh testified that every hour 205 children go missing, many of whom he said, would be found murdered. He failed to explain that that 95 percent of those missing were confirmed runaways, of whom 95 percent would return home within fourteen days.[28] Instead, headlines screamed: "205 MISSING CHILDREN EVERY HOUR!"

"The unbelievable and unaccounted for figure of fifty thousand children disappear annually and are abducted for reasons of foul play," Walsh claimed in his testimony.[29] "This country is littered with mutilated, decapitated, raped, and strangled children," Walsh warned.[30]

On February 3, 1984, in her nationally syndicated column, Ann Landers published a letter written by the executive director of the Adam Walsh Center. It opened, "Dear Ann: Consider these chilling statistics: Every hour 205 American children are reported missing. This means 4,920 per day and 1.8 million per year."[31]

It was spooky stuff and mothers across the nation huddled up their children behind locked doors. But where did that 50,000 figure that Walsh cited come from? According to recent research by John Gill, it was Senator Claiborne Pell, Democrat from Rhode Island, who in 1981 was the first public official to formally claim that the Department of Health and Human Services stated that 50,000 children vanish each year. Officials at HHS denied making that estimate and Pell's staff doesn't remember which official they spoke to.[32]

As the hearing progressed, all kinds of speculative statements were entered into the record and presented at press conferences. The most prevalent trend was to combine the FBI's Uniform Crime Reports homicide categories of *unknown* and *stranger* into one figure, pumping up the percentage of killings that appeared to be motiveless murders by unknown perpetrators, presumably roaming serial killers. Using this kind of "fuzzy math," it was claimed that nearly 25 percent of all murders—a total of 4,000 to 5,000 each year—could be attributed to serial killers. The only thing that could save us now was funding from Congress.

This claim was gleefully picked up by the press and true-crime authors. Even serious academic studies on serial murder bought into this big number. For example, an often-cited work by Holmes and De Burger states that in 1988

> [b]etween 3,500 and 5,000 persons are slain by serial murderers each year in this country. We emphasize that this is an estimate, but we believe that it represents a reliable approximation, given the data available and the input of various experts now engaged in efforts to deal with this problem. (italics in original)[33]

This figure is still being thrust on us today. The back cover art of a recently published edition of Michael Newton's *Encyclopedia of Serial Killers* features a specially highlighted box with a blurb promoting the book: "The starting point for any serious study of the serial or addicted killers who claim an estimated 3,500 victims each year—and evade detection . . . "[34]

But these numbers were never realistic and by now everyone should know it. The total maximum number of all known serial killer victims in the United States over a span of 195 years between 1800 and 1995 is estimated at only 3,860 tops.[35] Of this total, a maximum of 1,398 victims were murdered between 1975 and 1995, at an average rate of 70 victims a year. Even if we account for unknown victims, that figure is nowhere near the 3,500 annual number so often bandied about. But 3,500 victims a year sells better than 70. As Joel Best put it in his analysis of child abduction statistics in the 1980s, "Three principles seem clear: Big numbers are better than small numbers; official numbers are better than unofficial numbers; and big, official numbers are best of all."[36]

For the record, a study of 1,498 child murders in California between 1981 and 1990 determined that not stranger serial killers, as John Walsh claimed, but relatives, *predominately parents,* are the most frequent killers of children up to age nine. Strangers were involved in only 14.6 percent of homicides of children between ages five and nine; and 28.7 percent of

those between ages ten and fourteen. The offender relationship was unknown in 10.4 and 20.1 percent of homicides in the two age groups, respectively. Acquaintances murdered 30.2 percent and 39.2 percent of
victims in each age group, and females comprised 36.4 percent and 18.7
percent of the killers, while relatives including parents killed 44.8 percent
and 11.9 percent, respectively.[37] Of children between ages ten and fourteen
the motive behind their murder was a dispute in 60.9 percent of the cases,
a firearm was used in 64.2 percent, and a public place was the location in
51.5 percent. In summary, young children are killed at home by relatives,
while more mobile and independent older adolescent children are increasingly killed by acquaintances first, and then by strangers in public places.

The incredible stranger child abduction figures of 30,000 to 45,000 so
often cited became more frequently challenged in the late 1980s. People
began to wonder: Where were these abductions occurring? Why were they
not being reported in the papers? Where were the anecdotal accounts? Who
were the serial killers committing these abductions? Finally Congress spon-
sored a program to determine exact statistical data on missing and abducted children called the National Incidence Studies of Missing, Abducted,
Runaway, and Thrownaway Children (NISMART).

The study determined that there were two definitions of "abduction":
a legal one and a stereotypical one held by the public. In public perception a
child abduction occurs when a victim is taken away by a stranger a great distance, held for ransom, kept overnight or longer, or killed. Crimes such as
the 1993 abduction-murder of Polly Klaas or the recently resolved kidnapping of Elizabeth Smart fit the public perception of the threat posed by
strangers to children. But the law is broader than the public's perception.
For example, California courts define abduction as when a victim is lured
or forcibly moved farther than twenty feet or held longer than half an
hour if no movement occurs.[38] So when the FBI reported an annual average of 90,000 forcible rapes in the 1980s, in which teenage girls comprised
commonly a third to a half of the victims, still defined as children, the circumstances of many of these crimes easily fit the legal definition of child
abduction. Thus the figure of 30,000 to 45,000 "abducted children" emerged
under those kinds of definitions. But this was not what the public was
thinking in their definition of the type of child abduction they feared.

The NISMART study reevaluated child abduction statistics in the context of the public perception of abduction. The study determined that in a

twelve-year period between 1976 and 1988, an average of 43 to 147 children were victimized yearly in the United States in the stereotypical public perception of abduction. That brings the statistic more in line with the highly rare anecdotal and press reports of stranger abductions of children that we hear about. The reality is that the abduction and murder of children by strangers is a very rare crime. The degree of fear and concern generated by exaggerated and misrepresented statistics during the early 1980s far exceeded the reality of the danger. This fear persists to this day, despite the extremely low probability of such threats to children. Of course, this fact is of little consolation to the parents of the 43 to 147 children who on average every year are abducted by strangers.

Back in 1981–1983, as the committee hearings unfolded in Washington, the press darted like schools of fish to the Senate hearings and the various press conferences. Articles in large-circulation magazines such as *Time, Newsweek, Life, Omni, Psychology Today, Playboy,* and *Penthouse,* painted a picture of the United States plagued by an "epidemic" of senseless random homicides committed by roaming anonymous monsters who often victimized our children.

All those fearful and perhaps exaggerated cries came to some fruition. In 1982 Congress passed the Missing Children's Act and in 1984 the Missing Children's Assistance Act. President Ronald Reagan personally announced the establishment of the National Center for the Analysis of Violent Crime (NCAVC), to be housed at the FBI Quantico Behavioral Sciences Unit. The data collected by the BSU sexual killer study is applied today in a program known as VICAP (Violent Criminal Apprehension Program). When police suspect that a serial offender is loose in their jurisdiction, they can fill out a standard VICAP questionnaire consisting of 188 questions about their homicide case and submit it to the Investigative Support Unit requesting a profile of the unknown offender. (See Chapter 9 for a more detailed account of profiling and its problems.) The fill-in-the-blanks questions on the form range from the description of the location of where the victim's body was found down to the details of the nature of the assault and mutilation of the victim, the condition of the suspect's car, and his method of approaching the victim if it is known.

The result of a VICAP crime report is twofold. First, a computer analysis of the responses can identify patterns that may link the offender to other crimes he may have previously committed anywhere in North America. Each serial killer is known to have his own personal "signature" of which he is often not aware, and a properly completed VICAP questionnaire can identify this signature, while the computer can match it to other incidents.

Second, the data supplied by the VICAP report allows analysts to profile the killer, something that the FBI has developed into a reasonably effective but not entirely perfect technique. An analysis of the data in the report can often identify a high probability of the killer's race, age, social status, employment, intelligence, and sexual preference; how he dresses, and even the type of car he drives. Successful profiling can greatly narrow the field of suspects.

This means that there is an identifiable method to the madness committed by serial killers. Since the BSU study was completed, much has become known as to how and why serial murderers come to develop and act on their killing addiction.

Previous Serial Killer "Epidemics"

Let us return once more to the question of the rising wave of serial murders over the last thirty years. Is it real, or is it exaggerated media hype intended to address political agendas and sell papers? Philip Jenkins, a professor at Penn State, is probably the most recognized debunker of serial homicide statistics. Jenkins, for example, cites working lists of all known serial killers compiled by the Justice Department for use at the Behavioral Sciences Unit. He noted that in 1992, the FBI list of serial killers in the United States from 1900 to 1970 contained 447 names and an additional 365 names from 1970 to 1992, linked to 2,636 known victims and suspected in an additional 1,839. But after combing through the lists, Jenkins found enormous faults of duplication—for example, each of the convicted killers in the Manson Family was assigned the same list of victims, making the number of victims of spree killing in 1969 three times greater than it really was.[39] Jenkins found case after case of similar such multiplication of victims in the use of "suspected victim" categories and discredited confessions such as Henry Lee Lucas's confession of 360 murders.

So the good news is that there are fewer serial killers and victims in recent times than the FBI claims.

The bad news, according to Jenkins, is that the apparent rise in serial murder in the last three decades, while not as big as once thought, is nevertheless real—and worse, it is not our first. It merely follows several previous waves of serial killer epidemics over the last hundred years, each bigger than the last. Jenkins identified two previous periods during which there were surging waves of serial homicides: 1911–1915 and 1935–1941. He found that the FBI list, while duplicating some of the more modern serial homicide cases, entirely overlooked the existence of earlier ones.[40]

The FBI study, for example, lists a total of thirteen serial homicide cases in a twenty-five-year period between 1900 and 1924. But by merely looking through back issues of the *New York Times*, Jenkins identified a wave of seventeen cases just in the short period of five years between 1911 and 1915! Clearly the FBI was underestimating the prevalence of serial murder in America in earlier years.

Henry Lee Moore, for example, between 1911 and 1912, was a traveling serial killer who murdered more than twenty-three people—entire families. But little is known about him—he is a mere footnote. In September 1911, using an axe, Moore killed six victims in Colorado Springs—a man, two women, and four children. In October he killed three people in Monmouth, Illinois, and then he slaughtered a family of five in Ellsworth, Kansas, the same month. In June 1912, he killed a couple in Paola, Kansas, and several days later he killed seven people, including four children, in Villisca, Iowa. Moore then returned home to Columbia, Missouri, where he murdered his mother and grandmother. At this point he was arrested and prosecuted in December 1912. But Moore was not immediately linked to the previous crimes until a federal agent investigating the Villisca homicides was informed by his father, a warden of the Leavenworth Penitentiary with contacts throughout the prison system, of the nature of Henry Lee Moore's crimes in Missouri.

In another case, in Atlanta between May 1911 and May 1912 twenty light-skinned black women were murdered on the streets in Jack-the-Ripper-style mutilations. Between May 20 and July 1, 1911, the unknown killer murdered the first seven victims—one every Saturday night like clockwork.

In Denver and Colorado Springs in 1911–1912, seven women were bludgeoned to death with the perpetrator never being caught.

Between January 1911 and April 1912, forty-nine victims were killed in unsolved axe murders in Texas and Louisiana. Very similar to the Moore murders, entire families were wiped out: a mother and her three children hacked to death in their beds in Rayne, Louisiana, in January 1911; ten miles away in Crowley, Louisiana, three members of the Byers family in February 1911; two weeks later, a family of four in Lafayette. In April the killer struck in San Antonio, Texas, killing a family of five. All the victims were killed in their beds at night and nothing was stolen from their homes. In November 1911 the killer returned to Lafayette and killed a family of six; in January 1912 a woman and her three children were killed in Crowley. Two days later, at Lake Charles, a family of five were killed in their beds, and a note was left behind: "When He maketh the Inquisition for Blood, He forgetteth not the cry of the humble—human five."

In February 1912 the killer murdered a woman and her three children while they slept in their beds in Beaumont, Texas. In March, a man and a woman and her four children were hacked to death in Glidden, Texas, while they slept. In April a family of five were killed in San Antonio again, and two nights later, three were killed in Hempstead, Texas. The murders were never solved.

In New York City a "ripper" killed a five-year-old girl on an errand inside her apartment building on March 19, 1915. He sent taunting letters to the victim's mother and the police, signing himself as "H. B. Richmond, Jack-the-Ripper" and threatening to kill again. On May 3 he killed a four-year-old boy playing in a hallway and stuffed his body under a tenement staircase. The offender was never identified.

Again in New York City, in 1915 the corpses of fifteen newborn infants were recovered, suspected to be linked to some sort of "baby farm" operation.

These murders were all spectacular crimes, some widely reported in their time, others not, but all forgotten today. Jack the Ripper with his five victims is immortalized, but the Louisiana-Texas axe murderer with forty-nine victims is entirely forgotten. The primary difference is that London was the center of a huge newspaper industry while Louisiana and Texas were not. The story of Jack the Ripper was retold and entered popular myth and literature—while the Louisiana-Texas axe murderer faded from public consciousness. Serial murder "epidemics" are as much about reporting as they are about killing.

The Global Rise of Serial Murder

The rise in cases of serial murder in the last three decades is not a uniquely American problem. Although the United States is the primary location for serial murders, it does not exclusively harbor this trend. While 76 percent of all recently reported serial killings in the world took place in the United States, 21 percent occurred in Europe, where England led with 28 percent of the European total, followed by Germany with 27 percent and France at 13 percent.[41]

Serial murder was once considered only an American phenomenon, but Europe is also increasingly reporting a resurgent rise in the rate of serial murders. In England, police uncovered twelve murders committed between 1971 and 1987 by Rosemary and Fred West in Gloucester, England, including that of their sixteen-year-old daughter, who vanished in 1987.

In another case, the residents of a London apartment building complained that their toilets were not flushing properly. When a drain company operator inspected the plumbing he found it blocked by greasy fragments of human remains. Dennis Nilsen, a former police constable who lived in the same building, confessed to killing sixteen young men, cutting them up into pieces, and flushing them down the toilet.

In 2000, English doctor Fred Shipman was convicted of murdering fifteen of his elderly patients, while the actual number of his victims is believed to be four hundred—making him the possibly the most prolific serial killer in recent history. (Once a serial killer is successfully convicted for a few murders, authorities often do not pursue further convictions in the same jurisdiction.)

In France, Paris police announced in 1998 the arrest of Guy Georges—the "Beast of Bastille"—who raped and murdered seven women. Described as "unstable," Georges is said to be a persistent sexual offender who had been living in cheap hotels and squats for some time. In court, Georges was described by the public prosecutor as "the incarnation of evil," and psychiatrists warned that he could not be cured of his desire to kill. Born and raised in Angers, he is also being questioned about three rapes and murders committed there between 1991 and 1994. All the victims were young women, some found tied to their beds with knife or razor cuts to their throats. In 2001 he was sentenced to life with no chance of parole for twenty-five years.

In Copenhagen, Denmark, two surgeons, one of them a police pathologist, were sentenced to life in prison for the murders of ten women. The police pathologist had performed the forensic autopsies on some of his own victims.

Italy is not immune to the current rise of serial murder in Europe, as illustrated by the well-known case of the Monster of Florence, who killed eight couples between 1968 and 1985 and mailed pieces of their bodies to police and the media. In another case, two young men in their twenties—"yuppies"—one the son of a renowned plastic surgeon in Verona, the other of a managing director of the Verona branch of a German insurance company—were charged with twenty-seven homicides. One victim was a priest who had a nail driven through his forehead followed by a chisel with a cross attached to it.

More recently, in Apulia, in September 1997 police arrested a suspect in the murders of at least eight elderly women, each of whom lived on the ground floor of her building. Meanwhile in Verona, Gianfranco Stavanin was convicted in 1998 of murdering and dismembering six women between 1991 and 1994 and burying their remains in nearby fields.

That same winter in 1998, Italy was electrified by a dramatic series of murders of women on trains along the vacation coast between Genoa and Monte Carlo. The killer would surprise women inside the washroom by opening the door with his own special key. After murdering his victim, he would relock the door and slip back to his compartment in the dark while the train was passing through a tunnel. By the time a conductor would get around to checking the locked toilet, the killer had long ago gotten off the train. Police eventually arrested forty-seven-year-old professional gambler and petty criminal Donato Bilancia and charged him with a total of seventeen homicides over a six-month period. His victims consisted of nine males and eight females and included not only women on the train and roadside prostitutes, but criminal associates and friends and acquaintances. One victim was strangled; the rest were shot.

But Belgium appears to be inexplicably emerging as Europe's newest serial slaughter hot zone. After awaiting trial for eight years, Marc Dutroux, 47, and his two accomplices, one of whom is his ex-wife Michel Martin, 44, finally went on trial in March 2004 for the horrific kidnapping, rape, and murder of four girls during the mid-1990s. Dutroux, a previously convicted rapist and pedophile is also charged with killing a fifth victim, an accomplice who Dutroux claims allowed the girls to die from starvation during their captivity in a secret dungeon. In court, Dutroux admitted to the raping of the kidnapped girls, some were as young as eight, but he denies killing them. The bodies of the girls and the accomplice were found on Dutroux's property. Police also rescued two girls, ages 12 and 14, found alive in a cage in Dutroux's house. Dutroux admitted to raping the twelve-year old victim at least twenty times during her seventy-nine-day captivity. Belgians have been angrily protesting the eight-year delay of the trial amidst allegations of the existence of a highly placed and powerful pedophile ring in that country.

In another case, in October 1997 Belgian authorities charged a man identified as Andras Pandy—a seventy-year-old Protestant pastor from Hungary—with the murder of two of his ex-wives and four of his children. His daughter, Agnes, confessed to helping him kill five relatives—her mother, two brothers, a stepmother, and her daughter—and is now being investigated for possible links to the disappearance of others in the family. Authorities have also linked Agnes to the disappearance in 1993 of a twelve-year-old girl whose Hungarian mother had a relationship with Pastor Pandy. It was reported that Andras Pandy fostered an undetermined number of orphaned or homeless Romanian children in his home in Brussels. The children—who became orphaned or homeless in Romania's 1989 revolution that toppled communist dictator Nicolae Ceausescu—were taken in by a charity club named YDNAP (PANDY backward) founded by the pastor. They stayed under his care for varying periods of time, "and nobody knows what happened to them or if they returned home."

Also in Belgium, police admitted they were nowhere near finding the serial killer who scattered up to thirty bags of severed and precisely measured body parts of six women around the city of Mons. The city's public prosecutor's office said eight inspectors and a police commissioner had conducted seven hundred interviews and received six hundred items of information since the first bags were discovered in March 1997. The killer is believed to be a man, probably with local geographic and historical knowledge. Belgian authorities have called on the FBI for help profiling the elusive killer. The serial killer seems to be taunting authorities by leaving the dismembered remains of his victims in places with emotive names. The remains have been left in the Rue du Depot (Dump), near the River Haine (Hate), on the Chemin de l'Inquietude (the path of Worry), and on the banks of the River Trouille (Jitters). The last of the bags found containing body parts was on Rue

St. Symphorien, named after a third-century French saint who was decapitated and whose relics are in church nearby. Apparently the killer did not dismember the bodies by hand. He rolled his victims through a machine—used for chopping logs—with circular blades placed at twelve-inch intervals. Each body fragment so far found measures exactly one foot.

Until recently the Third World accounted for only 3 percent of the world's reported serial murders, but by now that number must have climbed.[42] Because these regions have police systems that are underfinanced—or focused on political repression—and huge populations of impoverished, underprivileged, and unwanted people, Third World serial killers individually murder extraordinary numbers of victims.

Pedro Alonso Lopez is another of the twentieth century's most prolific serial killers. A native of Colombia, he is believed to have murdered three hundred girls in Colombia, Peru, and Ecuador. His prostitute mother threw him out of their home at age eight for fondling his younger sister. He was then picked up by a pedophile and sodomized against his will. By the time he was eighteen he had been gang-raped in prison and retaliated by killing three of his assailants. After his release he migrated to Peru, where he killed at least one hundred girls, until he was confronted by an angry mob in a marketplace when he attempted to walk away with a victim. He moved on to Ecuador, where he said girls were "more gentle and trusting, more innocent." He murdered three girls a week until he was captured in 1980, when a flood exposed some fifty-three buried victims, all girls ages eight to twelve.

In 1999, police in Colombia arrested Luis Alfredo Garavito in connection with the murders of 140 children. Police recovered 114 mutilated bodies of mostly boys between ages eight and sixteen. Garavito was the oldest of seven children. He was repeatedly beaten by his father and raped by two male neighbors. Garavito was also a heavy alcoholic and was treated for depression and suicidal tendencies. He said he committed most of the murders after heavy drinking. Garavito had just five years of schooling and left home at age sixteen, working first as a store clerk and then as a street vendor who sold religious icons and prayer cards. Prosecutors said Garavito found most of his victims on the streets, gaining their confidence by giving them soft drinks and money.[43]

On March 16, 2000, a Pakistani court in Lahore sentenced Javed Iqbal to death for the murder of more than a hundred children. His three accomplices, including a thirteen-year-old boy identified only as Sabir, also were found guilty. Sabir was sentenced to forty-two years in jail; the other two accomplices were sentenced to death. Iqbal wrote in a letter to the police that he killed the children, who were mostly beggars, in retaliation for the abuse they inflicted on him following a previous arrest when he was accused of sodomy. On October 25, 2001, Iqbal and Sabir were found dead in their cell. Their apparent suicides by poison—as stated by prison authorities—came just four days after Pakistan's highest Islamic court had agreed to hear Iqbal's appeal against the death sentence.

South Africa, somewhere between the Third and First Worlds, for some reason has recently hosted a remarkably high number of serial killers in recent years—estimated to be as high as thirty-five. Recently captured or currently believed to be on the loose in South Africa are Lazarus Mazikane and Kaizer Motshegwa, charged with fifty-one rape-murders of women and children in Nasrec; Moses Sithole, thirty-eight victims; Cedric Maake, the Wemmer Pan Killer, twenty-seven victims; Norman Afzal Simons, the Station Strangler, twenty-two victims; Sipho Agmatir Thwala, the Phoenix Strangler, nineteen victims; the River Monster, ten victims; and Simon Majola and Themba Nkosi, the Bruma Lake serial killers, eight victims.[44] In 1999, South Africa had a murder rate of 53 per 100,000, compared to 6 per 100,000 in the United States, and apparently has the second-highest rate of serial homicide after the United States.[45]

China, which is rapidly capitalizing, is also reporting cases of serial murder. Cement truck driver Hua Ruizhuo was executed last year for picking up fourteen prostitutes near the Great Wall Sheraton Hotel in Beijing, handcuffing them in his van, raping them, and leaving their bodies in garbage dumps around the city.

A gang of four murderers in the central province of Henan murdered seventy-one people and evaded capture for months in 2000. Their modus operandi was to break into homes using battering rams. Once inside, they killed the inhabitants, frequently castrating male victims with cleavers. They left behind calling cards: cloth masks with eye holes burned out by cigarettes.

In 2001, Duan Guocheng, a twenty-nine-year-old security guard in the Hunan province, was charged with the murders of thirteen women—many of whom were wearing red dresses when they were killed.

In July 2003, two serial killers in separate incidents in China were accused of targeting migratory street workers and vagrants. One twenty-nine-year-old man is charged with killing sixteen vagrants, while another twenty-year-old is charged with killing ten street workers (migratory junk and garbage collectors from rural areas who often live without a permit in major Chinese cities and are disliked by the wealthier urban populace).

Why the Rising Wave of Serial Killing 1970–2000?

While we understand that waves of serial murder come and go, what we do not know is *why* there has been such a rise in cases in the last three decades. Some criminologists suggest that there are not more serial killers, but more potential victims. Steven Egger, who coined the term "linkage blindness" and is the former project director of New York State's serial killer computer analysis program HALT* and the current dean of the School of Health and Human Services at the University of Illinois, is today one of the leading proponents of the victim-driven scenario behind the rise in serial death.

Egger argues that there is an increased incidence of social encouragement to kill a type of person who, when murdered, is "less-dead" than other categories of homicide victims. Prostitutes, cruising homosexuals, homeless transients, runaway youths, senior citizens, and inner-city poor, according to Egger, are perceived by our society as "less-dead" than a white college girl from a middle-class suburb. Egger explains:

> The victims of serial killers, viewed when alive as a devalued strata of humanity, become "less-dead" (since for many they were less-alive before their death and now they become the "never-were") and their demise becomes the elimination of sores or blemishes cleansed by those who dare to wash away these undesirable elements . . . [46]

The serial murders of five University of Florida students in Gainesville inspired breathless national coverage by *Time* magazine and network television, while the systematic killings of eleven crack-addicted black prostitutes in Detroit hardly made page three anywhere—nobody cared, for they are the "less-dead."

---

* HALT (Homicide Assessment and Lead Tracking System) is similar in principle to VICAP and is now called ViCAPS in New York State.

Certainly when one begins to digest the backgrounds of serial killer victims, it does become evident that a large proportion of victims are prostitutes, inner-city poor, homeless drifters, cruising gays, and runaway kids—all marginalized members of our society about whom few are concerned and whose deaths some even celebrate. As Gary Ridgway, the recently confessed Green River Killer of forty-eight prostitutes, commented to police, "I thought I was doing you guys a favor, killing, killing the prostitutes. Here you guys can't control them, but I can."

Only the frequent presence of female college students and children among categories of victims preferred by serial killers does the "less-dead" characterization falter. More traditional views argue that the frequent types of victims "facilitate" their own murders by the lifestyles they lead. A serial killer desiring to kill a female can easily lure a prostitute into a vulnerable situation. College girls and children, by virtue of the impetuous nature of youth, become easy targets as well. Traditionalists argue that it is a matter of convenience, not social marginalization, that certain types of victims are selected.

While this callousness toward the underprivileged in our society is not new, Egger argues that our culture today actually encourages the serial murderer to increasingly target the "less-dead." A killing culture is being defined by true-crime literature, fiction, movie entertainment, and news coverage, which all focus on the serial killer's skills in eluding the police and the nature of his acts, while the victims are mere props in the story—or worse, justify their own deaths.

Egger, for example, despises the portrayal of the two serial killers in the movie *The Silence of the Lambs,* which essentially introduced into popular culture the concept of serial killers and profiling in the early 1990s. Egger was appalled that audiences identified with the clever, sophisticated, and cultured Dr. Hannibal "the Cannibal" Lecter played by Anthony Hopkins, and that he became the *real* star of the movie, not Jodie Foster as FBI Agent Starling. Egger is concerned that

[i]t was not only the brilliance of Anthony Hopkins that transformed this serial killer from a cruel, sadistic animal to an antihero. Acting skills notwithstanding, the public is preprogrammed to identify with or even laud the role of the serial killer in our society.[47]

The Chianti-sipping Lecter was a "good" serial killer, while the sexually confused, dirty, poverty-ridden, rural shack-dwelling, pseudotranssexual Buffalo Bill, who kept his victims in a stinking pit and skinned them, was the "bad" serial killer. Buffalo Bill was himself "less-alive." As one critic pointed out, many would enjoy the company of the cannibal Dr. Lecter at a dinner party (as long as they weren't on the menu), but who would want to be even seen in public with Buffalo Bill?

Egger argues that such demarcation between "acceptable" and "unacceptable" serial murder paves the way for our society to attach a value to the serial killer, raising him in status above "ordinary" killers who slay their spouses:

> For many, the serial killer is a symbol of courage, individuality, and unique cleverness. Many will quickly transform the killer into a figure who allows them to fantasize rebellion or the lashing out at society's ills. For some, the serial killer may become a symbol of swift and effective justice, cleansing society of its crime-ridden vermin. The serial killer's skills in eluding police for long periods of time transcends the very reason that he is being hunted. The killer's elusiveness overshadows his trail of grief and horror.[48]

Social critic Mark Seltzer also subscribes to a version of this viewpoint. According to him, serial murder culture in the United States has supplanted an earlier uniquely American cultural institution:

> Serial murder and its representations have by now largely replaced the Western as the most popular genre-fiction of the body and of bodily violence in our culture . . . the Western was really about serial killing all along.[49]

Seltzer links the popularity of true-crime literature, movie-of-the-week crime stories, and news accounts of serial murder to what he calls a Wound Culture—"the public fascination with torn and open bodies and opened persons, a collective gathering around shock, trauma, and the wound."

This kind of cultural insemination of serial murderers is echoed in historian Angus McLaren's analysis of the nineteenth-century serial murderer Dr. Thomas Neill Cream, who killed women coming to him seeking abortions. McLaren proposes that Dr. Cream's crimes "were determined largely by the society that produced them." In Cream's time and place, Victorian London, single pregnant women seeking an abortion were the focus of the most intense scorn and disdain. The serial killer, according to McLaren, rather than being perceived as an outcast disconnected from society, is "likely best understood not so much as an 'outlaw' as an 'oversocialized' individual who saw himself simply carrying out sentences that society at large leveled."[50]

Mark Seltzer suggests that serial killers today are fed and nurtured in a similar cultural dialogue, to which they respond with their own homicidal contributions in a process that he calls "mimetic compulsion." Or, as once put more simply by the late Robert Kennedy, "society gets the kind of criminal it deserves."

This kind of culturalist scenario explaining the increased serial murder rate is a perspective rapidly gaining currency as we begin a new millennium.

Today there is a creeping nonchalance toward serial murder cases, especially if the victims are society's throwaways. The arrest of Gary Ridgway—the Green River Killer—and his guilty plea to the murders of forty-eight prostitutes garnered routine media coverage. Although most can identify Ted Bundy or Andrew Cunanan, few people can identify serial killers with names like Kendall "Stinky" Francois or William Lester Suff, despite their relatively high number of victims.

Twenty-seven-year-old Francois killed eight prostitutes from 1996 to 1998 and stored their corpses in his attic, but he and his victims hardly made the news. Moreover, Francois was doing his killing in Poughkeepsie, New York, a town on the Hudson River halfway between Albany and New York City—too far south to enter the Albany television market and too far north to be covered by the New York City TV footprint. That's like saying it never happened. And of course, by the end of the 1990s, eight victims was a relatively mediocre performance if numbers count for anything: There was no "hook" to the story—he was not eating his victims, or even taking a bite and spitting it out—he was just strangling them and stacking their corpses in plastic garbage bags up in his attic while his parents complained about the smell. (Dead raccoons, he told them.)

Even William Lester Suff with his thirteen victims in the Lake Elsinore region of California from 1986 to 1992 is relatively obscure, having killed again outside the convenient Los Angeles television footprint. Suff killed drug-addicted street prostitutes and left their bodies behind strip mall garbage Dumpsters, posed so as to call attention to their drug habits. But Suff went on trial in the middle of the O. J. Simpson case; what are thirteen dead crack whores compared to two shiny-white Starbucks victims in Brentwood at the hands of an enraged celebrity? And how about Joel Rifkin, who murdered seventeen street hookers in the New York–Long Island area? The media abandoned his story in the rush to cover the deaths of six "respectably employed" train commuters at the hands of Colin Ferguson. The trial of Joel Rifkin was wrapped up in relative obscurity despite the seventeen murder victims. We might not even know his name if an episode of *Seinfeld* had not made it a butt of jokes.

For the press covering serial murder these days it is not the sheer number of snuffed-out lives that count, but their celebrity status or visible credit rating—the trade-off comes in at around one SUV in the garage for every five dead hookers in the Dumpster.

TWO

A BRIEF HISTORY OF SERIAL HOMICIDE:

Two Thousand Years of Murder
from Rome to Boston

These crimes and offenses I committed solely for my evil pleasure and evil delight, to no other end or with no other intention, without anyone's counsel and only in accordance with my imagination.
—GILLES DE RAIS, Confession, 1440

I made fools of them.
—ALBERT DESALVO, The Boston Strangler

Although not all serial killers are sex murderers, a significantly great proportion are. Historically, sexual crime can be defined as assault and/or homicide accompanying or substituting for sexual activity. The very act of cutting, dismembering, binding, torturing, and/or killing is often more important to the sex murderer than the actual sex act. This somewhat differentiates a sexual murderer from a "rapist-killer" who as an afterthought murders his victim to prevent her from reporting him to the police. The psychological dynamic is entirely different, and the sexual killer is more predisposed to repeat his crimes in a serial pattern.

Until the mid-eighteenth century, sex crime of any kind was virtually unknown, or at least largely unreported. One reason for this is the proposition that sex crime is a "leisure activity" requiring available time to develop and dwell on sexual fantasies and the freedom to act upon them. Prior to the industrial age the majority of people were just too busy to be fantasizing about sex. Most were desperately trying to feed themselves and survive various life-threatening dangers in the form of invading armies, bandits, revolts, and plagues. (This may account for the lower rate of serial murder in the nonindustrialized Third World, where the standard of living is much more tenuous for the average citizen.)

Rome—Empire of Hedonistic Killing

In the ancient world, the commission of serial murder was the exclusive prerogative of Roman Caesars, emperors, and barbarian nomadic chieftains who exercised absolute power over their subjects. In a sense, that kind of ancient imperial power over a human life is what a serial killer seeks today. It is difficult, however, to construct a modern criminal dynamic for the killings perpetrated by ancient despots such as Nero and Caligula. During an era when death circuses were attended by thousands of spectators in arenas, accusing Roman emperors of serial homicide would be like handing out traffic tickets at the Daytona Speedway.

Throughout the Roman Empire were hundreds of stadiums where systematic death was put on public display as a form of entertainment. The biggest facility, the Coliseum in Rome, held 50,000 spectators seated in various classes of tiers. There was a system of assigned seating with tickets, not much different from a stadium of today. Betting was big and the carnage was sexually charged, with prostitutes plying their trade beneath the coliseum arches. But unlike sporting events today, the gladiatorial games allowed for audience participation in the form of spectator voting with the classic thumbs up/down gesture as to whether a defeated gladiator would live or die.* Thus in a some senses, the games were a form of mass participatory serial murder. This is not a twentieth-century hindsight viewpoint; the Romans themselves were aware of this.[51] Athenagoras, in *Embassy 35*, states that "seeing a man killed in the arena is much like killing him." Seneca wrote, "Throwing a man to the lions is like tearing him apart with your own teeth."[52] Lactantius in *Divine Institutes* (6.20.9–14) defines the death game spectator as a *particeps*—"participant."

The audiences were certainly obsessed with attending these death spectacles, which would last all day long, sometimes for weeks at a time. They

---

* Some classicists believe that thumbs up, toward the heavens, signified death, while thumbs down, to the earth, signified life.

lined up early in the morning and riots broke out when tickets were not distributed equitably, as they might today at rock concerts. In the morning the games featured either condemned prisoners exposed to attacks of wild animals or combat between trained and well-armed gladiators where the crowd could by their vote decide to save a defeated gladiator who they felt fought well or put to death one who disappointed them.

At noon, however, there was a special spectacle that the crowds apparently enjoyed the most—combat between prisoners condemned to death, wearing no armor and often only one of the pair armed with a dagger. There were never any survivors—the victor was disarmed and set upon by the next armed prisoner. It is said that the crowds favored this spectacle, because unlike with the gladiators, whose faces were often hidden by a helmet, the crowds could see the faces of the dying prisoners. The Roman writer Seneca observed, "In the morning they throw men to the lion and bears; at noon, they throw them to the spectators."[53]

The Romans were highly aware of the different degrees of violence and had unique terms for them. Excessive violence with a purpose, such as crucifixion or mass public executions in arenas was classified as *crudelitas,* and was considered to be rational and have an objective, such as to prevent rebellion or to punish criminals. But irrational violence without profit *(compendium),* killing for its own sake, was called *feritas.* This violence was attributed to unreasonable *ira* (rage), and Seneca in his writings linked unlimited power to unlimited luxury, which he argued was the cause of excessive *ira.*[54] Thus we can already see in the Roman era a belief that hedonistic murder is linked to an excess of leisure.

The spectators in Rome were pathologically engaged with the killing taking place and displayed addictive obsessions with the death. They derived a deep pleasure from the killing and a sense of power in their ability to choose life or death for the victims. The line between serial spectators and serial killers in the Coliseum was very thin.

Between the Roman games and Jack the Ripper, there are a few known cases of pathological serial killers. The ancient English epic *Beowulf,* believed to have been composed during the eighth century, describes a monstrous character named Grendel who for twelve years has been killing people by night and whose description is tantalizingly similar to the modern pathology of a serial killer: "crazed with evil anger"; "deprived of joys"; "He grieves not at all for his wicked deeds."[55]

In the fifteen centuries that followed the Roman Empire, there were various murderous tyrants, chieftains, bandits, pirates, and emperors, but it is hard to distinguish their acts from political and financial gains. We know little of their personal pathologies. There were excessively zealous inquisitors of the Catholic Church with a suspiciously high propensity for submitting women suspected of witchcraft to torture and death, but again theological imperatives of those times cloud the question of personal pathology.

In later history, prior to the industrial age, Europe's two most notorious individual sexual serial killers were aristocrats with plenty of leisure time on their hands: Marshal Gilles de Rais in fifteenth-century France and Countess Elizabeth Báthory in seventeenth-century Hungary. That those two were condemned for their crimes, despite their privilege and power, indicate the shift that society had taken since the era of the Roman games. The nature of their killing foretold of modern times to come.

Gilles de Rais—Bluebeard, the Child Murderer

Gilles de Rais was born in 1404 into an aristocratic family near Nantes and came to be one of the richest men in France. He was the personal bodyguard and close companion of Jeanne d'Arc, at whose side he fought bravely, and it was whispered that he was her secret lover. When Jeanne d'Arc was wounded by a crossbow quarrel at the siege of Paris in September 1429, it was Gilles de Rais who valiantly carried her out of the range of further projectiles. For his valor, Gilles de Rais was appointed Marshal of France by the French king Charles VII and bestowed with a coat of arms of gold lilies on a blue field.

In 1432, at age twenty-eight, Gilles de Rais was ensconced back at his castles in Machecoul and Tiffauges south of Nantes. While Jeanne d'Arc was betrayed and burned at the stake, Gilles's service to France had made him enormously wealthy. His annual income surpassed 2.5 million francs a year and his capital was 4.5 million, making him among the richest people in Europe at the time. This figure does not include his holdings of art objects, books, furnishings, and tapestries. In his history of Gilles, George Bataille writes:

He rode preceded by a royal escort, accompanied by an "ecclesiastical as-
sembly." A herald of arms, two hundred men, and trumpeters announced
him; the canons in chapel, a kind of bishop, cantors, and the children in his
music school made up his retinue on horseback, glittering with the richest
ornaments. Gilles de Rais wanted to be dazzling, to the point of ruinous
expenditure. In providing for the necessities that his delirium commanded,
he liquidated an immense fortune without thinking. Some sort of dementia
was at the heart of his propensity to spend money; he underwrote great
theatrical performances accompanied by gifts of food and drink. He was
compelled to fascinate people at all costs, but he lacked what a criminal
quite often lacks on this order of things; this makes him recognize, in his
confession, his excessive display of what necessarily should have remained hidden: *his crimes . . .* [56]

It was precisely in this period that peasant children, mostly boys, began vanishing in the regions around Gilles de Rais's castles. There was no
mystery as to where the children were going. His servants had taken in
many as pages to Gilles's household. In the fifteenth century for a peasant
boy there were only two means of escaping crushing poverty—joining the
Church as a cleric or monk or going into the service of a local lord. Many
parents were happy that their son caught the eye of Gilles's henchmen.
They were overjoyed to accept the offer of giving up their child as a page.
The depositions given at Gilles de Rais's trial eight years later describe a
situation where beggar boys flocked to the gates of Gilles's castle hoping
to be taken in. The most attractive would be chosen and then never seen
again. There was the story of a thirteen-year-old boy who had been taken
into the castle to be made a page and who returned to visit his parents carrying a loaf of bread from the castle's bakery. He glowingly described his
treatment in the service of the count but after he returned to the castle he
was never heard from again. When parents inquired of their missing children, they were told that they had been assigned to more distant castles
belonging to Gilles or that they had happily entered the service of faraway
lords who on their visits to Gilles took a liking to the lads. At one point
parents were told that the English had demanded twenty-four male children as ransom for a captured French lord.

Other children were simply snatched up by Gilles's passing entourage
while they were tending cattle in the fields, walking in the streets on their

way to church or on an errand for their parents or employers. One boy regularly delivered bread to the castle—until one day he simply did not return from a delivery. Another was left at home to care for his younger siblings. When his parents returned he had vanished. Witnesses would later testify that although the entire region was now gripped in a mass fear for its children and that there were even rumors that "they ate children" at Gilles de Rais's castle in Machecoul, nobody dared to raise a voice of suspicion or complaint against the great lord. In the archives of France are still preserved a series of witness depositions, some of them corroborated by several additional witnesses, describing the disappearance of at least thirty-seven children:[57]

> The witnesses declare that it was public and common knowledge that children were put to death in the said castle.[58]

> Certain neighbors of his had told Barbe and his wife that they ought to watch over their child, who was at risk of being snatched and they were very frightened about him; in fact, the witness had even been at Saint-Jean-d'Angély, and someone asked him where he was from, and when he replied that he was from Machecoul, that person marveled [was shocked], telling him that they ate little children there. [In Old French: *sur ce, l'on lui avait dit, en se merveillant, qu'on y mangeoit les petis enffants.*][59]

In 1440 Gilles de Rais became embroiled in a dispute over the sale of some land. The party with whom Gilles was in dispute transferred the land to his brother who was a priest. In a fit of anger, Gilles de Rais rode to the church where the priest was celebrating mass and with an armed escort burst into the church, forcing the priest to relinquish the disputed land. As his attack on the priest was a grave ecclesiastical offense, the offices of the Inquisition immediately investigated Gilles. It was not long before the accounts of missing children reached the Church authorities. On September 14, 1440, Gilles de Rais was arrested and taken to Nantes. During the subsequent ecclesiastical and civil trials, the horrific fate of the missing children, estimated to number between 140 and 800, came to light. (In one of the ecclesiastical indictments, it was charged specifically that he "killed treacherously, cruelly, and inhumanly one hundred and forty, or more, children, boys and girls, or had them killed . . . ")

According to witnesses, Gilles de Rais would approach his victims very gradually after they were presented to him. At first he would treat them as his favorite servants, giving them much attention and remarking on their handsome beauty. De Rais would next caress the child and then begin grasping and pinching. At first if the child took fear and became upset, Gilles would dismiss his actions as playful and assure the child that he meant no harm. As soon as the boy would regain his self-composure, Gilles would pounce on the child and sodomize him. In the transcripts of the trial, which survive to this day, one of Gilles's servants testified:

The accused exercised his lust once or twice on the children, then he killed them sometimes with his own hand or had them killed . . . sometimes they were decapitated and dismembered; sometimes he cut their throats leaving the head attached to the body; sometimes he broke their necks with a club; sometimes he cut their throats or some other parts of their neck, so that their blood flowed . . .

Often he loved to gaze at the severed heads and showed them to the witness and to Etienne Corrillaut, asking them which of the heads was the most beautiful, the head severed just then or the one cut off the previous day. And he often kissed the head that pleased him the most, and took delight in it.

The witness heard Gilles say that he took more pleasure in the murder of the children, and in seeing their heads and their members removed, and watching them languish, and seeing their blood flow than in knowing them carnally . . . while they were dying, he committed with them the vice of sodomy.[60]

Gilles de Rais himself confessed:

Because of my passion and my sensual delectation I took and caused to be taken a great number of children—how many I cannot say precisely, children whom I killed and caused to be killed; with them, I committed the vice and the sin of sodomy . . . and . . . I ejaculated spermatic seed in the most culpable manner on the belly of the children, before as well as after their deaths, and also while they were dying. I, alone, or with the help of my accomplices [list of names of de Rais's servants] have inflicted various kinds and manners of torture on these children. Sometimes I beheaded them with daggers, with poignards, with knives; sometimes I beat them violently on the head with a stick or with other contusive instruments . . . sometimes I suspended them in my room from a pole or by a hook and cords and strangled them; and when they were languishing, I committed on them sodomitic vice . . . When the children were dead, I embraced them, and I gazed at those which had the most beautiful heads and the loveliest members, and I caused their bodies to be cruelly opened and took delight in viewing their interior organs; and was delighted to see them dying, and sat on their bellies and delighted in watching them die thus and I laughed at them with Corrillaut and Henriet, after which I caused the children to be burned and converted their cadavers into dust . . . These crimes and offenses I committed solely for my evil pleasure and evil delight, to no other end or with no other intention, without anyone's counsel and only in accordance with my imagination.

During the ecclesiastical trial, there was some muddled testimony that concerned satanic rites associated with alchemistic practices, intended to solve the financial ruin approaching Gilles. Perhaps these accusations were merely an attempt before the era of psychiatric theory to somehow find some rational explanation for these murders.

Gilles de Rais was sentenced to death by both ecclesiastical and secular authorities, and on October 26, 1440, he was hanged and then burned. His last words were reported to be, "there is no sin, no matter how great, that God cannot pardon." His accomplices were executed with him and their bodies were left to burn away. Gilles de Rais, however, requested that his body be taken down before it burned completely and be buried, allowing him in Christian theology the possibility of resurrection on the Final Judgment Day. Due to his high rank, the request was granted and he was buried at a Carmelite church in Nantes.

The details of Gilles de Rais's assaults on his victims are indistinguishable from those of some serial killers today.

Elizabeth Báthory—The Female Vampire Killer

With the kind of weird balance history sometimes provides all on its own, the other infamous serial killer from premodern times was a woman—

Countess Elizabeth Báthory of Transylvania. Born in 1560 to George Báthory (Ecsed branch) and Anna Báthory (Somlyo branch), Elizabeth was a product of the intermarriage between the dwindling Hungarian noble families. The Báthory family was one of the richest and most powerful Protestant families in Hungary. From her family came two of the most important ruling princes of Transylvania, a number of war heroes and church officials of Hungary, and a great empire builder, Stephan Báthory, prince of Transylvania and king of Poland. Elizabeth's other relatives included an uncle rumored to be addicted to secret rituals and worship of Satan; her aunt Klara, a well-known bisexual who enjoyed torturing servants; and Elizabeth's brother, Stephan, who was a drunkard and a lecher.

The countess had a reputation for sadistic treatment of her servants, whom she would torture for the slightest mistake. Elizabeth, with her own hands, tore apart the mouth of one servant girl who had made an error while sewing. Every day, young servant girls who had committed some infraction were assembled in the basement of the castle for brutal torture. Elizabeth delighted in the torture of the young women and never missed a session. While torture of one's servants in seventeenth-century Hungary was not a crime, it was by then considered "impolite." Thus when traveling and visiting other aristocrats, the first thing the countess did was to have a private room secured where she could torture her servants in privacy without offending her hosts. It was noted that the girls chosen for "punishment" seemed to be always those with the biggest breasts. Elizabeth was obviously sexually motivated in meting out her tortures.

Elizabeth was married at age fifteen to a fierce Hungarian knight, Count Gyorgy Thurzo, known as the "Black Hero of Hungary." Her husband, far from discouraging her sadistic practices, taught her some techniques of torture he had developed on the battlefield in the war against the Turks. It was, however, after he died that Elizabeth began her killing.

One day when Elizabeth's maid accidentally pulled her hair while combing it, the countess struck her so hard as to draw blood. A few drops splashed on Elizabeth's hand, and when she wiped them off it seemed to her that her skin appeared more transparent and rejuvenated. The countess became convinced that she had discovered a cosmetic secret for rejuvenating aging skin. Reportedly she ordered the girl's blood to be drained into a bathtub and bathed in it. For the next ten years, Elizabeth bathed in blood daily, believing that the ritual would preserve her skin from aging.*

The ruse she used for finding victims was similar to that of Gilles de Rais. Young peasant girls would be lured to Elizabeth's castle with promises of positions in the household staff. Upon their arrival they would be tortured by Elizabeth or her servants in nightlong sessions, and at dawn the countess would bathe in their blood.

In the countess's murderous service was her manservant, referred to only as Ficzko (which means "lad" in Hungarian); Helena Jo, the wet nurse; Dorothea Szentes (also called "Dorka"); and Katarina Beneczky, a washerwoman who came into the countess's employ late in her bloody career. Also, between 1604 and 1610, a mysterious woman named Anna Darvulia, who was believed to be a lesbian lover of Elizabeth's, taught her many new torturing techniques.

One accomplice testified that on some days Elizabeth had naked girls laid flat on the floor of her bedroom and tortured them so much that one could scoop up the blood by the pail afterward. Elizabeth had her servants bring up cinders in order to cover the pools of blood. A young maidservant who did not endure the tortures well and died very quickly was written out by the countess in her diary with the curt comment, "She was too small."

At one point in her life Elizabeth Báthory was so sick that she could not move from her bed and could not find the strength to torture her servant girls. She demanded that one of her female servants be brought before her. Dorothea Szentes, a burly, strong peasant woman, dragged one of Elizabeth's girls to her bedside and held her there. Elizabeth rose up on her bed and bit the girl on the cheek. Then she turned to the girl's shoulders, where she ripped out a piece of flesh with her teeth. After that, Elizabeth proceeded to bite the girl's breasts.

It is said that Elizabeth became particularly desperate about her aging. Convinced that peasant girls' blood was not pure enough, she began to murder young women of noble birth. At first she focused on daughters

---

* This is at least the legend. One source attributes the "bathing in blood" theme to the fact that Elizabeth was so covered in blood after torturing the girls that it appeared as if she had bathed in their blood.

of the impoverished families of fallen gentry, who were invited to become Elizabeth's companions. When questioned about the disappearance of the girls, she concocted a story that some of the girls had murdered other girls in her service and then committed suicide. Nonetheless, noble families began to refuse Elizabeth's offers to take their daughters into her court, and the countess's servants developed a ruse in which they would dress-up peasant girls in fine clothes and present them as nobility to Elizabeth.

In the beginning, Elizabeth saw to it that the dead girls were given proper Christian burials by the local Protestant pastor. But as the body count rose, the pastor refused to perform further funerals because too many girls were coming to him from Elizabeth who had died of "unknown and mysterious causes." She threatened him in order to keep him silent and continued to have the bodies buried secretly. Near the end, many bodies, mutilated and drained of blood, were disposed of in a haphazard manner in conspicuous locations such as nearby fields, wheat silos, the stream running behind the castle, and the kitchen vegetable garden. This gave rise to lurid vampire myths in the region.

Traveling between Vienna and northwest Hungary, Countess Elizabeth Báthory murdered some 650 young women over ten years. As in the case of Gilles de Rais, many people knew that girls were disappearing in Elizabeth's court, but no one dared to raise a voice of complaint against the countess, and those who did were quickly silenced by members of Elizabeth's powerful family.

So far, Elizabeth had been protected by two circumstances. First, throughout her life there was a degree of lawlessness in Hungary following the war with the Turks. The fact that her husband was a noted warrior in the battle against the Turks gave her powerful status. Second, Elizabeth was a Protestant, and Protestant-Catholic rivalry lead to a delicate balance of power in Hungary that nobody wanted to upset. All of that changed after the peace of Vienna in 1608, when Protestant and Catholic provinces were united under the Catholic Habsburg crown. This was followed by Protestant uprisings in Austria, which were brutally put down by the king. These factors eroded Countess Elizabeth Báthory's power, and the numerous reports and complaints about her began to gain momentum.

In the winter of 1610 Elizabeth still felt that her social position made her virtually untouchable before the law; she had her servants toss four murdered girls from the ramparts of Castle Cséjthe. This was done in full view of the Cséjthe villagers, who reported this latest atrocity to the king's officials.

The Hungarian parliament finally ordered an investigation, and officers of the crown searched Elizabeth's castle. There they found numerous bodies of young women, drained of blood, their hair torn out, their breasts cut off, and their genitals burned.

In 1611 Elizabeth's servants were tried for the murders and executed, but Elizabeth herself, still powerfully connected, was not put on trial. Although she was sentenced to death by an executive order, her sentence was commuted to life imprisonment in her castle. She was bricked up inside her bedchambers in Castle Cséjthe, with only a small port left open through which food could be passed to her. She died four years later at age fifty-five.

The entire episode was so embarrassing to Hungary's aristocracy that the matter was hushed up and kept secret until the 1720s, when a Jesuit scholar uncovered the transcripts of the official investigation.

Serial Sexual Crimes in Premodern History

Aside from the cases of Gilles de Rais and Elizabeth Báthory, there are few accounts in history of any pathological serial murder prior to the nineteenth century. In Scotland, in the Galloway region somewhere between 1560 and 1610, Sawney Beane and his family of cave-dwelling cannibals are said to have killed and eaten thousands of travelers over a forty-five-year period. His family, the product of incest consisting of eight sons, six daughters, eighteen grandsons, and fourteen granddaughters, fed on human flesh that was found by soldiers and pickled and smoked in the caves. They were all put to death in Leith without standing trial. The historic authenticity of this episode, however, has not been resolved with any finality, as no contemporary documentation for the event has been identified.[61]

In 1577 Nuremberg, German hangman Hans Schmidt wrote in his autobiography that he put Nicklaus Stüller to death because "First he shot a horse-soldier; secondly he cut open a pregnant woman alive in which was a dead child; thirdly he again cut open a pregnant woman in whom was a female child; fourthly he once more cut open a pregnant woman in whom were two male children."

During the same period in Cologne in 1589, Peter Stubbe (Stumpf) stood charged with the rape, murder, and cannibalization of fifteen women and children near the village of Bedburg over five years. Their remains were found scattered around the village fields. Some of his victims were pregnant women from whose wombs he tore out the fetus and ate it. One of his victims was his own infant child, the result of incest with his daughter, whom he killed and ate. Stubbe, it was charged, had made a pact with the devil to turn into a werewolf, in which form he would attack his victims. He was executed in Cologne on October 8, 1589.

Another case of "werewolf" serial homicides is recorded in France in 1603, when a fourteen-year-old boy, Jean Grenier, was arrested after being beaten back by a girl he had attacked. Grenier confessed that he would take the form of a werewolf while mutilating and eating young children and pretty girls. The judge of Chastellanie and Barony of La Roche Calais questioned the boy, paying particular attention to the issue of werewolves. According to the surviving transcripts:

> Asked what children he had killed and eaten while thus transformed into a wolf: said that once, as he was going from Coutras to Saint Anlaye he entered a house where he saw no one but found a one-year-old child in a cradle and took it by its throat between his teeth, carried it behind a garden fence, ate as much of it as he wanted.
>
> That near the parish of Saint Antoine de Pizon, he hurled himself upon a young girl wearing a black dress and watching over lambs, killed her and ate as much of her as he wanted. But here is something remarkable: he said that it was he who had pulled her dress down without tearing it. It has been observed that real wolves tear with their claws, and werewolves tear with their teeth, whereas men know how to despoil girls they wish to eat of their dresses without tearing them.[62]

That the girl's dress was not torn took on crucial forensic significance in this case. Physicians were called to examine the boy and concluded that he did not really turn into a werewolf, but only imagined he did, as a result of "demonic possession." In other words, he was insane. As a result, Jean Grenier was not put to death, but instead confined for life in a monastery.

The remaining few cases that are noted in history are either series of assassinations for political motives or murders by bandits, highwaymen, and pirates systematically killing off witnesses to their crimes. There were frequent accounts of serial killing for profit, including several of female killers poisoning their victims. Serial killers preying on victims for pathological need or pleasure were rarely if ever heard of, but we cannot rule out the possibility that legendary accounts of vampires and werewolves are actually factual descriptions of human serial killers.

The earliest recorded episode of a fetish-driven serial sex crime crops up in April 1790 in London. A "Monster" is reported by contemporary description, having committed a series of "nameless crimes, the possibility of whose existence no legislator has ever dreamed of." The Monster stalked well-dressed women in the streets, abused them with indecent language, and then slashed at their clothing. In some cases, he wore some kind of knife apparatus on his knees, allowing him to approach women in a crowd and slash at their clothing discreetly from below. More than fifty women were attacked this way between 1788 and 1790. Occasionally the assailant would cut too deeply and wound his victims, but many avoided being injured by the fashion of the day, consisting of multiple thick petticoats and bloomer-type underwear.

London was as shocked and alarmed by these extraordinary and inexplicable attacks as they would be by Jack the Ripper a hundred years later. Rewards were offered for the capture of the Monster and descriptions of his activities were posted everywhere, but they varied. The attacks appeared to escalate when some women on the street were approached by a man holding a small bouquet of artificial flowers who would ask them to smell it. Those who bent over to do so would be slashed on the face with something sharp hidden in the bouquet.

In June 1790, one of the victims thought she recognized her assailant, and he was arrested. He turned out to be an artificial-flower maker named Renwick Williams. Not all the victims identified him, and his trial was very complex because nobody knew what to charge him with. The prosecution spoke of "a crime that is so new in the annals of mankind, an act so inexplicable, so unnatural, that one might have regarded it, out of respect for human nature, as impossible." Due to the peculiarities of the criminal code at that time, attempted murder was merely a misdemeanor, and the authorities were hard pressed to find an appropriate felony with which to charge Renwick Williams. At first they considered the Coventry Act, which made it a felony to lie in wait with the purpose of maiming or disfiguring a person. But there was no evidence that the Monster ambushed his victims. The Black Act made it a felony to go about armed while in disguise, but Williams was not obviously disguised. Finally the magistrates discovered a 1721 act that was passed when English weavers, in protest against cloth being imported from India, slashed the clothes of those they saw wearing it. The act made it a felony punishable by transportation (usually to Australia) for seven years, to "assault any person in the public streets, with intent to tear, spoil, cut, burn, or deface the garment or clothes of such person, provided the act be done in pursuance of such intention."[63]

Williams was convicted of the charge, but a superior court decided that it did not apply to his case. He was tried again on the misdemeanor of attempted murder and sentenced to six years in prison. He denied being the Monster to the end. Upon his release, Williams married, fathered a child, and vanished from history.

In the decades that followed, several similar cases are on record in France and Germany. In Paris in 1819, women on the street were attacked and cut about the thighs and buttocks by *piqueurs*. The term *picquerism* is still used today to describe stabbing or slashing committed as a substitute for sex. At the same time in Augsburg, Germany, a *Mädchenschneider*— "girl cutter"—began to cut and slash young women in the buttocks, arms, and legs. His reign of terror lasted eighteen years, claiming some fifty victims, until the arrest of a wealthy thirty-five-year-old wine merchant named Carl Bartle. In his home, authorities discovered an extensive collection of edged weapons. Bartle confessed an aversion and disgust for women and stated that since age nineteen he would have an orgasm at the sight of blood. Like Williams, he was sentenced to six years in prison.

In the area of Bozen and Innsbruck, several women were stabbed with a small penknife in 1828 and 1829. The perpetrator, when arrested, also confessed to a sexual compulsion to stab women, which was enhanced by the sight of dripping blood. In Leipzig, similar attacks took place in the 1860s. In Bremen in 1880, a twenty-nine-year-old hairdresser, Theophil Mary, was charged with slashing the breasts of thirty-five women he had confronted on the streets. Previously he had committed a series of attacks in Strasbourg, but moved when the authorities intensified their search for the offender.

All of these offenses seemed a rehearsal for the attacks committed by Jack the Ripper in London in 1888. For some reason, all these perpetrators never crossed the line to killing their victims. Their attacks ranged from hesitant slashing of clothing to violent stabs to the women's bodies, but while they persisted for years, they never escalated to homicide.

Slouching Toward Whitechapel:
The Rise of Sexual Murder

It was not until the nineteenth century, with the advent of leisure time for all classes, that the middle and lower classes began to indulge to any extent in sex crime and serial homicide. Sex crime was no longer the prerogative of only aristocrats or demented vagrants.

In 1808, police in Regensdorf in Bavaria arrested fortune-teller Andrew Bichel for murdering women who came to his premises seeking employment as servants. Two bodies were found buried beneath the woodshed, and chests of women's clothing were discovered in Bichel's house. It was determined that Bichel had a fetish for female clothing and killed his victims for it. Bichel would request that the girls being interviewed bring their wardrobes with them. He persuaded some of the girls to have their eyes covered and their hands tied behind their backs in order to show them their future in a magic mirror. He then stabbed them in the neck.

One of the earliest documented sex murders was committed in the small town of Alton in England in July 1867. The perpetrator represented a new class with earned leisure time on its hands—the middle class. A young solicitor's clerk named Frederick Baker approached an eight-year-old girl he knew and persuaded her to go for a walk. Several hours later when the girl had failed to return home and her friends informed her mother that she had gone off with Baker, the mother set out to look for her daughter. She encountered Baker returning to the town. He told her in a very calm and self-possessed manner that her daughter had gone to buy candies. The child's body was found in a field several hours later, beheaded and cut up into many pieces. Her genitals were missing and were never found. Baker was immediately arrested but claimed to be innocent. In his office diary, however, police found an entry reading: "Killed a young girl today. It was fine and hot." Baker was tried and executed. (During his trial, he stated that he meant to write: "Killed, a young girl, today. [The weather] was fine and hot.")

Had Baker lived in a larger urban community where he was not known, he might have gone on to continue killing. When he encountered the girl's mother, he was calm and collected, and his clothes were clean despite the fact that he had just dismembered a body. That suggested that Baker must have stripped off his clothes in a lucid and premeditated manner prior to butchering his victim. His behavior, when questioned by the police, was cool and calm, and he persistently denied committing the crime.

It is in Europe in the 1860s that the first modern pathological serial sexual killings begin to crop up in history. In France, Joseph Philippe murdered six prostitutes, while in Vittoria, Spain, a man named Gruyo strangled six prostitutes over a period of ten years. In Italy in December 1870, a fourteen-year-old girl, Johanna Motta, set out to a neighboring village but failed to return. She was discovered lying by a path in the fields, with her abdomen cut open and her torn-out intestines and genitals near by. She had been suffocated by dirt forced into her mouth and appeared to be strangled. Nearby, under a pile of straw, were found remnants of her clothing and a piece of flesh cut from her calf.

In August 1871, a twenty-eight-year-old woman, Fregeni, was found by her husband in a field when she failed to return home. She had been strangled and her intestines were hanging out through a deep wound in her abdomen.

The next day, nineteen-year-old Maria Previtali reported that her cousin, twenty-two-year-old Vincenzo Verzeni, had dragged her out into a field of grain and attempted to strangle her. When he stood up to see if anyone was coming, she managed to talk her cousin into letting her go. Verzeni was arrested and he confessed:

I had an unspeakable delight in strangling women, experiencing during the act erections and real sexual pleasure. It was even a pleasure only to smell female clothing. The feeling of pleasure while strangling them was much greater than that which I experienced while masturbating. I took great delight in drinking Motta's blood. It also gave me the greatest pleasure to pull the hairpins out of the hair of my victims.

I took the clothing and intestines, because of the pleasure it gave me to smell and touch them. At last my mother came to suspect me, because she noticed spots of semen on my shirt after each murder or attempt at one. I am not crazy, but in the moment of strangling my victims I saw nothing else. After the commission of the deeds I was satisfied and felt well. It never occurred to me to touch or look at the genitals and such things. It satisfied me to seize the women by the neck and suck their blood. To this very day I am ignorant of how a woman is formed. During the strangling and after it, I pressed myself on the entire body without thinking of one part more than another.[64]

Verzeni admitted that he experienced sexual pleasure whenever he choked a woman. Previously he had experienced orgasms while pressing his victims' throats without killing them, but in the case of the two murder victims his sexual satisfaction became so delayed that they died. He sucked the blood of his victims and had torn a piece from Motta's calf to take home and roast, but hid it under a haystack for fear that his mother might suspect him. Verzeni stated that at age twelve he discovered that he derived sexual pleasure from wringing the necks of chickens. In the four years before the murders he had attempted to strangle three other women, including his former nurse while she slept sick in bed.

In the 1870s, physical features were linked to criminal character; therefore, close attention was paid to Verzeni's physiology. (Later in this book, we will see how a hundred years later, counseling psychologist Dr. Joel Norris found frequent physical abnormalities in serial killers he observed.) The clinical assessment of Verzeni concluded:

His cranium is of more than average size, but asymmetrical. The right frontal bone is narrower and lower than the left, the right frontal prominence being less developed, and the right ear smaller than the left (by 1 centimeter in length and 3 centimeters in breadth); both ears are defective in the inferior half of the helix; the right temporal artery is somewhat atheromatous. It seems probable that Verzeni had a bad ancestry—two uncles are cretins; a third, microcephalic, beardless and one testicle wanting, the other atrophic . . .

Verzeni's family is bigoted and low-minded. He himself has ordinary intelligence; knows how to defend himself well; seeks to prove an *alibi* and cast suspicion on others. There is nothing in his past that points to mental disease, but his character is peculiar. He is silent and inclined to be solitary. In prison he is cynical. He masturbates, and makes every effort to gain sight of women.[65]

The description of the first known sexual serial killer is remarkably typical of the ones of today. Verzeni was of average intelligence and showed no signs of mental disease but was "peculiar and inclined to be solitary." Vincenzo Verzeni was sentenced to life imprisonment in 1872.

The same year in Vinuville, France, a young man named Eusebius Pieydagnelle surrendered to authorities and confessed to killing seven people. He explained that he was obsessed with blood and would have an orgasm at the sight and smell of it. All of his victims were extremely mutilated. According to the evidence presented in court, Eusebius came from a "highly respectable family" and was well educated. His home was located across the street from a butcher shop; according to Eusebius, "The smell of fresh blood, and appetizing meat, the bloody lumps—all this fascinated me and I began to envy the butcher's assistant, because he could work at the block, with rolled up sleeves and bloody hands." Although his parents were opposed, Eusebius found employment with the butcher, intending to apprentice. He was overjoyed at the opportunity to butcher animals all day long. But his father eventually took Eusebius away and apprenticed him to a notary. This threw Eusebius into a deep depression and he began killing people; his first victim was a fifteen-year-old girl whom he stabbed and mutilated. He killed six more times, the last victim being the butcher he first worked for. Then he surrendered.

Across the ocean in the United States, in 1874 in Boston, a fourteen-year-old youth named Jesse Pomroy was sentenced to life imprisonment for the torture murders of a ten-year-old girl and a four-year-old boy. The boy had been found with thirty-one knife wounds; the girl, who had disappeared the month before, was found buried in the basement of the house that Pomroy lived in. Because of his youth, Pomroy was sentenced to life imprisonment. He served the first forty-one years of his sentence in solitary confinement and died on a prison farm in 1932 at age seventy-two.

The same year in Boston as well, Tomas Piper, a church bell-ringer in his midtwenties, battered to death and raped two women and a five-year-old girl. A few days before his hanging in 1876, he confessed to an additional four homicides.

• • •

At the time these crimes occurred, none of them were recognized as sex crimes. The killers were all characterized as "monsters" with animal-like appetites. They were paralleled with vampire and werewolf legends—they were no longer humans. It was during this period that Austrian psychiatrist Richard von Krafft-Ebing was working with the Berlin courts and witnessing all manners of sexual crimes. Krafft-Ebing was inspired to write *Psychopathia Sexualis*, a textbook on sexual abnormalities, including serial homicide, in which he identified and catalogued the sexual nature of homicides committed by so-called "monsters," which he termed "joy murder" or "lust murder" *(lustmord)*. Krafft-Ebing maintained that in such murders, the vicious mutilation of victims, and the killing itself, was sexually motivated and a substitute for normal sex.

Written in the 1880s, some of Krafft-Ebing's conclusions are still hauntingly applicable today. The authorities, he wrote, are ill-equipped to combat sex crime:

> This contest is unequal; because only a certain number of sexual crimes can be combated, and the infractions of the laws by so powerful a natural instinct can be but little influenced by punishment. It also lies in the nature of the sexual crimes that but a part of them ever reach the knowledge of the authorities. Public sentiment, in that it looks upon them as disgraceful, lends much aid.
>
> Criminal statistics prove the sad fact that sexual crimes are progressively increasing in our modern civilization. This is particularly the case with immoral acts with children under the age of fourteen.[66]

Statistics in France had indicated 136 cases of sexual assault on children in 1826 but 805 in 1867. In England there were 167 assaults during 1830–1834, but 1,395 for 1855–1857.

JACK THE RIPPER AND AFTER

Jack the Ripper—known in his time as the Whitechapel Murderer—is probably the most infamous serial killer of all time. He struck at the height of the Victorian era in London's East End, butchering at least five prostitutes between August and November 1888. He made headlines worldwide and even today he continues to capture the imaginations of countless readers and moviegoers—and other serial killers as well. He appears as a character in at least twenty-eight major motion pictures, hundreds of fiction and non-fiction books, and several specialized books about other books on Jack the Ripper or studies of the press coverage he received in his time.[67] There would be no point to dealing at any length here with Jack the Ripper's crimes in the face of the torrent of material still being produced about him today. It is sufficient to say that his crimes, committed in a newspaper publishing capital, received unprecedented coverage. He was raised to mythical proportions for his abilities to evade the authorities and for his choice of prostitutes as victims whom few would pity: He did not kill children or "innocent" women. He set the stage for crime literature where the serial killer takes the leading role in an almost heroic capacity.

The early victims were killed on the street by having their throats slit, and were hastily mutilated. But as he progressed, Jack the Ripper gradually became more proficient at gaining control over his victims. The last victim, twenty-five-year-old Mary Jane Kelly, was found in her own room where the killer had privacy to unleash his deepest and darkest fantasies. London police surgeon Dr. Thomas Bond wrote the report describing the condition of Kelly's body as it was discovered at the crime scene:

> The body was lying naked in the middle of the bed, the shoulders flat, but the axis of the body inclined to the left side of the bed. The head was turned on the left cheek. The left arm was close to the body with the forearm flexed at a right angle & lying across the abdomen. The right arm was slightly abducted from the body & rested on the mattress, the elbow bent & and the forearm supine with the fingers clenched. The legs were wide apart, the left thigh at right angles to the trunk & the right forming an obtuse angle with the pubes.
>
> The whole of the surface of the abdomen & thighs was removed & the abdominal Cavity emptied of its viscera. The breasts were cut off, the arms mutilated by several jagged wounds & the face hacked beyond recognition of the features. The tissues of the neck were severed all round down to the bone.
>
> The viscera were found in various parts viz: the uterus & Kidneys with one breast under the head, the other breast by the right foot, the Liver be-

tween the feet, the intestines by the right side & the spleen by the left side of the body. The flaps removed from the abdomen and thighs were on a table . . . the neck was cut through the skin & other tissues right down to the vertebrae the 5th & 6th being deeply notched . . . The skin & tissues of the abdomen from the costal arch to the pubes were removed in three large flaps . . . The left thigh was stripped of skin, fascia & muscles as far as the knee. The Pericardium was open below & the Heart absent.[68]

Mary Jane Kelly's missing heart was never recovered and Jack the Ripper was never captured, leaving behind more than a century of speculation as to his identity and to why he stopped killing.

What was clear was that Jack the Ripper was not some frenzied out-of-control individual, but someone who was able to disguise his insanity and appear normal to those around him. Jack the Ripper was ushering in the twentieth-century phenomenon of the serial killer.

While Jack the Ripper was a typically "territorial" type of serial killer, choosing his victims in London's East End, France's Vacher the Ripper was typically "migratory," killing in different regions of the country. Joseph Vacher was a twenty-eight-year-old vagrant when he was charged in 1897 for the murder of a seventeen-year-old shepherd boy. The victim had been strangled and afterward his abdomen had been cut open. Vacher confessed to eleven previously unsolved homicides that had occurred in different parts of France between 1894 and 1897, and was suspected in fifteen more.

In 1893 Vacher had been discharged from military service after displaying confused talk, persecution mania, and threatening language. The same year he wounded a girl who had refused to marry him and then shot himself in the head. He survived his suicide attempt, which left him deaf in one ear and with facial paralysis, and was confined in an insane asylum. He was declared "cured" and released on April 1, 1894.

On March 20, 1894, he strangled a twenty-one-year-old woman, cut her throat, tore out a portion of her right breast, trampled upon her abdomen, and had intercourse with the corpse. In November he strangled a thirteen-year-old girl and in May 1895 he murdered a seventeen-year-old girl. In August he strangled and raped a fifty-eight-year-old woman; shortly afterward he cut the throat of a sixteen-year-old girl and attempted to rip her abdomen open. In September he killed a fifteen-year-old boy, cut off his genitals, and sexually assaulted the corpse. Traveling through France, he killed women, girls, and boys, by either cutting their throats or strangling them. He mutilated and violated their corpses, taking away with him their genitals.

On August 4, 1897, Vacher attacked a woman gathering pinecones but she successfully resisted him, shouting for her husband and children. They overpowered Vacher and took him into custody. Vacher was sentenced to three months' imprisonment for indecent assault, but during his incarceration he wrote the authorities with a confession to eleven murders. Although Vacher insisted he was insane, a panel of psychiatrists pronounced him sane. He was executed in December 1898.

EXPLAINING MUTILATION AND PICQUERISM

The motives behind the extraordinary and brutal mutilation of female victims with edged-weapons remain a mystery even today. It is an act that seems to be largely perpetrated by angry heterosexual males on females or homosexual males on males—in other words, an act directed by males onto the object of their sexual desire.

Some argue that the formation of a serial killer is rooted to gender identification involving a boy's ability to successfully negotiate his masculine autonomy from his mother—a challenge not faced by females. When a boy cannot achieve this autonomy or when there is no solid foundation for him from which to negotiate this autonomy, a sense of rage develops in the child, and he subsequently carries the anger into adolescence and adulthood.

A serial killer's sexual assault on a victim can take one, or both, of two forms of expression. First, there are the primary mechanisms: intercourse and oral copulation. The killer does whatever is physically necessary to ejaculate during his attack. Frequently, however, no evidence of ejaculate is visible at a crime scene. It is here that the killer engages in secondary sexual mechanisms. These are a substitution for the primary act, a type of sexually delayed gratification. The actions that the killer performs will later lead to his climax when he is in a safe place. It is not a question of safety, however, but one of control. Having committed his act, and taken his souvenirs from the victim, the killer escapes to later masturbate until his sexual energy is drained. In this manner he exercises maximum control over his own sexuality and over his victim and is able to sustain himself between murders.

These secondary mechanisms take the form of torture, bondage, the posing of the victim's body in humiliating positions, cannibalism, stabbing, slashing, and mutilation. The preference to use a knife for mutilating a victim beyond what is necessary to kill is called *picquerism*. The killer expresses his sexuality by penetrating the victim with a knife. The victim's screams, the bloodletting, and the odors all create for the murderer a harmonic sexual experience. Some killers ejaculate uncontrollably without touching their genitals as they stab or hack at their victims.

Some experts associate picquerism with cultural construction of femininity, with its association with the body, bleeding, and birth, which link women with a mortality that provokes a dual reaction: anxious fear accompanied by erotic desire. If this duality slips out of control, the consequences can be horrific. Klaus Theweleit writes of dismembered murder victims:

> It is as if two male compulsions were tearing at the women with equal strength. One is trying to push them away, to keep them at arm's length (defense); the other wants to penetrate them, to have them very near. Both compulsions seem to find satisfaction in the act of killing, where the man pushes the woman far away (takes her life), and gets very close to her (penetrates her with a bullet, stabs, clubs, etc.) . . . Once she . . . is reduced to a pulp, a shapeless, bloody mass, the man can breathe a sigh of relief.[69]

As we become familiar with cases of serial murder in these pages, we shall see that this theory may have some validity to it.

WHY THE RISE OF SEXUAL HOMICIDE?

The question remains: Why did sexual homicide and serial murder arise in the nineteenth century? Some may argue that these crimes had always been with us but simply had not been recognized or reported, or were disguised as werewolf and vampire myths. Nonetheless, when one looks at the few systematic records of pre-nineteenth-century crime, such as England's *Newgate Calendar*, there are few references to sexual murder or "monsters."

Another theory relates the rise of sexual crime with growing population density. In experiments with rats, researchers discovered that 5 percent of the animals were dominant. When put into highly crowded conditions, this 5 percent began to behave "criminally" by raping female rats, instead of going through their usual complex and protective courting practices. The rats also began to kill and cannibalize infant rats. These studies, however, do not fully explain the phenomenon because some of the earliest serial murders were occurring in the countryside and not in the densely populated cities.

English writer Colin Wilson suggests that two factors may have contributed to the rise of sexual serial murder—the expansion of the female workforce and a certain type of pornographic literature.[70]

Wilson maintains that today every man knows that the majority of women that one encounters in the city are unavailable. However, during much of the nineteenth century, the reverse was true. Thousands of impoverished, urbanized women turned to prostitution and were all available to any man with a coin in his pocket. But by the last two decades of the century, it was discovered that women made better typists than men did, that they were excellent shop clerks, and so on. Now men were faced with a large population of gainfully employed and *unavailable* women, to which was added the Victorian-era philosophy that sex was something forbidden and prohibited. Women became taboo objects of a forbidden desire—a guaranteed formula for a volatile cocktail of confused and lethally misdirected libido.

Colin Wilson also traces the nature of pornographic literature, noting that there were fundamental shifts in theme. In the eighteenth century, pornography described sex explicitly, but freely. It was something to be indulged in sensually, like a good meal. In the nineteenth century, pornographic literature took its cue from the Marquis de Sade. It described sex as something forbidden—a taboo to be overcome only by voyeurism, illicit seduction, bondage, force, and rape. In the nineteenth century pornographic novel, the virtuous Victorian woman could enjoy sex only if she was overpowered. A common theme was the capture of traveling Victorian virgins by pirates or lustful Turks, where the women discover the pleasures of sex by being raped in a harem. Children are portrayed as sexual creatures intent on seducing the family butler. Scenes of bondage, flogging, and sex are intermixed; sex is almost always linked to pain and the loss of female virginity—often in childhood and accompanied by blood. Sold in cheap, popular, magazine-like multipart editions, in an age when print encompassed all available media, this literature had a tremendous impact on the imaginations of bored and frustrated males, no doubt among whom dwelled Jack the Ripper.

It is interesting that while so many medical, psychiatric, sexual, and philosophical terms refer to ancient Greek gods or Roman-era Latin expressions, *sadism* is entirely a modern term, taking its name from a late-eighteenth-century persona: the Marquis de Sade (1740–1814). As Michel Foucault points out:

> Sadism is not a name finally given to a practice as old as Eros; it is a massive cultural fact which appeared precisely at the end of the eighteenth century, and which constitutes one of the greatest conversions of Western imagination: unreason transformed into delirium of the heart, madness of desire, the insane dialogue of love and death in the limitless presumption of appetite.[71]

It should be noted that to this day, no clear link between the cause of sexual crime and pornography has been established. Some even suggest that pornography acts as a release from sexual tensions that might otherwise lead to criminal acts. What is evident, however, is that those already predisposed to committing sexual crimes are also heavy consumers of pornography. In the FBI study of sexual killers, the highest common denominator of various childhood and adolescent factors was their consumption of pornography—81 percent.[72] (We will discuss this issue further in Chapter 6.)

Into the Twentieth Century

Whatever the reasons, sex crime and serial murder continued to rise at a steady rate into the twentieth century. Each decade brought with it a new twist in serial homicide.

In 1916, in a small Hungarian village during World War I, authorities arrived to search out hidden caches of gasoline. The villagers told them to look in the house of Bela Kiss, who was at the time serving in the army at the front. The man was disliked in the village and his housekeeper, whom he had fired for snooping, had gossiped earlier that she saw metal oil drums stored in his house. When police broke the seals to Kiss's villa, they discovered seven oil drums, each containing a dead woman. They had all been strangled. The house was filled with women's clothing and pawn tickets—Kiss had lured his victims through newspaper advertisements offering marriage agency services. When the police came to arrest Kiss, they discovered that he had been wounded and had died in a hospital. Medical records, however, revealed that the man who died was too young to be Kiss, who must have exchanged his identity disk with a dying soldier and escaped. Kiss was never captured.

Postwar Weimar, Germany, became legendary for its serial killers. Fritz Haarmann, age forty-five, was convicted of raping and murdering twenty-seven young men in Hanover between 1918 and 1924. Haarmann, who was a police agent and private investigator, lured schoolboys or drifters from the Hanover railway station back to his apartment. There he attacked his victims and killed them by chewing through their throats. Afterward he sold their flesh to local butcher shops and restaurants, claiming it was pork, while dumping their bones into the river behind his apartment. It was the finding of numerous skulls in the river that led to Haarmann's eventual arrest.

Haarmann confessed to police:

I never intended to kill those youths. Some of the boys had come before. I wanted to protect them from myself because I knew what would happen if I had my way with them. I cried out, "Submit to me but do not let me loose control." When I would go out of control I would bite them and suck their necks. Some of the boys at the Café Kröpcke liked to practice "terminal sex" and "breath play" (*"dämpfen" und "Luft abstellen"*–sexual asphyxiation: also know as "scarfing" or "bagging"). Sometimes we struggled for hours this way. It was sometimes difficult for me to get an erection. Lately it has happened more often. It used to worry me; "God oh God, where is it going to end?" I would throw myself with my full weight on these youths. They were worn out by the excesses and the debauchery. I would bit through their Adam's apple and probably strangle and throttle them with my hands. I would collapse on the corpse. I would then go and make myself some strong black coffee. I would put the body on the floor and cover the face with a cloth so that he would not gaze back at me. I would open the abdomen with two cuts and empty the intestines into a bucket. I would dip a towel into the abdominal cavity and keep doing it until it had soaked up all the blood. Then I would make three cuts from the ribs towards the shoulders, grip the ribs and force them open until the bones around the shoulders broke. Then I would cut into that area. I could then extract the heart, lungs, and kidneys and chop them up and put them in my bucket. I would then sever the legs and then the arms. I would clean the flesh off the bones and put it in my waxed cloth bag. The remaining flesh went under the bed or in the cubbyhole. It would take me five or six trips to take everything out and dump it down the toilet or into the river. I would cut off the penis after I had emptied and cleaned the chest and stomach cavities. I would chop it up into lots of little pieces. I always hated doing this, but I could not help myself—my obsession was much stronger than the horror of the cutting and chopping.

I would take apart the heads last. I used a small kitchen knife to peel away the scalp and cut it up into little strips and squares. I would put the skull face down on a straw mat and wrap it in rags so that it would make less noise. I would then smash it with the blunt edge of an ax until the joins in the skull split apart. The brain went in the bucket and the bone chips into the river opposite the castle . . . I gave the clothes away or sold them.[73]

Haarmann was quickly tried and executed in 1925.

Peter Kürten, the "Vampire of Düsseldorf," stabbed, strangled, and battered at least nine and maybe as many as thirty victims between 1913 and 1930. Sometimes Kürten's victims went willingly with him to have sex, during which he would suddenly attack them with a knife. At other times, Kürten ambushed his victims, frequently children, on the streets and in parks. Kürten was executed in 1931.

While Kürten and Haarmann's cases are both well documented because they went to trial, several other cases in Germany during the same period are more obscure. In Berlin, George Karl Grossman is believed to have killed as many as fifty people between 1913 and 1920 and sold their flesh at a hot dog stand he kept at the railway station. He apparently found his victims in the same station where he sold their remains to hungry passengers. He committed suicide, however, when he was arrested, and thus his crimes remain obscured in myth and gossip.

In Silesia meanwhile, in 1924, police found the remains of at least thirty men and women pickled in jars in the kitchens of Karl Denke's inn.

He had been serving the flesh of some of the guests at his inn to other guests. Denke kept carefully written records of various body weights of his victims. Denke also committed suicide before he could be brought to trial.

Bruno Ludke is thought to have killed as many as eighty-five women between the late 1920s and 1943, when he was arrested for strangling a woman near his home. Ludke stabbed or strangled all his victims and had sex with the corpses. He pleaded not guilty by reason of insanity and was turned over to the Nazi SS for medical experiments; he died on April 8, 1944. Again, because the Nazis tended to suppress crime news in Germany, little detail is known about Ludke's activities.

These serial murders in Germany had a tremendous impact on popular culture in the country. Fritz Lang's movie *M*, with Peter Lorre in the role of a serial child murderer, touched a nerve in Germany and remains a cinema classic today.* Lurid paintings at the time by George Grosz and Otto Dix portrayed bloody scenes of mutilation, dismemberment, and sex murder.

Although many have suggested that the serial murders in Germany were the result of the total collapse of German society following its defeat in World War I, they overlook the fact that some of the Weimar-era serial killers began killing before the war ended, and most had sex crime records going back to long before the war. It is more likely that the postwar chaos unleashed serial killers who were already predisposed to commit their crimes. A similar situation seemed to happen in Russia in the wake of the collapse of communism—the country was plagued by serial cannibalistic sex crimes. Whether there are any links between the nature of the serial murders and the collapse of the two regimes is an open question at this time.

During the first half of the twentieth century, England and France had few serial murderers comparable in gruesome viciousness to those of Jack the Ripper or the Weimar killers. Between 1910 and 1914, George Smith in England killed three of his seven wives, while in France, Henri Desiré Landru killed eleven potential brides between 1915 and 1922. Dr. Marcel

---

* Forty-seven years later, in Los Angeles, Peter Lorre's daughter was confronted by the serial killer team of Kenneth Bianchi and Angelo Buono—the Hillside Stranglers. Posing as police detectives, they intended to rape and murder her like their previous victims, but when they looked through her purse they discovered the identity of her father. They immediately released her.

Petiot in Paris killed at least sixty-three war refugees between 1941 and 1944. All of these serial murders seemed to be profit-motivated.

Between 1943 and 1953 in London, John Christie murdered an infant and six females, including his wife, for sexual motives. Peter Manuel, a petty thief with a history of sexual crimes, began killing women after his fiancée rejected him upon discovering his criminal record. He killed nine people, including several males, in different parts of Scotland and England in 1959.

Back in the United States

Except for the cases of Jesse Pomroy and Tomas Piper, the United States reported few cases of serial sexual homicide before 1900. But in the entrepreneurial tradition of nineteenth-century America, there were many cases of profit-motivated serial homicides, such as those of the Bender Clan, who killed at least twelve travelers in Kansas in 1872–1873, and Herman Mudgett, who constructed a custom-designed "murder hotel" in Chicago during the World's Fair and is believed to have killed at least twenty-seven victims.

By the twentieth century, serial murder in the United States was catching up with European patterns. Earle Leonard Nelson raped and murdered twenty-seven landladies between February 1926 and June 1927. Nelson was a migratory serial killer, leaving multiple victims in San Francisco, San Jose, Santa Barbara, Oakland, Portland, Oregon, Seattle, Kansas City, Philadelphia, Buffalo, Detroit, Chicago, and finally Winnipeg, Canada, where he was apprehended, tried, and hanged. Nelson was twenty-nine when he began killing, but he had a criminal record going back to age twenty-one, when he was arrested for attempted rape. We will see that Nelson also fit a certain characteristic that many serial killers have—a history of head injury. When Nelson was ten, he was dragged under a streetcar, resulting in severe head trauma.

In New York City in 1928, the grandfatherly Albert Fish, fifty-eight years old at the time and the father of six children, befriended the Budd family. He originally had come in response to a newspaper advertisement placed by one of the Budd sons seeking work. Using a false name, Fish visited the family several times and finally offered the son work at his ficg Island farm, no doubt intending to kill him. But at the last minute, the Budds' twelve-year-old girl, Grace, enchanted Fish. He told the trusting parents that his sister was having a children's birthday party and offered to take Grace to the party while the son was packing his suitcase to leave for the supposed farm. The last the Budds saw of their daughter Grace was her walking off toward the subway holding the kindly old man's hand. A massive police investigation turned up no clues.

Six years later, the girl's mother received a letter from Fish revealing what happened to her daughter. Fish wrote [with original spelling and punctuation]:

My Dear Mrs. Budd,

In 1894 a friend of mine shipped as a deck hand on the Steamer Tacoma, Capt. John Davis. They sailed from San Francisco for Hong Kong China. On arriving there he and two others went ashore and got drunk. When they returned the boat was gone. At that time there was a famine in China. Meat of any kind was from $1–3 Dollars a pound. So great was the suffering among the very poor that all children under 12 were sold to the Butchers to be cut up and used for food in order to keep others from starving. A boy or girl under 14 was not safe in the street. You could go in any shop and ask for steak-chops-or stew meat. Part of the naked body of a boy or a girl would be brought out and just what you wanted cut from it. A boy or girls behind which is the sweetest part of the body and sold as veal cutlet brought the highest price. John staid there so long he acquired a taste for human flesh. On his return to N.Y. he stole two boys one 7 one 11. Took them to his home stripped them naked tied them in a closet. Then burned everything they had on. Several times every day and night he spanked them-tortured them to make their meat good and tender. First he killed the 11 yr old boy, because he had the fattest ass and of course the most meat on it. Every part of his body was Cooked and eaten except head-bones and guts. He was Roasted in the oven (all of his ass), boiled, broiled, fried, stewed. The little boy was next, went the same way. At that time, I was living at 409 E 100 st., near-right side. He told me so often how good Human flesh was I made up my mind to taste it. On Sunday June the 3-1928 I called on you at 406 W 15 St. Brought you pot cheese-strawberries.

We had lunch. Grace sat in my lap and kissed me. I made up my mind to eat her. On the pretense of taking her to a party. You said Yes she could go. I took her to an empty house in Westchester I had already picked out. When we got there, I told her to remain outside. She picked wildflowers. I went upstairs and stripped all my clothes off. I knew if I did not I would get her blood on them. When all was ready I went to the window and Called her. Then I hid in a closet until she was in the room. When she saw me all naked she began to cry and tried to run downstairs. I grabbed her and she said she would tell her mamma. First I stripped her naked. How she did kick-bite and scratch. I choked her to death, then cut her in small pieces so I could take my meat to my rooms, Cook and eat it. How sweet and tender her little ass was roasted in the oven. It took me 9 days to eat her entire body. I did not fuck her tho I could of had I wished. She died a virgin.

The police managed to trace the letter back to Fish by its particular stationery and arrested him. He confessed to molesting more than four hundred children over twenty-years, and is believed to have murdered somewhere between six and fifteen children. Fish was executed in January 1936.

Minnesota-born Carl Panzram was thirty-nine when he was executed after killing twenty-one people. Panzram was a personality of almost mythical proportions—he committed his first burglary at age eleven and remained a professional criminal the rest of his life. In 1920, he brazenly burglarized forty thousand dollars' worth of property from former U.S. president William Howard Taft's house. In jail, he terrorized the guards and administration by inciting riots and burning down the kitchen and factory in one of the jails. At one point, he broke out of jail, stole a yacht, and sailed it to Africa and Europe. He lured sailors on board his vessel, then sodomized them, killed them, and threw their bodies into the water. In prison, Panzram wrote a book openly describing his sex crimes, confessing to some one thousand homosexual rapes. Panzram stated, "My motto is: Rob them all, rape them all, and kill them all."

In 1929, Panzram was sentenced to twenty-five years in prison for burglary and threatened in the courtroom to "kill the first person who bothers me." Ten months later, he beat in the head of a fellow prisoner with an iron bar. For this crime he received the death sentence. When an anti–capital punishment group attempted to have Panzram's sentence commuted, he raged: "The only thanks you or your kind will ever get from me for your efforts on my behalf is that I wish you all had one neck and that I had my hands on it . . . I believe the only way to reform people is to kill them."

On September 11, 1930, Panzram was led out to the gallows and there asked if he had any last words. He replied, "Yes, hurry it up, you hoosier bastard. I could hang a dozen men while you're fooling around."

Many cases of serial murder were never solved and remain on the record as fragmentary reports. Moreover, as some of these murders occurred exclusively in black communities, the press often ignored them unless the victims were light-skinned blacks. In Atlanta, for example, between May 1911 and May 1912, an unknown killer stalked light-skinned black women on the street. He cut the throats of and mutilated twenty victims before he inexplicably ceased killing. Meanwhile, in Louisiana and Texas, between January 1911 and April 1912, somebody axe-murdered forty-nine victims. Again, nobody was convicted of the crime.

In Cleveland, Ohio, between 1935 and 1938, somebody killed and mutilated prostitutes and derelicts of both sexes. A total of twelve bodies were found before the murders mysteriously ceased. In Alaska, between 1930 and 1931, somebody tracked fishermen and hunters to remote locations and then killed them there. The murders were never solved.

During the 1940s and 1950s, the phenomenon of serial killings seemed to decline in frequency and intensity, but the nature of the crimes became more bizarre. In Tulsa, Oklahoma, Charles Floyd stalked and killed seven women between 1942 and 1948 because they had red hair. Jarvis Roosevelt Catoe, an African-American taxi driver, confessed in 1941 to strangling nine women in New York and Washington. In 1946 in Chicago, William Heirens killed two women and an eleven-year-old girl. On a wall in the apartment of one of the victims, he wrote in lipstick, "For Heaven's sake catch me before I kill more. I cannot control myself." In Los Angeles, Harvey Glatman in 1957–1958 hired models to pose for him and murdered them after taking their picture—he killed three women. In 1957 in rural Wisconsin, Ed Gein was arrested for killing two local women and cannibalizing their corpses. In Virginia and Maryland in 1959, Melvin Rees flashed his headlights at night to pull over motorists. He killed the men and raped the women. He killed a total of nine victims, an all-time high for any identified serial killer in the United States during the two decades between 1940 and 1960.

It would be Albert DeSalvo—the Boston Strangler—who bridged for us old-world-era serial homicide with the post-JFK epoch.

Albert DeSalvo—"The Boston Strangler"

There has recently been some serious controversy as to whether Albert De-Salvo really was the Boston Strangler. In 2000, the families of DeSalvo and of Mary Sullivan, his purported last victim, jointly exhumed her body and conducted DNA tests on trace material recovered from her corpse. The material, appearing to be traces of seminal fluid buried with the body for forty years, did not match the DNA pattern taken from DeSalvo's surviving brother. But the testing was privately done and has not so far changed the state position that DeSalvo is indeed the confessed Boston Strangler. There are some conflicting reports as to whether DeSalvo's brother is willing to cooperate with authorities in a state-sponsored DNA test.

If not the deeds, than at least the canonical story of Albert DeSalvo, who allegedly murdered thirteen women between 1962 and 1964, capped the industrial age of serial murder and ushered us forward into the new Ted Bundy epoch. Despite numerous cases of serial killings around the world since 1888, Jack the Ripper held his place as the worst in popular memory until the early 1960s. But in 1962 his primacy was shaken by the Boston Strangler, at least in the United States.

Like Jack the Ripper, the Boston Strangler focused on a very small "killing ground." He killed in so-called lace curtain neighborhoods of Boston's lower-middle-class districts. His victims lived among the dense rows of inexpensive low-rise apartment buildings. This type of focused killing had the effect of terrorizing the city, and as the press announced each new victim of the Boston Strangler, his reputation became legendary. After his confession, in the days before made-for-TV movies, Hollywood chose him as a subject worthy of a film. Twentieth Century Fox's *The Boston Strangler* starred Tony Curtis as the killer and Henry Fonda as the detective who pursued him. While many know the moniker "Boston Strangler," few remember the name of the man behind it: Albert DeSalvo.

• • •

Albert Henry DeSalvo was born on September 3, 1931 in Chelsea, Massachusetts. His mother, Charlotte, came from an old respectable "Yankee" family; her father was an officer in the Boston Fire Department. Charlotte was fifteen when she married Albert's father, Frank DeSalvo, a brutal alcoholic delinquent (69 percent of sexual killers in a FBI study report a history of alcohol abuse in the family). The father was arrested eighteen times (50 percent of sexual killers had a parent with a criminal record). DeSalvo's description of his childhood is horrendous. His earliest childhood memories are of his father beating his mother. He witnessed him once knocking out her tooth and breaking her finger. DeSalvo said that he himself was beaten severely by his father and once sold to a farmer in Maine along with his two sisters for nine dollars (42 percent of sexual murderers report physical abuse in childhood). After six months his mother found them. When Albert was twelve years old his father was jailed, and afterward his mother divorced him. (47 percent of serial killers report their father leaving before age twelve.)

The historiography of serial murder is inconsistent. Often descriptions of cases are written quickly and focus on the more lurid aspects of events. Attention to detail, authenticity, and fact is minimal and definitive case information is often locked up in inaccessible police archives. Such is the case for the question of Albert's relationship with his mother. Dr. James A. Brussel, a renowned criminal psychiatrist who interviewed DeSalvo, wrote in 1968, "The mother, Albert said, was not the warm and loving woman who might have made his life tolerable. She was, at best, indifferent to the boy. She was out of the house most nights. 'There was no home life. She didn't stop the nightly beatings.' "[74] On the other hand, DeSalvo's biographer, Frank Gerold, wrote that Albert was his mother's favorite (he had two brothers and three sisters) and that as an adult, he would visit his mother as often as possible.

Like 71 percent of the serial killers in the FBI study, Albert felt isolated in childhood: "I never allowed myself to get close to anyone . . . Maybe I wasn't able . . . I recall, I used to run away as a kid. I hid out in a junk yard. There was a dog there: Queenie . . . tough . . . bit everyone. Maybe I was looking for affection, but I slept with that dog night after night, and it never bit me."

According to Dr. Brussel, Albert's father used to bring prostitutes home, and the children witnessed him having sex with them. (Thirty-five percent of serial sex killers report witnessing disturbing parental sex acts.) When Albert was five or six, he and his brothers and sisters began attempting sex acts. The circumstances of Albert and his sisters being sold to a farmer by their father are unclear, and Albert never talked about what happened during the six months they were there.

Albert claims that he began to have steady sex at age eight with girls and women and that he prostituted himself to homosexuals:

> Some of them was amazed at how I could come and then five minutes later come again. The queers loved that they would pay for it, too, which was all right with me since I needed the dough and there was some relief from the urge that was pushing me to sex all the time, but it really was Woman that I wanted—not any special one, just Woman with what a woman has, not just to come, but to have the breasts and body to play with, to bite and kiss, then to go into . . . didn't even care so much what she looked like, how old she was . . . it was Woman and not a pretty woman, or any special woman, but Woman that I wanted, even then.[75]

Like 36 percent of the sex killers in the FBI study, DeSalvo tortured animals when he was a child. Like 81 percent of the surveyed killers, DeSalvo began to steal in early adolescence. At the age of twelve he was sentenced for burglary to ten months in the Lyman School for Boys, a reformatory in Boston. His IQ was tested at the time and recorded as 93—low average. DeSalvo said that in reformatory one "can learn about every form of sexual perversion." Just as with serial killers Ed Kemper and Henry Lee Lucas and thousands of other young men, early incarceration of DeSalvo served to better educate him in criminal techniques and expose him to darker frontiers of aberrant sexuality.

Once he was released from Lyman, DeSalvo began to commit a flurry of burglaries, never getting caught. There was a distinct sexual character to his burglaries. DeSalvo said, "There was something exciting, thrilling, about going into somebody's home . . . I think now, too, that it had something to do with going into the bedrooms where women had been sleeping, or were sleeping and there was times when I would get a rail [erection] on just standing there outside the bedroom door listening to some woman breathe . . . so you see what urge was all part of this and it was only a matter of time before I would feel strong and tough enough to go into the bedroom where the woman was there and make her let me do what I wanted with her."[76]

Once again there is a weak historiography on Albert DeSalvo's school years. Dr. Brussel describes DeSalvo as a "model pupil" who pleased his teachers by cheerfully running errands for them and getting them coffee and sandwiches. DeSalvo told him, "I bulled [bullshitted] my way through. I always tried to be tops, like in book sales or where you got recognition or a certificate for doing something. I was always number one. Teachers knew I wasn't doing my schoolwork properly . . . I actually had no schooling. I was jealous; I was looking for recognition."

Earl James, however, in his police manual on the apprehension of serial killers, wrote: "Albert DeSalvo began school when he was six years old. During his early school years, he suffered from some medical problems. He had tonsillitis and some other childhood diseases. Because of these illnesses, he missed a great deal of school. He failed second grade and was put into a special education class when he was in fifth grade."[77]

In 1948, at age sixteen, DeSalvo graduated from junior high school. His teachers there have no memory of him. DeSalvo went to work on Cape Cod as a dishwasher in a motel. He spent most of his free time on a roof watching couples through windows. As with many serial killers, his first sexual aberration was ostensibly a minor one—voyeurism.

In September 1948, when he turned seventeen, DeSalvo enlisted in the army and was sent to Germany. In the military DeSalvo apparently did well. He was trained as a military policeman, achieved the rank of sergeant, and was made colonel's orderly twenty-seven times. He also discovered that he had abilities as a boxer and became the U.S. Army middleweight champion of Europe twice.

DeSalvo also claimed that he had numerous affairs with officers' wives and that he practiced bondage with some of them. DeSalvo said that he was sought out by women and offered money or jewelry for his "stud" services. He claims that while he was able to satiate his growing sexual appetite, he was seeking love in his life.

In 1953, now twenty-two years old, DeSalvo married a pretty German girl from Frankfurt named Irmgard. He was intensely in love with her, but she was not a good match for his sexual appetite. DeSalvo recalled that she was innocent and scared of sex because of her strict family upbringing. He said he needed to have sex five or six times a day, often immediately after just having sex. She did not like it, he said, and he used to constantly ask himself what was wrong with him.

In April 1954, DeSalvo returned to the United States with his bride. He was stationed at Fort Dix, New Jersey.

In December 1954, at about 9:00 P.M., DeSalvo knocked at the door of a house where there was a woman whose husband was working a night shift. DeSalvo told her that he was driving by her house and saw a prowler looking through the window. She allowed him into the house to look around but then became suspicious when DeSalvo began to ask when her husband would be coming home. She locked herself into another room. DeSalvo left the house and sat in his car parked in her driveway. The woman wrote down his license plate number.

Tracing the license plate, New Jersey State Police questioned DeSalvo several days later. DeSalvo told them that he was driving around looking for a place to rent when he saw a prowler at the woman's house and had only wanted to help. There was nothing to charge DeSalvo with and no further action was taken.

On January 3, 1955, at about 2:00 P.M., a young mother went out to do some quick food shopping and left her nine-year-old daughter and two younger brothers alone. When she returned, the daughter told her that a soldier had come by "for the rent." Since the family owned the house, this struck the mother as strange. On further questioning, the girl said that the soldier had felt and touched her chest and genital areas.

When the New Jersey State Police were called, they immediately remembered the soldier they had questioned just a few days earlier. The little girl and her brothers identified him. DeSalvo was charged with carnal abuse of a child and released on a $1,000 bond. The case, however, never went to trial because the mother did not want her daughter to go through the trauma of testifying. All charges were subsequently dropped.

It was in this period, in 1955, that Irmgard gave birth to DeSalvo's daughter, Judy. She was born with a deformity of the legs that required special braces locking her limbs into a froglike position. DeSalvo tenderly massaged the legs of his daughter and tried to give the braces a more cheerful character by tying pretty colored bows around them.

Perhaps because of the sex crime charge or perhaps because of the birth of a crippled child, Irmgard withdrew from DeSalvo further. Referring to his murdering as having "stolen" life, DeSalvo wrote to his wife years later while in prison:

> You will admit that if you treated me differently like you told me all those years we lost, the love I had been searching for, that we first had when we were married. Yes, Irm, I stole them. But why. What happened when Judy was born and we found out she may never walk. How you cried, Al please no more babies. Irm from that day you changed. All your love went to Judy. You were frigid and cold to me, and you can't deny this. That's why we were always fighting about sex because you were afraid to have a baby. Because you thought it would be born abnormal.

In 1956, Albert DeSalvo received an honorable discharge from the U.S. Army. It is unclear whether he left the army as his own choice, or whether the charges in New Jersey had something to do with it. He returned to live in Chelsea with his wife and daughter and was arrested there in 1958 for a minor burglary.

In 1959, a son, Michael, was born. DeSalvo worked in a shipyard as a laborer to support his family. DeSalvo recalls attempting to lead a conventional life, being a provider for his family, but always being overpowered by his compulsions in the end. He said he was trying to "bring out the best" in himself, yet the "sickness" was always with him, forcing him to go out and "do things I knew was wrong."

In 1960, DeSalvo began committing a series of almost comical sex offenses in the Boston district of Cambridge. Posing as a talent scout for a modeling agency, DeSalvo asked women for permission to measure them. While wrapping a measuring tape around their bust and hips, he would touch and fondle them. Many women did not even notice DeSalvo's touch; complaints started to be filed with the police from angry women only when they realized that no photographer was coming to shoot their pictures. DeSalvo became known as the Measuring Man.

In March 1961, police observed DeSalvo breaking into a house in Cambridge and arrested him. DeSalvo confessed that before he was caught he had tried to break into an apartment where he had previously "measured" two women. He said he wanted to break into their apartment and wait for them to come home. Asked why, DeSalvo said nothing further.

DeSalvo was charged with lewdness, assault and battery, attempted breaking and entering, confining and putting in fear, and engaging in an unnatural and lascivious act. He was convicted of only assault and battery and attempted breaking and entering. He was sentenced to eighteen months in prison, and his term was reduced to eleven months for good behavior.

After he had committed the murders, DeSalvo commented on his Measuring Man activities:

> Mostly, I got a big kick out of those girls around Harvard. I'm not good-looking, I'm not educated, but I was able to put something over on high class people. I know that they look down on people who come from my background. They think they are better than me. They was all college kids and I never had anything in my life but I outsmarted them. I was supposed to feel that they was better than me because they was college people . . . when I told them they could be models that was like saying the same thing: you are better than me, you are better than anybody, you can be a model . . . Anybody with any sense could've found out. They never asked me for proof.
>
> They was times when I was doing that Measuring Man thing that I hated them girls for being so stupid and I wanted to do something to them . . . something that would make them think, even for a little while . . . that would let them know that I was as good as they was, maybe better and smarter.[78]

DeSalvo had been given a psychiatric examination at Bridgewater mental hospital, and it was recommended that he be put into a psychiatric unit instead of prison. It might have worked in this case, because it appears that DeSalvo was aware of his compulsions and sincerely wanted to be free of them.

When DeSalvo was in jail he told the psychiatrist of his slavish love for Irmgard: "I can hardly wait to get out so I can be with her and treat her the way a wife should be treated even if it means washing her feet." But when he got home, Irmgard rejected him totally. She said that he was "dirty and sickening" and called him an animal.

Two months after his release from prison, Albert DeSalvo left his house on June 14, 1962, telling his wife he was going fishing. Instead he ended up wandering into a low-rise apartment complex with scaffolding outside. He knocked on doors at random until Anna Slesers, a fifty-five-year-old woman of Latvian descent, came to her door. She appeared younger than her age and had brown, bobbed hair. She was trained in Latvia as an agronomist but in America she worked as a seamstress. DeSalvo told Slesers he was from a work crew and that some repairs were going to be done in her apartment. She let him in.

Slesers was later found lying on her back on a runner near the door to the bathroom. She was wearing a blue robe, which was spread open, exposing her nude body. Her legs were spread wide apart, her left leg bent at the knee. She had been struck on the head and there was a quantity of blood underneath her head. She was strangled with the cord of her robe, which was strangely tied around her neck with a bow under her chin. Although she appeared to have been raped, no seminal fluids were found in her vagina or at the scene.

Her wastebasket was missing and its contents were strewn on the floor. Drawers had been pulled open and some of their contents thrown on the floor. The police assumed that the murderer entered the premises to commit a burglary, and was discovered by the victim, who was then struck, raped, and killed by the burglar.

DeSalvo said that after killing Slesers, he went into the bathroom to wash up. He remembers that he was wearing gloves. He ransacked the apartment and took $20 he found on a cabinet. He later would say that was the only time he ever stole something from his victims—other than their lives.

He removed his bloodied jacket and shirt and, after dumping the contents of the wastebasket, put his garments in it. He turned off the record player, put on a raincoat he found hanging by the door, and walked out carrying the waste basket.

He walked by a police car on patrol, got into his car, and drove away. He stopped a man on the street and told him he was having an affair with a woman and that her husband had caught him and he had to run away without his shirt; would the man mind accompanying him to a store so that he could buy a shirt in case there were any problems with him walking in without a shirt? The man agreed.

Afterward, DeSalvo went to the ocean, tore the bloodied garments into strips, and dumped them in the surf. He then went home to have supper with his wife and kids.

DeSalvo described a tranquil, trancelike state after he killed:

It was all the same thing, always the same feeling. You was there. These things were going on. And the feeling after I got out of that apartment was as if it never happened. I got out and downstairs, and you could of said you saw me upstairs, and as far as I was concerned, it wasn't me. I can't explain it to you any other way. It's just so unreal . . . I was there. It was done. And yet if you talked with me an hour later, or half an hour later, it didn't mean nothing. It just didn't mean nothing.[79]

DeSalvo's first murder was highly proficient. He wore gloves and left no fingerprints behind. He parked his car a distance away from where he committed the murder. He quickly disposed of his bloodied clothing and he engaged a stranger who could later testify to an alibi if he had been caught that day. His training as a military policeman was paying off.

Two weeks later, on June 28, 1962, DeSalvo knocked on the door of eighty-five-year-old Mary Mullen. He told her he had been sent to do some work on her apartment. She inevitably let him in. It should be noted that all the victims of the Boston Strangler lived in economical low-rise apartments, which were almost always in need of some sort of repair. Whenever DeSalvo called to say he had been sent to do repair work or repainting, it always made perfect sense to the tenants.

When Mary Mullen turned her back on DeSalvo, he wrapped his arm around her throat. She apparently died instantly, perhaps of heart failure. DeSalvo laid her out on the couch and left. When her body was discovered, authorities declared her death as being of natural causes. It was only after DeSalvo confessed that the authorities realized Mary Mullen was a victim of the Boston Strangler.

On June 30, a Saturday, DeSalvo told his wife he had to go out on a job early in the morning. He drove around aimlessly until he arrived at an apartment building on Newhall Street in Lynn, where he had been before in his Measuring Man days. He randomly knocked at an apartment door on the second floor. Helen Blake, age sixty-five, answered the door still wearing her pajamas. Using his usual approach, DeSalvo told her he needed to check her windows for leaks. Just before he entered, DeSalvo picked up some milk bottles left by the door and handed them to Blake. He handled them carefully so as not to leave any fingerprints.

In the bedroom as they inspected the windows, DeSalvo grabbed Blake from behind and choked her. She fainted quickly. Holding her with one hand, he carefully took her glasses off and set them down. He laid her down on the bed, took off her pajamas, and raped her with a foreign object. He tied a nylon stocking and her bra tightly around her neck and strangled her. He then looped the garments into a bow, which he tied under her chin. This bow would become a signature of the Boston Strangler. Asked why he tied the bow, DeSalvo simply replied, "I don't know." Some analysts speculated that the bow was somehow connected to the bows he tied around the orthopedic braces of his crippled daughter, but the connection is tenuous.

DeSalvo killed his fourth victim later that same day. He drove into Boston, randomly chose an apartment, and began pressing buzzer buttons that had women's names on the address plates. Nina Nichols, age sixty-eight, was talking to her sister on the phone when DeSalvo buzzed. Her sister heard the buzzer, and Nina told her that she would call her right back. She never called back.

Nina Nichols was found posed on the floor, her legs spread wide apart, facing the entryway. Her pink housecoat and slip were pushed up to her waist and two stockings were tied around her throat in a bow under her chin. She had been raped with a wine bottle; seminal fluid was found on her thighs.

The apartment appeared to have been burglarized, with things strewn about and drawers pulled out. The desk drawer was pulled out and placed on the floor as if the killer carefully examined all the contents: stationery, stamps, pens, paper clips. Nothing, however, was found to be missing. Asked what he was looking for, DeSalvo again replied, "I don't know . . . I didn't have in my mind the idea of taking anything."

When DeSalvo was confessing to Nina's murder, he said that she had scratched him when he was strangling her and that the police must have found his skin under her fingernails. This revealed the extent to which DeSalvo was familiar with police investigative techniques.

At this point the police became aware that there was a multiple killer on the loose who had murdered three women (a fourth victim was thought to have died of natural causes.)

On August 19, 1962, DeSalvo murdered seventy-five-year-old Ida Irga. She was found on her back on the living room floor wearing a light night-dress that had been torn open, exposing her body. Her legs were spread wide apart and her feet were propped up on individual chairs. A pillow was placed beneath her buttocks and she was pointed in the direction of the door, so the sight of her exposed genitals would greet whoever would enter the apartment. A white pillowcase was tightly knotted around her throat. The posing of the victim had now become complex, but when DeSalvo was questioned about it, he could only say, "I just did it."

Within a day or two, DeSalvo killed his sixth victim, sixty-seven-year-old Jane Sullivan. The precise date of her murder is unclear, as her body was not discovered until August 30, some ten days after the murder. She was found in the bathtub in a kneeling position. Her face was beneath about six inches of water and her bare buttocks were exposed. Her cotton housecoat had been pulled up over her shoulder and her girdle was pushed above her waist. Her underwear was down around her ankles. She was strangled with her own nylon stockings. The victim had been killed in another room and then taken to the bathroom and posed.

Such posing is a sign that the FBI describes as a *disorganized*-personality serial killer. (See Chapters 3 and 9.) Often the posing of the victim has some obscure meaning known only to the perpetrator. DeSalvo's random targeting of apartment buildings also is a mark of a disorganized offender, as is his frequent use of weapons found at the crime scene—articles of clothing. At the same time, however, DeSalvo carried gloves with him, took meticulous care never to leave any fingerprints, and talked his way into the victims' apartments, all characteristics of the *organized* personality. DeSalvo was that rare creature defined as a *mixed*-personality killer—both predictable and unpredictable at the same time—a homicide investigator's worst nightmare. It made DeSalvo a unique case in forensic history, and DeSalvo was now about to go a step further.

After committing six homicides in a period of two months, DeSalvo suddenly stopped killing for four months. Then on December 5, 1962, he murdered Sophie Clark, a victim who defied the odds—she was black and twenty years old. It is rare for a sexual murderer to cross racial lines—usually whites kill whites, blacks kill blacks, and so forth. Even more rare was that having established a consistent pattern by murdering six elderly women, DeSalvo suddenly murdered a twenty-year-old. It caused havoc in the investigation, as detectives became divided on the issue whether there was one killer or two different stranglers. (Today this question is still being pondered about DeSalvo.)

December 5 was DeSalvo's wedding anniversary, and that might have triggered his killing again. DeSalvo gained entry into Sophie Clark's apartment using the usual repairman routine. He said, "I gave her fast talk, I told her I'd set her up in modeling. I'd give her twenty to thirty dollars an hour." He then asked her to turn around so he could get a better look at her figure. As she turned her back to him, he grabbed her around the throat with his arm.

Clark was found on the living room rug. Three of her nylon stockings were tightly tied around her neck, as was also her white slip and a belt. A gag was stuffed into her mouth. She was on her back, her bathrobe open, and she was naked except for a pair of black stockings, a garter, and loafer shoes. Her legs were spread wide open and her bra had been ripped from her during the attack. A sanitary napkin was tossed under a chair nearby. Her glasses were broken. Seminal fluid was found in her vagina.

After DeSalvo killed her, he remained behind in the apartment leafing through her magazines and record collection. Then, without taking anything, he quietly slipped out. Sophie Clark's apartment was two blocks away from Anna Slesers's, his first victim.

On December 31, 1962, DeSalvo killed his seventh victim—twenty-three-year-old Patricia Bissette. Again, DeSalvo defied the odds: The victim was found in her bedroom lying face up on her bed, her legs together, and covered by a bedspread snugly drawn up to her chin—diametrically opposite to the grotesque and humiliating posing that had been committed previously. A victim who is found covered this way often reflects a sense of guilt or remorse in the killer. Later DeSalvo said, "She was so different, I didn't want to see her like that, naked and . . . She talked to me like a man, she treated me like a man."

DeSalvo had knocked on her door, pretending to be somebody who lived upstairs looking for one of her roommates. He had already gotten the names from the mailbox below. Bissette invited him in to wait and made some coffee. DeSalvo said that she was nice to him, treating him "like a man" and that he talked himself out of hurting her. He tried to find an excuse to leave her apartment and offered to go out and get some donuts, but Bissette said it was not necessary. DeSalvo said that at that moment he knew that he did not want it to happen but it would.

Despite his fuzzy warm sentiments for Bissette, he raped her and strangled her with her stockings, leaving them tied in what by then the police were calling the "Strangler's Bow."

DeSalvo had this to say about Bissette's murder:

> I don't know if I done this for a sex act or for hatred or for what reason. I think I did this not as a sex act but out of hate for her—not her in particular, but for a woman. I don't think that a sex act is anything to do. It is what everybody does, from the top to the bottom of the world, but that is not what I mean. It is one thing to do it when a woman wants you to do it and another when she don't, you understand me? If women do not want you to do what is right and natural then it is dirty if they don't. You are really an animal if you do it just the same, is what I mean, you see? But all I can say is that when I saw her body the sex act came in. I did not enjoy the sexual relations with this woman. I was thinking too much about that she would not have wanted me to do it. There was no thrill at all.[80]

For once, DeSalvo had come up with some valuable insight into his motives. Rape and other sex crimes are rarely committed out of a desperate lack of sex. Bundy was an attractive man with many girlfriends, and DeSalvo was able to seduce countless women, yet both used extreme violence in compelling the victims into sexual acts. In such cases, the sexual act is merely a component of the aggressive impulse. Sex and rape are used as a weapon to batter the victim, and not for the purpose of sexual gratification. Many cannot understand why an individual would rape a seventy-five-year-old woman because they cannot imagine such a woman as sexually attractive. In fact, however, sexual attractiveness or desire has nothing to do with it—it is a purely aggressive and hateful act against a victim. (Likewise in prison, male-on-male rape has less to do with homosexual desire than with aggressive dominance. Very few prison rapists are homosexuals.)[81]

On February 18, 1963, DeSalvo gained entry into the apartment of a twenty-nine-year-old woman. She was sick with the flu and at first didn't want to let him in. He told her that he was from the construction crew working on the roof and that he needed to shut her water off. Indeed, there was a crew working on the roof and the woman finally let him enter. When he grabbed her, however, she bit his finger down to the bone and began desperately screaming. DeSalvo ran away. But the victim could not come forth with a useful description.

By now the police were in a frenzy and were meticulously checking every sex offender released from prisons and mental hospitals in the last two years. Unfortunately, DeSalvo had been convicted of assault and battery and breaking and entering, and therefore his name did not appear on the list of sex offenders.

On March 9, 1963, DeSalvo killed his ninth victim, sixty-nine-year-old Mary Brown. On his way into her building, he picked up a piece of brass pipe. Once he gained entry into her apartment, he struck her with the pipe. He then ripped her dress open, exposing her breasts. He picked up a sheet, threw it over her head, and then battered her skull with the pipe. Afterward he picked up a fork and thrust it into her breast.

On May 5, 1963, he killed twenty-three-year-old Beverly Samans. She was found lying on her back on a convertible sofa bed. She was nude except for a lace blouse draped around her shoulders, and her legs were spread apart. Her wrists were tied behind her and she was gagged. A nylon stocking and two handkerchiefs were knotted around her neck. Again, DeSalvo surprised the police with his versatility—Beverly Samans was stabbed more than twenty times.

Beverly Samans, who was partially deaf, was a month away from getting her master's degree in rehabilitation counseling. In her typewriter was her thesis, titled *Factors Pertaining to the Etiology of Male Homosexuality*. For some reason, perhaps because of the bite he had received from his previous victim, DeSalvo did not grab Samans by the throat from behind. Instead he drew his knife and confronted her face-to-face.

Samans tried to put her counseling education in practice to save her life: She attempted to negotiate with DeSalvo, agreeing to let him "play around with her" but no intercourse. When DeSalvo began to rape her anyway, she complained to him that he had exceeded their agreed-upon limit. DeSalvo became enraged because, he said, she began to remind him of his wife, with whom making love was "like asking a dead dog to move." DeSalvo said Samans made him feel unclean and unwanted. Making matters worse, because Samans was partially deaf but DeSalvo did not know it, she could not hear all of his instructions. He became enraged when no matter "how hard he tried to please her" his victim complained and struggled. Enraged, he stabbed her twenty-two times.

On September 8, 1963, DeSalvo killed his eleventh victim, fifty-eight-year-old Evelyn Corbin. He arrived at her door after trying several other apartments and failing to find a suitable victim. DeSalvo told her that the superintendent had sent him to check for leaks in the windows. At first she wouldn't let him in. Often in such cases, DeSalvo used a clever twist of psychology: "Well, if you don't want the work done, I'll go. It's your apartment."

Like all the others, Corbin eventually opened her door to DeSalvo. Once inside, DeSalvo drew his knife and put it to her neck. He said that the first thing she asked was, "You're not the Boston Strangler, are you?" DeSalvo assured her he was not and took her into the bedroom.

Corbin told DeSalvo that she was not well and could not have intercourse. DeSalvo sat down on the edge of the bed and had Corbin kneel before him on a pillow on the floor and perform oral sex.

DeSalvo then told her that he was going to tie her up and leave. He made her promise to give him time to go and not make a sound. He tied her hands in front of her and laid her down on the bed. He then stuffed a pair of panties in her mouth, straddled her body sitting on her hands, placed a pillow over her face, and strangled her with his hands. Finally he took some nylon stockings from her drawer and tied them in a bow. He spread her legs open in a forty-five-degree angle and tied another bow around the victim's left ankle.

On November 24, 1963, while most of America had come to a halt because of the assassination of President Kennedy two days previously, DeSalvo killed his twelfth victim: twenty-three-year-old Joann Graff. Despite the fact that victim was very wary and would not even permit the landlord to enter her apartment, DeSalvo talked his way in.

Graff was found lying at a diagonal across the bed with her legs spread apart. She was strangled. Two nylon stockings were intertwined with the victim's black leotard tied in a bow around her neck. DeSalvo said that afterward he drove home, washed up, played with the kids, had supper, and watched television. The murder of Lee Harvey Oswald was broadcast live on network TV that day.

On January 4, 1964, police found DeSalvo's thirteenth and last victim: nineteen-year-old Mary Sullivan. She was found on her bed in a propped-up position. Under her buttocks was a pillow. Her back rested against the headboard and her head was resting on her right shoulder. Seminal fluid was dripping from her mouth onto her right breast. Both of her breasts were exposed. Her knees were bent and raised and her legs spread apart. A broomstick handle was inserted into her vagina. There were seminal stains on the blanket. A stocking was tied tightly around her throat and covered by a scarf tied in a large bow. Next to the victim's left toes was placed a greeting card: "Happy New Year."

The Boston Strangler was finished. DeSalvo now took on a new persona: the "Green Man." Wearing green work pants and shirt, he broke and entered into women's apartments, tied them up, and raped them. Often he ejaculated as soon as he tied up and touched his victim, and did not have intercourse. He apologized to the victim and loosened her bindings before he left.

In the eleven months during which he committed his Green Man attacks, DeSalvo never killed any of his victims. On November 3, 1964, a detective recognized a victim's description of the Green Man as being similar to the Measuring Man. DeSalvo's mug shots were shown to the victim and she quickly identified DeSalvo as the Green Man. DeSalvo was arrested and held at the Bridgewater Mental Hospital.

The police had no idea that they had the Boston Strangler in their custody. Because so many victims were elderly women, police were looking for a "mother hater"—somebody who was still living with a domineering mother. DeSalvo's psychiatric prison records indicated that he had a good and loving relationship with his mother (despite Brussel's assertion that she was "indifferent" to Albert). It was only in the spring of 1965, while still in custody, that DeSalvo began making his confessions. The police realized that they had had the Boston Strangler in their custody for six months already.

DeSalvo made a deal with the authorities: He would plead guilty to the Green Man rapes and take a life sentence if no murder charges would be brought against him as the Boston Strangler. Thus, in the end, nobody was officially charged or convicted for the thirteen murders.

Many in the law enforcement community were unconvinced that DeSalvo was a killer. They pointed out that DeSalvo did not need to kill for sex because he was adept at both seducing and raping females. The problem is that it is a slightly outdated notion that offenders rape for sex—in fact, rape as much as seduction or killing could have easily been a question of control or rage for DeSalvo, not sex.

The question remains, however: why did DeSalvo kill—and more important, why did he stop on his own? Psychiatrist James Brussel was brought in from New York by the Boston police prior to DeSalvo's capture, as were several other psychiatrists. Brussel had been successful at profiling other criminals and had gained a formidable reputation in being able to project a killer's personality by studying his crimes. (See Chapter 9.)

The panel of psychiatrists, Brussel recalls, were all deeply divided as to the personality of the killer. A faction insisted that there were two different killers. They all agreed that the killer had a mother-hate complex and that he was probably suffering from impotency. At the conference after the murder of Mary Sullivan, Brussel recalls that he felt very uneasy—as if a solution were at the tip of his fingers, yet eluding him. Brussel heard one of the psychiatrists say, " . . . and this trail of semen, ranging from the thighs of the early victims to the mouth of the most recent, could hardly have been left by a single man." He suddenly came to the solution, Brussel states, by following the trail of semen, figuratively. Brussel concluded that over the two-year killing period, DeSalvo was psychosexually maturing—passing from puberty to manhood in a most monstrous way.

Brussel noted that DeSalvo's first five victims, elderly women, were not raped but manipulated or penetrated by a foreign object. Brussel saw this as sexuality typical of a small boy coveting his mother's love and curious about her body and by association the bodies of women in general. But with the alleged absence of his mother's love, DeSalvo expressed these longings with a rage—thus his murder and molestation of the first five victims.

Then, after a four-month hiatus, he turned his attention to younger women and girls. According to Brussel, DeSalvo was in a stage now resembling puberty, attempting intercourse but achieving only a half-potent immature kind of interaction.

In the end, DeSalvo grew up and "cured" himself through murder, Brussel concluded. He writes:

The last one, Mary Sullivan, was subjected to the final and complete indignity. The semen was in her mouth. The Strangler had said, symbolically, I

throw my sex in your face. And where the sex should have been, he scorn-
fully thrust the handle of a broom . . .

I think he has finished . . . He's been seeking two things: to grow up
sexually, and to avenge himself for his mother's rejection of him or whatever
caused his hang-up. I believe he has succeeded on both counts.

"With Mary Sullivan," I said, "he perpetrated the final indignity, the final
revenge. He threw his sex in her face. He used a broom handle to say that
her sex no longer troubled him; he scorned it. I think Mary Sullivan may turn
out to be his last victim. I think he has, in a way, 'cured' himself of his overtly
sexual difficulties—though not of his other emotional problems."[82]

Brussel's theory is a fascinating one but problematic in certain areas.
First, Brussel maintains that DeSalvo had a negative relationship with his
mother. Other sources say the opposite, that DeSalvo loved and cherished
his mother and that he was her favorite. If his mother was indifferent, why
did she spend six months looking for her children after her husband sold
them to a farmer? Second, unless Brussel was representing DeSalvo's point
of view, Brussel perhaps attaches too much of a value judgment on oral
sex by referring to it as an "indignity" and to the vagina as "where the sex
should have been." Finally, if DeSalvo had been having extensive sex since
adolescence and was such a prolific seducer, why would he engage in these
few acts of "immature child-like" sex, followed by murder? Of course,
there is a distinct possibility that DeSalvo was fantasizing about his sexual exploits. Perhaps women did not throw their jewelry at him in exchange for sex, and perhaps he was not the big bisexual neighborhood
stud-muffin he claims he was. The only accounts of DeSalvo's sexual history come from DeSalvo himself. What if Irmgard was his first sexual
partner?

Canadian anthropologist and serial murder expert Elliott Leyton rejects the psychoanalytic model of Albert DeSalvo for a socioeconomic one.
Leyton points out that DeSalvo made numerous statements attesting that he
felt he came from very low-class status. Like his father, DeSalvo "married
up" in class—Irmgard came from a respectable European middle-class family just as DeSalvo's mother came from a respectable old middle-class
Boston "Yankee" family. In the end, Irmgard rejected DeSalvo.

When he was arrested as the Measuring Man, DeSalvo told police:

I been a poor boy all my life, I come from a bad home, you know all that, why should I kid you? Look, I don't know anything about modeling or cameras . . . I'm not educated and these girls was all college graduates, understand me? I made fools of them . . . I made them do what I wanted and accept me and listen to me.

DeSalvo preyed on victims in lower-middle-class and student low-rise apartment blocks, but for DeSalvo it was a step up. He thought of striking in a wealthier neighborhood called Swampscott, but didn't have the confidence:

Now Swampscott . . . is a fancy place with big houses and lots of them smart and educated broads like I used to fool over around Harvard Square but they grew up and got married and now they got kids . . . and anyway I don't go to Swampscott because I don't like the way they make me feel like an animal, those kinds of broads, and that is why I always put something over their faces and eyes so that they can't look at me.[83]

During his interrogation, DeSalvo turned to one of the state attorneys and said:

You are a man, you know what I mean, sure you have been to them high-class colleges and you got all them big excuses, but you have had that thing in your pants too—I think this is one of the troubles, sir, that guys like you, who have played with yourselves, who have looked with real lust on women, some of them far too young, way out of your range of possibility with a great deal of lust are afraid to admit it because somehow it takes you down from the goddamn pedestal on which society places you—but you are only a man.

Let me say this, sir, to you who sits across the table from me with such a shocked face, just let me say this . . . I ain't got nothing to lose no more, you know, and I couldn't give less of a goddamn for your world which is a nice society for you as long as you have money . . . have you ever thought of what it would be like for your ass if you didn't have dough? I bet you ain't.

At one point DeSalvo suggested that he stopped killing because his Irmgard treated him better, but even then he expressed it in socioeconomic terms: "My wife was treating me better. I was building up, you might say, my better self, the better side of me. I was very good at my job, they liked me, I got two raises."

DeSalvo had wanted to confess earlier, but according to him, his wife had threatened to commit suicide and kill the children if he confessed to being the strangler. At some point DeSalvo began to believe that his wife never really loved him and was kind to him in the last months only because of his increased income. This angered him so much that he confessed to being the Boston Strangler. He told his wife, "Our last two months together you made me feel for the first time like a man. You gave me love I never dreamed you had to give. But why—only because you had just about everything you dreamed of . . . everything you wanted, house fixed up, all the money coming in." Confession was his revenge.

Leyton wrote that in the end, DeSalvo found what he was searching for in all those apartments in the last victim's home—the Happy New Year card—the ultimate insult to society, placed at the foot of society's precious young woman, raped and dead.

Whether Brussel's psychoanalytic model or Leyton's socioeconomic theory is more valid, we will probably never know. Any hope of further questioning Albert DeSalvo vanished on November 26, 1973, when he was stabbed through the heart in his prison cell. His murder remains unsolved, as does the mystery of exactly why he began killing and why he ceased.

America Tumbles into the Sixties:
1966, "The Year the World Went Mad"

In the wake of the Boston Strangler, the escalation of violence that swept through America during the 1960s was dramatic and heralded by two notorious acts of mass murder in 1966: in Chicago, Richard Speck killed eight nurses in a dormitory, and in Texas, sniper Charles Whitman killed sixteen people. Both events shocked the nation and were major headline news stories. Serial crime historian Michael Newton recently wrote:

Reporter Charles Kuralt once labeled 1966 "the year the world went mad," prophetic words as we reflect upon a quarter-century of random killers run amok. That year, God died on the cover of *Time Magazine* and the Church of Satan opened its doors in San Francisco; the sexual revolution and hippie-drug subculture burst into the headlines; the Vietnam war entered American living rooms through a television tube and brought thousands of protesters into the streets.[84]

From the assassination of President Kennedy, the disorder in the streets over the war in Vietnam, and racial rioting to the oil crisis of the early 1970s and the disillusionment of Watergate, America suffered a cultural collapse comparable to that of postwar Germany or post-Soviet Russia. In economic and political terms, the inflation-driven collapse perhaps was not as severe as those of Germany and Russia—but in social terms, it was as drastic. America of the 1950s was as different in spirit and values from the America of the 1970s as was the Soviet Union from today's Russian republics or imperial Germany from the Weimar government. Something in those kinds of radical cultural transitions unleashes serial murderers. Perhaps it's a collapse of once-treasured values, or a loss of any vision of a future, but those already predisposed to kill seem more likely to act in such times.

Today we stand on the brink of even worse times. The American dream of each generation advancing to the next socioeconomic class is stalled. In fact, a huge proportion of Americans have actually fallen back from the status of their parents and are faring worse. Real income continues to shrink. The middle class is no longer the safe-haven destination of the impoverished nor the guaranteed springboard to better things. Oceans are no longer a guarantee of physical safety, education of advancement, and corporate employment of financial security. For some, the only dream remaining is a dream of continual murder.

PART TWO

THE METHOD AND MADNESS

THREE

CLASSIFYING SERIAL KILLERS:

The Typologies of Monstrosity

I'm the only Ph.D. in serial murder.
—TED BUNDY

You could smell the blood.
—RICHARD RAMIREZ

They say that the twentieth century is an age of specialization; if that is true, then it certainly applies to serial killers. Each serial killer falls into a specific category and rarely do his murders cross the parameters defining the categories. This kind of categorization has become important in police investigations because it helps identify the probable characteristics of a suspect in a process the police use called *criminal profiling*. (See Chapter 9 for a more detailed treatment on profiling and some of the controversies surrounding it.)

There is no single universally accepted system for categorizing serial killers. It varies depending upon the individual investigator, criminologist, or forensic psychologist who is proposing the categories. In the next two chapters we will explore some of the more frequently cited categories used in classifying serial killers.

Probably the most common and familiar is the FBI's *organized/disorganized* classifications. The FBI's behavioral specialists have compiled the *Crime*

Classification Manual, which categorizes murder into four main groups: *criminal enterprise homicide* (category 100); *personal cause homicide* (category 120); *sexual homicide* (category 130); and *group cause homicide* (category 140). These groups are then further divided up into some forty subcategories. Thus, for example, under personal cause homicide, category 122.01 is *spontaneous domestic homicide* while category 123.01 is *argument murder.* Category 101 under criminal enterprise homicide is *contract killing* while category 107 is *insurance inheritance-related* death.[85]

There is no separate category for serial killing; serial homicides fall into the various categories depending upon their type. The most common group where serial homicides frequently occur is category 130: sexual homicide. That group is divided into subcategories that include the following:

131: organized sexual homicide

132: disorganized sexual homicide

133: mixed sexual homicide

Thus a singular or serial sex killer will be first categorized as *organized, disorganized* or *mixed.* These three categories are the fundamental building blocks of serial killer identification and profiling used by the FBI and by police agencies that adopt the FBI system.

Organized Killers

The organized offender plans his murders and his escape carefully. He thinks through his crimes, often for weeks, months, and even years, before acting. He evolves his fantasy gradually and is aware of his growing compulsion to act out his murderous desire. He scrupulously targets his victims and stalks them for as long as necessary. He gains control over them at the crime scene. Often he takes his victims to another location and disposes of the body in such a manner that it may never be found. The killer is methodical and orderly in his crime. There are usually three separate crime scenes: where the victim was confronted, where the victim was killed, and where the victim's body was disposed of.

The organized serial killer is dangerous and difficult to track for the police. Usually he is socially competent and gainfully employed as a skilled worker. He approaches his victims by socializing with them, charming them, or tricking them into a situation where he can overpower them. He owns a car and is mobile, often is married or lives with a partner, and is sometimes the father of children. He follows the reports of his crimes in the media and may change jobs or move to a different city to avoid being detected. He is intelligent, often educated, cunning, and controlled. He brings his own weapons and restraints such as rope, handcuffs, or tape to the scene of the crime, and afterward he destroys evidence left behind. He is sometimes schooled in police investigative methods. The organized serial killer is a perfectionist, constantly improving his technique with each additional murder. The longer he kills, the more difficult he becomes to capture.

Disorganized Killers

The disorganized serial killer is diametrically opposite the organized one. He too is difficult to catch because while the organized killer is predictable in a certain way, the disorganized one is not. The police cannot second-guess the disorganized offender because he himself does not make any careful plans and does not know when he will kill next. He has vague and intense murderous fantasies, but he does not develop a thought-out plan of action. The disorganized serial killer usually attacks his victims spontaneously—his act is often a crime of opportunity. The victim is frequently overcome by a violent "blitz" attack and the weapon is often an object found near by—a pipe, a rock, a branch. The killer is usually socially inept, is unemployed or unskilled, does not own a car, and kills near his home. He is often of below-average intelligence or psychotic. The victim's body is usually left where the confrontation and attack took place, and the killer makes no attempt to hide it. The corpse is often subjected to extraordinary and frenzied mutilation. The offender often keeps souvenirs from the victim's belongings, clothes, and even parts of the victim's body. He makes little or no effort to cover his tracks, destroy evidence, disguise himself, or develop an escape plan. Often the offender is isolated from other people and living alone, and therefore, there is nobody from whom to hide incriminating objects or behavior. Evidence might be found in his premises out in the open or even on display.

Mixed-Category Killers

The FBI system also classifies homicides as a mixture of both organized and disorganized. The reason for this could be two or more killers working as a team. An attack may begin organized but be interrupted and deteriorate into chaos. The youthfulness of the offender or the use of drugs or alcohol can alter a personality of the offender from one crime to another. Critics of the organized/disorganized model argue that the "mixed" classification demonstrates the weakness of the system—too many serial killers do not fit into the neat categories and are thus classified "mixed"—a meaningless classification.

How these three categories manifest themselves in actual behavior is best illustrated with some actual case studies of offenders that reflect these organized/disorganized/mixed characteristics.

Ted Bundy: The Ultimate Organized Serial Killer

All roads in the empire of serial killers lead to Ted Bundy. Bundy was so organized that the police never located the crime scenes where his first seventeen victims were actually killed. Six of his victims remain missing to this day. Bundy referred to himself as "the only Ph.D. in serial murder."

What serial killers from Jack the Ripper to the Boston Strangler are to "then," Ted Bundy is to "now." He is *the* American psycho: the very essence of both fact and myth in a simultaneous representation of everything we know and think we know the new breed of serial killers are. Bundy is special because he was attractive, educated, and like us—that is, those of us who represent some kind of middle-class aspirations linked to the promise held out by our belief in a college education and hard work.

Albert DeSalvo, whom you met previously, sold by his father to some farmer at age nine, and the killers you will meet later in this book—Ed Gein, all alone on his remote Wisconsin farm; crazy young Herb Mullin and the voices in his head; Henry Lee Lucas in a shack with his glass eye; Jerry Brudos hunched down in his basement workshop with body parts in the freezer—all dwell in a world that we think serial killers *should* come from: a dark insane place that does not belong to us. *Our* world is going to work on Monday morning, showing up in class on time, mowing the grass, going to the weekend barbecue, paying the rent and credit card bills at the end of the month, going out on Friday night, and knowing more or less where we will be six months from now. In our world, serial killers came from the outside as predators, not as neighbors from next door or among our dinner guests. That is, until we met law school student and crisis prevention counselor Ted Bundy.

Bundy's story has been told in minute detail in numerous contradictory books and summarized in countless encyclopedias of murder. He was an archetypical organized killer and could also be classified as a "power/control" or "anger-excitation" killer type. (See the next chapter for more details on these categories.) I'll try to summarize here the essential history of his case and try to knead out some of the contradictory kinks between the various histories.

Ted Bundy was born as Theodore Robert Cowell on November 24, 1946, in Burlington, Vermont, to Louise Cowell, age twenty-two. From birth Bundy was already in a category in which the FBI survey found 43 percent of sexual and serial killers: he had only one parent. His mother was single and had become pregnant in Philadelphia. The story of who the father was remained obscure. The Cowell family were very strict Methodists and deeply shamed by Louise's pregnancy. In September she went away to the Elizabeth Lund Home for Unwed Mothers in Vermont, accompanied by a local church minister's wife. After giving birth to Ted in November, Louise returned to Philadelphia, leaving Ted behind in Vermont for three months.

Back in Philadelphia, her father, Sam Cowell, pretended to adopt Ted as his son from some unknown orphanage. Louise, it is said, pretended to be his sister. Nobody knows for sure when Ted unraveled the mystery of his birth history because he gave conflicting stories about it afterward.

Most biographies of Bundy simply state that Ted and his mother lived in Philadelphia for four years and then Louise moved to Tacoma, Washington—clear across the continent. In Tacoma she was employed as a church secretary and met and married John Culpepper Bundy, a hospital cook, from whom Ted took his surname.

Reports and memories of Bundy's childhood in his biographies are relatively mundane and undramatic: Bundy was ashamed of his family's lower-class status; he was embarrassed to be seen in the family's working-

class Rambler automobile and had fantasies of being adopted by TV cowboy actor Roy Rogers. Bundy missed his grandfather; Bundy wanted to live
with his great-uncle Jack, a university music professor in Tacoma who had a
grand piano in his house. When Bundy was eight he was no longer allowed
to jump into bed with his mother and stepfather; Bundy was threatened by
the birth of four other children after his mother married John; Bundy's
playmates remember that he had a short temper. Nothing in the biographies
indicates that Bundy grew up in anything but a loving and nurturing family,
or that his mother or stepfather treated him any differently from his four
siblings. His stepfather was reported to have a short temper, but there are
no reports that he abused Ted or his mother, nor did Ted Bundy make any
such claims. Ted Bundy's brothers and sisters apparently had an excellent
relationship with their elder half-brother. Bundy's mother maintains that
because he was her first-born, she was especially attentive to Ted.

His classmates from public school remember Bundy as an intelligent,
happy, and popular child with many friends and a good academic record.
One of his friends recalled that Bundy had a very subtle and intelligent
"on the mark" sense of humor. Bundy had a paper route.

Once in high school, people's recollections of Bundy suddenly become
more clouded. Bundy is said to have been withdrawn and his academic
progress was mediocre. He no longer was as popular as in junior high
school. His friend recalled that he lost his confidence and appeared
tongue-tied in social situations, not only with girls but with meeting new
people in general.

Bundy later recalled that in high school he felt alienated from his old
friends, feeling that they had somehow moved on but he did not. As far as
learning appropriate social behaviors, Bundy felt that he had "hit a wall"
when he got to high school and wondered whether it was perhaps a genetic thing. He claimed he did not have any role models at home to help
him in school.[86]

For some mysterious reason that nobody can seem to explain, once
Bundy got to high school he no longer fit in. There was nothing really wrong
with him, yet he became isolated. A woman who today is an attorney and
went to high school with Bundy remembers that when Bundy was seventeen he was well known and popular but not in the "top crowd." She remembers him as being shy. That she remembers him at all is to Bundy's
credit—so many serial killers are invisible in their adolescence.

He had only one date with a girl, and Bundy said that in high school sex was "over his head"—he knew or understood little about it. In prison, Bundy said that in matters of high school male-female relationships he was "dense," not understanding when a woman was particularly interested in him. Remarking on comments that he was handsome, Bundy said he did not believe that about himself. He remembered not understanding how friendships worked or what underlay social interaction.

The descriptions of Bundy in many ways are those of a typical high school student—just so, so typical. He was not among the most popular students at his school and he was not among the despised losers—in other words, again he was like most of us. He was not mocked, rejected, or sneered at, but neither was he the most popular kid in school.

There is one dark tremor in Bundy's adolescence. When he was fourteen, eight-year-old Ann Marie Burr vanished near his Tacoma neighborhood. Many years later police would suspect that Bundy might have been responsible.

After Bundy was executed in Florida's electric chair in 1989, investigative journalist Myra MacPherson attempted to dig deeper into Bundy's history to solve the mystery of how his homicidal personality was formed. MacPherson was puzzled by how Bundy's biographies leapt from his mother's time in Philadelphia to her sudden departure four years later to Tacoma, Washington. Nothing was said about the four years that child Ted lived with his grandparents.[87]

Ann Rule, for example, in her brilliantly definitive portrait of Bundy and his crimes, *The Stranger Beside Me,* after stating that little Ted was told to call his grandparents "Mother" and "Father," devotes only one short paragraph to his relationship with his grandfather:

> Ted adored his grandfather Cowell. He identified with him, respected him, and clung to him in times of trouble.[88]

After interviewing Ted Bundy for months, the authors of *The Only Living Witness* had only this to say about the first four years of Bundy's life, during which, if some psychologists are correct, 75 percent of a person's life knowledge is acquired:

Just before his fourth birthday, Teddy and his mother left Philadelphia to join her uncle and his family in Tacoma, Washington. Later, a story attributed to the adult Ted Bundy had it that Louise posed as his older sister, not his mother. This is not so; he always knew her as Mom. However, the little boy was angry and confused about being torn from his grandfather, who doted upon him, and his grandfather's comfortable old house.[89]

When MacPherson interviewed Bundy's surviving relatives, a disturbing picture began to emerge about his roots. Bundy's grandfather apparently had an explosive temper and was even feared by his brothers, one of whom said, "I always thought he was crazy." The grandfather often struck his wife. The grandmother was severely depressed and repeatedly hospitalized and given shock treatments. One of Ted's cousins reported that the grandfather, who was a church deacon, kept a large collection of pornography and that little Ted one day found it and pored over the images.

Apparently, Ted was in fact calling his grandfather and grandmother "Daddy" and "Mommy" and perceiving his real mother as his older sister. Bundy's great-aunt said that the other members of the family were suspicious about Ted's "adoption" by Louise's parents. Her mother was not well enough to care for a child, and everybody suspected that Ted was actually Louise's child.

Nobody knows exactly when Bundy discovered his true birth history, and Bundy told conflicting stories about it. In some versions he found out when he was in university that his "sister" was in fact his mother, but his school friends claim that there was never any question of Louise Bundy being anybody but his "mom." Another friend recalls that Bundy told him when they were in high school that he was born illegitimate.

MacPherson writes that only recently did Bundy's mother admit that her father on occasion beat her mother. Did little Ted witness his "father" with the porno collection beating his "mother"? And why did his "sister" suddenly, when he was four, take him away clear across the country and become his new mother? Moreover, upon her arrival in Tacoma, his mother changed Ted's last name to Nelson. No satisfactory explanation has yet been given for that shift of identities. MacPherson hints at all sorts of dark possibilities as to why the identity of Ted's supposed real father has never been discussed. Nor do we know the reasons why Louise suddenly packed up and left Philadelphia when Ted was four.

Several psychiatrists who interviewed Bundy argue that he may have shown symptoms of somebody who witnessed something horrific and traumatic in his early childhood, and had been suppressing and sublimating that memory since. MacPherson also uncovered the story of three-year-old Ted lifting the covers of his fifteen-year-old aunt's bed as she slept and slipping in three butcher knives beside her. According to Ted's aunt:

> He just stood there and grinned. I shooed him out of the room and took the implements back down to the kitchen and told my mother about it. I remember thinking at the time that I was the only one who thought it was strange. Nobody did anything.

If MacPherson's premise is correct, then unpleasant but minor episodes in Bundy's childhood take on a different context and magnitude. Just like the 81 percent of the killers in the FBI study, Bundy in his adolescence showed a history of stealing. Researchers found an index card listing Bundy as a juvenile suspect in some burglaries, but the details of the incidents were destroyed when Bundy turned eighteen. His high school friends remember that Bundy forged ski lift tickets and that all his skiing gear was stolen. Skiing was one of the few group activities in which Bundy participated and excelled in. Years later some of his victims would be dumped along the mountain roads leading to the region's ski areas. Bundy's exposure to pornography as a child, if true, then pegs him in another 81 percent of childhood experiences reported by serial sex killers.

The isolation, the feeling of being different from the rest, puts Bundy into a category reported by 77 percent of all killers in the FBI study. When Bundy graduated from high school in 1965 he was one of the first members of the baby boom generation—his class was the biggest in the school's history, with 740 students. That too must have contributed to his sense of anonymity and isolation.

It seems that from a very young age, Bundy was obsessed with being too poor, with being too low in the social class structure. His dreams of being adopted by Roy Rogers had less to do with his role as a cowboy on TV as with his personal wealth as a successful television actor. Little Ted wanted to live rich. He also dreamed of living with his great-uncle Jack, who had a grand piano in his house, a symbol for Ted of wealth. When his mother took Ted as a child to buy clothes, he apparently pulled his mother to the most expensive fashion items. Even after he was arrested for murder, he wrote letters from jail lamenting the absence of "chilled Chablis." Many years later, when asked what he felt when he killed, he once replied, "How do you describe the taste of bouillabaisse? Some remember clams, other mullet." He even affected a strange little aristocratic accent that was vaguely English—he was a young Anthony Hopkins–Hannibal Lecter before the character was ever written.

While his snobbery and obsession with class in themselves did not make him kill, they might have instilled in him unrealistic expectations that he could not live up to. He was already infected with a deep sense of insecurity, perhaps because of some early childhood trauma in Philadelphia, and the humiliation and shock of failing to realize his expectations led to his withdrawal into that secret world of fantasy that serial killers retreat to.

Bundy was most to the point when he dismissed reports of him being handsome and popular. In the end it did not matter what Bundy's circumstances really were; what counted was what Bundy thought and perceived them to be. Bundy could have been superstar attractive—but if he did not *feel* that way, of what consequence was it?

After graduating from high school, Bundy entered the University of Puget Sound in 1965. Like most first-year university students Bundy was lost in a series of huge, impersonal, crowded introductory classes and lectures. Bundy recalled that as a lonely year for him. He no longer had his neighborhood buddies to hang out with and did not feel socially adept enough to make new friends. Bundy lived at home his first year in college. His mother recalled that he got good grades but did not get involved with social life at school. Every day he came home, studied, slept, and went back to school.

In the spring of 1966 Ted Bundy met the love of his life. Her name was Stephanie* and she was older than him and ahead of Bundy in school by two years at the University of Washington. She was a tall, beautiful, elegant young woman with long dark hair parted down the middle. She came from a wealthy family in San Francisco—exactly the kind of background that Bundy aspired to. She was everything that Bundy dreamt of. For some time, Bundy admired her from afar but was too shy to approach her.

---

* A pseudonym.

One day he found out that Stephanie was going skiing and he noncha-lantly asked her to give him a ride in her car. On the ski slopes, Bundy was confident and masterful. On the ride back home in the car, Bundy charmed Stephanie and they became lovers. She was, perhaps, Bundy's first sexual experience.

Bundy worked hard at romancing Stephanie. Beatrice Sloan, a sixty-year-old widow whom Bundy befriended, lent him her car so that he could impress Stephanie. Mrs. Sloan remembers Bundy as a "lovable rascal" and sympathized with his need to impress his girlfriend. Once she lent Bundy her best crystal and silverware when he cooked a gourmet meal for Stephanie. Ted and Stephanie became a steady couple.

For his second year, Bundy transferred to Stephanie's university and enrolled in Chinese language studies. He said he chose the most exotic and obscure area of study to separate himself from the crowd. That year was probably the happiest of Bundy's life. He excelled in his learning of the Chinese language. He showed off his girlfriend to his neighborhood friends and family.

Yet years later, Bundy stated that it was precisely in this happiest pe-riod of his life that he began to act out a compulsion that was sparked in-advertently. Walking down a street one evening, entirely by chance he saw through a window a woman undressing. The sight so excited him that he began to compulsively seek out opportunities to peep through windows. Bundy recalled that this was not an overwhelming compulsion; he would not break a date, postpone an important meeting, or rearrange his life in any way. His voyeuristic forays fit the dictates of his daily routine. But he said that he devoted, nonetheless, an enormous amount of time and en-ergy to fitting his window-peeping activities into his schedule; he became very adept at it and highly addicted to it.

In the spring of 1967 Stephanie graduated, and it is said that by that time she was getting bored with Bundy. She felt he was too childish, too imma-ture. It bothered her when he sneaked up on her, tapped her on the shoulder, and vanished before she could turn around. Perhaps, despite Bundy's claims that they did not affect his normal life, his voyeuristic activities were mak-ing him a less attentive lover. Later, when Bundy began to kill, his other lovers reported the onset of a "sexual laziness," a cold, perfunctory per-formance. Hoping to ease herself out of her relationship with Bundy, Stephanie told him that she intended to go back home to San Francisco upon her graduation. To her surprise and dismay, Bundy told her he had been offered a scholarship at Stanford University in San Francisco for a summer session in Chinese studies. He followed her down to California.

Once in San Francisco, Bundy fell apart. It is hard to determine what happened first: his failure at Stanford or his outright rejection at the hands of Stephanie. He stopped showing up to lectures and doing his class work at Stanford, and he failed his courses. Stephanie, in the meantime, had begun working in a brokerage house in San Francisco. One day as she emerged from her building for lunch, there was the familiar tap on her shoulder. When she turned around, Bundy was hiding behind a corner like a little boy. Stephanie told him she did not want to see him anymore.

Bundy was devastated on his return to Tacoma. His brother recalls that before the breakup with Stephanie, Ted was always in charge of his emotions. He had never seen his brother so upset and moody.

Somewhere in this period, Bundy confessed that he began to attempt to disable women's cars by deflating the tires or stealing the distributor cap. It never worked, he remembers, because around the college there were plenty of men who would quickly help a woman with car troubles. He said, however, that he did not have any idea what he would have done if he had actually succeeded in trapping a woman by this method. Bundy said he was toying with danger, just exploring how far things could go.

Bundy was now actively taking his fantasies out on "test runs"—a phase that incipient serial killers go through prior to committing their first murder. His voyeuristic activities, meanwhile, put him into an activity in which 71 percent of the FBI's surveyed killers engage in before they committed their first murder.

In the autumn of 1967, Bundy returned for his third year of university. He abandoned Chinese language studies and began studying urban planning. He could not concentrate on studies and by December he had quit school. He spent the winter traveling around the country. Later, investigators would trace his travels, but found no evidence that Bundy committed any homicides during this period. In the spring of 1968, Bundy returned to Seattle, rented a small apartment, and took a job as a night stocker in a supermarket.

During this period, Bundy became a practiced thief. Most of his clothes, furniture, appliances, stereo, TV, and even a huge plant were stolen. Bundy did not steal as a professional thief to later sell the items he took—he kept and used everything he stole, and stole only items of the highest quality. Sometimes he stole from stores; at other times he burgled summer houses along the beach near Seattle. Bundy also recalled that alcohol became an important tool in his thievery, as it lowered his inhibitions and made him appear less nervous than he really was.

Bundy said that he also became an avid consumer of violent pornography. Bundy talked about his taste for porn developing over a period beginning from his juvenile high school years. He said that he began with an attraction to normal sexual imagery found in magazines like *Playboy,* but slowly his taste began to mutate toward imagery of a more violent nature.

Bundy also confessed to being an avid reader of pulp detective magazines, of the type that Ed Gein, John Joubert, and Harvey Glatman were reading. Bundy says he was excited by the stories and images of abused females and was also getting an education in police procedures and crime techniques—what worked and what did not. (See Chapter 6 for more about the suspected role of detective magazines in serial killing.)

It is very likely that Bundy was nearing the point of committing a homicide linked to his fantasies. He was already experiencing numerous stressors: His girlfriend had rejected him, he had failed the previous year at college and had to drop out, he was employed at a dead-end job. The only thing needed was the final trigger—one more rejection, an accidental confrontation with somebody during a burglary, anything could have set him off on his murderous career that spring of 1968. Instead, Bundy put the pieces of his life together and started anew.

What makes the case of Bundy so fascinating, again, is how typical his experiences, desires, and goals were of many young, ambitious, urban men and women—he truly could be any one of us. Among my generation of males, few were not familiar with the cheery, wholesome "girl next door" nudes published in *Playboy* that Bundy refers to. Most of us eventually turned to dating the real girl next door. And so did Bundy at first.

Later in early adulthood, many of us had an unhappy romance, a bad year in college, or some other major disappointment. And so did Bundy. And perhaps at those bitter moments, some of us fantasized about doing something dramatic, something unacceptable, perhaps even violent. Bundy started to toy with his fantasies—peeking into windows, disabling women's cars, exploring how far things could go. This is what begins to distinguish him from the rest of us, even before he began to kill: his willingness to tinker his desires into reality, to start exploring that dark fantasy road to see where it leads.

Yet Bundy did not go down that road easily. Like the rest of us, Bundy attempted to deal with his disappointment, heal from his hurt, and go on with his life, doing the best he could in "chasing the dream." What makes Bundy so fascinating is his resilience and drive, so lacking in most other serial killers. Bundy attempted to do what is expected of us—get back up on his feet and keep moving.

One morning in the spring of 1968 Bundy was on his way to break into some beach houses. On a street corner near one of the houses, Bundy ran into an acquaintance from high school and they struck up a conversation. He told Bundy that he was working for Art Fletcher, a local Republican politician making a bid for the office of lieutenant governor of Washington State. Several of Bundy's other acquaintances were already working for Fletcher, and he was invited to come by. His friend remembered that in high school Bundy had had an active interest in election politics. Shortly afterward, Bundy was offered a job on Fletcher's election staff.

Bundy recalled that he found politics a way to be instantly a part of something. There was a social life that came with it. He said he did not have the money for a tennis club membership, but politics gave him access to influential levels of society.

In 1968, Art Fletcher was running in the same series of elections that Robert Kennedy was in before he was assassinated. Fletcher was so impressed by Bundy that he selected him as his personal driver and bodyguard. Bundy was remembered as an able, intelligent worker, whose appearance was always meticulous but studiously casual. Nobody knew that Bundy was shoplifting the fine clothes he wore. Unfortunately, in November Fletcher came in second, and within days after the election, Bundy no longer had employment.

Bundy quickly secured a job as a salesperson in the same Seattle department store from which he used to shoplift. There he quickly gained a reputation as an excellent salesman, especially adept with female customers. Apparently he could sell them anything.

In the meantime, Bundy remained in touch with his lost love, Stephanie, in San Francisco. He occasionally wrote or phoned her, and apparently when Stephanie passed through Seattle to visit relatives in Vancouver, British Columbia, she called Bundy to say hello. There seemed to be no sense of desperation or drama in Bundy's letters or calls to her.

After saving some money, Bundy quit his job at the department store and in the winter of 1969 he traveled to Philadelphia, where he had spent his first four years. There he enrolled in Temple University, taking theatrical arts classes. He got good grades in acting and stage makeup, skills that he would put to use in the near future. Nothing else is known about his winter there.

In the summer of 1969 Bundy returned to Seattle and took an apartment in a University District rooming house run by a couple. They took an instant liking to Bundy and remember him as a quiet and helpful tenant. He kept his room neat and tidy and helped out with small chores around the house. He was often invited down to their kitchen for lunch or coffee. He took various temporary jobs, one of which was as a messenger for a legal firm.

In September, Bundy walked into a college tavern around the corner from where he lived and spotted a pretty girl with several of her friends. Her name was Liz Kendall; she was a twenty-four-year-old divorcée with a three-year-old daughter, and she worked as a medical secretary. She had long, dark hair and came from a wealthy family in Salt Lake City, Utah. Ted told her he was a law student and was writing a book about Vietnam. Liz bitterly recalls that Bundy was so charming and handsome that by the end of the evening, "I was already planning the wedding and naming the kids."

They became a steady couple and Liz and her daughter would go on many trips and outings with Bundy. Liz was a very insecure and jealous woman. Her recent divorce had made her even more insecure, and as such she was perfect for Ted. Within three months they were engaged to be married and took out a marriage license. But as things began to get serious, Bundy dramatically tore up the license and confessed to Liz that he in fact was a failed student and was not writing a book. Liz forgave him for his lies, and offered to finance his return to the university.

In the summer of 1970 Ted Bundy began to work as a delivery truck driver for a small medical equipment company. At the same time, he enrolled in the department of psychology at the University of Washington. That summer Bundy was hailed as a hero when he rescued a three-and-half-year-old girl who fell into a lake. His psychology professors had nothing but praise for Bundy. In a letter of recommendation, one of them wrote:

> Mr. Bundy is undoubtedly one of the top undergraduate students in our department. Indeed, I would place him in the top 1% of undergraduate students with whom I have interacted both here at the University of Washington and at Purdue University. He is exceedingly bright, personable, highly motivated, and conscientious. He conducts himself more like a young professional than like a student. He has the capacity for hard work and because of his intellectual curiosity is a pleasure to interact with . . . As a result of his undergraduate psychology major, Mr. Bundy has become intensely interested in studying psychological variables which influence jury decisions. He and I are currently engaged in a research project in which we are attempting to study experimentally some of the variables which influence jury decisions.

Another professor of psychology gushed:

> It is clear that other students use him as a standard to emulate . . . His personal characteristics are all of the highest standards. Ted is a mature young man who is very responsible and emotionally stable (but not emotionally flat as many students appear—he does get excited or upset appropriately in various situations) . . . I am at a loss to delineate any real weakness he has.

In the meantime, Liz Kendall continued seeing Bundy, later stating that he was a considerate, romantic, and gentle lover during this period. She was welcomed in the Bundy household and often she and Ted went to the family's A-frame cabin in the mountains. Everyone assumed that it was just a matter of time before she and Ted were married.

In September 1971, Bundy began his last year of psychology training. He left the medical equipment delivery job and was employed as a counselor at the Seattle Crisis Clinic. This was a twenty-four-hour facility that people who felt suicidal or were in some kind of crisis could telephone and get counseling and advice. It was mostly staffed by volunteers and supervised by paid psychology students like Bundy.

At about the same time, Ann Rule began working at the clinic as a volunteer on Tuesday nights and was paired with Bundy. Rule was in her forties, with four children and in the middle of a divorce. She was a former Seattle police officer who had quit the force and began attending college to study creative writing. She became a prolific writer of true-crime articles for pulp detective magazines such as *True Detective,* the very same ones that Bundy was so avidly consuming. When she met Bundy she had already published some eight hundred articles. She was also a commissioned deputy sheriff in several counties of Washington State, where she was hired to write crime synopses for various investigations in progress. In her best-selling book about her friendship with Bundy, *The Stranger Beside Me,* she wrote, "I liked him immediately. It would have been hard not to."

Rule wrote honestly about her early impressions of Bundy:

> If, as many people believe today, Ted Bundy took lives, he also saved lives. I know he did, because I was there when he did it.
>
> I can picture him today as clearly as if it were only yesterday, see him hunched over the phone, talking steadily, reassuringly . . . he was never brusque, never hurried . . . He was one of those rare people who listen with full attention, who evince a genuine caring by their very stance. You could tell things to Ted that you might never tell anyone else.[90]

Whereas some people stated that they saw Bundy occasionally flare up in anger, Rule says she never saw that in him:

> I never saw that anger. I never saw any anger at all. I cannot remember everything that Ted and I talked about, try as I might, but I do know we never argued. Ted's treatment of me was the kind of old-world gallantry that he invariably showed toward any woman I ever saw him with, and I found it appealing. He always insisted on seeing me safely to my car when my shift at the Crisis Clinic was over in the wee hours of the morning. He stood by until I was safely inside my car, doors locked and engine started, waving to me as I headed for home twenty miles away. He often told me, "Be careful. I don't want anything to happen to you."[91]

Tiny, subtle, almost imperceptible cracks began to manifest themselves in Bundy's personality. What is terrifying is that these cracks took on meaning only once Bundy's crimes were revealed. Ann Rule recalls that at Bundy's request, she brought him copies of articles she wrote for *True Detective.*

At one point, Bundy specifically asked her for articles on rape because he needed the information for a psychology "research project." His girlfriend, Liz, recalls one night pulling a pair of rubber surgical gloves from the pocket of his jacket. A friend remembered glimpsing a pair of handcuffs in Bundy's car trunk and when asking him what they were for, Bundy gave some vague story about finding them in the garbage.

In the spring of 1972, Bundy graduated with a degree in psychology and applied to law school. Although his marks were good, Bundy fared poorly on the Law School Aptitude Test (LSAT) and, as a result, was turned down by every law school he applied to. Bundy went to work as a counselor in the psychiatric outpatient unit of Seattle's Harbourview Hospital. He did not last there very long. It was reported that he was cold and nearly abusive with his patients and tended to lecture them rather than offer counsel. Moreover, some of the staff actually began to suspect that Bundy was phoning the patients at home during the night and making anonymous threats.

Despite Bundy's professed attachment to Liz, he was having an affair with another counselor at the hospital. She told police, years later, that when she was making love with Bundy one day, he shoved his forearm under her chin and began to choke her.

Perhaps sensing an oncoming crash like the one that occurred after his disastrous romance with Stephanie, Bundy turned to politics once more for refuge. It was an election year in 1972 and Bundy went to work for the incumbent governor, Dan Evans. Sometimes he was sent out to reconnoiter the opposition's rallies. Bundy wore disguises such as wigs and false mustaches on these jobs. He began to display a remarkable chameleon-like ability to radically change his features by getting a haircut, growing a beard, or even parting his hair differently. Several people commented that Bundy was a true changeling.

Once again, Bundy seemed to have regained equilibrium despite his failure at his first job after graduation and rejection from law school. After the election was over, he was rewarded for his good work on the governor's campaign. Bundy's curriculum vitae for 1972–1973 reads as follows:

- Crime Commission Assistant Director: October 1972 to January 1973. As assistant to the director of the Seattle Crime Prevention Commission, suggested and did the preliminary investigation for the Commission's investigation into assaults against women, and "white collar" (economic) crime. Wrote press releases, speeches, and newspaper articles for the Commission. Participated extensively in the planning of the Commission's activities for 1973.

- Criminal Corrections Consultant: January 1973. Currently retained by the King County Office of Law and Justice Planning to identify recidivism rates for offenders who have been found guilty of misdemeanors and gross misdemeanors in the twelve county District Courts. The purpose of the study is to determine the nature and number of offenses committed subsequent to a conviction in District Court.

In May 1973 Bundy was hired as a consultant by the state Republican Party central committee to analyze cost overruns in government spending. He worked for the committee chairman, Ross Davis, and was often a guest at his home. Davis remembers Bundy as "smart, aggressive, exceptionally so, and a believer in the system." His wife Lisa recalls, "He didn't talk much about himself, but I didn't feel he was trying to hide anything. He spoke of his mother and family in loving terms." Occasionally Ted Bundy babysat the couple's children, and he ate dinner at their house at least once a week.

Bundy also reapplied to law school and with some aggressive lobbying he was accepted at the Utah College of Law in Salt Lake City—he was scheduled to begin classes there in September. Somewhere in this period, Ted Bundy also bought a car—a bronze-colored Volkswagen Beetle. It was the second time he had bought that model. Bundy apparently liked the auto for its classless status; it was an inexpensive vehicle, but sometimes preferred by the wealthy as a stylish second car for errands in the city.

That summer, Bundy was sent to California for a Republican Party conference, and while there he decided to look up his lost love, Stephanie. Bundy was no longer a "loser." He projected now the aura of a "take charge" man: a college graduate with political ambitions, outspoken, confident, and about to enter law school. Stephanie liked what she saw and they rekindled their romance.

By August 1973, Bundy had truly surpassed some formidable setbacks and obstacles. He had achieved much: From a disappointed and failed college-boy reject, Bundy built himself into a psychological counselor, a respected political hand, an often-invited dinner guest, a rescuer of lives, a student of law; somebody who, some said, might very well be a future state governor. And now he reconquered his first and true love, the woman he had lost five years ago. True, there were a few rough spots along the way, such as his burglaries and window peeping; and true, there was a cloud on the horizon—he was now deeply involved with two women and he would have to deal with that. Otherwise, though, Bundy appeared to be healed. Who would have thought that six months from now he would begin brutally raping and murdering women.

At the last minute Bundy switched law schools. Over the summer his friends from the Republican Party argued that it was not wise for Bundy to go to a law school in Utah if he had plans for a political career in Washington State. Bundy applied and was admitted to the school of law at the University of Puget Sound in Tacoma, Washington. He wrote the University of Utah, telling them that he had been in a serious car accident and could not attend classes that year. Why he told that lie is unclear, but perhaps he was embarrassed, after lobbying the university so hard for admission, to switch schools at the last minute.

Some biographies of Bundy link this change of schools with his subsequent outbreak of killing. The story goes that when Bundy arrived at the law school in Tacoma, he discovered that it was located in an anonymous office building. It was not an "Ivy League" institution as he had imagined, but a drab, third-class school, and it is theorized that the snob in Bundy revolted—he immediately began to fail in all his classes, in a collapse very similar to the one six years earlier in San Francisco. Bundy's biographers maintain that this new intolerable failure triggered his homicidal crimes. But it is highly improbable that Bundy went through an application process to the school in Tacoma without visiting its facilities. Moreover, if he was applying late to the school, he probably would have had to go there in person to deliver his application materials, and since his family lived in Tacoma, it would have been a convenient trip. (Seattle is about a thirty-minute drive from Tacoma.) It is improbable that Bundy was surprised by anything he saw at the school when he started classes. Something else must have happened.

We know that in the last seven years Bundy had been window-peeping and trolling aimlessly at night in the residential neighborhoods near the university, seeking some sort of satisfaction out of his fantasies. Nobody knows for how long the fantasies themselves had existed; probably since childhood or early adolescence. At points, it appears that Bundy took his fantasies on "test runs," as when he disabled women's cars. These points probably marked cycles that came and went, but intensified with every reappearance. Bundy described them as cyclical depressions: "Not mood swings, just changes," he said. He said he had no difficulty projecting a false cheerfulness for short periods of time while at the same time hiding a huge part of his life that nobody knew about.

Many biographers of Bundy associate his failure at Stanford in the summer of 1967 with his breakup with the girl of his dreams, Stephanie. We are not sure, however, at what point in the sequence of events Stephanie actually began to withdraw from Bundy. In fact, events might have happened the other way around—his collapse at Stanford might be associated more with his success, rather than with some failure with Stephanie. Prior to meeting Stephanie, Bundy already had notions and fantasies of what his ideal woman would be like; Stephanie seemed to fulfill those criteria. But as we all know, real-life lovers rarely match the ones in our fantasies. It is precisely after Bundy began dating Stephanie that he said he "inadvertently" began his nocturnal trolling. It was when he successfully realized his fantasy of acquiring a beautiful girlfriend that he might have realized that it was not enough. It was not what he really wanted. That was exactly when he began to prowl in the night.

Bundy claimed that violent pornography began to slowly solidify his vague fantasies and compulsions into concrete ideas and actions. Perhaps, but most likely Bundy was in a state of denial when he said that. Bundy's violent fantasies were probably formulated much earlier, but he had the intelligence and education to be embarrassed about them—perhaps he even suppressed the early memory of them.

The pressure on Bundy was coming from three sides: the violent fantasies that he *really* wanted to fulfill; the attempts to realize ambitions that he felt he *should have* realized; and the anxiety, perhaps guilt, at the contents of his violent fantasies. A less intelligent, less thinking, or less ambitious person than Bundy might not have thought or worried much about the inappropriateness of his violent desires. Perhaps Bundy was even worried that his fantasies, if they ever took control of him, would be socially embarrassing and ruinous to his career plans—which is exactly what happened.

It was no doubt a fantasy of Bundy's that he could get his girlfriend from six years ago to fall in love with him again, and remarkably, she did, fulfilling that fantasy. It was truly an extraordinary achievement no matter how you look at it. It is very possible that everything that Bundy had done in the last six years, he did with the purpose of regaining the love of Stephanie. The evidence is there: His failed studies in urban planning in the fall of 1967 resulted only because he was too late in applying to architectural school—Stephanie had expressed to him her admiration of architects.

Now in the fall of 1973, Bundy had reconquered his lost love. Stephanie flew to Seattle to spend time with Ted. To make sure that Liz would not stumble upon them, Ted checked Stephanie into a hotel in Seattle.

Without Liz ever finding out, Ted and Stephanie became engaged to be married, and he brought her to the Davis house for dinner and introduced her as his fiancée. Bundy borrowed their car and took Stephanie on a romantic trip into the mountains where they used to go skiing in their college days. At the end of the trip, Lisa Davis took some photographs of Ted and Stephanie with their arms around each other in front of the Davis house, and then drove Stephanie to the airport.

Almost immediately, as soon as Bundy reunited with Stephanie, his life began to fall apart, beginning with a dismal performance at law school. It is probable that when Stephanie agreed to marry him, Bundy must have realized that his fantasy in reality was meaningless—it was false. Bundy once said, "I always felt somehow lost in my life."

Bundy must have felt that there was something else that he truly wanted to be doing other than becoming a lawyer to win the heart of a beautiful dark-haired woman. All he really wanted, deep down, was just to possess her body; he did not need her love and companionship, he realized. When he was on death row, Bundy explained that he received no pleasure from harming or causing pain to his victims. He did not torture them. What really fascinated him was the hunt for his victims and their capture and, as he said, "possessing them physically as one would possess a potted plant, a painting, or a Porsche."

Bundy's cyclical disappointment upon realizing his goals is typical of the cyclical psychology of serial murder. When serial killers "realize" their murderous goals by killing, they frequently find the experience of murder disappointing and need to commit another in some improved way, hoping for a better payoff to the fantasy.

• • •

Ann Rule writes that in December 1973, she saw Bundy at a Christmas party. This time he was there with his girlfriend, Liz, and he introduced her to Rule. She assumed that Bundy had gotten over Stephanie and that Liz and Ted were living together. Liz told her she was returning home to Salt Lake City for the Christmas holidays, while Ted was going to stay in Seattle to study.

As soon as Liz left to visit her parents in Utah, Stephanie arrived in Seattle to spend time with her fiancée and discuss their marriage plans. Later, Stephanie testified that Bundy had changed radically since their last time together in September. He did not buy her any Christmas presents, but showed her a very expensive chess set he bought for a friend. He was very unenthusiastic about the expensive presents she had bought him. His lovemaking was very cool and mechanical. Once he left her alone for an entire day to work on a "school project."

He told Stephanie that there was another woman and that although it was over with her, she called often and that he needed to "get loose" of her before he could devote himself to Stephanie. When Stephanie attempted to discuss their marriage plans, he dodged the issue and went into a tirade about his illegitimate birth history. On the last evening before she returned to San Francisco, they did not make love, Stephanie said. Stunned and confused, she flew home on January 2, 1974.

On January 4, an eighteen-year-old woman went to bed in her basement apartment in a big old house near the University of Washington. When she failed to appear for breakfast the next morning, her housemates assumed she was sleeping late. By midafternoon they began to worry and went downstairs to investigate. They found her door unlocked and saw her sleeping in her bed, but not responding to their calls. As they approached closer they discovered to their horror that her face and hair were matted with blood. Somebody had detached a heavy metal rod from her bed frame and fractured her skull with it. Then the intruder inserted into her a vaginal probe, a speculum, the kind that is carried by medical supply houses, and brutally wrenched her genitals apart, seriously injuring them. She remained in a coma for ten days, and when she awoke she remembered nothing of the attack. It must have occurred while she slept. She remained brain-damaged for the rest of her life.

Bundy, the former medical supply house delivery driver, is today believed to have committed this crime.

On the night of January 31, 1974, Lynda Healy, a psychology student at the University of Washington, went to bed in her basement apartment in a big house shared by several college girls. Lynda worked part-time announcing ski reports at a local radio station and needed to get up very early in the morning. One of her housemates, Barbara Little, who also had a basement apartment right next to Lynda, heard Lynda's electric alarm clock go off as usual at 5:30 A.M. Barbara rolled over and went back to sleep.

About half an hour later, Barbara's own alarm went off. As she got up, Barbara was surprised to hear Lynda's alarm still buzzing incessantly next door. She went into Lynda's room and turned on the light. Everything seemed to be in order, although Barbara was surprised to note that Lynda had made her bed before she left—usually she made it only after she got home from classes. Barbara turned Lynda's alarm clock off. The radio station phoned, saying that Lynda had not arrived. Barbara assured the station that Lynda had left already and would be there shortly.

As her roommates woke up that morning, each noticed something strange. Lynda's bike, which she used for transportation to the university, was still in the basement. They also found, to their surprise, that the side door leading to the basement was unlocked—this was unusual. They then hurried off to the university and spent the day going to their different classes, each assuming that one of the others saw Lynda during the day. When that evening they got home and found that Lynda's family had arrived for a supper that she had planned, and that Lynda still had not appeared, they called the police.

The police began to carefully search Lynda's room. When they pulled the bedspread back they discovered Lynda's pillow soaked in blood and missing its case. Her horrified roommates told the police that the bed had been made differently from the way Lynda did it—she pulled the sheet over the pillow, whereas now the sheet was tucked under. In the back of her closet they found Lynda's nightgown, the neck and shoulder area caked with blood. The clothing she had worn the night before—a pair of jeans, a blouse, and boots—were missing, as was her knapsack. The police surmised that somebody had entered the house, knocked Lynda unconscious, dressed her, made her bed, and carried her away. Not a single clue was left behind by her abductor—not one fingerprint, strand of hair, or witness sighting. Nothing.

Bundy was connected to Healy. Bundy's cousin was a friend of Healy's and Bundy was in three of Healy's psychology classes at the University of Washington—but so were four hundred other students.

Back in San Francisco, Stephanie was beside herself with confusion and anger. It was now mid-February, nearly six weeks since she had last seen Ted, and he hadn't phoned or written once. Finally she telephoned Ted in Seattle and when he answered the phone she berated him for not calling her. Bundy sounded drunk and dazed, she said. He didn't say anything except, "Well, far out, you know." And then he hung up on Stephanie. They would never speak to each other again.

On March 12, 1974, in Olympia, near the same place where Kathy Devine had vanished back in November, nineteen-year-old Donna Gail Manson disappeared. She lived on the campus of Evergreen State College, and around 7:00 P.M. she left her dormitory to attend a jazz concert being held on the campus. She never arrived. There were no witnesses, and no clues, and her body was never found.

On April 17, Susan Rancourt, who lived in a dormitory on the campus of Central Washington State College at Ellesburg, was planning to see a German film with some friends. She had a meeting with her instructors first, and told her friends she would meet them at the movie. Before leaving for the meeting, she loaded up a washing machine in one of the dorm's laundry rooms. She planned to put the clothes in the dryer upon her return from the movie. After the meeting was over, she left in the direction toward the building where the film was being screened, carrying a binder full of papers. She never arrived at the movie, and her washing was found the next day in the laundry room, still wet. Police attempted to retrace her movements. Rancourt was a student of karate and would have fought back at any attempt to kidnap her. Police surmised that her papers would have been found scattered somewhere. The police found no traces of her movements.

For the next few days, police took reports of every strange or suspicious incident that students at the college could remember. There were many such reports, and among them were two reports of a young, handsome, neatly dressed man, with his left arm set in a cast and driving a bronze-colored Volkswagen bug. Twice he approached different female students in front of the college library, asking them to help him carry his books to his car. The first woman reported that as she approached his Volkswagen, she noticed that the front passenger seat was missing. For some reason that she could not explain, she felt suddenly afraid, and she placed the books on the hood of the car and hurried off feeling embarrassed by her "irrational" anxiety. It saved her life.

The other woman said that after she carried the books to the car, the man told her he had problems starting the vehicle. Would she mind getting behind the wheel and turning the ignition while he fiddled with the engine in the back of the Volkswagen? Again, something caused her to feel uneasy about getting into the man's car, and she left, saying she was in a hurry and could not help him more.

These reports were among many, none of which really at the time offered any significant clue or meaning to Rancourt's disappearance. They were filed away.

Ted made no mention to Liz of his engagement to Stephanie. Nor did he tell Liz that he was failing miserably in his classes and that he had already reapplied to the law school at the University of Utah, without informing them that he was attending school in Tacoma. Liz, however, could not help but notice how his lovemaking had changed. Ted now wanted to tie her up spread-eagled to the bed with her pantyhose. When she consented to this kinky sex play, she noticed that he went directly to the drawer where she kept her hose without asking her where to find it. The third time she agreed to be tied up, Bundy began choking her and she refused to be tied again. Then Ted started to demand anal sex; after trying it several times and not liking it, she refused that as well. Bundy sulked. Liz, meanwhile, was puzzled by this sudden shift in his sexuality—it was so much unlike him.

•   •   •

The next attack happened in Corvallis, Oregon, on May 6, about two hundred miles south of Seattle, at Oregon State University. Kathy Parks, age twenty-two, agreed to meet some friends for a late-night coffee at the Student Union Building, but she never arrived. Kathy stepped out of her campus dormitory at about 11:00 P.M. and vanished along the way. Nobody saw anything.

On June 1, Brenda Ball, twenty-two years old, who had graduated from Highline Community College two weeks earlier, vanished. She was an independent young woman who could take care of herself. That night she was drinking at the Flame Tavern, a seedy and rough bar just outside Seattle. At 2:00 A.M. when the bar closed, Brenda was in the parking lot trying to get a ride home. One of the musicians from the band talked to her briefly but was going in a different direction. That was the last time she was seen. Because Brenda was such a free spirit, nobody became worried when she was missing. It took seventeen days before her roommate was concerned enough to report her absence to the police. There were no clues or witnesses—just like the other women, Brenda vanished as into thin air.

Liz, meanwhile, was seeing Ted's behavior get stranger and stranger. One night she woke up to find Ted secretly inspecting her body under the sheets with a flashlight—hauntingly similar to the recollections of Ted's aunt when he was a small boy and she awoke to discover him placing knives under her sheets as she slept.

Although they kept separate apartments, Liz and Ted almost lived together. His things were often at her house, and they often drove each other's cars. One day when looking for something in the closet, Liz stumbled upon a box of powder used to make medical casts, which Bundy had obviously stolen years ago when he was a driver for the medical equipment house. She also found a pair of crutches. On another day at Ted's apartment, she accidentally came across a bag of women's underwear. She was embarrassed by her find, and did not say anything to Ted. On yet another occasion, she discovered a heavy wrench carefully taped under the seat of Bundy's Volkswagen.

•   •   •

On June 11 at the University of Washington, eighteen-year-old Georgann Hawkins disappeared. She lived in a sorority house on the campus and was visiting friends in various other houses on the campus complex. It was around midnight, but on the warm June night, the campus was full of students socializing outside. Friends escorted Georgann back to her house and saw her get within fifty feet of her door. Another friend leaned out the window of a nearby fraternity house and briefly spoke to Georgann. That was the last she was seen. Later the police investigation found a report of a young man on crutches with a broken leg asking several young women if they would help him carry some books to a Volkswagen parked nearby.

Shortly before he was executed, Bundy revealed what he had done to Georgann. He confessed that he had parked his Volkswagen in the shadows near some bushes by the fraternity houses. He laid a crowbar and some handcuffs on the ground near the rear of the car. Hobbling around on his crutches, he asked numerous women to help him carry his books to his car until Georgann agreed to do so. They chatted amiably as they made their way to the car. As Georgann approached the cute little "love bug" Volkswagen to deposit the books through the passenger door, Bundy scooped up the crowbar from the ground and knocked her unconscious from behind. He handcuffed her and dragged her into the Volkswagen, laying her on the floor in the space from which he had removed the passenger seat.

Bundy drove out into the countryside with the unconscious Georgann on the floor. At some point during the trip she regained consciousness and according to Bundy began to speak about a Spanish test she was supposedly taking the next day—she was obviously raving. Bundy drove out onto a dirt road, dragged her out of the car into a clearing, and struck her unconscious again with the crowbar. He then took a length of cord he kept in his car and strangled her to death. He dragged her body some thirty feet away from the car into a small grove of trees, and there he carefully undressed her. Fifteen years later, on the eve of his execution, he remembered undoing a pin that had kept her pants closed—a detail police had kept confidential. He then had sex with Georgann's corpse until dawn.

In the morning Bundy drove away from the site, throwing out along the way various items of Georgann's clothing and his killing tools. By the afternoon he realized that he had made a mistake. He returned to the murder site and, retracing his route, he recovered most of the items that he had thrown from his car. One thing perplexed Bundy: He could not find one of Georgann's shoes. To his horror, Bundy realized that they might be back at the location where he kidnapped her. Fearing that police were searching the area and might have a description of a Volkwagen parked there last night, Bundy rode a bike back to the kidnap site. There he discovered Georgann's other shoe and an earring that had come off when he struck her. He took away the remaining clues to Georgann's fate before police could find them.

Three days later, Bundy returned to where he had left Georgann and had sex with her decomposing corpse one more time. Then he severed her head with a hacksaw and buried it in the ground about fifty feet away. Police never learned any of this until the last days prior to Bundy's execution.

Ted Bundy had failed his first year of law school, but cleverly he decided to repeat the year at Salt Lake City, where he was admitted the year before. Without telling them he had attended school for a year in Tacoma, Bundy wrote that he had sufficiently recovered from his "car accident" and was ready to start. He was admitted into the first year and scheduled to start in September.

While Ted waited for school to begin in the autumn, he went to work that summer at the Department of Emergency Services (DES), whose function was to respond to disasters and coordinate search and rescue efforts. The summer of 1974 was the year that the OPEC oil embargo hit the United States, and the DES was responsible for allocating the dwindling fuel supplies in Washington State. Bundy was assigned to calculate a special project budget for the DES by the end of the summer.

Bundy's arrival at the DES attracted a lot of attention. The women thought he was very attractive and the men were impressed with his political connections and knowledge of how to get things done with the state bureaucracy.

One former employee at the DES, Larry Diamond, remembered feeling jealous of Bundy and how everybody, including the males, was taken with him. While most men talked about women in the context of fantasy, Bundy did not. It was as if Bundy "compartmentalized" them, according to Diamond. Eventually Diamond concluded that perhaps Bundy had one major flaw: He was too perfect. Diamond explained, "Ted was almost one-dimensional if I think about it. It's like there's a very beautiful store-front that's attractive and lures you in. But when you get inside to see the merchandise, it is sparse to say the least."[92]

Larry Diamond's perception was very acute and his metaphor of a beautiful storefront an apt one—except that it was not a scarcity of mer-chandise that waited behind the beautiful exterior, but horrific death. It is hard to say whether Diamond was more perceptive than others in the past, or whether Bundy, in the middle of his series of brutal rapes and homi-cides, was losing his grip on his carefully composed mask of sanity.

Bundy was about to get strange on his girlfriend, Liz. On the weekend of July 6 they went river rafting. They drank a few beers and were quietly drifting along the river enjoying the peaceful and sunny day. Suddenly Bundy lunged at Liz and pushed her under the water. When she came up shouting at him, he simply would not respond, which deeply unnerved her. He was becoming a total stranger to her. Later he said to her, "Can't you take a joke?"

The following Saturday, Liz phoned Ted at his parents' house in Tacoma and asked if he was free on Sunday. Ted told her he'd be busy. The next morning, July 14, as she was getting ready to go to church, Ted un-expectedly appeared at her house and wanted to know what she was go-ing to be doing that day. She told him the name of a small park she was going to, hoping that he would join her there. He never showed up.

Fifteen miles east of Seattle lies Lake Sammamish State Park, a par-adise of lakes, forests, rivers, and recreational facilities. It is a popular des-tination for picnickers, swimmers, and sunbathers. That weekend a local brewery was sponsoring a beer party at "Lake Sam," as locals knew it. At the other end of the park was the annual Seattle Police Department picnic. There were some 40,000 visitors that day at Lake Sam.

Janice Graham later told police that a man approached her with a bro-ken arm at about noon that Sunday. He was dressed all in white—white T-shirt, socks, tennis shoes, and shorts. He asked her if she would help him load his small sailboat onto the roof of his car. She agreed and began to walk with him. She said he was very friendly, polite, and charming. He told her he injured his arm playing racquetball and they chatted the entire route. When they got to his car, a bronze-colored Volkswagen, Janice saw no boat or trailer. "It's at my parents' house, just at the top of the hill," the stranger said, asking her to get into his car.

Janice refused because some friends were waiting for her. He should have told her, she said, that the boat was at his parents' house. The stranger was not at all upset, he apologized and walked back with her from the parking lot. Janice later told the police, "He was very polite at all times. Very sincere. Easy to talk to. He was real friendly and he had a nice smile."

In an interview, Bundy talked about encountering his victims in his third person manner:

> BUNDY: Conversation, to remove himself from the personal aspects of the encounter, the interchange. Chattering and flattering and entertaining, as if seen through a motion picture screen. He would be engaging in the patter just for the purpose of making the whole encounter seem legitimate and to keep her at ease. He didn't want this girl to get second thoughts about going with him to his place. And, also, he was afraid if he started thinking about what he was going to do he'd become more nervous or lose his concentration or in some way betray himself.

> QUESTION: So there's a very delicate balance between being cool and the excitement?

> BUNDY: Well, it's a critical balance, not a delicate balance. It became almost like acting a role. It wasn't difficult. The more an actor acts in a role, the better he becomes at it, the more he is apt to feel comfortable in it, to be able to do things spontaneously. And get better, as it were, in his role.[93]

Shortly after meeting her friends, Janice Graham saw that the stranger had found somebody else to help him. He was walking back toward his car next to a young woman with a bicycle. Janice wondered where she was going to put her bicycle for the trip to get the man's boat.

Twenty-three-year old Jan Ott, a Seattle probation officer, bicycled that day to Lake Sammamish for some sunbathing and swimming. She found a spot on the edge of the lake, not too far from several couples who were enjoying the sun, and spread out her towel. One couple testified that she was there for about half an hour when a handsome young man approached her. He was dressed entirely in white and his left arm was in a sling, encased in a cast from his wrist to past his elbow. He spoke with a slight

English accent. He asked Jan if she could help him load his boat. Just to show how fast serial killers learn and adapt, this time Bundy told Ott that the boat was at his "parents' house." She did not leave immediately with him and they talked for about ten minutes. Witnesses overheard him introducing himself as "Ted." Eventually Jan got up and left with the handsome stranger. Several couples testified that they overheard him telling her that there was room in his car for her bike and talking about how easy it would be for him to teach her how to sail in a single afternoon. Jan Ott was reported missing the next day by her roommate. Her bike was never found.

It wasn't over yet. About two hours after Ott walked off with the stranger, several women reported being approached near the park washrooms by a man dressed in white with a broken arm needing help with his sailboat. One woman turned him down because he grabbed at her while asking for help with his boat. Another saw him watching her before he approached her with his request and practically ran from him. Bundy was like some kind of killing animal loose in a herd of prey.

Nineteen-year-old Denise Naslund and her boyfriend, Kenny Little, were sunning themselves in the park. At one point Denise got up to go to the washroom. Kenny fell asleep. When he woke up, Denise still had not returned—her purse lay nearby where she had left it. Kenny attempted to report Denise's disappearance to the park police, but was told that only family could file a missing person report. He drove back to her parents' house and they called the police. Witnesses later recalled seeing Denise in the washrooms, but afterward there was nothing.

Liz remembers Ted phoning her that Sunday late in the afternoon— about an hour after Denise's boyfriend discovered that she had disappeared. Ted invited Liz out to dinner—he was starving, he told her. He arrived about ten minutes later and they drove to a bowling alley reputed to serve some of the best hamburgers in Seattle. Liz was amazed to see Ted gobble down two hamburgers. He looked like he was under stress, she said. His eyes were all puffed up and when she asked him about it, he said he had a cold and was tired. Nonetheless, he insisted on driving back to Liz's house and transferring a ski rack that he had borrowed from his car to hers.

•   •   •

By this time, the various police agencies had met and although they had little tangible evidence, they had good reason to suspect that the kidnappings were committed by the same individual. The police had identified distinct similarities in the student victims:

- Long hair, parted down the middle

- Caucasian, fair-complexioned

- Above-average intelligence

- Slender, attractive, highly talented

- Each had vanished within a week of midterm or final exams at local colleges

- Loving and stable families

- Vanished at night

- Each girl was single

- Each girl was wearing jeans or pants when she disappeared

- Construction work was going on at each campus where a girl disappeared

- No physical evidence in any of the disappearances

The police reviewed the witness statements and isolated the reports of a man wearing a cast and driving a Volkswagen. The disappearances at Lake Sammamish now gave them a name: Ted. But that was all they had, and the police did not agree among themselves that the same man had committed the crimes.

Using witness descriptions from the Lake Sammamish disappearances, newspapers published police sketches of the suspect and the information that he was driving a Volkswagen and might be called Ted. A lot of people ribbed Bundy about the fact that he had a Volkswagen, was called Ted, and looked like the individual in the sketches. Everyone felt safe kidding Bundy about it, because few believed that he could even be remotely capable of committing those kinds of crimes.

That summer, Ann Rule was among the first to call the police with Ted

Bundy's name. She remembers that she did not know whether Ted had bought a car since she had seen him last, but it appeared to her that Ted resembled the police sketches published in the papers. She had a friend on the police force run Bundy's name through vehicle registration records and was shocked to find out that "her" Ted also drove a Volkswagen.

Liz was also seeing the resemblance and could not shake the memory of finding the box of medical cast material. She made an anonymous call to the police. But neither Ann Rule nor Liz Kendall, despite their suspicions, was convinced that Ted was a killer. Rule continued her friendship with Bundy, and Liz continued working on marriage plans with him.

The police meanwhile, filed Bundy's name with the other 3,000 names reported to them as possible suspects.

On August 2, in Vancouver, Washington, twenty-year-old Carol Valenzuela vanished, but it was thought that she left on her own and no alarm was raised about her disappearance.

Ted Bundy, in the meantime, at the end of the month packed his things and moved to Salt Lake City in Utah to attend law school there. No further disappearances were reported in the State of Washington.

On September 7, in the Issaquah hills about a mile from Lake Sammamish, hunters discovered the remains of Jan Ott and Denise Naslund. There was not much to find—their bodies had been torn apart by coyotes, rodents, and possibly bears. Their flesh was mostly stripped away, and bones and tufts of hair were scattered all over the area. It took the police days to assemble enough bones to identify the women. Worse yet, the police anthropologists discovered extra female bones—there was a third victim. To this day, her identity remains unknown but it could have been Georgann Hawkins, whose body was never officially found.

Then in October the body of Carol Valenzuela was discovered near Olympia, Washington, in the rugged territory close to the Oregon border. She too had been consumed by animals. Lying near her, the police found the body of another woman believed to be aged between eighteen and twenty-two. Her identity has never been established either.

In the Salt Lake City area, young women began disappearing on October 2. The first was sixteen-year-old Nancy Wilcox, who on a night when she had argued with her parents was seen getting into a Volkswagen bug. She was listed as a runaway at first. Her body was never found. Salt Lake City is some seven hundred miles south of Seattle, and nobody in Utah even remotely thought of making a connection between the Volkswagen and the crimes in the north, nor was there any national database like VICAP today to make that link.

On October 18, Melissa Smith, age seventeen, the daughter of a police chief of a small town near Salt Lake City, vanished. She went out around 9:00 P.M. to eat a pizza with a friend. Afterward she was seen at a few teen hangouts around the town and was reported at one point to be seen hitchhiking.

Her body was found ten days later, the first of the series of victims to be found reasonably intact enough to perform an autopsy. Her skull had been fractured by a heavy blow, and she had been strangled by one of her knee-high socks tightly wrapped around her throat. Her head and shoulders showed multiple bruises and lacerations. She had been raped and sodomized, and afterward sticks had been pushed into her vagina. Her makeup was completely undisturbed and her long fingernails were undamaged. This led the police to believe that the killer may have kept her in an unconscious state for several days, applying her makeup himself and repeatedly raping her before finally strangling her.

On October 31, Halloween night, seventeen-year-old Laura Aime disappeared. She was at a party, got bored, and decided to hitchhike downtown to get some cigarettes. Her body was found the next month in a canyon. Her jaw had been broken and her skull was fractured. She had been raped and sodomized, and one of her stockings was wrapped tightly around her throat. There were vaginal puncture wounds from a sharp instrument, believed to be an ice pick, thrust into her genitals. The one thing that immediately struck the police was that her hair was freshly shampooed and free of blood from her cranial wounds. Again, as with Melissa Smith, it appeared that the killer had kept the teenager in an unconscious state, shampooing her hair, raping her, and then strangling her.

On November 8, Carol DaRonch was approached in a shopping mall by Ted Bundy posing as a police officer and lured into his car. As he attempted to put a pair of handcuffs on her, she managed kick free of him and flee. DaRonch is the only known victim of Ted Bundy's to escape.

Later that same night, at an evening performance by a high school drama club, young women and girls were approached by an impeccably dressed man and asked to come into the parking lot and identify a car, or help him start a car. The request made no sense and the man appeared very nervous and would not look the women in the eye. Everybody refused the stranger's request. His actions attracted the attention of a few people among the audience of 1,500 and they kept an eye on him that evening. During the intermission they saw him leave, and were happy to see that he did not return when the play began again. However, when the play ended and the lights went up, they were surprised to see that he was back in the auditorium, although now his shirttail was hanging out and his hair seemed somewhat disordered.

Dean and Belva Kent were among those who never noticed the man. They were sitting with their daughter, seventeen-year-old Debra Kent. During the intermission, Debra left the auditorium to pick up her brother from a nearby skating rink. She used the school pay phone to call him and say she was on her way and walked out of the school toward her parents' car. She then vanished. The car was found parked as it was when they first arrived at the school. Debra's body was never found.

Thirteen murders in ten months, and there were more to come. While the police in Utah hunkered down for what they expected to be more murders in December, nothing happened. Ted was back in Seattle for the Christmas holiday.

In Seattle, after the discovery of the first bodies, the investigation had mobilized into a major effort. The police had a list of 3,000 names that had been phoned in—including Ted Bundy's four times by now. The 3,000 names were fed into a computer. The names of Volkswagen owners in Washington State were added, the names of all the friends of victims, names from their address books, class lists of all the missing girls' fellow students, all mental patients in the state for the last ten years, known sex offenders, names of motel guests near Lake Sammamish, and even names of people renting horses to ride in the district. The computer was then programmed to print out any names that appeared twice. Nearly six hundred names emerged. The computer was asked to print out any names that appeared four times—and the computer responded with four hundred names, including Ted Bundy's. This time, the computer was asked to print out five coincidental appearances of the same name. The computer identified twenty-five names for the police to investigate. Bundy was not one of them.

The sameness of Bundy's crimes becomes numbing to describe. Clever kidnappings, no witnesses, no physical evidence. The victim was rendered unconscious by a powerful blow to the head with a blunt weapon, raped and sodomized, and then strangled.

After the Christmas holidays, Bundy returned to Utah. The next disappearance happened over in the next state—Colorado. Caryn Campbell and her boyfriend were staying at a ski lodge. In the evening they were in the lobby sitting by the fireplace when Caryn went upstairs to get a magazine from her room. She never made it. Her magazine was found untouched. A month later her body was discovered a few miles from the lodge, partially consumed by animals. Her skull had been fractured and it appeared as if she had been strangled.

In March, back in Washington State, forestry students working on the slopes of Taylor Mountain found a skull. It was identified as Brenda Ball, the girl who had gone missing at the Flame Tavern some thirty miles away. Two hundred police officers began making a painstaking search along the slopes of Taylor Mountain. Their search would yield scattered fragments from the heads of three other victims: Susan Rancourt, who disappeared on her way to a movie at her campus, ninety miles away; Kathy Parks, who disappeared while going for a coffee at her campus, 260 miles away; and Lynda Healy, the first girl who had vanished from her basement apartment. Four girls, killed at four different locations at four different times, their heads dumped on Taylor Mountain—the killer's private graveyard. He spent months returning to the same location, arriving each time with a new head. Even for seasoned police officers, it was a horrific find.

At the time a junior investigator, Robert D. Keppel, suggested that the killer was cutting off the victims' heads and keeping them for a while before dumping them on Taylor Mountain. The notion was dismissed at the time by the supervisors because no neck vertebrae were found at the scene. Typically, intentional decapitations are made with a cut below the base of the skull, leaving a fragment of the vertebrae at the scene. Senior police officials instead insisted that animals had dragged the other bones away beyond the search perimeter, never adequately explaining why animals left precisely only fragments of the heads.

Keppel later recalled:

> My own theory—considered outrageous—was that, for a period of time, the killer had parked the skulls at another location, where they decayed individually, and then dumped his entire load just inside the edge of the forest. The physical evidence, which consisted of leaves in skulls from one previous leaf fall, the growth of the maple branches through and around the skulls, and the lack of any tissue on the crania left me with the feeling that they were exposed to outdoor elements, in one place, where they decayed at the same rate. In other words, they were put someplace else for a period of time and then brought to Taylor Mountain; the killer was moving around the body parts of his victims. It seemed as though nobody wanted to consider my theory seriously—maybe because it gave too much credit to the ability of the killer to manipulate evidence and escape detection. They also probably didn't want to consider what it would take to catch a killer so remorseless that he could handle the body parts of his dead victims long after he had murdered them.[94]

Years later Bundy would confess to Keppel that he used a hacksaw to sever the victim's heads and that he kept them in his apartment. The bodies he dumped at other undisclosed locations, which he would visit from time to time to see how the animals had devoured them. Ted also admitted that he burned Donna Manson's head in the fireplace of Liz Kendall's home.

On March 15, in Vail, Colorado, twenty-six-year-old Julie Cunningham went out at about 9:00 P.M. to meet a friend at a nearby bar for a drink. She never arrived and her body was never found.

On April 6, in Grand Junction, Colorado, twenty-five-year-old Denise Oliverson set out on her bicycle from her apartment to her parents' house. Her body was never found.

On April 15, eighteen-year-old Melanie Cooley vanished in Denver.

●   ●   ●

In May, three friends from last summer's work at the Washington Department of Emergency Services—Carole Ann Boone, Alice Thissen, and Joe McLean—came to spend a week with Bundy. They went swimming and horseback riding and remember that Bundy seemed to be in high spirits. In the evenings Bundy prepared gourmet meals for his guests while Mozart played on his stereo.

In prison, referring to himself in the third person, Bundy explained that his desire to kill was akin to a hobby—it was not something you did all the time, "like collecting stamps. He doesn't retain the taste of glue, so to speak, all day long."

In June, Bundy was back in Seattle. He spent a lot of time with Liz Kendall discussing marriage plans and helped his former landlords, Ernst and Frieda Rogers, put in a garden at the rooming house. Near the end of the month he left Seattle.

On July 1, Shelley Robertson, twenty-four, vanished in Golden, Colorado, after being last seen at a service station; much later that same day, about seven hours away, in Farmington, Utah, near Salt Lake City, twenty-one-year-old Nancy Baird vanished, also from a service station. Ted Bundy was on his way back to Salt Lake City.

On Saturday, August 16, 1975, at 2:30 A.M., a Utah Highway Patrol officer was sitting in his cruiser in front of his own house in the Salt Lake City suburb of Granger when he saw a Volkswagen drive by. It was a small neighborhood where there was little traffic, and even less at night, and almost every vehicle was known—this auto was not. The officer let the car pass without taking any action. Ten minutes later, the car passed by again and this time the policeman turned on his high beams to read the license plate. As soon as he did that, the Volkswagen turned off its lights and began to drive away quickly. After a short pursuit, the highway patrolman had the Volkswagen pull over into a service station parking lot. Ted Bundy stepped out of the car.

Bundy was relaxed and calm, but appeared confused as to why he was stopped by the police. He told the officer he had been at a movie and got lost on his way home. When the patrolman asked the name of the movie playing at the theater, Bundy made his fatal mistake—he gave the wrong title. A few minutes later, another patrol car arrived, summoned by radio.

Bundy's trunk was searched. Inside they found a pair of handcuffs, a mask made from pantyhose, an ice pick, short lengths of rope, and torn strips of sheets.

Bundy was taken into custody, charged with evading police, finger-printed, and sent home. He was told to expect a warrant charging him with possession of burglary tools.

On the following Tuesday, police officers from various Utah agencies gathered for their weekly review of arrests. It was a boring procedure as the various arrests of that week were reviewed and notes compared. But when Salt Lake City detectives heard the mention of a Volkswagen and a pair of handcuffs, they immediately became alert.

Slowly, step by step, Ted Bundy was first charged with possession of burglary tools, and then, after being identified by Carol DaRonch, he was charged with attempted kidnapping. Bundy remained free on bail during his trial in the winter of 1976, but once he was convicted in the spring, he found himself in prison. Because Bundy had no previous criminal record, his sentence was fairly light—one to fifteen years, meaning that he could be paroled after serving only three years. But soon after Bundy began serv-ing his sentence in Utah, he was charged with murder in Colorado. He found himself transferred to Aspen, Colorado, to stand trial for the mur-der of Caryn Campbell, who had disappeared at the ski lodge. By now the police had assembled a formidable collection of evidence consisting of gas receipts, phone bills, credit card slips, hair samples, and witnesses who linked Bundy's movements and presence with the murder of Caryn Camp-bell. Bundy was now in serious trouble.

Ted Bundy's story should have ended there; perhaps if it had, Bundy might have remained in history as just another serial murderer with seventeen kills. Instead of becoming a household name and a movie of the week, Bundy could have become another Gerald Stano—a guy who killed forty-one women between 1969 and 1980, twice as many as Bundy, but nobody has heard of him other than true-crime buffs. But Bundy made a spectac-ular escape by jumping from a second floor window of the Aspen court-house during a lunch break, which guaranteed him superstar status in the future. He disappeared into the mountains for nearly a week before he was recaptured after getting lost and coming back down into Aspen. At the time, the full extent of Bundy's crimes was not known, and Bundy was treated as a local hero and outlaw.

Remarkably, after escaping once, Bundy escaped a second time. On this occasion he managed to saw his way through the steel ceiling of his jailhouse cell on the night of December 30, 1977. This time, instead of heading into the mountains, Bundy went directly to the airport. By the time the authorities realized that Bundy had escaped, he was already in Chicago. From there, he slowly made his way to the college town of Ann Arbor, but did not like it there, and moved to Tallahassee, Florida. He took a room in a student house near Florida State University and survived by shoplifting and stealing credit cards.

Within sixteen days of his escape, in the middle of the night of January 15, 1978, Bundy slipped into a campus sorority house carrying a log and walked from room to room battering the heads of sleeping women. He bit the nipple off one woman and sodomized her with an aerosol bottle of hair spray before killing her. In total, two women were killed and two were severely injured. A few minutes later at another house nearby, he battered a fifth woman, but failed to kill her.

Bundy's crimes had become frenzied. The attack on five women in one night was unlike Bundy's previous carefully executed crimes. His attack was characteristic of a disorganized personality: The weapon was a piece of branch taken from a woodpile at the back of the sorority house. The bite marks left on one of the victims were a valuable piece of evidence that would be effortlessly matched with Bundy's teeth. The women were found at the crime scene, unlike Bundy's other victims.

Bundy was reaching the "burnout" stage. This is the stage in which some serial killers quietly surrender to the police; others commit suicide; some go underground, never to be heard from again; others, like Bundy, increase the frenzy of their killing and become sloppy, as if hoping that the police will capture them.

On February 9, Bundy kidnapped and killed a girl who is believed to be his last victim—twelve-year-old Kimberly Leach. She was snatched in front of her school. Her body was found in April in an abandoned hog shed— she had been raped and sodomized and then strangled. By then Bundy was already in custody. He was pulled over on February 12 while driving a stolen car in a drunken state. Earlier that day he had been caught four times committing petty crimes but managed to talk his way out of trouble every time. While in custody, he was identified. Ted Bundy would never leave Florida again.

Bundy was a thinking person, and no doubt after he had been arrested the first time and jailed, he must have thought a lot about his crimes. He considered himself lucky when he escaped to Florida, for in Colorado he was on trial for murder but had not yet been convicted. He knew that his compulsion was the ruin of his life. Bundy believed that the two years in jail had cured him of his homicidal desires; certainly in the first weeks he lived in Florida, he attempted to stay away from situations in which he might be tempted to kill. However, at some stage he must have suddenly felt the pangs of his compulsion once again, and by that point in his life he knew that he could not resist.

Bundy must have been smart enough to know that sooner or later his compulsion would lead to his capture, and therefore he began to gorge himself on killing, no longer caring if he was leaving evidence behind or not.

Bundy's conclusions about his own crimes are intelligent but banal. Bundy attributed his crimes to "peculiar circumstances of society and of the twentieth century in America."[95]

He said, "Living in large centers of population and living with lots of people, you can get used to dealing with strangers. It's the anonymity factor. And that has a twofold effect. First of all, if you're among strangers you're less likely to remember them or care what they're doing or know what they should or should not be doing. If they should or shouldn't be there. Secondly, you're conditioned almost not to be afraid to deal with strangers."[96]

Bundy was charged with the sorority house murders and the murder of Kimberly Leach. The trials were held separately, were televised, and cost the State of Florida $9 million. Bundy acted as his own defense counsel.

His friend Carole Boone, whom he had met the summer he worked at the Department of Emergency Services, became his lover.

When Bundy was convicted for murder, he and Boone requested permission from Florida's prison authority to get married. Permission was refused. Bundy then pulled off a coup by performing the marriage ceremony himself. Boone filled out the necessary marriage licenses at the courthouse.

She was then called to the stand by Bundy to testify as a character witness during his sentencing hearing. During the examination, Bundy suddenly asked her if she would marry him and she replied, yes. Bundy then responded that he, too, wanted to marry her. A notary hired by Boone sat among the courtroom spectators and witnessed the exchange of vows. Under Florida law, Bundy and Boone were now legally married, and thus Boone had the right to ask for contact visits in prison with her husband Ted. Although such visits were restricted to a kiss, a hug, and holding hands under the watchful eyes of guards, prisoners often managed to engineer some way to have sex with their visitor. Boone claimed that she and Bundy conceived a child during one of these contact visits. If true, then Bundy had a daughter in the autumn of 1981.

While on death row awaiting execution, he was asked if he felt guilty about the murders he had committed. Guilt, he said, is an illusionary mechanism to control people and is unhealthy and does terrible things to people's bodies. Bundy replied that he felt as sorry for those who felt guilt as he did for drug addicts or businessmen who craved money. It solves nothing. It only hurts you, he said.

Bundy had committed many of his murders in King County in Washington State. In 1982 a new serial killer took his place there—the Green River Killer. Robert D. Keppel was now a senior investigator when Bundy offered to profile the Green River Killer for him. Keppel accepted and secretly met with Bundy, not only to take advantage of Bundy's expertise in serial murder but to also probe further into Bundy's own crimes and possible locations where missing victims might be found. Keppel found Bundy's insight into serial killers perceptive. At the same time he marveled at Bundy's ego and his sense of superiority over the Green River Killer. Keppel said, "The Leonardo da Vinci of serial murder was Theodore Robert Bundy's perception of himself."

Bundy himself proclaimed, "I'm the only Ph.D. in serial murder. Over the years I've read everything I can get my hands on about it. The subject fascinates me."

Bundy explained his crimes in the context of young urban professional ambition when he said, "Society wants to believe it can identify evil people, or bad or harmful people, but it's not practical. There are no stereotypes. The thing is that some people are just psychologically less ready for failure than others."

•   •   •

After years of numerous appeals and motions, Bundy was executed in January 1989. Carole Boone and Ted's daughter had vanished from the public eye several years earlier, and it is not known if they stayed in contact with Bundy. Ted may have died alone. On Florida campuses, students hosted "Bundy-Qs" and chanted, "Fry, Bundy, Fry" on the day he was electrocuted.

The Disorganized Serial Killer: Miguel Rivera—"Charlie Chop-Off"

An example of the disorganized class of serial killers, Miguel Rivera randomly attacked young boys in tenement buildings in East Harlem and on the Upper West Side of New York between March 1972 and August 1973. His first victim, an eight-year-old boy, was stabbed thirty-eight times and sodomized, and an attempt was made to cut off his penis. Three other boys were found in hallways, in basements, and on the rooftops of various tenements, stabbed to death and their genitals cut off. Local children dubbed the serial killer "Charlie Chop-Off." Witness testimony produced a description of a Puerto Rican suspect who was attempting to persuade young boys to run errands for him. Following a failed attempt to kidnap a nine-year-old boy in May 1974, Miguel Rivera, who exhibited severe signs of mental illness, was arrested. Rivera claimed that God had told him to transform little boys into girls. The hidden logic and erratic behavior of the disorganized serial killer makes it difficult for police to narrow down a suspect, even though he often makes no attempt to cover up his crimes.

Herbert Mullin, whose case is described in the next chapter (see the "Visionary" section), is also a classic case study of the disorganized class of serial killer, as is Richard Chase, described in Chapter 9.

The Mixed-Category Serial Killer: Richard Ramirez—The "Night Stalker"

Richard Ramirez, who committed most of his crimes in Los Angeles, is an example of a mixed-category murderer. Between June 1984 and August

1985, nineteen people were brutally killed inside their homes by a mysterious intruder who was dubbed the "Night Stalker" by the press. Men were shot or strangled, while women were brutally raped and mutilated. He gouged out one victim's eyes with a spoon and took them away with him. One night, he killed three victims, on other nights, he left without killing his victims. At the crime scenes, the Night Stalker left occult symbols such as an inverted pentagram drawn on a wall with a victim's lipstick. Some crime scenes were signed "Jack the Knife." One victim who survived reported that as she was being raped, he forced her to recite, "I love Satan." When asked where they hid their valuables, victims were ordered to "swear on Satan" that they were telling the truth. The crimes were committed completely at random, and the killer made unsuccessful attempts to disguise his fingerprints. His victims often saw his face, and he left them alive as often as he killed them. Outside the windows of the houses he entered, he left behind his shoe prints. When the FBI's Behavioral Sciences Unit was asked to profile the crime scenes, they responded that the crimes were unique and did not conform to anything they had seen before.

In 1985 California installed a new $25 million computer system—Cal-ID—that could automatically search out fingerprints from previous crimes and match them to prints on record. The official story is that within several minutes of being online, the computer used the prints left behind by the Night Stalker to identify him as Richard Ramirez, a twenty-five-year-old petty burglar from El Paso, Texas. The real story is that police had first developed leads from several street informants who dealt in stolen goods. They revealed that a burglar they knew named Rick, Ricardo, or Richard Ramirez was weird enough to be the Night Stalker. Police ran those names through the computer and quickly came up with a match on a fingerprint from an abandoned car connected to one of the crimes.[97]

Pictures of Ramirez were widely publicized in California, and it was not long before he was sighted on a street in a residential Los Angeles neighborhood. The police had to rescue him from a mob intent on beating him to death.

Richard Ramirez was a mentally disturbed drifter with a cocaine addiction who frequented the skid row district around the Los Angeles bus station. He was the youngest brother in a devout Catholic Mexican family. Ramirez's father was a former Mexican police officer and a domineering and tyrannical parent whose temper frightened all the kids. His mother was deeply religious, frequently praying, lighting candles, and regularly attending church.

We will later see that frequently serial killers sustained head injuries as children; Ramirez was accidentally knocked unconscious twice as a child. He also had epileptic seizures. When Ramirez was seven or eight he might have witnessed his older brothers being sexually molested by a neighbor. Neither he nor his brothers can remember whether Ramirez himself was victimized. Ramirez is remembered as shy and sweet, and his teenage girlfriend with whom he had a relationship several years before the murders also remembers him as a gentle and sweet lover. Girls at his school remember Ramirez as being "nice."

When Ramirez was twelve years old he began to hang out with his cousin Mike, a Green Beret who had recently returned from two tours of duty in Vietnam. They frequently smoked marijuana together, and Mike regaled the impressionable Richard with war stories. According to Ramirez, his cousin showed him black-and-white Polaroids of Vietnamese women forced to perform fellatio on soldiers. Other photographs showed the severed heads of the same women. Ramirez said that he became highly aroused at the sight of those images. On May 4, 1974, while on a visit at Mike's house, Richard saw his cousin shoot his wife to death in cold blood. Mike told him never to say that he had been there and sent him home. Ramirez remained mute about what he had seen, while Mike was found not guilty by reason of insanity and committed to a mental facility.

Several days after the shooting, Richard visited the apartment with his parents to retrieve some of Mike's property. Ramirez recently recalled: "That day I went back to that apartment, it was like some kind of mystical experience. It was all quiet and still and hot in there. You could smell the blood."

After witnessing the homicide, Richard began to steal and habitually smoke marijuana. His interest in school declined. Making matters worse, he went to Los Angeles to visit his older brother, a heroin-addicted thief who instructed Richard on the finer arts of burglary.

When he was thirteen, Richard moved away from home to live with another brother. There he began experimenting with hallucinogenic drugs such as LSD, mushrooms, and PCP—angel dust—a highly unstable and dangerous drug normally used as a horse tranquilizer. Richard became obsessed with slasher horror films such as *Halloween* and *Friday the 13th*. He was into heavy metal, especially the darker stuff from Judas Priest, Black Sabbath, Billy Idol, Ozzy Osborne, and AC/DC. Soon he dropped out of school.

In 1978 Richard left El Paso and returned to live in Los Angeles, settling into the cheap seedy hotels in the downtown tenderloin district. He became addicted to cocaine, which he would inject. In summary, Ramirez had head injuries, had epilepsy, had a tyrannical father and an overly religious mother, was perhaps sexually molested, was exposed to graphically violent images, witnessed a murder at age twelve in which he was complicit by his silence, smoked marijuana, consumed LSD and PCP, and entertained himself by watching horror films and listening to heavy metal, before he became addicted to the ultimate paranoia-inducing drug—cocaine, which he did not merely snort, but injected. Young Richard's brain no doubt was seriously fried and his soul battered when he added one more thing into the mix at age seventeen: In the summer of 1978 he read *The Satanic Bible* by Anton LaVey—a San Francisco self-styled satanist. So impressed was Richard that he stole a car and drove to San Francisco, where he sought out LaVey and attended his satanic rituals, during which he says he felt the hand of Satan touch him.

Between 1978 and 1984 Ramirez became almost entirely estranged from his family, including his brothers. He rarely contacted them and we know little about his activities. In mid-1983 his sister sought him out and found him living in a fleabag hotel near the L.A. bus station. He was still injecting cocaine and sustaining himself by committing burglaries. He told his sister that Satan was protecting him from arrest.

On June 27, 1984, he committed his first known murder, stabbing a woman to death as she slept in her bed. He would kill at least nineteen victims, raping, stabbing, shooting, mutilating, and bludgeoning them, before his capture on August 31, 1985.

At his trial Ramirez flashed press photographers with an inverted pentagram inked on his palm and chanted "Evil, evil . . ." When he was convicted and sentenced to death, he growled at the court, "I don't believe in the hypocritical, moralistic dogma of this so-called civilized society . . . I need not look beyond this room to see all the liars, haters, the killers, the crooks, the paranoid cowards; truly trematodes of the Earth, each one in his own legal profession. . . . You maggots make me sick; hypocrites one and all . . . And no one knows that better than those who kill for policy, clandestinely or openly, as do the governments of the world, which kill in the name of god and country or for whatever reason they deem appropriate . . . I don't need to hear all of society's rationalizations. I've heard them all before and the fact remains that what is, is. You don't understand me. You are not expected to. You are not capable of it . . . I am beyond your experience. I am beyond good and evil, legions of the night—night breed—repeat not the errors of the Night Stalker and show no mercy . . . I will be avenged. Lucifer dwells within all of us! . . . See you in Disneyland."

We can see that Ramirez fits both categories of organized and disorganized serial killers. He killed his victims in their homes at random, not always sure whom he would find when he entered houses. He overcame them with a fast "blitz"-type attack using extreme force. He left many of his victims alive, suggesting that when he made a decision to kill he made it spontaneously at the scene. He did not disguise his face and left forensic evidence behind, traits of a disorganized killer. On the other hand, Ramirez brought weapons to the scene and even carried a police frequency scanner, traits of an organized offender. Ramirez is a mixed-category serial killer in the FBI system.

In Chapter 9, which deals with profiling, we will return to a more extensive discussion of some of the problems of the organized/disorganized profiling system used by the FBI. Next, however, we explore how the dissatisfaction with the organized/disorganized model of serial killer behavior led to the evolution of alternate and more complex categories.

FOUR

THE EVOLUTION OF MONSTROSITY:

Visionary Missionary Hedonist Power-Assertive Anger-Retaliatory Munchausen Syndrome by Proxy Serial Spree Killers and Other Emerging Categories

It only took them a month to get me to kill.
—HERBERT MULLIN

I had to evict them from their human bodies.
—EDMUND KEMPER

Evolving Categories

The FBI model classifying offenders as *disorganized, organized,* or *mixed* was only the beginning of an effort to classify serial killers. While the FBI categories are used for investigative purposes, there are many other ways of classifying serial killers for psychological or criminological study. These categories are often more valid and accurate in their definition, because they are based on already identified serial killers about whom much is known—unlike the FBI system, which is focused on unknown killers for investigative goals. The most prevalent typologies in current use for studying offenders are those defined by criminologists Ronald Holmes, Stephan Holmes, and James De Burger, who based their classification system on motive, as opposed to the FBI's basis in method. Holmes, Holmes, and De Burger grouped serial killers into four distinct types with several subgroups, based on the motive or type of gratification the serial killer derived from his crime:

1. *Visionary:* These serial killers kill at the command of hallucinated external or internal voices or visions that they experience. Such individuals are almost always suffering from psychoses or other mental illness.

2. *Mission-oriented:* Some serial killers come to believe that it is their mission to rid the community of certain types of people: children, prostitutes, old people, or members of a specific race.

3. *Hedonistic:* These include killers who murder for financial gain (*comfort killers*), those who gain pleasure from mutilating or having sex with corpses, drinking their blood, or cannibalizing them (*lust killers*), and those who enjoy the actual act of killing (*thrill killers*). For the first two subtypes, the comfort and lust killers, murder is only a means to an end and in itself is less important than the acts accompanying or following the killing; for the third subtype, the thrill killer, the desire to kill is central to the motive.

4. *Power/control-oriented:* These are perhaps the most common of all serial killers, for whom the fundamental pleasure of their crime lies in the power and control they exert over their victims. They enjoy torturing their prey and find it sexually arousing, and murder is often the most satisfying and final expression of their power and control over their victim.[98]

We are going to look at these categories here in greater detail and see how they are manifested in actual cases.

VISIONARIES

These types of serial killers commit incomprehensible murders, leaving behind chaotic crime scenes. They often leave behind an abundance of physical evidence, but their victims frequently seem to fit no comprehensible pattern. That is because the killer's mind is completely disconnected from reality: Voices and visions drive the offender to kill for reasons secreted in the recesses of his madness. Sometimes these types of offenders are completely nonfunctional in society—living alone and having no contact with other people. In other cases, the offenders have episodic breaks with reality during which they kill but otherwise appear harmless or at worst, eccentric, to those around them. Most visionary serial killers genuinely suffer from mental illness and some are schizophrenic or psychotic (as opposed to *psychopathic,* which is a behavioral disorder, see Chapter 5). While almost all serial killers have a disturbed or difficult childhood to some degree, visionary killers might grow up in completely normal, supportive family settings. Because mental illness such as schizophrenia often first manifests itself in late adolescence or early adulthood, visionary killers are often young. While visionary killers do little to disguise their identity and leave behind evidence, they are difficult to apprehend because there is no clear method or motive to their crimes. They operate on an agenda entirely synched to the incomprehensible madness within them.

While most serial killers have an ideal victim in mind and kill for sexual purposes, the visionary killer selects his victims at random in a logic often indiscernible to an investigator. Visionary killers often kill close to home; because of their disturbed state of mind, they are unlikely to venture very far. Visionary killers almost exclusively fall into the FBI disorganized category because of the mental disorder driving their offenses.

Some serial killers have been known to pose as visionary killers, claiming to hear voices or have multiple personalities, in an attempt to secure a verdict of not guilty by reason of insanity.

Herbert William Mullin—"The Die Song"

Herbert Mullin was born in 1949 in Santa Cruz, California, and by most accounts grew up in a stable and nurturing, but perhaps too strict, Roman Catholic household. In high school he was smallish—five foot seven, weighing in at 120 pounds, but he was popular with both boys and girls. He played offensive guard on the school football team, was unfailingly polite and well mannered, got excellent grades, and was voted "most likely to succeed" by fellow students. The first indication of some kind of instability in Mullin cropped up at age sixteen, when a friend of his was killed in a road accident. Mullin set up a shrine for him in his bedroom and began to obsess that he might be a homosexual. When he turned seventeen Mullin began to hear distant voices—a classic symptom of paranoid schizophrenia, a disease that often begins to make its first appearance at this age.

Between ages eighteen and twenty-four, Mullin's life was punctuated by a series of hospitalizations in psychiatric facilities, relieved by periods of normalcy. He enrolled in Cabrillo College and earned an associate degree in arts, got an award in mechanical drawing, and designed the Santa Cruz tourist information booth, which stood in front of the Holiday Inn.

In 1968 he enrolled in San Jose State University, but his mental health began to decline rapidly. He was picked up several times by the sheriff's department, babbling to himself and wandering aimlessly. Making matters worse, Mullin became a user of marijuana and LSD, a potent hallucinogenic drug that mimics the symptoms of schizophrenia in healthy subjects. One can only imagine what it does in a user who already has schizophrenia—and no, it does not mimic sanity.

In 1969 on a visit to his sister, he began to mimic everything her husband did, and at other times he sat motionless, staring at them, refusing to say anything. The next morning his sister drove him to a mental health hospital and he checked himself in voluntarily. But as Mullin did not display any inclination to hurt himself or others, he was released in a week. To his credit, Mullin also ceased to consume drugs as his condition worsened.

He experimented with the hippie lifestyle for a period, adopting Eastern religions, growing his hair long, and wearing beads. Then he cut his hair short and put on a suit and tie. He approached strange women on the street, proposing marriage. Rejected, he traveled to San Francisco's gay neighborhood and propositioned men. He traveled to Hawaii and ended up in a mental hospital there. Back in California he was hospitalized several more times. He stood up in a Catholic church during a service and shouted out that it was not really Christian, but then shortly afterward he enrolled in studies for the Catholic priesthood.

He appeared at a boxing gym in San Francisco wearing a sombrero and carrying a Bible and proved himself to be a ferocious boxer. He was even considered to be a potential lightweight professional contender but suddenly dropped out. In Santa Cruz Mullin developed a crush on a local deputy sheriff and kept turning up at his office calling him "sweetheart." He continued doing this long after he had begun his series of murders.

A year after he had registered as a conscientious objector, Mullin joined the Marines with the help of his father, a former Marine colonel. He successfully completed basic training, but his mental condition made itself visible in the end, and he was quickly discharged. Who knows what the effect of Marine Corps combat drills had on the young schizophrenic, but he came to believe that American lives being sacrificed in the Vietnam War were saving California from the predicted great earthquake.*

In hindsight one must appreciate both the freewheeling and apocalyptic times that Mullin was living through in the late 1960s and early 1970s—and the role California played at their epicenter. With his bizarre behavior, Mullin must have been invisible in the do-your-own-thing rainbow of the Haight-Ashbury hippie culture that swept out of California and engulfed not only the nation but the rest of the Western world. But by the early 1970s it turned bad. Charlie Manson had long before abandoned Haight-Ashbury as a trip gone bad and unleashed his followers to commit a series of horrific murders in Los Angeles before retreating to the remote Death Valley desert. What was celebrated in the green fields of Woodstock was put to death on the black asphalt of Altamont, where during a Rolling Stones performance of "Sympathy for the Devil," Hell's Angels bikers beat a spectator to death in front of center stage.

In the late summer of 1972 as America stood by to reelect Richard Nixon, Mullin journeyed one more time to San Francisco and attempted to join a hippie art collective on Geary Street. He was just too bizarre for them and was sent packing by management. Michael Roberts, one of the artist residents there who had protested Mullin's expulsion, recalled, "He left the human race that day. It was the final rejection."

In September 1972, Mullin returned to his parents' home in Santa Cruz. He spent that month, according to witnesses, deeply contemplating the Bible. Mullin later stated that he discovered that killing was a biblical tradition, and that his father, the ex-Marine, had reinforced that in him. According to Mullin, his father used to urge, almost force him to go deer hunting to develop his masculinity. Mullin began to hear the disembodied voices of his parents ordering him to sacrifice lives to stave off the natural disaster threatening California's coast. Mullin stated, "It only took them a month to get me to kill."

On October 13, 1972, Mullin was driving down a highway when he

---

* Some accounts state that Mullin was rejected by the Marines *before* he went through basic training. See, for example, Ward Damio, *Urge to Kill,* New York: Pinnacle Books, 1974, pp. 168–169. Ressler and Shachtman, in *Whoever Fights Monsters* (New York: St. Martin's Press, 1992) state that he completed basic training.

noticed Lawrence White, a fifty-five-year-old vagrant, walking along the roadside. Mullin stopped his vehicle ahead of him, and when White approached him, Mullin killed him with blows to the head with a baseball bat. He then dragged White's body into the bush and left it there.

Soon Mullin began to hear his father's voice explaining that pollution was coming from inside people's bodies. He had just been reading accounts of Michaelangelo's dissections in Irving Stone's *The Agony and the Ecstasy* when on October 24 he picked up college student Mary Guilfoyle, who was hitchhiking. When she climbed into his vehicle, he plunged a knife into her chest, killing her. He then dragged her body out into the woods and cut open her abdomen, taking out her organs and inspecting them for traces of pollution. So he could better inspect the intestines, he strung them across the branches of a tree. Her body would not be found for months.

Even today, with all the advances in profiling, it is hard to imagine investigators linking these two seemingly different crimes to the same perpetrator or understanding the motives behind the mutilation of Mary Guilfoyle. Most likely they were attributed to Jack-the-Ripper-type sexual lust, but in fact, these were not sexual fantasies driving Mullin—they were not really even fantasies, but hallucinations.

Still deeply linked to his Catholic faith, Mullin went in the afternoon of November 2 to St. Mary's Church in Los Gatos, a suburb of Santa Cruz, to seek help from a priest. Father Henri Tomie at random entered the confessional booth to listen to Mullin. Mullin began to hallucinate that Father Tomie was asking Mullin to kill him. Mullin recalls that he told the priest that his father had been telepathically ordering him to sacrifice people.

In Mullin's recollection of the conversation, the priest asked him, "Herbert, do you read the Bible?"

"Yes."

"The commandments, where it says to honor thy father and mother?"

"Yes."

"Then you know how important it is to do as your father says."

"Yes."

"I think it is so important that I want to volunteer to be your next sacrifice," the priest said, according to Mullin.[99]

Mullin beat the priest, kicked him, and stabbed him six times in the chest and back, leaving him to die in the confessional booth.

On December 16, Mullin went to a Santa Cruz auto parts dealership that also sold handguns. He picked out a .22-caliber pistol and filled out the required gun purchase application form, giving his occupation as sketch artist and checking off truthfully "No" when asked if he had any felony convictions or narcotic addictions. (Both marijuana and LSD are not considered physically addictive, and he was off them anyway.) A week later he returned for the weapon, paying $22.99 for it.

After he became seriously mentally ill, Mullin ceased to use drugs. Now he became convinced that it was precisely those drugs that were the cause of his condition. On January 25, 1973, taking his handgun with him, Mullin went to find his former high school football teammate James Gianera, who had first shared a marijuana joint with him. Mistakenly, he arrived at a neighboring house instead. Kathy Francis was at home with her two children when Mullin knocked on her door. She knew Gianera and directed Mullin to his house. According to Mullin, she also told him that she and her children wanted to be sacrificed. She was found by police on the kitchen floor stabbed in the chest and shot through the head. Her two sons were found in their bunk bed, stabbed through the back and also shot in the head. The house appeared undisturbed.

Mullin then wandered over to James Gianera's house. After a brief conversation about old times and drug consumption, Mullin shot James dead. Gianera's wife, Joan, who was taking a shower upstairs, was shot dead as she tried to escape. Again the house was not disturbed. Police identified the same weapon in all five murders. They also determined that the two families were jointly involved in a small-time marijuana-dealing business, and classified their deaths as drug-business related.

Mullin was a disorganized visionary serial killer. His eight killings so far were mission-driven but entirely unplanned and haphazard. No connection would appear between the beating death of the vagrant, the mutilation of the college girl, the stabbing of the priest, and the multiple shootings of the five recent victims. Each crime appeared different not only in the method but also in the apparent motive. This kind of hidden logic is what makes disorganized serial killers not only difficult to apprehend, but sometimes even difficult to notice.

On February 10, 1973, Mullin came upon four teenagers camping in Cowell State Park, about two miles away from his parents' house. He shot all four dead, because, as he later explained, he believed they were disturbing the environment. Their bodies would not be found until a week after Mullin was already in custody.

On February 11, hunters finally discovered the remains of Mullin's second victim, her intestines hanging in the tree branches. On February 13, Mullin set out in his station wagon. Later there would be some speculation that Mullin was obsessed with the number thirteen, and indeed his first murder was committed on November 13, and his thirteenth victim would die on February 13.

Seventy-three-year-old Fred Perez had fought as a U.S. Marine in the Boxer Rebellion in China, and during the 1920s he had been a champion middleweight fighter in California. He had four children, seven grandchildren, and five great-grandchildren. Around 8:00 A.M. he was gardening in his front yard when Mullin stopped his car about 150 feet away. Perez's niece and a neighbor saw Mullin lean out from his window, brace a .22-caliber rifle, and squeeze off a single shot that hit Perez in the side of the chest. Mullin then calmly drove away as the neighbor phoned the police. The wound was so small that when a police officer arrived at the scene, he assumed that Perez was having a heart attack and assured him that he would be okay. But Perez died in his garden before paramedics could arrive.

With the description of the car on air, police quickly apprehended Mullin and seized both the rifle and the handgun still in his car. Mullin refused to cooperate with the police and at his arraignment he asserted his Fifth Amendment right not to incriminate himself. A week after his arrest, the bodies of the four teenagers were found and ballistics linked their deaths to Mullin.

It is debatable how disorganized a serial killer Mullin was. He defied the traditional definition in purchasing a weapon prior to his later homicides and bringing it with him to the scene where he committed his offenses. When arrested he steadfastly denied having committed the murders. Yet at the same time there is no evidence that Mullin planned his murders and stalked his victims. They were highly random, improvised acts of violence. Mullin would eventually be indicted for eleven murders. His lawyer, on the condition that Mullin not be charged, had to inform the police of the November murders of Lawrence White and Mary Guilfoyle. The police would not have linked them to Mullin otherwise.

Mullin was convinced that voices were directing him as the "savior of the world." Mullin explained, "Satan gets into people and makes them do things they don't want to do." By killing people (causing "small disasters"), Mullin believed that he was going to prevent the great disastrous earthquake and tidal wave that threatened California. The transcript of Mullin's police interrogation clearly shows the extent of his delusions:

MULLIN: We human beings, through the history of the world, have protected our continents from cataclysmic earthquakes by murder. In other words, a minor natural disaster avoids a major natural disaster.

QUESTION: But if murder is a natural disaster, then why should you be locked up for it, if it's natural and has a good effect?

MULLIN: Your laws. You see, the thing is, people get together, say, in the White House. People like to sing the die song, you know, people like to sing the die song. If I am president of my class when I graduate from high school, I can tell two, possibly three young male *homo sapiens* to die. I can sing that song to them and they'll have to kill themselves or be killed— an automobile accident, a knifing, a gunshot would. You ask me why this is? And I say, well, they have to do that in order to protect the ground from an earthquake, because all of the other people in the community had been dying all year long, and my class, we have to chip in so to speak to the darkness. We have to die also. And people would rather sing the die song than murder.

QUESTION: What is the die song?

MULLIN: Just that. I'm telling you to die. I'm telling you to kill yourself, or be killed so that my continent will not fall off into the ocean. See, it's all based on reincarnation, this dies to protect my strata.

Although Mullin was obviously insane, a California jury felt he was fit to stand trial—he was convicted of ten homicides (having committed thirteen). It is believed, however, that the jury deliberately chose to ignore his insanity, fearing that if he were committed to a hospital he would later be released back into the community (not an unfounded fear at the time of the Mullin case). Mullin was sentenced to life in prison.

MISSIONARIES

Missionary killers feel compelled to kill a certain type of victim whom they believe is worthy of death. Often the choice of victim is somehow influenced by the killer's past experience or current beliefs that lead him to conclude that a certain type of person is "undesirable." Prostitutes, homosexuals, homeless people, and members of a specific race are the most frequent candidates for missionary serial killers.

Missionary killers are highly organized, compulsively seeking out and stalking their victim type and killing them quickly. Usually no sexual offenses are associated with the crime, but there are exceptions, particularly in the murder of prostitutes. Missionary serial killers are often stable, gainfully employed, long-term residents of the geographical territory in which they kill. They are frequently intelligent and white-collar or professional workers. They usually refrain from posing or mutilating the corpse of their victim—the kill is the mission. The body is frequently found at the location of the murder, as the missionary killer has minimum contact with his victim because he is uncomfortable relating to the object of his hate in an attempt to lure the victim to another location.

Missionary serial killers sometimes team up into groups and can be arguably also classified as "cult serial killers" when they do.

Joseph P. Franklin

A former Klansman, Joseph Franklin was convicted in 1980 of four homicides: the sniper shooting of two black men jogging with a white woman in Salt Lake City, Utah, and the shooting of a black-white couple in Madison, Wisconsin. He is believed to have committed up to fifteen murders in seven states between 1977 and 1980—in one double homicide of a mixed-race couple, he was released after being arrested because of a lack of evidence. His victims were either blacks or interracial couples. He apparently killed one woman he picked up hitchhiking when she told him she had dated a Jamaican. Franklin stated, "Race-mixing is a sin against God and nature . . . I feel it is my duty as a servant of God to protect white womanhood from injury or degradation."

"The Zebra Killers"

The Zebra Killers, who were named for the interracial nature of their crimes, consisted of five black offenders who murdered fifteen white men, women, and youths in 1973 and 1974 in San Francisco over a span of 170 days. They belonged to an inner cult within the Elijah Mohammad's Nation of Islam movement called the "Death Angels." It was never ascertained how high in the movement approval and complicity in the Death Angels went. Membership, or "wings," in the Death Angels was open to anyone who killed ("stung") at least nine white men, five white women, or four white children. Once a member committed the required number of homicides, the member's photograph was posted on a bulletin board at Nation of Islam centers with a pair of wings drawn in extending from his back. In October 1973 there were apparently fifteen Death Angels in the California chapter of the Nation of Islam.[100]

The five new aspiring members of the cult patrolled in groups of two or three and killed their victims randomly at bus stops, in telephone booths, at a late-night laundry, or on the street. The men were "killing grafted snakes for Allah—blue-eyed devils." Although they were supposed to only kill, they robbed or raped their victims on several occasions, which was against the rules of the cult. Most victims were shot dead, some were stabbed and hacked, and a few victims were kidnapped and tortured. While the earlier Death Angel murders were discreet, the new batch were blatant and committed with the same weapon, allowing the police to quickly link the murders together and alarming the city of San Francisco.

One of the aspiring Angels allegedly flew to Chicago, where the Nation of Islam was headquartered, and demanded an early promotion into the Death Angels. Upon being rebuffed he intensified the killing spree. When a senior, yet unidentified member of the movement came to California and attempted to defuse the killings by agreeing to promote the aspirants into the Angels without their fully qualifying in the number of kills, it became his turn to be rebuffed. He was told by one of them that they would not be comfortable with other Death Angels, not having themselves equaled in the number of kills. They continued in the killing campaign.

In May 1974, one of the five aspiring Angels fell out with the group and turned state's evidence, implicating a number of fellow cult members.

Only four men—Jesse Cook, Larry Greene, Manuel Moore, and J. C. Simon—were indicted, and it turned out that two of them had no criminal record previously. After what was at that time California's longest trial, running more than a year, the four were sentenced to life in prison. It is believed that the Death Angels in California might have murdered as many as 135 men, 75 women, and 60 children, all of them white, but there was not sufficient evidence to charge the remaining fifteen to twenty people implicated in the cult.[101]

Ted Kaczynski—Harvard, the "Unabomber," and His Mission

Ted Kaczynski, who mailed and placed bombs targeting high-technology researchers and executives, supposedly believed that technology had advanced to a state where it posed a threat to mankind. A brilliant Ph.D. in mathematics, Kaczynski withdrew from society to a primitive cabin in Montana, from which he made his bomb-running forays into civilization for twenty years—during which he seriously injured several victims and killed three. Known only as the Unabomber, he persuaded several media outlets to publish his manifesto protesting against society's becoming too dominated by high technology and global corporate power interests. He was identified after his family recognized the phraseology in the manifesto and alerted the FBI.

There was some controversy over the effectiveness of the FBI profiling of Kaczynski (see Chapter 9). Moreover, there are some disturbing questions over Ted Kaczynski and the nature and motive of his crimes. A brilliant mathematician with a Harvard undergraduate degree and a Ph.D. from the University of Michigan and a one-time assistant professor at the University of California at Berkeley, Kaczynski is probably the most educated serial killer on record. When identified and captured, he showed no signs of organic mental illness. What made this brilliant man cross the line to kill?

Apprehended and tried by federal authorities, Kaczynski was portrayed as an unkempt hermit nutcase who suddenly "cracked" after teaching for two years at Berkeley and retreated into the wilderness to a Montana cabin, from which he emerged only to kill. Because Kaczynski's beliefs, and even his homicidal actions, garnered sympathy in some segments of society, it was important to discredit him and his mission as the actions of a crackpot.

The media coverage of Kaczynski's trial in Sacramento, from where this portrayal emerged, was highly controlled by the very corporate powers he so hated. Authority for press passes to the trial was delegated to a consortium of major news organizations, led by the Associated Press.[102] The consortium established the Unabom Trial Media Group, which issued press passes only to "bona fide" journalists. Furthermore, all courtroom passes were reserved exclusively for major media outlets, with only two passes available on a daily lottery basis to independent or small media organizations. The rest of the journalists could use a room where audio was pumped in on speakers from the courtroom—but only if they paid a $5,000 initiation fee and took out liability insurance costing another $1,500.[103] Very few independent journalists or writers could afford such a privilege.

The truth is slightly different. Kaczynski was hardly a hermit, and maintained friendly relationships with some of his neighbors and people in town. And while his cabin was primitive, it was hardly remote by Montana standards. Author Alston Chase, who actually took the trouble to go to the site of Kaczynski's cabin, writes:

> Ted's place, far from being a "wilderness," bordered on suburban. Standing outside his door, one could hear traffic on the Stemple Pass Road . . . Just a few hundred feet down the creek from Kaczynski stood a row of vacation cabins . . . And quite a few townsfolk liked Kaczynski.[104]

There was no "crack-up" at Berkeley—Kaczynski took the position there with the specific objective of financing a rural cabin and a planned retreat from society. Kaczynski's lifestyle might have been kooky compared to the New York–L.A. routine led by the journalists who reported on him. But deeper down, Kaczynski was no nuttier than the eminent American thinker Henry David Thoreau, who in 1845 went to live in a primitive cabin on Walden Pond, "not to walk in procession with pomp and parade, in a conspicuous place, but to walk even with the Builder of the universe, if I may,—not to live in this restless, nervous, bustling, trivial Nineteenth Century, but stand or sit thoughtfully while it goes by."[105] Kaczynski of course, did not sit thoughtfully. He killed coldly, wearing disguises as he planted lethal devices and cleverly left misleading evidence by wearing different-sized shoes attached like snowshoes below his regular ones.

Now that Kaczynski is locked away in a federal facility, all sorts of weird background is coming out about him. Recently it was discovered that Kaczynski was a survivor of a series of brutal personality-breaking psychological experiments in 1959, conducted at Harvard by Henry A. Murray, a towering figure in the world of intelligence agency personality analysis, brainwashing, and interrogation techniques. During World War II, Murray worked for the OSS, the precursor of the CIA, designing tests intended to identify the best recruits for clandestine work. Murray was particularly interested in how well recruits could withstand interrogation designed to break down their personalities.

In the 1950s, Murray served as an advisor to the U.S. Army on various drug tests on human subjects.[106] This was around the time that the CIA and the Department of Defense were experimenting with LSD. Harvard researcher Timothy Leary, the future civilian guru of LSD, recalled in his autobiography that Murray was "the wizard of personality assessment who, as OSS chief psychologist, had monitored military experiments on brainwashing and sodium amytal interrogation. Murray expressed a great interest in our drug-research project and offered his support."[107]

The sixty-six-year-old Henry Murray himself was experimenting with taking LSD when he subjected the brilliant but odd and lonely seventeen-year-old Harvard undergraduate student Ted Kaczynski to personality formation experiments. Students were asked to describe everything they fundamentally believed in, and then suddenly subjected to surprise attacks on their beliefs by hired lawyers. Murray described these as experiments in "stressful interpersonal disputations" or "dyadic interaction of alienated subjects."[108]

There is no documented proof that Murray was at the time working for any of the CIA programs focused on the use of LSD as a method for programming "Manchurian candidate" assassins, interrogating prisoners, and disabling chosen target victims. We know, however, that under code names MK-ULTRA and Project Artichoke, such programs existed. University psychiatric and psychology professors in the United States and Canada received grants from the CIA to conduct these experiments, and one such program at McGill University in Montreal became the subject of extensive lawsuits.

Whether Murray's experiments involving Kaczynski were part of the

CIA's mind-control research programs is unknown, but considering Murray's history as a veteran of military and intelligence personality and interrogation research programs, it is likely that they were. Between 1960 and 1966 the CIA funneled $456,000 to thirteen Harvard programs and unnamed professors in the departments of psychology, philosophy, and social relations.[109]

After Alston Chase wrote an article in June 2000 in *The Atlantic* about Kaczynski's participation in these experiments, Harvard quickly sealed the test records documenting what Kaczynski went through. Some of the other participants, however, recall the experiments as being devastating of their belief systems and personalities, although none of them became serial killers.

Perhaps most ironic is that Murray's "dyadic interaction of alienated subjects" became the foundation for the therapeutic programs during the 1970s and 1980s aimed at "curing" serial killers and other types of psychopathic offenders in criminal psychiatric facilities. By the end of the 1980s this type of therapy was under severe criticism, as it appeared to do more damage than good.[110]

We know from the journals that Kaczynski kept, and which were entered into evidence during the trial, that he had expressed anger and desire to kill years before he planted his first bomb.

> My motive for doing what I am going to do is simply personal revenge. I do not expect to accomplish anything by it. Of course, if my crime (and my reason for committing it) gets any public attention, it may help to stimulate public interest in the technology questions and thereby improve the changes for stopping technology before it is too late; but on the other hand most people will probably be repelled by my crime . . . I certainly don't claim to be an altruist or to be acting for the "good" (whatever that is) of the human race. I act merely from a desire for revenge. Of course, I would like to get revenge on the whole scientific and bureaucratic establishment, not to mention communists and others who threaten freedom, but, that being impossible, I have to content myself with just a little revenge.

After he started planting his bombs seven years later, he wrote again:

> I emphasize that my motivation is personal revenge. I don't pretend to any kind of philosophical or moralistic justification. The concept of morality is simply one of the psychological tools by which society controls people's behavior.

My ambition is to kill a scientist, big businessman, government official, or the like. I would also like to kill a Communist.

In the end, we see that Kaczynski was actually a nutter, but not the one that the press depicted him as. Somewhere inside him, beneath that Harvard-educated 170 IQ—or perhaps, as Alston Chase argues, because of it—lurked a homicidal psychopath. Typically, and especially of missionary-type serial killers, Kaczynski felt that he was somehow special and "entitled."

One thing we will see later in this book is that serial killers are frequently isolated and lonely children. Whether it is because of a domineering mother, a physical disability, a behavioral disorder, a mental handicap, or an overabundance of intelligence, serial killers as children and teens are frequently isolated from their siblings and playmates and increasingly live in a fantasy world. It is of course, a "chicken-or-egg" paradox—do children grow up to become serial killers because they are isolated, or are they isolated because there is something deadly wrong with their behavior in the first place? The problem is that millions of people have not killed, but have the same or worse childhood symptoms that serial killers frequently have: bedwetting, fire starting, animal cruelty, domineering mothers, broken families, head injuries, and isolation from peers. So while these things are often present in the childhoods of serial killers, they alone are not the solution to the puzzle—there is still an unknown factor sought by criminal psychologists to explain the existence of serial killers.

As we will also see in later chapters, serial killers often need some kind of trigger to set them off on the inevitable path to murder. Whether the psychological experiments in 1959 unleashed Kaczynski's rage to homicidal action by breaking down the remnants of his personality is not an easy question to answer. Sealed in Harvard's archives are the details of Kaczynski's time in the "dyadic interaction of alienated subjects" that Professor Murray was conducting. Obviously, Murray was not "deconstructing" the personalities of psychopaths at Harvard—he was experimenting on the personalities of ambitious, highly intelligent scholars, attacking their fundamental beliefs and personality traits. Kaczynski was definitely isolated from his childhood peers by both his intelligence and his parents' ambitious management of his intellectual development. Whatever rage he might have developed, his intelligence and acceptance of basic ethics might have kept it in check, until Murray's "dyad" got hold of him at the weakest and loneliest point in his life—away from home for the first time as a college undergraduate. That could be the elusive trigger in Kaczynski's murderous career—a trigger that, with his intelligence and sense of organization, he did not act on impetuously, but carefully and smartly, evading apprehension for nearly two decades.

HEDONIST COMFORT KILLERS

Hedonist comfort killers are perhaps the oldest recognized and simplest type of serial killer. They kill for profit and gain—for comfort. They were highly prevalent in previous centuries in times of anarchic disorder or in frontier territories where the institutions of justice were weak and the value of life was low. Pirates, bandits, urban slum landlords, baby-farm matrons, black widow husband poisoners, bluebeard wife murderers, landlady killers, innkeeper murderers, medical cadaver harvesters—all these categories dominate the descriptions of nonaristocratic serial killers from the past. These types of crimes continue to occur in rural areas or in economically depressed urban communities, where victims are often transients who are not missed. Organized-crime contract killings likewise unfold in a type of underworld anarchy and the victims, often other criminals, are not missed or valued.

Victims are frequently known to the killer. The killer is the victim's husband or wife, business partner, friend, or employer-employee or is in some kind of professional relationship with the victim. Victims are very carefully chosen for the profit their death will yield, and their murders are planned and their bodies carefully disposed of. The types of killers are divided between geocentric killers who lure victims to their place of residence or business and nomadic killers who seek out the victim. Victims are often killed quickly, and any mutilation of the corpse has to do with disposal as opposed to psychopathology. Female serial killers are frequently this type of killer. In some cases, complete strangers who randomly enter the offender's "kill zone" become victims.

Dr. Marcel Petiot

Hauntingly similar to the late-nineteenth-century profit-motivated murders by Herman Mudgett in Chicago, who killed victims in his custom-designed "murder hotel" during the World's Fair, were the crimes in 1941–1944 of Dr. Marcel Petiot in Paris. Petiot preyed on refugees, often Jews attempting to flee France during the war, claiming that for a price he could assist them in escaping German-occupied France. They came to his home, in which Petiot had built a soundproof room with a peephole. Petiot "inoculated" his victims with poison and then guided them to the soundproof room. He watched them die through the peephole, and afterward he buried their bodies in the basement or burned them in a furnace. The money the victims paid Petiot for his "help" was supplemented by their belongings, which he stole after their deaths. After his arrest he was found with 1,500 articles of clothing and forty-seven suitcases belonging to some of his victims. Nobody noticed the people disappearing, as it was thought that they had either escaped Paris or had been arrested and deported by the Germans.

In March 1944, when neighbors complained of rank black smoke emerging from Petiot's chimney, the fire department checked Petiot's apartment and stumbled upon the remains of forty-seven bodies in his house. Petiot cleverly evaded arrest by claiming that the bodies were German soldiers or collaborators whom he was disposing of at the orders of the Resistance. In the wartime confusion Petiot was allowed to go free, but subsequent investigations pieced together the identities of the victims, and in November 1944 he was arrested. He was convicted of twenty-seven homicides committed between 1941 and 1944, but was believed to have committed a total of sixty-three. He was guillotined on May 26, 1946.

HEDONIST LUST KILLERS

Hedonist lust killers are probably the scariest and most monstrous of all types of serial killers. Not all of them want to necessarily hurt or kill you—they simply want to wear your skin or eat your liver or have sex with your severed head. It's just that your life gets in the way. . . . Edmund Kemper, who murdered ten victims and had sex with their corpses and various mutilated body parts, explained that the actual killing of his victims had little to do with his fantasies. "I'm sorry to sound so cold about this," he said, "but what I needed to have was a particular experience with a person, and to possess them in the way I wanted to: I had to evict them from their human bodies." (See Chapter 5 for a case study of Kemper's offenses.)

Lust killers often have an ideal victim type in mind with fetishistic elements—type of footwear or clothing worn, color or style of hair, body shape, a "cheerleader type" or a "slutty type," and so on.

Lust killers often need intimate skin-to-skin contact in their killing, and use a knife or strangulation to murder. Necrophilia is a very frequent aspect of lust killer homicides. They are mostly highly organized, having gone through years of the process of transforming and rehearsing their often bizarre fantasies into reality. Lust killers are often aware that their victim choice is visible to police and may choose to travel to various jurisdictions in both their hunt for and disposal of victims. Because sometimes these killers consume certain body parts or focus on them, dismembered victims might be spread over different locations. The lust killer usually chooses different dumping grounds for each victim (unlike the power/control killer, who might like to keep his victims' corpses together at a choice location).

Jerry Brudos—The Fatal Shoe Fetishist

Brudos is a minor serial killer whose story, nonetheless, demonstrates the evolution of a hedonistic sexual serial killer and is worth summarizing in some detail here.*

In 1969, young women were vanishing in Oregon and police were very concerned. On March 27, nineteen-year-old Karen Sprinker went missing in Salem. She was home visiting from college and was to meet her mother for lunch at a downtown shopping center. Her mother waited for an hour, but Karen never arrived. Police found her car parked in the indoor garage of the department store where her mother was waiting. There were no signs of any violence at the vehicle.

The police surmised that Sprinker was kidnapped in broad daylight as she was walking from her car to the store downstairs to meet her mother.

---

* The case of Jerry Burdos is described in Michael Newton, *The Encyclopedia of Serial Killers;* Eric W. Hickey, *Serial Murderers and Their Victims;* and many other sources, but the most definitive account of the Burdos case was produced by Ann Rule (writing as Andy Stack), in *Lust Killer,* New York: Signet, 1983.

When the police subsequently surveyed shoppers in the center who might have been there when Sprinker went missing, they were told of a huge strange woman lurking around the garage—except that the woman, witnesses thought, was really a man dressed in female attire.

Next, twenty-two-year-old Linda Salee, a secretary at a moving company, went missing in Portland. She had been last seen at a shopping mall purchasing a birthday present for her boyfriend after work. But she never showed up to meet him later that evening.

When Salee failed to appear at work the next day and was reported missing, the police took the report very seriously and a search was made. Her car was found parked and locked at the mall with no signs of violence. Salee was not the first girl to disappear under similar circumstances. In the previous months, two other women had vanished.

Linda Salee was found three weeks later in a river about fifteen miles south of Corvallis, Oregon. A fisherman discovered her body bobbing in the river, firmly wedged against the current. The police had a difficult time extracting her corpse from the river because it was weighed down with a heavy automobile transmission box. Her body had been attached to the transmission with nylon cord and copper wire. The cord was tied off with a distinctive knot, while the copper wire was twisted in a manner in which electricians trim electrical lines. Cause of death was determined to be strangulation with a cord. One thing puzzled the medical examiner: There were two strange needle marks, one on each side of Salee's rib cage. The punctures were circled by small burns, which evidently had occurred after death.

Several days later, about twenty yards from where Linda Salee's body was found, police divers located the body of Karen Sprinker. Her body was lashed to a six-cylinder engine head, with the same type of cord and copper wire, knotted in the same electrician's manner. Her autopsy revealed that she too had been strangled with some kind of strap. She was clothed in the green skirt and sweater that her mother had reported her wearing the day she disappeared. She was also wearing the same cotton panties, but was clad in a bustier-type waist-long black bra many sizes too big for her. When the medical examiner removed the bra he discovered that it was stuffed with brown paper toweling. Karen Sprinker's breasts had been cut off and the toweling inserted to create the illusion of a big bosom. Clearly the two bodies were the work of the same killer.

Although the river yielded no further bodies, police in Oregon had on their hands two other cases of mysterious disappearances of young women. On January 26, 1968, in Portland, nineteen-year-old Linda Slawson went missing. She was selling encyclopedias door-to-door but when she did not show up at the sales office the next few days, nobody paid much attention. Encyclopedia sales were a very difficult and discouraging line of work—salespeople came and went all the time. Her family lived in Minnesota, so it took some time before she was reported missing. When the police checked with the encyclopedia company where she was making sales calls, the best they could do was give the police a neighborhood in Portland, but no specific addresses. Slawson had simply vanished, nobody sure exactly where and when.

Then on November 26, 1968, twenty-three-year-old Jan Whitney went missing while driving home for the Thanksgiving holidays from her college. Her car was found just outside Albany, Oregon, locked and parked at a highway rest area. There was a minor mechanical breakdown in the engine that would have prevented the car from being driven. Somebody had obviously offered Jan Whitney a ride.

With the recovery of two victims, both obviously murdered by the same killer, the police now began in earnest to search for a suspect. They knew he was probably a strong large male because he was able to carry bodies weighed down by engine parts. By the way he trimmed the wire binding the victims, police guessed that he might be an electrician. They had only one very tenuous lead. On April 22, in Salem, a day before Linda Salee disappeared while shopping for her boyfriend's gift, a fifteen-year-old girl reported that a huge man with sandy hair and freckles had attempted to force her into his vehicle—a small sports car. Other than that, the police had no further clues.

Police decided to work their way back to Karen Sprinker's college residence in Corvallis—perhaps her killer knew her from there. Investigators began a massive interview of all of Sprinker's fellow students—whom did she go out on dates with? Did she get any strange phone calls at the dormitory where she lived? The police then expanded their questioning to the contacts of other girls on the campus: Whom were they seeing? Had any of them been taken to strange places? Did they have contact with any weird individuals or receive unusual phone calls?

Several girls told the police that they were called by their first name to the communal phone at the dormitory. The caller was a man who said that he got their name from a friend of theirs, without ever mentioning the name of the friend. He said he had been a prisoner of war in Vietnam for three years and that he possessed clairvoyant powers. Would they like to meet him for a Coke? Most of the girls had turned him down and could not remember what name he gave on the phone. Obviously, he was simply calling and asking for a female first name on the chance that somebody with that name was living at the dormitory.

One girl, however, had agreed to see the man. She said she felt sorry for the poor ex-soldier and agreed to meet with him. They sat and talked in the dormitory lounge and then drove out in his car for a Coke. They spent a lot of time talking about the two girls found in the river, but she did not find that unusual—everybody was talking about it on the campus. He drove an old, dirty, beat-up station wagon with children's clothes in it—she thought he was married. He said only one strange thing to her: "How did you know I would bring you back home and not take you to the river and strangle you?"

The girl described him as a large man, more than six feet tall and heavy— sort of tubby. His hair was thinning and was a blondish-red, sandy color. He had a pale complexion and lots of freckles. The description matched that given by the fifteen-year-old kidnap attempt victim. The police told the college girl that if the man called again, she should agree to meet him at the dormitory and call them immediately.

On May 25, the man called. When police arrived, a large, tubby man was waiting for the girl downstairs in the lobby. He had committed no crime for which the police could arrest him, but they did question him there in the lobby before sending him on his way. He told them that he lived in Salem and that he was in Corvallis to mow a friend's lawn. He was an electrician by trade and he had a wife and two kids, he told the investigators. He appeared slightly embarrassed but otherwise was calm and cooperative.

Checking into the man's recent movements, police determined that in January 1968, he had lived in the same neighborhood in Portland where Linda Slawson was selling encyclopedias. In August he moved to Salem and was working a location on the same section of highway where Jan Whitney vanished. Currently he worked only six miles from the point in the river where the bodies were found, and he now lived just blocks away from the downtown shopping center where Karen Sprinker disappeared. He had a juvenile record for sex offenses. And he was an electrician. . . . There were just too many coincidences. And that is how Jerry Brudos came to the attention of the police.

Jerome Henry Brudos was born in Webster, South Dakota, on January 31, 1939. He was the younger of two brothers and apparently was unwanted by his mother, Eileen, who was hoping for a daughter as a second child. The father was a small, short-tempered man, but not abusive. They were a poor family and lived mostly on farms while the father held casual jobs in town.

The mother was extremely dominating and highly critical of Jerry. While her other son, Larry, could do no wrong, she constantly denigrated Jerry. Both the father and the older brother were aware of her dislike for her younger child, but both were equally intimidated by Eileen Brudos.

Little Jerry roamed around freely and liked to play in a junkyard near their home. One day when he was five years old he found a pair of women's shiny black patent leather high-heeled shoes; one of them still had a rhinestone-studded clasp. Jerry was both pleased and fascinated by the shoes—he had never seen a pair like that; his mother always wore flats. The little boy brought them home with him, slipped them on, and showed his mother. Her reaction was completely unexpected: She shrieked with outrage, telling the boy he was wicked and ordering him to take the shoes back to the dump.

Five-year-old Jerry Brudos could not understand what he had done wrong—the shoes came from a dump, and nobody wanted them. Yet by his mother's reaction, he saw that he was committing some sort of deeply forbidden act. Instead of throwing the shoes out, Jerry hid them. When his mother found them, she made a show of burning them and punishing Jerry harshly. A fetish was born.

The bonding between mother and child had already been disturbed by Eileen's distaste for Jerry. The boy attached himself to a kindly woman in the neighborhood and often fantasized that she was his real mother. The woman had diabetes and was very sick, and before long could no longer receive visits from Jerry. At the same time, Jerry also had a close friendship with a girl his own age who died from tuberculosis. He was devastated by the death of his girlfriend and grieved for a long time. These three events all occurred when Jerry was five years old, and for some inexplicable reason they became interconnected in his mind—he would not be able to speak of one without the others.

When Jerry was in the first grade, he stole his teacher's high-heeled shoes from her desk. Before he could take them home, he was caught and humiliated. On another occasion, a couple with a teenage daughter was visiting the Brudos home. The daughter did not feel too well. She laid down on Jerry's bed and fell asleep, still wearing her high-heeled shoes. Jerry recalls that he was transfixed and sexually aroused by the sight of the shoes and attempted to pry them off the sleeping girl. She awoke and told Jerry to get out of the room.

At school Jerry was a dull and sickly child. He failed the second grade and was often sick with sore throats and migraine headaches that made him vomit. He had two leg operations to correct circulation in his legs and had fungal infections in his toes and fingers. While his brother Larry passed school with A's, Jerry was considered a dull child, despite the fact that his IQ was tested at normal or above.

Sex was never discussed in the Brudos home, and Jerry never witnessed any signs of affection between his parents. Growing up on the farm, Jerry recalls that he saw farm animals having intercourse, but he never associated or linked the erotic feelings he had for shoes with human sexuality. For him, his obsession with shoes was something secret and forbidden— and highly pleasurable.

The family moved around a lot, and for a period they lived next door to a house where there lived a lot of daughters. Jerry and one of their brothers would sneak into the girls' rooms and fondle their clothing. Jerry discovered that touching female underclothes gave him the same arousing sensations that the shoes did. He loved the feel and the scent of female underwear, bras, and stockings. They were mysterious and forbidden totems arousing in him deep erotic feelings that he could not understand or explain.

Jerry Brudos, it must be remembered, was still a prepubescent boy. It is not unusual for some boys, at age five or even younger, to feel a sexual urge toward the female person, without understanding what it is that they are feeling or why. As the child does not know what to make of the pleasing yet frustrating urges he feels, they can sometimes be "short-circuited" to a number of other parallel, transient, and experimental emotions or fantasy scenarios. If these associations permanently fuse in the child's subconscious, they can become fetishes or paraphilias such as masochism or sadism, necrophilia, bestiality, and so forth, that the child will carry with him into adulthood. Psychologists are unsure what causes such a fusing in some children, but in the case of Brudos, it might have been his mother's hysterical reaction to his bringing home a pair of high-heeled shoes. Whatever sexual feeling he might have had at that moment could have become fused with guilt, rage, and unrequited desire for the rest of his life. The unfortunate events that followed in his childhood could have prevented him from ever growing out of it.

I do not want to make any kind of value judgment here on gender issues or alternative sexual lifestyles or on what is normal or abnormal, healthy or unhealthy. Let us say for the sake of argument that basic "normal" development will lead a child and adolescent to gradually discover increasing degrees of sexual pleasure from conventional affectionate contact with the opposite sex: touching, hugging, kissing, intercourse, and so on. If this development, however, is sidetracked or "short-circuited," the individual seeks sexual pleasure by focusing on areas that were fused to his or her sexual memories in childhood. These become fetishes or *paraphilias*—narrowly focused sexual obsessions with either inanimate objects or particular types of partners or activities accompanying sex that often exclude the enjoyment of sex in any other form. It also appears to be predominantly a male problem. (See Chapter 7 for more on types of paraphilias.) Paraphilias are often accompanied by deep shame, so deep that sometimes the offender finds it less shameful to kill the victim than to admit to a paraphiliac desire.

Sometimes these associations are minor and harmless and simply limit the individual in his relationship to the opposite sex—they become expressed as preferences for long-legged women, or for women with a certain body type, color of hair, scent, voice, and so forth.

Other times these paraphilias are more extensive. For example, a surprisingly common paraphilia among otherwise heterosexual males approaching middle age is a desire for sex with transsexuals: males who appear to be women with developed breasts but still have a penis. In many countries, entire neighborhoods are sometimes dedicated exclusively to prostitutes of this category. Why? Most likely the normal sexual urge of some male children toward the opposite sex is short-circuited by their ignorance of female anatomy—especially if they have no female siblings in the family or have not been exposed to full female frontal nudity in life or in pictorial form (to which many males growing up prior to the 1970s would not have been readily exposed). Instead, the male child fills in his imagination with what he knows best—his own body. He imagines the female form with the penis and fuses this imagery with his earliest and arguably most intense sexual sensations. What happens next, of course, remains a mystery. Upon discovering the true form of female genitals, some males react with aversion while others decide that what women really have is even better than what they imagined and go from there. Others, however, continue to associate an intense desire with their childhood memory of women with male genitals.

Paraphilias are powerful because they are so often linked to a primal sexual awakening in childhood that is frequently not even understood as "sex" but just as an overwhelming mysteriously pleasurable but unsatisfied urge. Some individuals spend the rest of their lives chasing the sexual dragon they experienced in childhood, never coming close to replicating the original sensation.

In some cases, these sexual associations are severe and debilitating and sometimes dangerous to others. They can be fused with sadistic or necrophiliac tendencies or with rage and humiliation, especially in individuals who were abused as children. Even harmless paraphilias can be given a dangerous edge under certain circumstances. Jerry Brudos had no opportunity for healthy social development, and his almost-comic shoe fetish became a motive for horrific murders. While in others, a fetish for shoes would be a harmless quirk, in Brudos it was streaked with feelings of hate, rejection, betrayal, anger, and frustration toward women. Brudos was a walking time bomb and as he staggered into puberty, it got only worse.

When Jerry's older brother was sixteen, he had assembled a large collection of pinup pictures that he kept hidden in a box. One day, Jerry found Larry's collection and was poring over it when his mother walked in on him. Again there was a hysterical scene and Jerry was severely punished. He never told his mother that the collection was Larry's and not his.

At age sixteen, Jerry had his first nocturnal ejaculation—a wet dream. When his mother discovered the seminal stains on his sheets, he was again punished. Jerry was forced to wash his own sheets by hand and sleep without sheets while they dried on the line.

Jerry Brudos said that around this period he began to develop violent fantasies toward females. Brudos began to dig a tunnel in a hillside near the farm on which they lived. It was his fantasy to kidnap and imprison a girl there. Brudos recalls that he had no specific idea of intercourse or rape at that time—he was just excited by the idea of possessing a female.

During this period, Brudos began to slip into neighbors' homes and steal shoes. He stole female underwear from clotheslines. He assembled a large collection of female garments, which he secreted from his mother. Years later, when police checked into the manufacture of the mysterious bra that one of Brudos's victims was found wearing, they discovered that it had not been on the market for years. It is possible that it came from Brudos' teenage-era collection.

Brudos stated in a psychiatric interview that touching female clothes gave him a "funny feeling" and he attempted to masturbate with it, but failed to ejaculate. He said he could only ejaculate in nocturnal emissions during his teenage years.

In 1955, Jerry Brudos was seventeen and had by now learned about intercourse. He became obsessed with seeing a naked girl, but Jerry was very shy and withdrawn around girls in school and the neighborhood. The situation was worsened by his hulking size and the onset of severe acne. Girls were repelled by the big, clumsy, ugly giant.

In August 1955, when the Brudos family was living in Salem, Oregon, Jerry crept into a neighbor's house where an eighteen-year-old girl lived and stole her underwear. The next day he went to her and told her he was working undercover with the police and that he could get her lingerie back for her. The story seemed absurd to the girl, but Jerry was convincing. He told her that he lived in the neighborhood where many thefts were taking place and that nobody would suspect a seventeen-year-old kid as an undercover agent. He told the girl to come to his house when he knew nobody would be home. Since Jerry was a year younger than she was and he seemed like a chubby clown, the girl felt no fear of him. She decided she had nothing to lose and went to Jerry's house.

When she knocked at his door, Brudos called to her from upstairs to come in. When she walked into his room, he jumped out of a closet wearing a mask and wielding a knife. He forced her to take her clothes off and then took photographs of her. After he finished he ran out of the room. The shaken girl was getting dressed as Jerry came running into the house without the mask. He told the girl that somebody had locked him in the barn and that he had just managed to break out. Did she see anyone, he asked. The girl knew it had been Brudos in the mask, and dashed from the house. As is often the case in sex crimes, the girl did not report the incident at the time.

In the meantime, Brudos developed the photographs and took great pleasure in handling the girl's lingerie as he gazed at her pictures. His only regret was that he could remember little of the actual crime—he said he was too nervous and too busy taking pictures to actually savor the possession he had of the victim.

In April 1956, Brudos struck again. He lured a girl from his school into his car, drove her out to a remote location, and ordered her to take her clothes off. When she refused, he dragged her out of the car and began beating her with his fists, breaking her nose and causing extensive bruising. Fortunately a couple was driving by in their car and stopped when they saw the scene. Brudos at first attempted to convince them that the girl accidentally fell out of the car and was hysterical because she was scared. Then he told them that he was driving by and saw the girl being attacked by a "weirdo" and that he had fought him off. The couple took the now-docile Brudos and his victim to the police.

Police searched Brudos's room and found his photographs and collection of female clothing. The girl in the pictures was contacted, and his assault from the previous August surfaced. Brudos was treated as a juvenile offender and sent for psychiatric evaluation to the Oregon State Hospital. The doctors found that Brudos was depressed and that his "judgment and insight are questionable." But he was not grossly mentally ill or suffering from hallucinations, delusions, or illusions. According to the psychiatrist, Brudos showed no evidence of homicidal or suicidal tendencies and was suffering from "adjustment reaction of adolescence with sexual deviation, fetishism."

Brudos lived at the psychiatric hospital but was allowed to attend high school during the day. He was talented in mathematics and science, but he performed below his abilities. Years later, when Brudos became infamous, nobody from high school could remember him—it was as if he did not exist. Like so many serial killers, he lived in isolation. After eight months of treatment, Brudos was released from hospital care and moved back to his unhappy home.

Brudos graduated from high school in 1958 and was said to have excelled in electronics. In March 1959, Brudos joined the army and was trained as a communications technician, but he received an early discharge in October 1959 after being found unfit for service. Brudos moved back in with his parents in their two-bedroom house in Corvallis, Oregon. While his brother, Larry, was away at college, Jerry was allowed to sleep in the second bedroom, but when Larry came home, he was relegated to a shed at the back of the house.

During this period, Jerry began to stalk and attack women whose shoes he was attracted to. He would choke them into unconsciousness and then run off with their shoes. He continued stealing women's garments from clotheslines and dwelled in his dark shed surrounded by female attire.

Despite Jerry's mental problems, he continued to excel in electronics. He became a licensed broadcast technician and was employed at a Corvallis radio station as their engineer. He was less of a loner than in high school and was friendly with several male employees at the station. He remained, however, terminally shy in the presence of women.

A young boy used to come to the radio station and hang around watching Jerry work and pestering him with questions. One day in 1962, Brudos jokingly told him to find him a girlfriend. To Jerry's surprise, the boy took him to a house where he introduced him to a pretty dark-haired seventeen-year-old girl with big eyes. Her name was Susan* and she was almost as shy as Jerry.

Despite her shyness, Susan had dated teenage boys her own age, but the twenty-three-year-old Brudos seemed different to her. He courted her, pulling out her chair, buying her gifts, opening doors for her, and treating

---

* A pseudonym.

her as a lady. She was impressed by his job at the radio station and the attention and admiration he gave her.

They slipped into sex effortlessly, according to Susan, who says that there never seemed anything strange about Jerry's sexual performance. He was tender and loving. She knew nothing of his fetishes or his past mental problems.

Before long, Susan was pregnant, and they decided to get married. The couple had already agreed that they would marry if she became pregnant. Brudos admitted that their relationship was not a big love affair, that Susan saw marriage as a way of escaping the restrictions of her strict parents, while he just needed somebody to sleep with. In 1962, the couple had a girl whom they named Karin.

Susan testified that nothing in Jerry's behavior changed. He continued to be kind and tender with her, and bought her presents on holidays and anniversaries. They seemed to have a fairly lively sex life. Even before they were married, Susan posed nude while Jerry snapped photographs of her. He developed them himself in his own darkroom. Often he asked Susan to pose in black high-heeled shoes. Jerry asked her to do the housework nude except for her shoes, and the two of them romped around the house naked. The first three years of their marriage appeared to be happy ones. Jerry, it appeared, had finally found his fantasy girl.

Yet there were problems that nagged at the marriage. First, Jerry could not hold down a job. He kept changing jobs, and in their seven-year marriage the Brudoses lived in twenty different houses. Secondly, Susan felt that Jerry was very distant and removed from their daughter, Karin. He avoided all physical contact with his daughter, spent no time with her, and paid her little attention.

By the third year of their marriage, Susan was twenty and was beginning to turn away from Jerry's requests. Wearing high heels hurt her back and she was too busy with their child and housework to be "dressing up" for Jerry. The sex was becoming monotonous and their daughter was getting too old, Susan felt, for them to be running around the house naked. Once again, Jerry Brudos began to feel rejected.

Susan says that Jerry became "depressed" and withdrawn when she did something to displease him, but she never witnessed him being angry or violent. Unknown to Susan, during these "depressions" Jerry went out prowling at night stealing women's garments. Brudos also began to experience more migraine headaches and the pain was more intense. He also claims that he began to have "blackouts."

People who worked with Jerry Brudos during this period remember a very mild-mannered and brilliant electronics technician. One of his former employers says that he felt that Brudos could have run any television or radio station in the country, but somehow he seemed to lack ambition. He was a dependable and valuable worker and presented himself as a family man who did not smoke or drink and never talked of women.

Despite their marital problems, in 1967 Susan became pregnant again. Brudos was very enthusiastic about her second pregnancy and wanted to be in the delivery room with Susan when the baby came. He felt betrayed by Susan when she told doctors not to allow him into the delivery room, later explaining to Jerry that she did not want him to see another man touching her. She did not think it was right.

A son, Jason, was born and Brudos, while continuing to ignore Karin, paid much attention to the infant, taking him along on errands and planning to teach the boy how to use his tools in the basement when he grew up. After Jason's birth, however, the couple drifted apart even further. Susan, although she never told Jerry, was now actually repelled at the idea of having sex with him. She spent a lot of time out with her girlfriends, while Jerry was in his basement workshop fiddling with his electrical and electronic projects. Jerry's mother, whom he openly hated, came over and babysat upstairs.

In 1967, another thing happened that may or may not have triggered Jerry Brudos on his path to serial murder. While repairing an electrical device he touched a live wire and received a tremendous jolt of power that knocked him off his feet. He was burned and dazed and sustained some neck injury. Brudos was very fortunate to have inexplicably survived the lethal current. As a result, Brudos would now suffer even more severe headaches, and would pass periods of time unable to work.

Shortly after the birth of his son and the accident, Jerry Brudos went out on one of his forays in which he knocked women down and stole their shoes. For some reason, however, this time he followed a woman back to her home. He waited until he thought she was asleep and broke into her apartment. When the woman awoke, Brudos pounced on her and strangled her into unconsciousness. He testified that her limp body aroused him to such an extent that he raped her. Brudos was now escalating into some kind of necrophiliac fantasy, even though he had not killed the woman. It is hard to say whether Brudos genuinely broke into the woman's apartment to steal her shoes or deliberately stalked her. His change in MO is curious—why not just knock her down as before and take the shoes? Regardless, Brudos left the apartment with the shoes, which he claimed were his favorite of all he had stolen.

A serial killer's first kill is often accidental or unplanned. It gives him the taste of blood, so to speak, and triggers his circular addiction for subsequent murders. We might wonder if there is such a thing as a "window" for some serial killers during which if they do not have an opportunity to commit their first murder, they never become serial killers. How many nonlethal sex offenders are separated only by chance from becoming serial killers? Some would say that it is just a matter of time for individuals destined to be serial killers—they will kill sooner or later; it is inevitable. Others say that some serial killers never start out with murder as part of their fantasy, and that the first homicide happens suddenly and unexpectedly during the commission of a lesser offense, but then, once committed, becomes incorporated into future offenses. The description is akin to human-eating lions and tigers, which, once they overcome their fear of people and get a taste of human flesh, never return to hunt wild game again.

We do know, by Jerry Brudos's own testimony, that by the end of 1967 he was fantasizing about keeping preserved female corpses in a freezer so he could dress them in his favorite lingerie and pose them at will. But the actual killing itself was never part of Brudos's prehomicidal fantasies.

One can only wonder what would have happened with Jerry Brudos if on January 20, 1968, encyclopedia saleswoman Linda Slawson had not gotten her addresses mixed up and accidentally called at the Brudos home, thinking she had an appointment there.

Jerry Brudos confessed to police that he was working in the yard when Slawson appeared at his house, saying she had an appointment. He showed her to the rear door and down to the basement, telling her he was interested in buying a set. Slawson must have been so eager to make a sale that she followed him down to her death. While Brudos's mother was upstairs watching his little girl, Slawson sat on a stool in Jerry's basement workshop and began her sales pitch. At some point Brudos slipped behind Slawson and struck her in the head with a two-by-four. He then strangled the young woman to death. He hid her body under the staircase, then went upstairs and asked his mother to go out and get some hamburgers.

Brudos then returned to the basement and took Slawson's corpse out from under the staircase. The psychological drive behind his murder is clear in the answer he gave police when asked whether he remembered what Slawson was wearing. He responded that he could not remember her outer clothing but listed off to the police the precise color and style of lingerie. He said that he tried out different lingerie on her from his collection, dressing the dead woman like a "big doll."[111]

Brudos kept the body into the night. Around 2:00 A.M. he loaded the corpse into his car and drove to a bridge over a river. He parked his car and took out the jack to make it look like he had a flat tire.

Just before he threw her over into the river he cut her foot off because he wanted to still keep some part of her. Brudos confessed to police that because he was right-handed he cut off her left foot. He took it home and kept it in his freezer. He would insert the frozen foot into different shoes from his collection and take pictures of it.[112]

One suspects that it was no coincidence that Jerry's mother was just a few feet away on the next floor upstairs when he killed his first victim. Here he was, under the nose of the woman who had punished him for bringing back a pair of old shoes from a garbage dump when he was five, now hacking those shoes off the legs of real women, with their feet still inside. It was almost too simple to be true.

In the spring of 1968, the Brudoses moved to Salem into a house just a few blocks away from the Oregon State Hospital, where Jerry had been committed as a teenager. The house they rented had a garage that stood separately across a narrow breezeway, and Jerry was overjoyed by the big space for his "workshop." He installed a heavy padlock on the door and an intercom. He told his wife never to go into the garage without calling him on the intercom. The reason, he said, was that he had set up a photo darkroom and if she opened the door, she might ruin the work he was doing.

Brudos bought a huge freezer and installed it in the garage. Susan complained that it was pointless to lock her away from the freezer when she needed to prepare dinner, but Brudos insisted she just tell him what she needed from the freezer and he would bring it to her. This annoyed Susan, as sometimes she just wanted to look over all the things in the freezer for an idea of what to prepare.

Susan noticed that Jerry was putting on more weight and getting fat and tubby. One day she jokingly told him he was getting too fat. Jerry left the room without saying a word and then returned about ten minutes later. Susan was shocked to see Jerry dressed in a bra with stuffing for breasts, a girdle with stockings, and huge high-heeled shoes. It was the strangest thing she had seen in her young life. Jerry asked her if he looked thinner now and Susan laughed nervously, not knowing what to say. After an awkward silence, Jerry left and returned as himself again. They never talked about it afterward and both behaved as if it never happened.

In November 1968, Jerry Brudos again killed unexpectedly. He encountered Jan Whitney on the highway by chance on his way from work. Her car had broken down and Brudos stopped. After inspecting the car, he said that he could fix it for her, but they would need to drive back to his house nearby for him to get his tools. Jan went along.

When they got to the house, Jerry told Jan that his wife had not come home yet and they would have to wait a few minutes for her to let him in so he could get his tools. Jan sat inside the car, which was parked in the driveway of Jerry's house. Brudos nonchalantly slipped into the backseat of the car behind Jan. In his statement to the police, Brudos said that he engaged Whitney in a little game, asking her if she could close her eyes and, without moving her hands to demonstrate, describe how to tie a shoelace. Whitney went for the challenge and as she sat there with her eyes closed attempting to describe how to tie a shoe, Brudos slipped a strap around her throat and strangled her in the car. He then raped her corpse in the car. Afterward he carried her body into his workshop and dressed her in some of the clothes from his collection, photographed her, and had sex with her corpse again. Afterward he hoisted her up from a hook in his garage ceiling. He decided to keep the corpse.

Brudos confessed to police that he kept Whitney's corpse hanging in the garage for days. He would rush home from work, dress the body up in various items of clothing, and have sex with it. He wanted something of her to keep and he cut off one of her breasts and experimented in preserving it. He stuffed it with sawdust and mounted it with tacks on a board like a trophy. He also tried taking a plastic mold from it in the hopes of producing lead paperweights but he was not satisfied with the result.[113]

Brudos got rid of Jan Whitney's body only after the police nearly discovered it accidentally. Leaving the corpse hanging from the hook in the ceiling, Brudos took Susan and the kids on a Thanksgiving weekend trip. While away, an automobile passing the Brudos house skidded and crashed into the garage, knocking a hole through the wall. When the police arrived at the scene, they actually shone a light through the hole to inspect the damage, but did not see the dead woman hanging from the ceiling. Not wanting to violate any constitutional rights by entering Jerry's property without his permission, the police left a card asking Jerry to call them when he got home. They needed to inspect the garage to determine damage for their report. When Jerry got home, he wrapped Jan's body in plastic and hid her in the water pump shed behind the garage. He then called the police and let them inspect the damage. Afterward he threw Jan Whitney's body into a river, weighed down with a heavy automotive part. Neither Whitney's nor Slawson's bodies were ever recovered, and Brudos refused to tell the police exactly where he dumped them.

In January 1969, Jerry Brudos celebrated his thirtieth birthday. Susan, in the meantime, began to witness her husband's behavior becoming progressively more bizarre. One day while hanging the laundry she walked into the garage unannounced and saw photographs of nude women in Jerry's development trays. Susan probably did not recognize that they were dead. Jerry told her that he was developing pictures for a "college kid" and reminded her not to enter the garage without telling him.

When Susan was away from the house, Jerry insisted that she telephone ahead before coming home. When asked why, he replied jokingly, so that he could get the blonde he had in the house out before she got home.

Then Susan found pictures of Jerry that he took of himself using a camera timer. He was lying on their bed dressed in different items of women's lingerie. His face was covered in the photographs but she recognized his huge body.

One day she found a plastic object that looked like a very realistic copy of a female breast. She asked Brudos what it was, and he explained to her that he had an idea for a novelty item—a female breast paperweight. It was eerie how realistic it looked. Susan testified that Jerry told her it did not come out the way he wanted and that later he made another one, slightly different. This one he put on the fireplace mantel in their living room, where police would later find it when they searched his home. At some point during this period, Brudos also acquired a handgun.

In March, Jerry Brudos went out looking for victims. Accidental en-counters were no longer satisfying enough—he now had the taste of blood and was trolling for suitable victims. Jerry Brudos told police that he came upon Karen Sprinker on her way to meet her mother in a department store restaurant. (That Brudos was identified and caught when police surveyed students in Sprinker's college residence was a remarkable coincidence—Sprinker might have even rebuffed his telephone invitation only to suc-cumb to him weeks later entirely at random in a different city.) Brudos was driving around the street when he spotted an attractive girl in a miniskirt and high heels entering a department store at about ten in the morning. Brudos parked his car in the store's multilevel garage and went down into the store. But he could not find the girl. On the way back to his car in the garage, Brudos spotted nineteen-year-old Karen Sprinker emerging from her car. It was late morning, just before lunch hour.

Brudos at first was not entirely satisfied with the victim he saw ap-proaching him. He recalled that he did not like the style of shoes she was wearing. But she was pretty and Brudos settled on her as victim just the same.[114]

Brudos confronted Sprinker with a pistol in the doorway of the de-partment store and forced her out through the indoor parking garage to his car. Although it was noon, nobody passed by at the moment. As her mother patiently waited below in the department store restaurant, Sprinker was being driven away from the parking complex by Brudos.

Brudos drove Sprinker back to his home through midday traffic. Upon arriving at his house, he walked her into his garage and raped her. After-ward he allowed her to use the bathroom in the house and then walked her back to the garage and forced her to pose in various items of clothing and shoes while he took photographs. He then killed her by attaching a rope around her neck through the hook in the ceiling and hoisting her up.

Brudos told police that he then went back into the house, but later re-turned to the garage to have sex with Sprinker's corpse. He cut off both her breasts and again experimented with taking molds from them but was still not satisfied with the results. He said that he did not like the bra Sprinker had worn so he picked out one of his favorite bras from his collection to dress her in but now that he had removed her breasts it did not fit. Brudos said he ended up stuffing it with paper towels so it would "look right."[115]

When police searched Brudos's house, they found the photographs that he took of his victims when they were alive and later, when they were dead. One picture showed one of the victims, dressed in a black lace slip, panties, and garter, hanging from a pulley on the ceiling—apparently dead. On the floor, Brudos placed a mirror so that it reflected the girl's crotch beneath the slip Brudos had dressed her in. One corner of the mirror reflected Brudos's drooling face gazing up at the girl—Brudos had accidentally photographed himself with his victim.

Brudos displayed a very typical pattern in serial murder: The first victim was killed unexpectedly without much planning; the second murder, ten months later, was more premeditated, but hesitating and virtually unplanned. The third murder, four months later, Brudos planned carefully and set out to commit, stalking his potential victim. Within a month of that killing, he began stalking his fourth victim.

His interaction with his victims likewise escalated. His first victim he only dressed and undressed like a doll; his second victim he raped only after she was dead; his third he raped before killing her. Brudos was "maturing" in his interaction with the women he attacked, in a pattern similarly observed in Albert DeSalvo, the Boston Strangler.

In Portland, twenty-two-year-old Linda Salee was on her way back to her car after purchasing a present for her boyfriend when Brudos approached her in the mall parking lot. He flashed a toy police badge and "arrested" her on "suspicion of shoplifting." Remarkably Salee said nothing as Brudos drove more than an hour to his house in Salem. Brudos said that it was as if she wanted to go with him.

Brudos drove the car with his victim right into his garage. His wife was home preparing dinner, so Brudos tied Salee up and went in to have supper. Brudos claims that when he returned to the garage he discovered that Salee had gotten loose of the ropes but had not attempted to escape or use the phone in the garage. This kind of passive behavior in shocked and traumatized victims is not uncommon.

Brudos then wrapped a strap around Salee's neck and began to strangle her. Salee at this point began to fight back, scratching and kicking, but it was too late. Brudos stated that he raped her just as she died or shortly afterward. Brudos then revealed the cause of the strange burn marks police found on Salee's body. Himself a surviving victim of an accidental electrocution, Brudos told police that he wanted to try an experiment using electricity. He confessed that he hung Salee on the hook like the other victims and stuck hypodermic needles into her rib cage. He then ran an electrical current through them to see if he could animate the corpse. Brudos was disappointed that the experiment did not work and only caused burns to the body. He had hoped, he said, that the corpse would "dance" or move in some way.[116]

Brudos told police he kept her corpse another day and a night, raping her again. But he did not cut her breasts because her nipples were not dark "like they should be." He attempted to make plastic molds of them, but failed.

Brudos's arrest was not easy, but he was arrogant and almost challenged police to find evidence to convict him. Several days after Brudos was identified when he called the girl at the dormitory, detectives came to visit him at his garage workshop. He freely let them come inside. They looked suspiciously at the strange hooks in the ceiling and the cord tied off in a knot exactly the same as the ones found on the ropes binding the bodies in the river. Brudos noticed the detectives eyeing the knot, and told them they could take the knot if they wanted—which is precisely what they did.

The fifteen-year-old girl that Brudos attempted to kidnap identified Brudos, and he was arrested on that charge. When police found a handgun in his vehicle, he was also charged with weapons offenses. But police did not have enough evidence to even search his garage—the photographs remained there while Brudos was being held on the other charges. At one point, Brudos even called Susan from jail and asked her to burn the container with the photographs and a bag of clothing, but she didn't.

Detectives skillfully interviewed Brudos, who at first followed his lawyer's advice and remained silent. In the end, however, Brudos needed to brag and he confessed to police. Subsequently his home and garage were searched and evidence recovered. He pleaded guilty and was sentenced to life.

His wife, Susan, was later charged as an accessory to murder and the children were taken away. She was found not guilty, recovered her children, and disappeared into obscurity. Brudos remained in love with Susan until the end.

Later Brudos appealed his conviction and is now eligible for parole. Today he denies that he committed any crimes and refuses to discuss them if asked. It is unlikely he will get released, but he keeps trying.

As of 1997, Brudos did not look like he had aged much since 1969. He was a model prisoner in the Oregon State Penitentiary, where he maintained the prison's record computer systems and installed the cable TV network. He was also in charge of repairing, stocking, and maintaining the vending machines. These are all highly privileged positions, a remarkable achievement considering he is a sex offender, on the lowest rung of a prison hierarchy. Sex offenders are often murdered by their fellow prisoners, many of whom have wives, girlfriends, and daughters of their own. In fact, several "accidents" have happened to Brudos in prison, but he refused to name any attackers. Inside a prison only one of two things count: intelligence or strength. Brudos has both, and perhaps with that rare combination he has managed to rise above his sex offender status. He is considered by guards as polite and not particularly dangerous—he wanders around the prison unsupervised.[117]

Ed Gein—The Original "Psycho"

Ed Gein, who killed in rural Wisconsin in the 1950s, is perhaps one of the more notorious hedonistic lust killers. He was the character on whom Robert Bloch's novel *Psycho* and Alfred Hitchcock's film of the same name were based, and part of the composite character of Buffalo Bill, the serial killer who skinned his victims in the novel and movie *The Silence of the Lambs*. Officially Gein is known to have killed two local women, which technically speaking excludes him from some definitions of serial killers that insist on three or more victims. But he was suspected in several other local homicides. He looked like a harmless farm-elf with one those flannel ear-flapped hats and his shirt buttoned to the top. His only reason to kill was that he needed to harvest human body parts—especially the husk of a female head and torso that he wore like a bodysuit.

Ed Gein lived alone on a farm after his mother and brother died and was known in the community as slightly odd but harmless. Nobody knew he had been robbing graves of freshly buried corpses for years. In 1954, however, he killed a local woman and dragged her body on a sled back to his farm. His crime was never detected.

In 1957, after Bernice Worden, a local town hardware store clerk, disappeared and somebody remembered seeing Gein in the premises earlier, the police visited his farm. They found a human heart in a pan on the stove; human entrails in the refrigerator; a shoebox with nine vulvas in it; another box containing four noses; a pair of stockings made from human skin; a soup bowl fashioned out of a human skull; a vest made from a female torso; skulls mounted on Ed Gein's bedposts; nine masks made out of the flesh of female faces, some hanging on the walls as decoration; a human scalp in a cereal box; a drum fashioned out of human skin; four chairs whose upholstery was made of human skin caked in dripping fat; various pieces of jewelry fashioned out of body parts; and ten female heads. Many of the artifacts had been rubbed down with oil to keep their luster; the human masks were made up with lipstick; a red ribbon was tied through one of the vulvas. In Ed Gein's summer kitchen, they found the headless and quartered corpse of Bernice Worden hanging from the rafters like a freshly killed deer.

Ed Gein had no particular compulsion to kill—what he needed was corpses. When during the hard winter months he could no longer dig into the frozen earth to uncover graves, he began killing to get his supply. Gein was certified insane and died in detention in 1984. One of his neighbors remarked, "Good old Ed. Kind of a loner and maybe a little bit odd with that sense of humor of his, but just the guy to call in to sit with the kiddies when me and the old lady want to go to the show." For years, children who visited Gein's house had been reporting to their parents that Gein had a collection of "shrunken heads" and strange masks hanging on walls, but the parents dismissed the stories as childish tales. None of the children ever reported Gein's behavior toward them as threatening or unusual in any way.

HEDONIST THRILL KILLERS

These types of offenders specifically derive sadistic pleasure from the *process* of killing—not the actual killing, but the acts leading up to it. To enjoy the act, they need to keep their victims immobilized and alive and aware of what is happening to them. They often kill in elaborate ritualized methods and sometimes take a respite and revive victims who lose consciousness before continuing their torture. (A surviving victim of Richard Cottingham testified that he wiped her face down with a cool, damp cloth between bouts of torture [see the Preface].) These sadistically driven killers derive pleasure from the pain and suffering their victims go through as they die. Once the victim is dead, they almost immediately lose interest. Postmortem mutilation and necrophiliac acts are not a frequent characteristic of this kind of murder.

Thrill murders often involve three distinct crime scenes—where the victim is captured, a highly controlled environment where the victim is tortured and killed, and finally a site where the victim is quickly dumped. Thrill killers are often attractive, intelligent, charismatic psychopathic personalities, relying on their charm to seduce and lure victims to their deaths. They may pose as police officers and "arrest" their victims. They are highly controlled and controlling, carefully selecting and stalking their desired victim type. They either maintain a carefully chosen location where they torture and murder their victims or customize a vehicle, frequently a van, for their killing. The body is often disposed of so as to deliberately lead investigators away from the killing scene.

Kenneth Bianchi and Angelo Buono— "The Hillside Stranglers"

Operating as a team, these two cousins terrorized Los Angeles between October 1977 and February 1978, committing a series of rapes and murders of women. Many of the victims were dumped on the sides of the Hollywood Hills, and the media dubbed the presumed killer "The Hillside Strangler." The police, however, knew because of seminal fluids and the positions of the bodies that two individuals were killing together. They withheld this information from the press.

The first victim was a black prostitute, Yolanda Washington, who walked the Sunset Boulevard area. Her naked body was found on October 18, 1977, on a hillside near the Ventura Freeway. Her murder merited a few lines in the newspapers in the back pages.

Fifteen-year-old Judy Miller went missing on October 31, 1977, in the Hollywood Boulevard area. She was a runaway, a drug user, and an occasional prostitute. Her body was found tossed in a flowerbed in La Crescenta. She had been vaginally and anally raped and traces of adhesive tape were found on her mouth, wrists, and ankles.

On November 6, 1977, the corpse of Lisa Teresa Kastin was found in Glendale. Unlike the other two victims, Kastin was not a runaway, drug user, or prostitute—she was working at two jobs: as a waitress and for her father's real estate company.

On November 10, 1977, the body of Jill Barcomb, eighteen, a convicted prostitute, was found off of Mulholland Drive. Kathleen Robertson, seventeen, also part of the Hollywood Boulevard street scene, was found on November 17. Kristina Weckler, twenty, an art student, was found on November 20—she had been tortured prior to being killed. On the same day, the police found the bodies of Sonja Johnson, fourteen, and Dollie Cepeda, twelve. They were last seen at a shopping mall together. On November 23, Jane King, twenty-eight, a struggling actress, was found in the Los Feliz extension area. November ended with the discovery of Lauren Wagner, eighteen, a business school student whose raped and strangled corpse was found off Cliff Drive. There was little doubt that the murders were linked: almost all the bodies were nude; raped by two individuals; previously bound, gagged, and handcuffed; and tossed off the sides of roads or highways, often at hill sites above Hollywood, out of view of any houses. The police were also worried that the killers might have been police officers or somebody very familiar with police procedures. Virtually no evidence accompanied the corpses, and they had been obviously carefully stripped to further reduce any possibility of forensic links.

On December 15, seventeen-year-old prostitute Kimberly Martin was dispatched by her call girl agency to the Tamarind Terrace apartments in Hollywood. She had joined the agency because she feared exposing herself on the streets with the Hillside Strangler on the loose. Her naked body was found on a deserted lot near Los Angeles City Hall. When the police checked the apartment she had been dispatched to, they found it vacant and broken into. The killers had placed the call from a library pay phone nearby and then waited for their victim in the apartment.

The last known victim was discovered on February 17, 1978, when somebody reported seeing a car halfway down a cliff off Angeles Crest Highway. When police investigated the vehicle, they found in the trunk the raped and sodomized nude body of Cindy Hudspeth, a twenty-year-old student and part-time waitress.

Then the murders ceased as mysteriously as they began.

•   •   •

Eleven months later, in Bellingham, Washington, some 1,000 miles north of Los Angeles, Karen Mandic and Diane Wilder, two university students, disappeared.

Mandic worked part-time in a store during the evenings, and the previous summer she had made friends with a security guard who had worked there for a short time. He was a friendly, popular, and handsome young man who went on to become a supervisor with a Bellingham security company. His name was Kenneth Bianchi and he was twenty-seven years old. He lived with a local girl named Kelli Boyd and they had an infant son on whom Kenneth doted.

One day in January, Bianchi mentioned to Karen Mandic that he had a great opportunity for her to make a hundred dollars for two hours' work. An alarm system in a house that his company was watching needed repair. The owners were away on a trip. Karen would be paid a hundred dollars to house-sit for two hours while the alarm was disconnected for repairs. Karen asked if she could bring her roommate, Diane Wilder, on the job. Of course she could, Bianchi told her. Only one thing: She must keep the job a secret until after it was done—nobody must know, not even her boyfriend. Karen however, told her boyfriend.

Karen Mandic and Diane Wilder were found raped and strangled in the trunk of their car parked on a dead-end street in Bellingham. The police didn't take long to make the connection to Kenneth Bianchi, and when his security company reported no knowledge of any alarm repair scheduled for the house in question, but the keys to the house missing, Bianchi was arrested.

As police gathered physical evidence from the house where the girls were lured to and murdered and from Kenneth Bianchi's apartment and his vehicle, there was little doubt that he had committed the crime. Yet nobody could quite believe it: Kelli Boyd maintained that Bianchi was a gentle lover and caring father to their son; the security company, run by a former police officer, reported that Bianchi was one of their best employees, a popular guard who was often requested by clients; and friends came forward maintaining that Bianchi was too gentle to have committed such brutal crimes.

The chief of police in Bellingham was a former Los Angeles–area police officer. During the Hillside stranglings, one of the victims was the daughter of a man he knew, and he had spoken to him at length about her murder. Through his contacts in Los Angeles, the chief was familiar with the series of murders there. Something about this murder reminded him of the crimes there. One of the first questions he put to Kelli was about Kenneth Bianchi's background. Kelli replied that she had met him in Los Angeles about eighteen months ago when she lived there. After she had the baby, she moved back home to Bellingham and Kenneth Bianchi had followed in May of last year—three months after the Hillside stranglings had ceased.

Within hours, the chief was on the phone to Los Angeles. The links began to come together quickly the more Kelli was interviewed. Kelli and Bianchi once lived at the Tamarind building where the call girl was lured to a vacant apartment. Kelli reported that at one point they did not have a phone, and that Kenneth placed phone calls from a pay phone in the Glendale library—the same pay phone used to make the appointment for the call girl. When Kelli first met Bianchi, he lived on Garfield Avenue, where two of the Hillside victims were last seen. As the evidence began to gather, Kenneth Bianchi was charged in the Los Angeles stranglings as well.

Bianchi claimed that he could not remember committing any crimes, and psychiatrists were called in to assess his claims. Under hypnosis, Bianchi began to reveal other personalities that were allegedly living inside him—including one named "Steve Walker." It was "Steve" who identified Bianchi's accomplice—his forty-four-year-old cousin in Los Angeles, Angelo Bouno.

Under hypnosis, "Steve" emerged, claiming that Kenneth was a stupid and mild little man, that "Steve" hated women and made Kenneth commit the murders. "Steve Walker" described in detail how Angelo Buono and Kenneth Bianchi posed as plainclothes policemen to lure women into their car. The prostitutes and runaways were "arrested." The two girls at the shopping mall were spotted shoplifting by Bianchi and Buono and were also "arrested."

One woman was lured out of her apartment when Bianchi called at her door and told her an accident had happened with her car in the street. She had met Bianchi before and did not hesitate to follow him out. Many of the victims were taken back to Angelo Buono's upholstery shop in

Glendale and raped and strangled there, before their bodies were stripped of all clothing and jewelry and tossed on hillsides by the two killers.

Another woman came to the shop to buy some seat covers for her car—she was overpowered, raped, and murdered. She was the last victim who was found in the trunk of her car, which was pushed down a hillside. Another victim was waiting for a bus when Kenneth Bianchi struck up a casual conversation with her and told her he and his partner were police officers at the end of their shift. The handsome Bianchi would be glad to give her a ride home if she did not mind taking a short detour while he dropped his partner off home first. The woman gladly went along. When they got to Buono's house, she was handcuffed and quickly hustled inside.

At one point, Buono and Bianchi "arrested" twenty-seven-year-old Catherine Lorre, the daughter of actor Peter Lorre, who portrayed a serial killer in the classic 1931 Fritz Lang movie *M*. When they found a picture of the woman sitting on Peter Lorre's lap among her identification, they let her go. Later she told police that they had approached her, flashing L.A. police badges (allegedly stolen by Buono from the set of a TV show).

Bianchi had almost convinced a board of six psychiatrists that he was legally insane and suffering from multiple personalities. The police, however, discovered that Bianchi owned a large collection of psychiatric textbooks and was an "amateur" psychiatrist who had actually opened a psychological counseling office in Los Angeles. It folded quickly when he could get only one patient. Bianchi had attempted to open the office with other legitimate psychiatrists and advertised seeking fellow tenants. One of the psychiatrists who responded to Bianchi and sent him a résumé was a doctor named Steve Walker, the police discovered. Bianchi then used the résumé to secure a copy of Walker's diploma, which he altered by inserting his own name. The "Steve Walker" that existed within Bianchi was supposed to have existed since his childhood, but Bianchi had received the real Steve Walker's résumé only a year previously.

Finally one psychiatrist broke through Bianchi's game. He hypnotized Bianchi and told him to hallucinate that his lawyer was in the room. Bianchi immediately reached out into empty space and shook hands with the nonexisting lawyer. The problem is that while hypnotized subjects can be made to hallucinate people and objects, they do not hallucinate physical contact with them. Bianchi was obviously pretending to be hypnotized and his insanity plea was rejected.

Kenneth Bianchi was born in 1951 in Rochester, New York, to a seventeen-year-old alcoholic who gave him up for adoption; thus there was a possibility of prenatal brain damage. He was adopted at age three months by Frances Bianchi, an overprotective, anxious, and hysterical woman. There is a rich record of psychiatric and medical reports on Bianchi as a child, who was constantly brought to doctors by his mother for various imagined complaints. One that was not imagined was his tendency to wet his pants and bed, a common childhood symptom among serial killers. A medical report on Kenneth when he was seven years old reads as follows:

> He had been admitted to the hospital on 12-15-58 with a diagnosis of genitourinary problems. His diagnoses now were: 1. Diverticulum, 2. Horseshoe kidney and 3. Transient hypertension. Dr. Townsend said that although these were physical problems for this boy, he also had many emotional problems. He proved to be "a little minx" on the floor. Everything went fine during the day except during visiting hours when his mother was there and then everything was wrong, especially for his mother's benefit. He would have one complaint after another and Mrs. Bianchi would take these up with any available nurse or doctor who happened to be handy. Having this child hospitalized proved to be a trying experience and Dr. Townsend wondered if his social or home environment could be considered at all adequate.

A doctor's report dated March 13, 1959, stated:

> The impression is gained that this mother is herself a seriously disturbed person, and her discussion about the handling of the child by various medical men indicates some apparent paranoid trends. It is apparent that she had been strongly controlling toward this boy, keeping him out of school very frequently, particularly in the last several months, because of her fear that he would develop a sore throat and begin to wet. It is not clear whether this mother can carry through successfully with a psychiatric evaluation, but it is felt that diagnostic study should be offered, in order to

clarify more fully the degree of personality disturbance on the part of the boy, the boy's presenting symptom, and the nature of the family relationships, including the degree of disturbance on the part of the mother in particular.

When Kenneth was twelve years old, another report stated:

. . . Kenneth is a deeply hostile boy who has extremely dependent needs which his mother fulfills. He depends upon his mother for his very survival and expends a great deal of energy keeping his hostility under control and under cover. He is very eager for other relationships and uses a great deal of denial in handling his own feelings. For example, he says that his mother and father are the best parents in the world.

He is a very lonely boy who wants to move away from his mother. He is very constricted however, and feels being hurt if he should move away from her. Mother seems to allow him only one friend in the house. There seems some basic confusion around his own identity. He tries very hard to placate his mother, but she always seems to be dissatisfied. To sum up, Dr. Dowling said that he is a severely repressed boy who is very anxious and very lonely. He felt that the only outlet whereby he could somehow get back at his mother was through his psychosomatic complaints. Dr. Dowling felt that without this defense of the use of his somatic complaints he might very well be a severely disturbed boy.

It is interesting how sparse and few are the mentions of Kenneth Bianchi's father—it is as if he did not exist. In the FBI sexual homicide study, 66 percent of sexual and serial killers interviewed reported their mothers as the dominant parent. Kenneth Bianchi's father was almost never home, holding down several jobs. When Kenneth was thirteen, his father dropped dead from overwork with a heart attack. Kenneth was apparently devastated by his death. The psychiatric reports speak for themselves. Kenneth Bianchi was one very angry child who was suppressing his anger under a mask of friendliness and compliance.

Some argue that the formation of a serial killer is rooted to gender identification involving a boy's ability to successfully negotiate his masculine autonomy from his mother. When a boy cannot achieve this autonomy or when there is no solid foundation for him from which to negotiate this autonomy, a sense of rage develops in the child, and he subsequently carries the anger into adolescence and adulthood, focusing it on females.

Kenneth Bianchi's high school history seems fairly untroubled. He was athletic and popular with girls. In 1971, Bianchi married, but his young wife left him for another man after eight months. Friends recall that Bianchi seemed to have trouble perceiving the reality of his marriage. During this time, Bianchi studied police sciences at college and worked as an ambulance attendant. He hoped to become a police officer. After his breakup with his wife, however, Bianchi led a depressed and lonely life.

Between 1971 and 1973, three girls were strangled in Rochester while on their way to do grocery shopping for their mothers. After Bianchi was identified as the Hillside Strangler, police in Rochester suspected that Bianchi might have been behind these killings—but they remain unsolved.

By 1975, Bianchi's mother was remarried and Kenneth had moved to Los Angeles to seek a new life. He moved in with his mother's nephew, his cousin, Angelo Buono.

Buono was forty at the time, the father of seven children, three times divorced on grounds of cruelty—he had a predilection for violent anal sex. He had an upholstery shop behind a small house in which he lived. Buono also seemed to attract a stream of young runaway girls.

At some point, Buono and Bianchi decided to get into the prostitution business. They began to lure young runaways into drugs and prostitution. As Hollywood was, for obvious reasons, a mecca for runaway teenagers from all over the United States, Buono and Bianchi had no problems finding suitable girls to pimp. However, they ran into several problems. One girl told a client of such horrific abuse at the hands of Buono and Bianchi, that he refused to let the girl return to them. Buono and Bianchi threatened the man, who responded by sending Hell's Angels bikers to threaten Buono. Buono was thoroughly terrorized.

Then Buono and Bianchi paid another prostitute for an alleged list of clients who regularly used prostitutes. The list turned out to be worthless. Shortly after this episode, Yolanda Washington, the first victim, a professional prostitute, was found strangled.

In the meantime, Bianchi had moved out into his own apartment and met Kelli Boyd, who worked as a secretary at the time. They became lovers, moved in together, and eventually had a child. Kelli recalls that Bianchi often went to his cousin's upholstery shop to "play cards," but she never accompanied him—she did not like Buono, who appeared to her as if he hated women. Otherwise, she remembers Kenneth as a childish and irresponsible man, but gentle and loving. She had not the slightest suspicion of his double life and was not convinced of it for the longest time, even after Bianchi's arrest.

After what was at that time Los Angeles's longest and most expensive criminal trial, Angelo Buono was convicted as the other Hillside Strangler. Because Bianchi had confessed to his crimes and testified against Buono, he was spared the death penalty. In the case of Buono, the jury felt reluctant to give him the death penalty while his partner got life. Buono denied having any involvement with the crimes to the end, but evidence linking him and Bianchi was fairly conclusive.

Kenneth Bianchi's story did not quite end, however, after his arrest. Bianchi seemed to have a strange hold over women, which only increased after he was accused of killing a string of women. Veronica Compton, a twenty-four-year-old fledgling playwright whose work was obsessed with sadomasochism and serial murder, began to write to Bianchi while he was in jail. Eventually she went to see him and they began a relationship. In the summer of 1980, Bianchi showed Compton how he strangled his victims and slipped her a sample of his sperm secreted in the finger of a rubber glove. Compton then flew to Bellingham and lured a woman to her motel room where she attempted to strangle her. This was in an era before DNA testing, and the plan was to kill the woman in the same way Bianchi killed the others and make it look as if the killer were still at large by leaving a sperm trace similar to Bianchi's. The victim, however, was more powerful than Compton and managed to escape. Compton was arrested shortly afterward. While in jail, Compton fell into a relationship through letters with another Los Angeles serial killer—Doug Clark, one of the Sunset Boulevard Killers. Compton was eventually convicted of premeditated attempted murder and sentenced to life imprisonment with no possibility of parole until 1994. She is currently an inmate in the Washington Correctional Center for Women and, in 2002, published a book, *Eating the Ashes: Seeking Rehabilitation Within the U.S. Penal System,* in which, according to the publisher, "she relates heart-rending images of lives in disarray and describes programs that have been successful in producing rehabilitation."[118]

It is interesting to note that Angelo Buono was the dominant partner of the two, and Kenneth Bianchi spent much of his energy attempting to

please and impress his older cousin. Yet Buono is not known to have committed any murders before Kenneth arrived in Los Angeles or after Kenneth's
departure for Bellingham. Buono, however, is said to have kept Kenneth's
enthusiasm in check and made sure that the crimes were so carefully committed that there was no chance of their being arrested. Eventually, Buono
grew tired of Bianchi and suggested that Bianchi go to Bellingham to join
Kelli. There Bianchi attempted to commit two murders on his own and was
quickly arrested. Without Bianchi, Buono would not kill, while without
Buono, Bianchi could not kill efficiently. That often is the interdependent
nature of serial killer partners.

POWER/CONTROL KILLERS

Power/control serial killers are highly organized and closely related to
sadistic thrill killers, with the difference that causing pain and suffering is
not the primary motive for their offense; controlling and dominating the victim is (but they may use pain as a method of control and torture as a token
of it). The actual pleasure of controlling the victim may begin before the victim even realizes it as the serial killer manipulates and seduces the victim.

These serial killers are often charming, charismatic, and intelligent,
gradually taking control over their victims before springing a physical capture. Again, they often pick a certain "type" of victim, but fetishistic elements are less important. The murder is often the ultimate expression of
the serial killer's control over his victim—but unlike the thrill killer, the
power/control killer does not necessarily lose his interest once the victim is
dead. The control often continues into death with the offender keeping the
corpses near him, sometimes in his home or in some safe place where they
can be revisited. Sometimes various postmortem sexual acts, mutilation,
and necrophilia also occur with the power/control killer.

John Wayne Gacy—"The Killer Clown"

On December 11, 1978, in Chicago, Elizabeth Piest went to pick up her
fifteen-year-old son, Robert, from a drugstore where he worked. It was her
birthday and a big party had been planned. Robert asked her to wait inside the store while he went out to the parking lot to speak with a con-

struction contractor about a summer job that would pay twice as much as he was currently earning. Robert had met the contractor when he came by to inspect the premises for some possible renovations. That was the last Elizabeth Piest ever saw of her son. He never returned to the store.

After the mother reported the disappearance, police went out to interview the contractor: John Wayne Gacy, age thirty-six, a short, chubby man with a double chin and a dark mustache. He was a successful building contractor, well known and respected in the community. He had been voted Jaycee (Junior Chamber of Commerce) "Man of the Year" in three different cities, led the Polish Constitution Day Parade one year in Chicago, and escorted President Carter's wife, Rosalynn, on one of her visits to the city. In his spare time, Gacy entertained sick children at a hospital, dressed as a clown named "Patches" or "Pogo." His act for the kids included the "handcuff trick," in which he cuffed a child to a bed and pretended to lose the key, and the "rope trick," in which he lassoed kids while they squealed with delight. He had lived in the same house since 1972, and neighbors described him as a helpful and friendly man who always decorated the house with elaborately strung Christmas lights. He shoveled snow for some of his elderly neighbors. He had been twice married and divorced and had two children.

Gacy would have been a very unlikely suspect had he not denied knowing Piest or being anywhere near the parking lot where the boy disappeared. When the police challenged him by saying that they had witnesses who saw him with Piest that day, Gacy admitted that perhaps he had been in the parking lot, but had nothing to do with the boy.

The police checked Gacy's records and discovered that he had been convicted of forcible sodomy of a minor in Iowa back in 1968, a crime for which he served eighteen months of a ten-year prison sentence. In 1970, similar charges were brought against him in Chicago, but were dropped when the youth failed to appear in court. In March 1978, a twenty-seven-year-old man complained to police that Gacy had invited him to smoke some marijuana in his car and then clapped a chloroform-soaked rag over his face. He said that he had been driven to Gacy's house and then whipped and repeatedly raped by him. Afterward Gacy released the man. The authorities could not secure enough evidence to bring Gacy to trial and the investigation lapsed.

Investigators surrounded Gacy with a tight ring of surveillance. At first Gacy challenged the police, telling the officers following him that their superiors were idiots and inviting them out for lunch. He would playfully tell the surveillance team his destination, and hung out his Christmas lights as usual at his house. But as the days progressed, Gacy began to show signs of stress—he stopped shaving and started drinking heavily and shouting at people. He hired two lawyers and filed a lawsuit charging the Chicago police with harassment and preventing him from conducting his business.

At one point, Gacy invited two detectives into his house for coffee, and one of them asked to use his bathroom as a ruse to poke around and see what he could find. The detective found nothing in the bathroom, but detected a distinct odor coming from the drain familiar to any experienced homicide investigator—the smell of decomposing human remains.

On December 21, the police searched his house and accused Gacy of holding Piest in it. Gacy denied the charge, but inexplicably admitted that in 1972 he had had a homosexual lover whom he killed in self-defense. He had buried the body in concrete in his garage, he told the police, and led them to the site, spray-painting a mark on the floor where the body lay. As the police searched the house, they found a trap door leading to a crawl space beneath Gacy's house. There they discovered three decomposing corpses and parts of others. Gacy was arrested while the police began tearing his house apart. They uncovered the bodies of twenty-eight males between ages fifteen and twenty. Gacy admitted to killing another five and dumping their bodies into the river. Later, Gacy retracted his confession, claiming that some unidentified other person, who had a key to his house, had put the bodies there to frame him. Gacy said his worst crime was perhaps running a cemetery without a license.

John Gacy was born in Chicago in 1942. His mother was Danish and his father was Polish. The father was a heavy drinker and beat Gacy mercilessly. Gacy also claims that at age five he was molested by a teenage girl and by a male construction contractor at age eight. When Gacy was eleven he was struck in the head by a swing, causing a blot clot in his brain that needed treatment. As a juvenile Gacy committed numerous petty thefts and apparently engaged in homosexual sex.

Gacy was relatively intelligent and graduated from business college. He began working as a shoe salesman and in 1964 married his first wife, whose father owned several Kentucky Fried Chicken restaurant franchises. Gacy became a manager in one of his father-in-law's restaurants. Gacy had two children, a son and a daughter, and became well known in the community in Iowa. The marriage ended in 1968 when at age twenty-six, Gacy was suddenly arrested for handcuffing one of his juvenile employees and sodomizing him. Gacy received a sentence of ten years but was such a model prisoner that he was released after eighteen months. In the meantime, his wife divorced him.

Upon his release in 1970, Gacy left Iowa and returned to Chicago, where he went into the contracting business. He was charged that year in another sexual assault on a youth, but the charges were dropped. After his 1978 arrest, Gacy confessed that he had committed his first murder in 1972, when he brought a man to his house from the bus station for sex. Gacy said that they argued and the man attacked him with a knife. Gacy claimed that he killed him in self-defense and buried him in a crawl space under the house.

Later that year, Gacy married for a second time. His wife, her three children, and her mother all moved in with Gacy. When his wife was not home, Gacy lured youths to his house, raped them, murdered them, and buried their bodies under the house. His wife and mother-in-law lived with Gacy for about four years and constantly complained of bad odors in the house. Gacy explained that the smells must have been coming from "dead rats." When his wife was not home, he poured concrete over the corpses in an attempt to cover the odors. Gacy also told authorities that he learned to stuff rags into the corpses' mouths to prevent reeking body fluids from escaping.

When Gacy's wife asked about wallets and clothing she was finding belonging to young men, Gacy shouted at her to mind her own business. He progressively became impotent with his wife and abusive. She finally moved out in February 1976 and subsequently divorced him. Gacy must have been relieved to see her go, because by then he was heavily addicted to killing.

From the testimony of several youths who had encountered Gacy, police learned that he cruised the streets looking for gay prostitutes or runaway kids or offered youths work with his construction business. Several youths testified that they went to his house for "job interviews," during which Gacy showed them pictures of him with the president's wife and offered to demonstrate to them his "handcuff trick." It appears that only those youths who refused to participate in the trick survived to tell their stories.

Gacy very gradually ensnared his victims. He plied them with marijuana and alcohol and began by showing them heterosexual porn movies. He then shifted to gay porn. If the guest did not object, Gacy then did his "hand-cuff trick." Once he had his victims imprisoned, he sodomized them. Gacy developed an elaborate ritual of torture in which he submerged his victims in a bathtub full of water with a plastic bag over their head and revived them before they died. Eventually they either died from the treatment or Gacy strangled them with his "rope trick." He looped a cord around the victim's throat, attached it to a stick, and slowly twisted the stick, tighten-ing the noose. Gacy confessed that as he killed his victims, he recited aloud the Twenty-Third Psalm: "The Lord is my shepherd . . . Even though I walk through the valley of the shadow of death, I will fear no evil . . ."

Curiously, the more Gacy killed, the higher a profile he kept in the community. His Pogo the Clown period was during the height of his kill-ing. He threw an annual block party for all the neighbors and plowed all the sidewalks in the neighborhood free of snow without being asked. A lo-cal Democratic Party official recalled, "He was always available for any chore, washing windows, setting up chairs for meetings—even fixing some-one's leaky faucet. I don't know anyone who didn't like him."

At one point after his arrest, Gacy claimed that there existed within him an "Other Guy tilt" who committed the murders. Tim Cahill writes:

> Maybe drugs and alcohol set loose the Other Guy tilt to his personality . . . There was, John told the docs, a lot of the Old Man in the Other Guy tilt. Now, take the Other Guy tilt during a blackout and apply it to some greedy little hustler. You would get an angry, punishing father, an irrational alco-holic father who had to strike out . . . The corpse would be found in the morning with the dawning of sobriety, and it would be hidden in a father's hiding place, in the basement, to be covered over and forgotten, like a fa-ther's hapless drunken ravings.[119]

Five bodies, including Robert Piest's, were never recovered. Gacy said he dumped them in the river. Because so many of Gacy's victims were run-away youths from different cities, police and forensic anthropologists spent several years attempting to identify the twenty-nine bodies recov-ered from Gacy's house. The police managed to link names with some of the victims, but eight remain unidentified to this day.

FBI profiler Robert Ressler, who interviewed Gacy after his conviction, states that Gacy told him that his victims were "worthless little queers and punks." Ressler challenged him on that—was he not a homosexual himself? Gacy responded that his victims were runaways while he was a successful businessman. Moreover, Gacy explained that he was too busy to wine and dine and romance women—he had to settle for quick sex with males.

Gacy said, "Everything they've got on me is circumstantial. Do you realize that there's not one person can put me with one of the victims before, during or after the crime . . . If you want to say I slept in the same house with a dead body, OK, fine, I'll buy that—but in the same room, no! And besides, the dead won't bother you—it's the living you've got to worry about."

Gacy lived on for another fifteen years, often granting interviews and receiving visitors. He became a jailhouse artist and several galleries exhibited his primitive paintings, many of Pogo the Clown. Gacy eventually set up a 900 number that people could call and hear a message he recorded proclaiming his innocence. He nearly married for a third time in 1986, one of the many women who wrote and visited him. John Wayne Gacy was executed by lethal injection on May 10, 1994, after all his appeals were exhausted.

Recent Revisions in Serial Killer Categories

The problem with all the classifications described so far is that the FBI system of organized/disorganized/mixed is proving to be too vague, with "mixed" being frequently a meaningless category. The visionary/missionary/hedonist/power-control categories are helpful in assessing motive, but do not contribute much to elements relating to the offender's identity. None of these categories, including those in the FBI-authored *Crime Classification Manual,* are actually used to classify crimes by any major North American homicide computerized tracking system such as the FBI's own VICAP; the Homicide Investigation Tracking System (HITS) in Washington, Oregon, and Idaho; or the Canadian Violent Crime Linkage Analysis System (ViCLAS).[120]

The most recently proposed new classification system comes from renowned criminologist Dr. Robert Keppel, a veteran of fifty serial murder investigations including those of Ted Bundy, the Atlanta child murders, and the Green River killings.[121] His system is focused on classifying sexual "signature" murderers, both single and serial, and is based on categories first developed in the 1980s by Roy Hazelwood and Ann Burgess for the FBI's classification of rapists. For investigative purposes, Keppel proposes the following classification of sexual serial killers divided into four categories: power-assertive, power-reassurance, anger-retaliatory, and anger-excitation.

POWER-ASSERTIVE KILLERS

Power-assertive killers commit crimes where a rape is planned but the murder is not, and the victim might be male or female. The killing occurs as a result of increasing aggression for the purpose of controlling the victim. The central motive to the crime is the assertion of a masculine power over a female or male victim. (Remember, sex and desire are actually low priorities in many rapes, which are mostly about aggression and control.)

These types of killers have a learning curve in which they evolve and improve their methods based on their previous experiences. The selection of victims is focused toward strangers who are taken by surprise when opportunity allows. Either the victims are found in the street or the perpetrator seeks them out in their homes or places of employment. If the victim is abducted on the street, the body is usually dumped elsewhere from where the victim was killed. If the victim is killed in his or her home, then the body is usually left there undisturbed by posing or postmortem mutilation. Clothing is torn off the victim and he or she may show signs of beating and pummeling. A weapon is brought to the crime scene, often a knife or rope, and is an important part of the masculine identity the offender forms for himself.

The degree of violence unleashed on the victim is governed by what the offender believes is short of perverse or deviant—therefore, mutilation of the victim is rare. Traces of ejaculate are commonly found at a power-assertive crime scene, with the perpetrator sometimes committing multiple rapes prior to killing the victim. After the murder, the offender maintains no links to the victim and leaves behind an organized crime scene carefully cleaned of forensic evidence. The killer feels that his self-image is beyond suspicion in a crime of this type and he emotionally detaches himself from it, allowing him to quickly repeat it. At the same time his need for power and recognition requires that he somehow be "credited" or suspected of the crime. He may reveal or hint at his role in the crime to friends, co-workers, cellmates, or even police.

Power-assertive killers are usually in their early twenties. They are obsessed with projecting a masculine image in a primitive kind of manner, while internally they are highly insecure in their masculinity. They often are body-builders, display tattoos, drive powerful well-maintained vehicles, carry weapons, participate in martial arts, and maintain a confident body posture and form. They are aggressive, arrogant, and condescending to others and function on the borderline of being loners. They are not perceived as "team players" by others. They may have a history of failed marriages and relationships and might be remembered by their former spouses as "control freaks."

They are typically high school dropouts with a limited sense of masculinity, which means that their taste in pornography is unimaginative— usually limited to traditional "soft" erotica of the type found in *Playboy* or *Penthouse*. They may have a military record but it will be poor and frequently terminated early because of a lack of "team" social skills. Their criminal record may show power-demonstrative crimes such as robbery, theft, and burglary.

POWER-REASSURANCE KILLERS

With power-reassurance killers, the rape is again planned while the murder is not. The main motivation of these types of killers is the realization of a seduction and conquest fantasy. The offender seeks from the victim reassurance that he is "pleasing" them or is "better" than other lovers. The murder occurs when the victim's behavior contradicts or interrupts the fantasy. The offender either becomes enraged or coldly kills the victim and then reintroduces the fantasy into the encounter. Postmortem mutilation and necrophilia sometimes result as the offender insists on realizing his fantasy. The murder occurs when a rape fails.

The power-reassurance killer selects and stalks his victims carefully, and sometimes they are a casual acquaintance or a neighbor. The victim is frequently ten or fifteen years younger or older than the offender. A same-age victim might be chosen if he or she has some type of mental or physical handicap. Central in the offender's mind is his fantasy and victim vulnerability and not a victim "type." He will custom-fit his fantasy to whatever victim he selects.

The offender uses threats and intimidation to gain control of the victim. He has a weapon learning curve—often bringing none to the first offense; a gun that he will not discharge to the second; and a knife to the third, which he may use to actually kill the victim. During the initiation of the rape, the offender might be described as polite and gentlemanly, asking if the victim is comfortable and enjoying himself or herself—the so-called "gentleman rapist." He is seeking reassurance of his sexual competency, and if he does not get it, he becomes violent and lethal.

Once the victim is killed, the offender may attempt to prolong the fantasy through necrophilia, mutilation, and ritualistic acts. Ejaculate is usually not found at the crime scene because the rape was unsuccessful and the fantasy interrupted. Again, as the killer finds some satisfaction in the postmortem acts and rituals, he is reinforced to repeat his crimes and increase his lethality in subsequent acts. He may take souvenirs and collect newspaper clippings in an attempt to maintain his fantasy relationship with the victim.

The offender is frequently in his mid twenties and has a fantasy life so intense and contradictory to reality that he may appear emotionally disturbed or unintelligent. Feeding on fantasy, he lives alone in isolation with no male or female friends and is perceived as a weird loner. He is incapable of the social interaction required to develop a sexual relationship or romantic partnership. He deeply fears rejection and prefers to focus his sexual energy through fantasy and substitute solitary sexual acts such as window peeping, fondling of clothing, pyromania, or kleptomania. He may have an extensive police record relating to these activities. His fantasies often emerge at a very young age and are buttressed by other environmental challenges and difficulties in his childhood.

He usually completes his education but is perceived as an underachiever. His military record likewise will show a history of an obedient but undistinguished soldier.

He is immature and lives life as an observer, not a participant. He lacks self-confidence and with his parents may live on a subsistence-level income or be employed in minimum-wage menial jobs. Familiarity is crucial to his confidence and he often works, lives, and commits his crimes in the same neighborhood. His most common means of transportation is walking, but if he owns a car, it will be run-down and poorly maintained. He leaves behind a disorganized crime scene.

ANGER-RETALIATORY KILLERS

With anger-retaliatory killers, both the rape and the murder are planned. The murder often involves "overkill"—excessive violence beyond what is necessary to kill the victim, who is usually female. The primary motive driving the killer is his need to avenge, get even with, or retaliate against a female, or her substitute, who somehow offended the killer in his perception. The rage is often inspired by a female with power presently or in the past over the offender—his mother, wife, teacher, or work supervisor. The rage is triggered when either the same female or another, in his perception, criticizes, scolds, humiliates, rejects, belittles, or somehow disrespects him, but the focus of his attack will be most likely an unsuspecting substitute victim.

The substitute victim will probably be the same age as or older than the offender and was previously selected as a potential victim. The offender would have seen the victim in the vicinity of his neighborhood or his place of work and noted her address and vulnerability level. Once angered, the offender usually walks to the crime scene to attack his preselected symbolic victim. If the offender uses a vehicle, he may drive to the scene but walk the last two or three hundred feet.

On some occasions, the anger-retaliatory killer may strike at the actual person who has angered him. In these cases, the victim is almost always younger than the offender or a child.

The offender may use some kind of ruse to get into the victim's premises and then stage a confrontation with the victim, acting inappropriately to elicit a negative response from the victim. He unleashes a blitz attack, striking the victim in the face and mouth. As the attack escalates, he may use some object found at the scene to pummel or stab the victim. Ejaculate might not be found at the scene, as the primary focus of the attack is the assault on the victim. The offender's age, emotional maturity, and experience govern whether he will be able to get an erection during the attack.

The assault will continue until the killer's anger is satiated, even if the victim is long dead. When he is finished, the killer will position the body in a submissive pose: on its side away from the door, facedown, or with something covering the eyes. The crime scene is disorganized and the murder weapon is often found near the victim. Before leaving, the offender frequently takes some souvenir or token from the victim. He experiences no sense of guilt because he transfers blame for the murder to the victim and easily slips into a serial pattern of offenses.

The anger-retaliatory killer is usually in his mid to late twenties, impulsive, quick-tempered, and egotistically self-centered. He may be perceived as having an explosive personality. He is not a loner, but maintains shallow social relations, sometimes only limited to drinking buddies, and rarely reveals anything about himself to them. He may play team contact sports.

He feels both dependent and resistant in his relationships with women and often uses violence to resolve the conflict. If he is married, there will probably be a history of spousal abuse and extra marital relations. He may have a police record reflecting impulsive offenses such as assault, reckless driving, and threatening.

He is sexually frustrated and frequently impotent and has highly eroticized his anger, linking it to his sexual inadequacy. He does not consume pornography but he may exhibit some curiosity toward soft erotica like *Playboy*.

He had disciplinary problems in high school and is frequently an underachiever or dropout. Likewise, if he has a military record, there are often disciplinary problems and early termination of service. In general there is a history of conflicts with authority.

ANGER-EXCITATION KILLERS

Anger-excitation killers plan both the rape and the murder. The primary motive is to inflict pain and terror on the male or female victim for the sexual gratification of the perpetrator. The crime is characterized by prolonged torture and mutilation of the victim, generally before death. The murder itself is on a lower priority for the offender, who focuses on the process leading up to it. The offender has highly specialized and elaborate fantasies focused on his need to express power and control. The crime is highly ritualized and often played out in a tightly scripted scenario, which evolves and is perfected victim by victim.

The victim is often a stranger who fits into an ideal victim type for the perpetrator: a student, a prostitute, a child, an elderly person, a "slut," a nurse, and so on. The offender might alternatively show partiality in his victim preference: blond hair, long legs, blue eyes, small stature. There might be fetishistic elements as well: a type of shoe worn by the victim, color of clothing, and so on. The offender often approaches, seduces, and charms the victim. He maintains the ruse until he can isolate the victim from safety. At that point, the offender's behavior vacillates between friendly and threatening until he entirely drops his mask. He may very calmly and matter-of-factly tell the victim, "I am now going to rape and torture you for three days and then I am going to kill you slowly and painfully," to savor the fear in the victim.

Once the offender senses the fear, he begins a highly ritualized session of torture and degradation based on a complex of fantasies that the offender might have developed since early childhood. The offender may attempt to rape the victim and ejaculate at the moment of the death.

After death, there are frequently secondary sexual assaults: insertion of objects, mutilation, and harvesting of body parts. The body might be left in a bizarre state of dress or undress, reflecting some fetishistic focus. Items of clothing might be cut away, taken, or found neatly folded nearby. Often clothing, body parts, or other souvenirs are taken away and used for repetitive sessions of compulsive masturbation by the offender. It could be said that the offense continues in the offender's comfort zone, far away from the victim's body, and does not cease until the offender is emotionally satiated and completes his masturbatory arc.

The anger-excitation killer maintains a "murder kit," consisting of a murder weapon, restraints, and instruments of torture, which he brings with him to the crime scene and carefully packs up and takes away afterward for safekeeping. The offender is highly alert to leaving behind possible forensic evidence, and frequently moves the body from the murder scene to another location and conceals it. He tends to commit his offenses and dump the bodies away from his residence or place of work. He may, however, then interject himself into the search for the victim or the police investigation of the murder in order to stimulate himself further.

The anger-excitation killer's age is variable but usually he is a mature individual who often commits his first murder by age thirty-five. He is often a physically attractive, bright, and seemingly social individual. He appears to be law-abiding and conventional. He may frequently have a good marriage and be a doting father to his children, and be gainfully employed in a position requiring minimal supervision, or he may be self-employed in a semiskilled trade such as carpentry or mechanics. He shows signs of being compulsively organized and may have had several years of college education or graduated. If he has military service, his record is usually good and he may have been selected as a potential candidate for officer training.

Essentially, the anger-excitation killer lives a double life, carefully separating his conventional life from his fantasy-driven one. He probably maintains a private space where he keeps his murder kit, souvenirs, and other fetishistic tokens—a kind of dark secret chamber of horrors in the basement, the attic, a closet, the garage, or some nearby abandoned structure. He will be a consumer of sadistic pornographic literature and imagery.

Offense Distribution of the Proposed Categories

In October 1995 there were 41,584 inmates in the Michigan corrections system, of which 14 percent were serving terms for homicide (5,928 killers). Of those, 2,476 offenders—42 percent of all the murderers—had committed sexual homicides. Unfortunately the study did not differentiate between single and serial offenders.[122] The distribution among categories indicated that power-assertive offenders consisted of 38 percent of sexual killers, anger-retaliatory 34 percent, power-reassurance 21 percent, and anger-excitation a mere 7 percent.

Other Classifications and Typologies

While the types described previously seem to be the most often cited in serial homicide analysis, serial killers can be shuffled into many different categories and types. These categories can be based on all sorts of criteria: psychological, pathological, criminal, social, and even astrological. One astrological study found that many serial killers were born under the sign of Gemini or Sagittarius: Jeffrey Dahmer, David Berkowitz (Son of Sam), Wayne Williams, Danny Rolling (the Gainesville Ripper), Peter Sutcliffe, Arthur Shawcross, and Richard Chase (the Vampire Killer) were Geminis, while Dennis Nilsen, Ted Bundy, and Edmund Kemper were Sagittarians.[123]

Serial killers can be classed by their gender or social identity: gay killers, female killers, team killers, cult killers, professional killers, medical killers, family killers, and so on.

Female Serial Killers

So far I have been using the pronoun *he* when referring to serial killers, simply to facilitate the flow of words. However, I should be referring to serial killers as *he or she,* because nearly one out of five serial murderers are women. In fact, they are often more deadly and more prolific than typical male serial killers. Female serial killers are described as the "quiet killers" because they rarely leave bodies dumped by the roadside, which alarm a community. Their killing careers last twice as long as men's: eight years for women to the male serial killer's average of just over four years.[124] Their killing is often committed at home or in a professional setting such as a hospital, retirement home, boardinghouse, or hotel, where sometimes it is not even noticed or recognized as a murder.

A study of incarcerated female non-serial murderers found that on average 77 percent were unemployed when they committed their offense, 65 percent were black, and 76 percent had children, and their median age was twenty-seven.[125] Female killers are young and poor, and often function in a socioeconomic class where interpersonal violence is more frequent and "acceptable."

The statistics for specifically female serial killers are substantially different: 95 percent were white, their median age was thirty, and only 10 percent were known to be unemployed, while 10 percent were professionals, 10 percent were skilled workers, 15 percent were semiskilled, and 11 percent were other, such as self-employed or business proprietors (and 41 percent unknown).[126] Their higher socioeconomic class, where interpersonal violence is less acceptable, suggests some kind of psychopathology behind their crimes. Poor unemployed women living in a society where often responding with interpersonal violence is the only way to survive may commit a spontaneous homicide in the heat of a moment. But the more middle-class female serial killers contemplated and planned their murders carefully.

The motives of female serial killers are substantially different from those of the female single killer or even the male serial killer. On average,

74 percent of female serial killers were at least in part motivated by personal financial gain, a sad reflection on their middle-class aspirations.[127]

FEMALE SEXUAL SERIAL KILLERS AS ACCOMPLICES

While there are arguably no cases of a single female sexual serial killer operating in a similar manner to the men described in this book, there are numerous cases of women participating in sexually sadistic serial murders as accomplices of a male partner. The male is often the dominant one in the team and commits the actual homicides, but not always. Nearly 44 percent of female serial killers committed their crimes as an accomplice, often in the company of a male partner.

During the mid-1930's, American psychologist Abraham Maslow undertook a number of studies of sexual behavior related to dominance. He noted that in captivity, the most dominant monkeys engaged in almost constant sex, and that the nature of that sex was often "abnormal"—male monkeys mounting other males and even instances of dominant females mounting males. Maslow concluded that sex in those circumstances was often an expression of dominance rather than of the primates' sex drive. He also noted that when a new monkey was introduced into the group, the lower-dominance monkeys would act extremely violently toward it. Maslow linked these attacks to low-esteem violence of the type seen in human beings.

Maslow then turned his attention to young college girls, whom he interviewed at great length. In 1939, Maslow concluded that female sexuality is also linked to dominance. He found that people fall into one of three categories: high-dominance, medium-dominance, and low-dominance.

High-dominance women were more promiscuous, sexually adventurous, and uninhibited. Medium-dominance women tended to also be very sexual but usually related to one male partner at a time. Low-dominance women had a very low opinion of sex, engaged in it infrequently, and felt that its only purpose was for reproduction. Maslow noted that the sexual characteristics of each category had nothing to do with sexual desire: While the sex drive was equally intense in each type, the amount of sex that the women actually engaged in differed.

Maslow also discovered that women preferred males who were slightly more dominant than themselves but within the same dominance group.

High-dominance women rejected most males because of their lower dominance. One woman who claimed that she could have an orgasm by simply looking at an attractive male explained to Maslow that she couldn't have an orgasm when having sex with some males because they were too weak and she could not imagine herself "giving in to them."

Medium-dominance women found high-dominance men too frightening, while low-dominance women found the medium-dominance man intimidating. Each mated with slightly more dominant men but from within their dominance class. For Maslow, this was the normal course of male-female relationships and is often applicable to homosexual relationships as well.

In certain situations, however, partners from different dominance groups mate, and a very severe dynamic emerges in the relationship. The reason that such mating occurs is usually some type of emotional disorder that leads an individual to seek a mate from a different dominance class. High-dominance individuals with personality disorders, needing to sadistically dominate their mate, may seek out partners in lower-dominance categories, while lower-dominance individuals with personality disorders, compelled perhaps to act out an abusive scenario, may seek out higher category mates. Often the result is a slavelike, almost hypnotic relationship between the two parties where one partner totally dominates the other, yet both are desperately dependent upon each other. Sometimes the one vital element that a dominant partner lacks to unleash his or her homicidal fantasies is provided by the submissive partner.

Gwendolyn Graham and Catherine May Wood

Gwendolyn Graham and Catherine May Wood are a rare case in which two women teamed up in a series of sexual murders. Wood was a recently divorced 450-pound supervisor in a nursing home when she entered into a lesbian relationship with Graham, a nurse's aide. The dominant Graham told Wood that it would be a sexual thrill to murder six elderly patients in the home so that their last names would spell out the word *murder*. Their spelling game failed when some of the patients did not die as easily as the couple hoped. Nevertheless, using a wet washcloth to suffocate the patients, Graham killed five victims while Wood stood guard. After each murder, the couple immediately retired to a vacant room in the nursing home and had sex. In exchange for her testimony, Wood received a twenty-to-forty-year sentence, while Graham was given six life sentences. (The sixth sentence was for conspiracy to commit murder.)

Myra Hindley and Ian Brady—"The Moors Murderers"

In England between 1963 and 1965, Ian Brady and Myra Hindley murdered nine children and youths. When Brady was twenty-three he was working as a stock clerk at a chemical company, where he met a typist— eighteen-year-old Myra Hindley. Myra was described as a perfectly normal girl who loved animals and children and brightly colored lipstick. She fell in love with the "intellectual," dark, and brooding Brady.

Myra lost her virginity to Brady and became his slavish girlfriend. A converted Catholic, Myra was soon convinced by Brady of the nonexistence of God. She was completely enthralled with the older and "sophisticated" Brady, who read intellectual books, sported black shirts, and was learning German. Myra said, "Within months he had convinced me there was no God at all: He could have told me that the earth was flat, the moon was made of green cheese and the sun rose in the west, I would have believed him, such was his power of persuasion, his softly convincing means of speech which fascinated me, because I could never fully comprehend, only browse at the odd sentence here and there, believing it to be gospel truth."

According to Myra, in July 1963 Brady began to talk to her of committing a perfect murder as proof of their superiority. On July 12, Myra and Brady set out to commit their perfect crime. Myra drove a van while Brady followed her on his motorcycle. It was Myra's job to pick up a female hitchhiker; she was successful in luring sixteen-year-old Pauline Reade into the vehicle. Myra told Pauline that she was on her way to the moors—the bleak, windy, grassy expanses of wasteland outside Manchester. She had lost a glove there, Myra said, and if Pauline would help her find it, she would give her some record albums as a reward. Pauline agreed and the two set out to the deserted moors, followed discreetly by Brady on his motorbike.

At the moors, Brady attacked Pauline, raped her, and cut her throat. Although Myra claims that she was in the van when the rape and murder took place, in an open letter from prison in 1990, Brady stated that Myra also committed sexual acts on Pauline. Afterward, using a spade that they had brought with them in the van for the occasion, Myra and Brady buried Pauline's body on the moors.

On November 23, 1963, using the same ruse, they murdered a twelve-year-old boy, John Kilbride. Myra stated that Brady raped the boy and strangled him because the knife was too dull to cut his throat. Police were later able to find Kilbride's grave by identifying prominent land features in a photograph of Myra posing on the grave with her dog. Later when Myra was under arrest and was told that her dog died in police custody, she remarked, "They're nothing but bloody murderers."

On June 16, 1964, they murdered another twelve-year-old boy, Keith Bennett, using the same methods. After being raped and strangled, he was buried on the moors and his body, despite numerous efforts, including some with the help of Myra and Brady, has never been found.

It would be a year and a half before the couple would kill again. On December 26, 1965, they kidnapped ten-year-old Lesley Ann Downey and took her back to their house. There Brady set up a light and camera and forced the girl to pose for pornographic photographs. Then, turning on a tape recorder to record the child's screams, Brady raped the girl. According to Brady's 1990 letter, Myra "insisted upon killing Lesley Ann Downey with her own hands, using a two-foot length of silk cord, which she later used to enjoy toying with in public, in the secret knowledge of what it had been used for."

In October 1965, Brady decided he wanted to form a gang, and began to talk with Myra's unemployed brother-in-law, David Smith, about committing a hold-up. On the evening of October 6th, Smith dropped by the house and complained of having no money. Brady suggested: "We'll have to roll a queer." He went out and came back later with seventeen-year-old Edward Evans. Brady struck Evans with an ax and strangled him. He made Smith hold the ax so that his fingerprints would be on the weapon and then the two of them wrapped the corpse in plastic and cleaned up the blood. Myra and Brady then went to bed while Smith wandered off home in a state of shock. At home he told his wife what had occurred and they immediately called the police.

The next morning the police raided Brady's house and found the corpse in a spare bedroom still wrapped in plastic. In the spine of a prayer book, the police found a key to a train station locker where they discovered the pictures and tape recording of Leslie Ann Downey. The tapes were played in court during Ian Brady's and Myra Hindley's trial. Both were sentenced to life imprisonment.

The crimes of Brady and Hindley touched so raw a nerve in England that even in 1997 their crimes remain a sensitive issue. When in September, British Royal Academy of Arts held an exhibition of young artists' works that included a thirteen-foot portrait of Myra Hindley by painter Marcus Harvey, objections were raised. The family of one of Hindley's victims appealed to the Academy to exclude the work. On the opening day of the show, the portrait was splashed with paint, ink, and eggs and had to be withdrawn for a week for restoration.

Myra Hindley died in prison at the age of sixty in November 2002, while Ian Brady is still confined in a psychiatric facility where he has recently written a book entitled *The Gates of Janus: An Analysis of Serial Murder.*

Karla Homolka and Paul Bernardo— Sex, Death, and Videotape

Karla Homolka and Paul Bernardo have been called the Ken and Barbie Killers. When arrested, he was twenty-eight and she was twenty-two years old. Paul Bernardo was blond, blue-eyed, tall, athletic, intelligent, and handsome with what many described as an angelic face. Karla also had a head full of thick blond tresses and was blue-eyed, smart, and petite with a well-proportioned body and good looks. He was a university-educated accountant and she was a recent high school graduate who worked as a veterinarian's assistant. Both were brought up in anonymous middle-class suburbs, attended typically middle-class suburban schools, and frequented typical high school and college student events and parties. Everything about them was typical: Their taste and style were not too high class and not too low class—they were upscale shopping mall mediocre.

They met when Karla was seventeen and Paul was twenty-three, and they engaged in sex within hours of their first encounter. After a several-year engagement, Paul and Karla were married in a lavish, but again entirely mediocre style that could have, and probably did, come from the pages of some popular bridal magazine. They left the church in a horse-drawn carriage and honeymooned in Hawaii.

They settled to live in one of those typical, affluent, middle-sized towns that dot the fertile belt of southern Ontario known as the "Golden Horseshoe" between Toronto and Niagara Falls. They rented a perfect little lakeside Cape Cod–style house for $1,200 a month and furnished it with typically Canadian pine furniture.

Atypically, by the time Paul and Karla left for their honeymoon, they had already together raped, tortured, and murdered two adolescent girls, one of whom was Karla's fifteen-year-old sister Tammy. Upon their return from Hawaii they kidnapped, raped, and killed a third girl. They recorded all three crimes on videotape.

So perfectly respectable, attractive, and inoffensively middle-class were the couple that nobody suspected them of anything, even though their first victim, Karla's younger sister, showed signs of anesthetic drug influence and had been raped. Even for hardened police investigators, it was inconceivable that the "Ken and Barbie" couple before them could have had anything to do with the girl's death.

In 1993, Karla arrived at a hospital with black eyes and a swollen face, accusing her husband, Paul, of severely beating her with a flashlight. Shortly afterward, Paul was arrested for a series of brutal rapes in Toronto, committed more than a year earlier and in which he was not exactly suspected but not cleared either. A sample of his DNA was collected, but it would be more than a year before the overworked and under-funded provincial lab could process and match all the samples.

Karla suddenly confessed that Paul was also responsible for the kidnapping, rape, and murder of two young teenage girls and the accidental death of her own younger sister, Tammy, while raping her on Christmas night in her parents' basement rec room. Karla had provided the veterinary drugs that had knocked her sister out. As the two videotaped the assault, they took turns molesting and raping the girl, who then in her unconscious state choked on her vomit and died.

As the details of the rapes and murders began to emerge, Karla claimed "battered-wife syndrome," saying that she had been forced to participate in these crimes. She agreed to testify against her husband in exchange for a lighter sentence. No sooner had the prosecution signed and sealed the deal with Karla, than the videotapes surfaced showing Karla lustfully participating in the torture and rapes of the victims. One fifteen-year-old victim, Kristen French, was seen being repeatedly raped, sodomized, and tortured over a three-day period, sometimes by Bernardo alone, sometimes by both of them. But it was too late to undo the deal the prosecution team had made.

During the trial Bernardo claimed that it was Karla who actually murdered the girls because she was jealous of the attention he was lavishing on the captives. Karla was certainly aware of and entirely indifferent to the victims. As Bernardo beat, raped, sodomized, and tormented fourteen-year-old Leslie Mahaffy in their bedroom, Karla took little breaks downstairs in the living room reading the Bret Easton Ellis novel *American Psycho* until Paul called her to come up and hold the video camera. When asked in court how she could possibly read while a girl was being tortured and raped upstairs, Karla incredulously replied that she was quite capable of doing two things at same time.

It was revealed at the trial that Karla shaved the hair from the head of one of the dead girls rather than throw away a carpet that might have picked up hair traces from the victim (to the great confusion of profilers, who interpreted the hair shaving as a "signature"). Marks of what appeared to be her knee imprints were found on one victim's back. The videotapes did not show the actual murders, however. In the end, the jury chose to believe that Bernardo was most likely the killer: He had committed a series of very violent rapes and dismembered one of the dead victims.

Karla Homolka, who has been happily taking university courses while in prison, is due to be released very shortly, having nearly finished her entire fourteen-year term, while Bernardo is serving a life sentence.

Carol Bundy and Douglas Clark— "The Sunset Boulevard Killers"

In 1980 in Los Angeles, Douglas Clark and Carol Bundy were involved in the murders of at least six young women who were either hitchhiking or working as prostitutes in the Sunset Boulevard area. Clark enjoyed carefully shooting his victims in the head when they were performing oral sex on him. He then had sex with their cadavers. Carol accompanied Clark on at least one of the murders, sitting in the backseat of the car and watching as Clark murdered the victim in the front. On another occasion Clark brought home a severed female head and asked Carol to set the victim's hair and apply some makeup; he then had sex with the head in the shower. Eventually Carol killed a male victim and severed his head in a futile attempt to impress Clark, whose interest in her was waning.

Charlene and Gerald Gallego

The bisexual Charlene Gallego tested in prison at an IQ of 160. She was a talented violin player and college graduate from a wealthy California family. One evening while buying drugs at a club, she met Gerald Gallego. He had a lengthy record of sex offenses beginning at the tender age of thirteen, when he raped a seven-year-old girl. Moreover, he had a criminal pedigree going back to his father, who had killed two law enforcement officers and was the first person executed in Mississippi State's gas chamber when Gerald was nine years old. Charlene was instantly attracted to Gerald Gallego's "outlaw" persona and married him.

Once again, she was probably a high-dominance woman who needed a high-dominance man—Gerald was perfect. He fantasized along with Charlene about keeping virginal young sex slaves at a remote country house. On his daughter's (from another marriage) fourteenth birthday, he sodomized her and raped her friend as Charlene watched.

Things went wrong when one night both of them seduced a sixteen-year-old go-go dancer. The three-way sex was fine, but the next day after coming back from work, Gallego found Charlene and the dancer having sex together. He became enraged, threw the girl out, and stopped having sex with Charlene. Charlene then suggested that they kidnap, rape, and murder young girls.

Killing between September 1978 and November 1980, they often kidnapped girls from Sacramento shopping malls. They also killed in Nevada and Oregon, often beating in the heads of their victims with a tire iron or shooting them with a .25-caliber pistol. They buried one victim alive, a pregnant woman. In three instances, they kidnapped two women at a time. Gerald shared the victims with Charlene, who liked to bite one girl as another performed oral sex on Charlene. She bit the nipple off one of the victims.

At one point, Charlene got into a gunfight with Gerald when he started raping their two young teenage captives in the back "without waiting for her" while she was driving the van. The couple shot at each other until Charlene grazed Gerald's arm.

Charlene was seven months pregnant in 1980 when their car was identified during their kidnapping and murder of a high school couple during
a prom night. When police showed up at their door, the couple were such
unlikely suspects that police left even though the suspected car was parked
in their driveway. When police returned several hours later, the Gallegos
had already fled.

They were eventually apprehended and Gerald Gallego was sentenced
to death, while Charlene Gallego, in a pattern that should be familiar to the
reader by now, received a sixteen-year sentence, testifying against Gerald.

While in prison she continued her education, studying a range of subjects from psychology to business to Icelandic literature. "She's a pretty intellectual woman," said Nevada District Judge Richard Wagner, who was
the lead prosecutor in Gallego's Nevada trial. "She has a phenomenal
mind, which made her a tremendous witness. . . . She had almost a photo-
graphic memory about the victims, down to their shoes and clothes."

On July 17, 1997, Charlene was set free and reverted to her family
name of Williams. In an interview she claimed that she was as much a victim of Gallego as the other girls: "There were victims who died and there
were victims who lived. It's taken me a hell of a long time to realize that
I'm one of the ones who lived."

Charlene said of Gerald Gallego, "He portrayed to my parents that he
was a super family guy. But soon it was like being in the middle of a mud
puddle. You can't see your way out because he eliminated things in my life
piece by piece, person by person, until all I had around me were members
of his family, and they're all like him, every one of them. . . . Prison was
freedom compared to being with him."

Gerald Gallego recently died of cancer in the midst of his attempts to get
a new trial. On November 20, 1999, a Nevada farmer uncovered a shallow
grave containing the bodies of fourteen-year-old Brenda Judd and thirteen-
year-old Sandra Colley, missing since 1979, two of the ten known victims
of Charlene and Gerald.

There are remarkably frequent cases of women, some of them well educated
and with "normal" family backgrounds, emerging as willing accomplices
in sadistic rapes and murders of children, men, and women. Other noted
sexual killer couples include and Fred and Rosemary West in England, who

sexually murdered at least ten women and young girls, including their daughter, between 1971 and 1987; Debra Denise Brown and Alton Coleman, who bludgeoned, shot, tortured, and raped eight victims age seven and up in Ohio, Illinois, and Michigan in 1988; and Judith and Alvin Neelley, who called themselves "The Night Rider and Lady Sundance" and robbed, raped, and murdered fifteen women in Alabama, Tennessee, and Georgia in 1980–1982.

Aileen Wuornos—The Single Female Sexual Serial Killer Who Wasn't

There seem to be virtually no records of single female sexual serial killers operating in the way male serial killers described in this book do. Even the case of Aileen Wuornos, often cited as an example of a male-type female serial killer, seems to lack the sexual pathology of a male sexual killer. Wuornos was a thirty-five-year-old Florida roadside prostitute who was convicted for shooting six men. Although she robbed her dead victims, her motive appears to have been revenge or rage induced as a result of a lifetime of real and perceived abuse.

Throughout the period of the murders, numerous other lesser charges were laid against her under different aliases for threatening people with a weapon, assault, vandalism of her apartment, and other minor offenses. She constantly traveled with a loaded handgun. In one town she was charged with making threatening calls to a supermarket chain over a lottery ticket dispute, and in another with assaulting a bus driver over a fare dispute. Addicted to cocaine and possibly crystal meth, she was wired up into a highly aggressive state of rage.

Her victims were elderly male motorists. Either they mistook her for a woman needing assistance or a hitchhiker, or they picked up Wuornos for sex. Their bodies were found dumped in remote areas, often shot several times in the back and the head, and their pockets turned inside out or their clothes stolen in their entirety. Their vehicles were found elsewhere, with property removed from them. There was no evidence, however, of torture or mutilation of the victims.

At her trial Wuornos claimed that she shot these victims in self-defense when they attempted to rape and assault her during her encounters with them. Indeed, it turned out that her first victim, Richard Mallory, had served ten years for a violent rape. The other five victims, however, had no records of sexual assaults. The likely scenario is that Wuornos shot Mallory in self-defense and found herself afterward in a raging addiction to kill more. Perhaps some real or imagined slight during her encounter with her elderly victims triggered her murderous acts. Perhaps they reminded her of her grandfather, who abused her and who she thought was actually her father until age thirteen. Wuornos was raped at age fourteen and gave birth to a son, who was given up for adoption. From age fifteen she led a life of prostitution and drug addiction and claimed she was raped five more times before age eighteen.

During her trial Wuornos became a cause for some factions of the feminist movement, who believed that her crimes were a response to systemic abuse at the hands of men. Whether or not Wuornos is to be believed—and certainly her claims are plausible—her childhood and adolescent history is comparable to that of many male serial killers who did not get a break from the justice system. Neither did Wuornos: She was executed in Florida on October 9, 2002.

Wuornos is often presented as a sexual killer because the offenses took place in the context of her prostitution. But it is highly debatable whether her killings gave Wuornos any sexual gratification in the way male sexual serial killers derive theirs.

OTHER TYPES OF FEMALE SERIAL KILLERS

BLACK WIDOWS

Black widows are probably the most common type of female serial killer. These women focus on victims with whom they establish extensive relationships—their husbands, children, and lovers. Almost 85 percent of these types of serial killers use poison to murder their victims.[128] Their motive is material gain—they acquire or inherit the property of their victims or collect on their insured lives.

ANGELS OF DEATH

Angels of death are women who kill victims in their care: nurses who kill babies, patients, or elderly victims, or childcare workers who murder children in their care. Their motives range from profit to the attention and praise they get when they revive a patient who suffers a medical emergency they secretly induce. Others derive a sense of power and thrill from taking life. Some are missionaries, believing that certain types of patients do not deserve to live, while others have a misguided sense of mercy, believing that they save their patients from unnecessary suffering by killing them.

MUNCHAUSEN SYNDROME BY PROXY

Hieronymus Karl Friedrich von Munchausen was an eighteenth-century German baron and mercenary officer in the Russian cavalry. On his return from the Russo-Turkish wars, the baron entertained friends and neighbors with stories of his many exploits. Over time, his stories grew more and more expansive, and finally quite outlandish. Munchausen became somewhat famous after a collection of his tales was published.

Almost a century later, an unusual behavior pattern among young men gained recognition in the writings of Charcot. In 1877, he described adults who, through self-inflicted injuries or bogus medical documents, attempted to gain hospitalization and treatment. Charcot called this condition *mania operativa passiva*.

Seventy-four years later, in 1951, Asher described a similar pattern of self-abuse in which individuals fabricated histories of illness. These fabrications invariably led to complex medical investigations, hospitalizations, and at times needless surgery. Remembering Baron von Munchausen and his apocryphal tales, Asher named this condition *Munchausen syndrome*.

Today, Munchausen syndrome is a recognized psychiatric disorder. The American Psychiatric Association's *Diagnostic and Statistical Manual of Mental Disorders* (*DSM III-R*) describes it as the "intentional production of physical symptoms."

The term *Munchausen syndrome by proxy* (MSBP) was coined in a 1976 report describing four children who were so severely abused that they were dwarfed. In 1977, Meadow described a somewhat less extreme form of child abuse in which mothers deliberately induced or falsely reported illnesses in their children. He also referred to this behavior as MSBP.[129]

In an extreme case of MSBP, Marybeth Tinning in Schenectady, New York, was arrested after eight of her children died one-by-one between 1972 and 1985. The children all appeared to succumb to Sudden Infant Death Syndrome (SIDS) and authorities at first did not suspect the apparently loving mother who grieved for her children.

Marybeth responded to all these deaths with a round of dramatic funeral announcements and a gathering of all her friends and relatives. Both her birth and death announcements put her in the center of attention. One relative said, "Every funeral was a party for her, with hardly a tear shed."

Concerned relatives forced a careful autopsy when the eighth child in Marybeth's care, her nine-month-old daughter, died of what appeared to be SIDS once again. The autopsy revealed that the child was in fact suffocated.

Marybeth Tinning confessed to the murder of the infant and to the murders of two other children, but not the others. She also confessed that she was attempting to poison her husband. In 1987, Tinning was sentenced to twenty years to life.

Kathryn A. Hanon, an investigator with the Orlando Police Department and a specialist in Munchausen syndrome by proxy abuse cases, writes: "MSBP offenders are uncharacteristically calm in view of the victims' baffling medical symptoms, and they welcome medical tests that are painful to the children. They also maintain a high degree of involvement in the care of their children during treatment and will excessively praise the medical staff. They seem very knowledgeable of the victims' illnesses, which may indicate some medical study or training. They may also have a history of the same illnesses being exhibited by their victims."[130]

The Spree Serial Killer:
A New Emerging Breed of Murderer

Serial killers were at one time called "mass killers." But today a mass murderer is an individual who at some point "snaps" mentally and explodes in a murderous rage, killing multiple victims during a single incident. Sometimes such mass slaughters begin with the offender killing members of his own family or other people close to him before proceeding to other victims. Often these outbreaks are nothing more than a form of selfish suicide, where the mass killer intends to take others with him into his own death.

Only half of all mass killers survive their outbreaks—the other half are shot by police or commit suicide when they run out of either victims or ammunition. These outbreaks of killing usually last for short periods of time, anywhere from a few minutes to a day, with the killer rarely going to sleep after he commits his first homicide. The killer proceeds from murder to murder in a nonstop fashion. Charles Whitman, who shot sixteen people from a clock tower in Texas; James Huberty, who killed twenty-one victims at a McDonald's restaurant in California; Colin Ferguson, who killed six people on a commuter train in New York; and Columbine teenage gunmen Eric Harris and Dylan Klebold, who killed twelve fellow students and a teacher, are all mass killers.

Spree killers, on the other hand, tend to stretch their killing out over a longer period of time, stopping to rest and sleep and often changing locations. Generally speaking, spree killers often murder while committing other felonies. The killing is secondary to their other crimes. Frequently they are escapees from justice and are highly mobile. They do not fit the classic serial killer pattern: There is no cooling-off period where they slip back into their daily routine lives and identities before going out to secretly kill again. Spree killers are often identified outlaws on the run and they do not lead the double life of a serial killer. Usually spree killers commit their crimes over a period of a few weeks before they are apprehended or killed.

Now, however, we are seeing a new category emerging—the spree serial killer. These are serial killers who live only one identity—that of a killer. They seem to have no cooling-off period; they do not return to a normal routine but remain focused on evading capture and perpetuating their compulsion to kill. Often they are fugitives, but the reasons for their flight are not other crimes, but their very acts of serial murder.

These murderers become more difficult to discern from the typical serial killer because ostensibly, by killing multiple victims on different days, they meet the classic definition of a serial killer. There are, however, subtle differences. Typical serial killers have a cycle in which their desire to kill grows and builds, and is followed by a period of depression and release after the murder. (See Chapter 8.) Some serial killers promise themselves during this postkill period that they will never murder again. They go back to the patterns of their normal life after the murder—they return home to their families, they report to work the next day, and so on. Before long they begin the cycle anew. The spree serial killer might not go through this cycle—instead he immediately launches into preparing for his next murder; he becomes a "full-time" killer and makes no attempt to lead a "normal" life.

What spree killers share with mass murderers is a mental "snapping" point of no return. They bear stress and pressure for months or years, but once something triggers their killing they never return back to their previous lives.

The murders by Andrew Cunanan in 1997 and more recently the Washington, D.C., beltway sniper killings in 2002 define this category of spree serial killer, but like everything in the history of serial homicide, it is not exactly new. Christopher Wilder, Alton Coleman, and Paul John Knowles are serial killers in the past who today can be reclassified as spree serial killers. They remained highly focused on killing, committed felonies in order to sustain their killing careers, and led no routine life or maintained no identity other than that of serial killer.

Wilder is a particularly interesting personality because he became a spree serial killer after his first series of murders were uncovered. Until then he maintained an identity as a wealthy Florida builder, photographer, and amateur race car driver. Once discovered, he abandoned all that and hit the road as a fugitive, continuing to commit new murders until police shot him dead.

Andrew Cunanan

More than any other killer, Andrew Cunanan made us recognize this category of spree serial killers when he murdered Gianni Versace on the morning of July 15, 1997. The fifty-year-old fashion mogul was returning to his house in Miami Beach after having a coffee and buying some newspapers at a local cafe. As Versace approached the gates of his house on Ocean Drive, twenty-seven-year-old Cunanan stepped up from the sidewalk and fired a shot through Versace's left cheek with a powerful .40-caliber handgun. With Versace collapsed on the ground, Cunanan coldly fired a second shot through the back of his head.

A hotel security camera around the corner recorded the presumed assassin running down the street, and witness statements had him entering a municipal parking garage a few blocks away from Versace's house. In the garage, police found a pickup truck with clothing and Andrew Cunanan's passport. The truck belonged to another murder victim, killed six weeks earlier. At that murder scene, in New Jersey, police found a vehicle belonging to yet a third murder victim, killed in Chicago five days previously. And in Chicago, police had found yet another vehicle that connected Cunanan to a double homicide in Minnesota. A trail of murder victims' automobiles (and the same handgun) linked Andrew Cunanan to five murders across the United States between April 29 and July 15, 1997. On July 23, the manhunt for Cunanan ended when he shot himself dead while holed up in a houseboat he had broken into moored several miles away from the scene of Versace's murder.

Andrew Cunanan had been almost universally described as a serial killer, for indeed he killed five victims on five different dates. Others, however, categorize him as a spree serial killer. His first two victims were both individuals he knew and was close to. He never attempted to cover his identity as a murderer, and after his first killing he lived on the road as an "outlaw." Moreover, Cunanan's murders lacked a consistent serial killer's signature—the subconscious imprint of a definitive, elaborate, identifiable, and evolving fantasy that a serial killer leaves on each of his victims. For example, Cunanan's victim in Chicago, believed to be a stranger, was extensively mutilated, tortured, and bound by Cunanan, while his victim in New Jersey was quickly shot for his vehicle, with no sexual fantasies involved. Because the victim was apparently killed for only his vehicle, some clinicians describe that murder as "serial functional." Versace's "execution-style" murder also differed radically from the murder in Chicago. As a matter of fact, had Cunanan's friendship with the first two victims not tied him to those murders, and vehicles and ballistics not linked him to the other three homicides, investigators might not have been inclined to link the murders. (On the other hand, confusing matters is the fact that both Versace and the Chicago victim, developer Lee Miglin, were both high-profile, middle-aged, extremely wealthy entrepreneurs. Victim selection is also part of a "signature.")

Finally, when Cunanan was discovered at the houseboat by a caretaker and knew that his capture would be imminent, he shot himself dead—a typical conclusion for a serial spree killer.

There is, of course, one question in the midst of all this—what happens when a spree killer does not get apprehended? Does he at some point "cool down"? Does he then return to a killing cycle again? The psychological histories of both mass and serial killers are remarkably similar in their buildup of "stressors" before they commit their first murder. Fantasy and sex, however, play a lesser role in the classical spree–mass killer profile. This is not so in the case of spree serial killers, whose psychopathology parallels those of classic serial killers.

Andrew Phillip Cunanan was born on August 31, 1969 and grew up in Rancho Bernardo, California, an upper-middle-class suburban community in the hills north of San Diego. He was the youngest son of Filipino Modesto Cunanan and Italian Marie Ann Celino. His father was a retired US navy officer who became a stockbroker. Andrew had two older sisters and a brother.

His sisters and brother recall that Andrew was very intelligent and pampered by their father. He had the master bedroom in the house and was given credit cards at age seven with which to entertain his friends. He was the family "star," memorizing almost the entire contents of encyclopedias. They remember him as a happy and nonviolent child. They insist that their Catholic family suspected that Andrew was gay and would have accepted it if they had confirmed it.

Whether the family would have accepted it or not, the fact remains that Cunanan himself felt that he needed to lead a double and fractured life as a teenager. Moreover, it might have been worse: There is fragmentary evidence that he might have been sexually abused in his adolescence by a priest at the time he was serving as an altar boy. A sexual abuse hotline in 1996 logged calls from somebody using the same pseudonym that Cunanan later used, warning about a sexually abusive priest in San Diego. The priest was apparently charged, but not convicted, of abuse of other youths during the same period that Cunanan served as an altar boy. The evidence is admittedly tenuous, but nonetheless, entirely plausible.

Cunanan graduated from the prestigious catholic Bishop's School, an elite preparatory school in La Jolla, a wealthy neighborhood of San Diego. His classmates remember him being openly and flamboyantly gay, once appearing at a school function dressed in a red patent-leather jumpsuit, a gift from a much older man who was his date. Cunanan was voted by his fellow students as "Least Likely to Be Forgotten" in the 1987 school yearbook. The young Cunanan was an above-average student, reading the Bible and teaching himself Spanish. He was already fluent in French.

In later years, some of the well-educated and professional people he encountered remarked that they were impressed by his brilliance and his ability to absorb information. He was a witty conversationalist and a pleasure to have at a dinner party. He could recall the provenance of a painting, from when it had been painted to the history of its subsequent owners; he was fluent in the intricacies of political issues and could describe the texture of exotic gourmet delicacies or what was the most luxurious hotel to stay at in Morocco or the best restaurant on Capri.

In 1988, Cunanan began studying at the University of California at San Diego, majoring in art history. He was full of hope and promise with the keys to a great future: a solid upper-middle-class background, wealth, prep school education, charm, vigor, and charisma. And then it suddenly collapsed.

Cunanan's father, "Pete" Modesto was accused of embezzling $106,000 from the brokerage where he worked.[131] Faced with a possible criminal indictment, with Andrew his youngest child now nineteen years of age, Modesto had few qualms about what he did next: He packed his bags and left for the Philippines, abandoning the family. Marie Ann divorced him and sold the house. After Modesto's liabilities were deducted, $3,000 remained from the sale.

No doubt Modesto had underestimated Andrew's capacity to overcome this disaster and continue with his promising future. Andrew dropped out of college and went to the Philippines to join his father. There he was overwhelmed by what he perceived as the abject squalor in which Modesto was now living. He returned to San Diego and moved in with his mother in a small $750-a-month rented condominium in Rancho Bernardo. During this period, Cunanan's history shows some capacity for violence—he got into an argument with his mother and pushed her so violently against a wall that her shoulder was dislocated.

To get by Andrew worked sporadically as a discount drugstore clerk. Mostly, however, he sought out older men to replace the love and financial security his father had once provided him.

Between 1990 and 1996, Andrew Cunanan cruised the gay communities of San Diego and San Francisco, making his living as a upscale gigolo for refined, professional, older men. He was well known in the San Diego gay social set. Restaurateur Michael Williams said, "Andrew did his homework. He would investigate older, wealthy gay men who didn't have families, and he would place himself in those circles. That was his living."

On October 21, 1990, Cunanan encountered Versace at a reception at the Colossus nightclub in San Francisco, when Versace had designed costumes for the opera company. Versace apparently thought he had met Cunanan somewhere before, and they briefly exchanged words before Versace moved on. Despite all sorts of fragmentary reports that Versace had more contacts with Cunanan, other than the short encounter in San Francisco, there is no evidence of any contact between Cunanan and Versace.

Through the years Cunanan told fantastic stories about his life, claiming he was the son of a Hollywood movie mogul, spinning tales of his family's wealth, and claiming ownership of sugar plantations in the Philippines and a villa in the French Riviera. Cunanan said his father was a Filipino general close to the fallen dictator Marcos and that he was bisexual as well, with a young lover whom Andrew claimed he resented. Cunanan said that he had a pilot's license and that he was a personal pilot to a Filipino senator whom he flew in the senator's decaying airplane, which was nicknamed the "Buddy Holly death plane."

In later years he lived and socialized under assumed names: Andrew Phillip De Silva and, at other times, Drew Cunningham. Many of his acquaintances in San Diego did not even know that his real name was Cunanan. However, they remembered Cunanan picking up $1,000 dinner tabs and leaving $200 tips, smoking $10 Davidoff cigars, and never drinking anything stronger than cranberry juice. He was the center of attention and welcomed young gay men arriving in San Diego and fixed them up with contacts.

When not living off rich older men, he worked as a male prostitute through an escort agency that charged a paltry $140 a night, 40 percent of which Cunanan dutifully forwarded to the agency. But clients were very pleased with Cunanan, and he began to get cross-country referrals from the agency.

In 1996 Cunanan was living in La Jolla with Ron Grundy,* a conservative retired millionaire and art collector in his sixties. Cunanan convinced Grundy to sell his home in Scottsdale, Arizona, and buy an oceanfront

---

* A pseudonym.

house in La Jolla. The house had been previously owned by an older friend of Cunanan's, Lincoln Aston, who in 1995 was bludgeoned to death by another man.

From Grundy, Cunanan received an allowance of $2,000 a month and a $30,000 1996 Infiniti I30t automobile, and he was given plenty of free time to pursue his own friendships. He and Grundy often flew to New York for Broadway shows and spent the summer of 1996 in Paris and the south of France.

In September 1996, however, Grundy and Cunanan split. The exact circumstances of the breakup are obscure. Cunanan claimed that he left Grundy because he was too cheap—that he refused to fly first class and would not buy Cunanan a Mercedes 500SL he desired. Others report that Cunanan was upset by the split. In any case, Grundy let Cunanan keep the Infiniti. Cunanan moved into an apartment he shared with two room-mates. He was now just eight months away from his first two murders.

While Cunanan performed as a gigolo to the aging millionaire Grundy, he was really in love with another man—thirty-three-year-old David Madson, whom he met in San Francisco in December 1995. Madson was a talented designer of retail banking centers for a Minneapolis company. He traveled all over the country, designing storelike banking facilities for malls and shopping plazas. He would become Cunanan's second murder victim in April 1997.

Cunanan also formed a nonsexual friendship with twenty-eight-year-old Jeffrey Trail. Trail was a former U.S. Navy officer and small-arms instructor who had served on a guided-missile cruiser in the Persian Gulf and was in training with the California Highway Patrol when Cunanan met him. Cunanan, who had fantasies of being a naval officer himself, admired Trail and claimed that he was his best and oldest friend. It was a strange friendship, because Trail was straitlaced and a conservative opponent of drugs, while Cunanan consumed drugs liberally and was a flamboyant attention-grabbing liar. Jeffrey Trail would be Cunanan's first murder victim.

By September 1996, Cunanan's relationship had fallen apart not only with Grundy but with Madson and Trail as well. Madson had dropped Cunanan back in the spring when Cunanan began disappearing for ten days at a time, presumably to service Grundy. When Cunanan broke up with Grundy in September, he attempted to rekindle his romance with Madson, but was turned down.

Many say that Cunanan was quickly losing his youthful good looks and was growing fat and ugly, a kiss of death for any gigolo's career. A testament as to how fat Cunanan was by the end is the police report mentioning Cunanan's bloodied jeans at the scene of Trail's murder. The formerly slim Cunanan was wearing size 36 jeans.

To continue maintaining his lifestyle, Cunanan began intensively dealing in drugs, mostly pharmaceuticals. He also started smoking crack cocaine. There is no crazier nor more deadly drug than crack. Crack really does all the things that antidrug crusaders for decades claimed other drugs did: makes you insane, paranoid, totally out of control, crazy-homicidal-suicidal.

In the summer of 1996, Jeffrey Trail had cut Cunanan off from his friendship. Cunanan told several people that Trail was angry with him because he became connected with Cunanan's drug-dealing business and was forced to resign from the California Highway Patrol training program. Trail's acquaintances vehemently deny this, stating that Trail was very conservative and would never become involved in drug traffic. Nonetheless, Trail's sudden resignation from the highway patrol remains a bit of a mystery. Rejected by both Trail and Madson, getting tubby and disheveled, Cunanan began to disintegrate through the winter of 1996–1997. He had to sell his car to pay for his lifestyle, having racked up $50,000 in credit card debt.

Cunanan began a subtle mind game with Madson, telling him that Madson was his only path to reforming himself. Although they were no longer lovers, Madson continued to see Cunanan and meet with him in San Francisco. He told people that he couldn't abandon Cunanan as he was trying to change his life around.

Both Jeffrey Trail and David Madson coincidentally then moved to Minneapolis, Minnesota, 2,000 miles away from San Diego. Although Trail and Madson knew each other through their relationships with Cunanan, they were never lovers; each had their own boyfriends in Minneapolis. Cunanan was despondent.

On the Easter weekend of April 1997, Cunanan joined David Madson in Los Angeles. Madson was there to meet with two friends from San Francisco who were getting married soon. Madson was to give away the bride. Cunanan took two $395 rooms at the Chateau Marmont and insisted that everybody stay with him. The couple later remembered that

Cunanan seemed to be in a manic state, promising to pay $15,000 for the wedding reception of a couple he had just met. Madson and Cunanan argued when Cunanan made sexual advances toward Madson.

Cunanan was beginning to slide into a disturbed state of mind. At a party given by Madson, Cunanan set fire to a pile of paper napkins at the table and walked away. After a screening of *Pulp Fiction* in San Diego, people noticed how animated and excited Cunanan was over the scene where a man has his head blown apart in the backseat of a car by a gunshot. On a beach he scooped up some live crabs and burned their eyes out.

Cunanan announced that he was moving to San Francisco to start a new life. He told several people that before moving, he needed to see Jeffrey Trail about some "unfinished business." Cunanan went to the airport and purchased an airline ticket for Minneapolis. He had to plead and persuade the ticket clerk to put the purchase on his credit card—he was way over his limit. An acquaintance recalled, "Andrew said that he would call in a few days if he needed a ride home from the airport, but that call never came." Nobody knew that that the ticket Cunanan purchased for Minneapolis was one-way.

Both Jeffrey Trail and David Madson were patient and accommodating with Cunanan on his visit. Trail described Cunanan as being like a "disliked relative" who had to be hosted out of obligation. On Friday, April 25, David Madson picked up Cunanan from the airport and took him back to his apartment, where he was going to spend the night. It was understood that Cunanan was in Minneapolis for the weekend and was going to fly home on Monday morning. Friday night, Madson and Cunanan met with friends for dinner. Cunanan had Madson show everybody a Cartier watch that Cunanan had given him "for being a great friend."

On Saturday, Madson and Cunanan went out to dinner again, but Cunanan spent the night in Jeffrey Trail's apartment, who left a key for him. Trail had told Cunanan that he wasn't going to be able to see him much that weekend because his boyfriend, Jon Hackett, was celebrating his birthday. Trail spent Saturday night over at Hackett's place, perhaps even as a favor to Madson, to take Cunanan off his hands for a night.

On Sunday morning, a friend of Madson's called and asked how things were going with Cunanan. Madson said everything was fine and that Cunanan had stayed at Trail's apartment but would be coming back tonight to his place.

On Sunday morning, Cunanan answered several calls at Trail's apartment and took messages for him. He then returned to Madson's apartment, presumably to spend the last night there before returning to California the next morning.

On Sunday afternoon, Trail appeared at a baseball game and then he and Hackett had dinner at home that evening. They decided to go dancing but before they left, Trail found a message on his answering machine from Cunanan, asking him to come by and see him at Madson's apartment. Trail told Hackett he would go over and see Cunanan for about twenty minutes—they had something they needed to talk about. He would then meet Hackett at a nightclub between 10:00 and 10:30 P.M. The caller ID on Madson's phone shows that Cunanan admitted somebody into the building, no doubt Trail, at 9:45 P.M. Trail failed to meet Hackett later that night.

Jeffrey Trail was a twenty-eight-year-old adult, so it was not a simple matter to report him missing to the police. Not only would police require a seventy-two-hour waiting period before they would activate an investigation, but they would want a report from Jeffrey Trail's parents or relatives, not a boyfriend. Hackett was not sure whether Trail's parents knew that their son was gay, and did not want to call them. Thus Trail's disappearance went unreported for several days.

Nor was David Madson to be seen anywhere. He failed to report to work on Monday. When on Tuesday he did not come in to work, two of his fellow workers visited his apartment. They heard Madson's dog scratching on the other side of the door. At 4:00 P.M. on Tuesday, the superintendent used his passkey to look into Madson's apartment. Madson was nowhere to be seen, but Jeffrey Trail was found dead, rolled up in a carpet. He had been struck in the head with a claw hammer some twenty-five to thirty times; his watch had stopped at 9:55. The hammer was apparently taken from a toolbox that stood open nearby. Two sets of footprints tramped through the blood and gore. Madson's dog appeared calm and fed. Witnesses reported that they had seen Madson and Cunanan coming in and out of the apartment for the last two days.

On Monday evening Cunanan was seen back at Trail's apartment. He presumably went there with Trail's keys and stole his .40-caliber handgun. Cunanan and Madson spent two days with Trail's body in Madson's apartment. When people began calling at the door, Cunanan and Madson drove off in Madson's Jeep Cherokee.

There has been no end of speculation why Madson stayed with Cunanan. The shock of finding Trail dead in his apartment might have un-hinged Madson. Perhaps Cunanan threatened him with the handgun—he may have taken it earlier on Sunday from Trail's apartment.

On May 3, about forty miles outside Minneapolis, fishermen found the body of David Madson on the shore of East Rush Lake. He had been shot once through the back and once through the eye. A third shot had grazed his cheek. Cunanan had killed the two people whom he said he loved most in his life.

Lee Miglin, seventy-five years old, was a prominent real estate devel-oper in Chicago. He had no known connections to the gay community or known homosexual predilections. On May 4, his wife returned from a trip and was surprised that he did not come to the airport to pick her up. When she arrived home by taxi, she found her husband's body stuffed un-der a car in their garage. Miglin had suffered some forty-nine separate in-juries—every rib in his body was broken and his head was nearly severed. There were fifteen blows to his head and Miglin had been run over by his car at least five times. His face was wrapped in a plastic bag fastened with duct tape. A small opening was left at the nostrils through which he could breathe. A pair of pruning shears were plunged into his chest and his throat had been carved through with a gardening saw. Cunanan had spent the night sleeping in Miglin's house, made himself some sandwiches, and shaved in the bathroom. It is believed that Cunanan struck at Miglin's house at random when he saw Miglin through an open garage door as he drove by. Madson's jeep was found parked near Miglin's house, while Miglin's 1994 Lexus was missing.

There are two troubling factors about Miglin's death. First, Miglin fit perfectly the social profile of the kind of men that Cunanan used to service as a gigolo. It was a remarkable twist of luck for Cunanan to have been able to zero in on that type of victim at random. Second, witnesses stated that one of the stories Cunanan had told months earlier was that he was going into the movie soundproofing business with Duke Miglin, the vic-tim's twenty-five-year-old son. Duke Miglin, however, vehemently denied that he had ever met Cunanan or that he was gay. The Miglin family also reiterated that Lee Miglin was exclusively heterosexual.

On May 9, in New Jersey, forty-five-year-old William Reese, a ceme-tery caretaker, did not come home for dinner. His wife drove to the ceme-tery and found him on the office floor, dead with a single shot to the head.

Miglin's Lexus was parked in the cemetery but Reese's red Chevrolet pickup truck was missing. Reese's murder was described as "functional." He was killed for his vehicle. The murder of Reese is perhaps the most tragic, for if Cunanan had only known how to hot-wire a car, Resse probably would not have been murdered.

During the night of May 10, a license plate was stolen from a Toyota in Florence, South Carolina. The plates would be found attached to the truck that Cunanan stole from Reese.

On May 12, Cunanan checked in at the Normandy Plaza, a shabby hotel in Miami about four miles north of Versace's home. Cunanan paid $230 in cash weekly for his room. The management of the hotel says he went out every night but never brought anybody back with him. He frequently changed his appearance, including the color of his hair, the manager said.

The parking records at the municipal lot near Versace's house show that Cunanan parked the truck there on June 10 and did not move it. It accumulated nearly $130 in daily parking charges. This suggests that Cunanan had already decided to stalk and kill Versace more than a month before the murder.

On June 12, the FBI put Cunanan on its Ten Most Wanted List and distributed his picture. Several sightings of Cunanan were reported from all over the United States, but several came from Miami. Police were slow to respond.

On July 7, Cunanan pawned a gold coin in a Miami pawnshop, using his own name. The coin was rare enough to attract the attention of the police, but remarkably they failed to recognize Cunanan's name. The coin was later traced to Lee Miglin's collection.

On July 10, Gianni Versace arrived in Miami after being away on business. Witnesses later testified to seeing Cunanan in various clubs and restaurants that Versace might have conceivably patronized. One of them was the 11th Street Diner, where Miami's chief of police was known to lunch.

Chicago police captain and serial killer specialist Tom Cronin stated, "Down deep inside, the publicity is more sexual to him than anything else. Right after one or two of these homicides, he probably goes to a gay bar in the afternoon when the news comes on and his face is on TV, and he's sitting there drinking a beer and loving it. You hide in plain view."

After invisibly lurking around Miami for more than two months, Cunanan struck on the morning of July 15, killing Gianni Versace. Nothing is known about Cunanan's state of mind between the first four murders and the day he committed the fifth two months later. Cunanan disappeared within minutes of Versace's murder, presumably breaking into several boats to hide. Police intercepted phone calls he made to a friend, attempting to secure a false passport to get out of the country. But in the end, Cunanan was cornered on a houseboat in Miami. On July 23, when a caretaker entered the house-boat, Cunanan was upstairs in the bedroom. He shot himself with Trail's .40-caliber handgun as the caretaker was opening the door downstairs.

In certain aspects, a homosexual can be more prepared to lead the life of a serial killer: He frequently has practice from childhood of concealing the nature of his sexuality and leading a secret life. Who knows what else was going on in Andrew Cunanan's head, aside from his homosexuality? Cunanan might have felt betrayed by men he held important to him in his life—perhaps violated by his priest, abandoned by his father. In his last year, he was rejected by Grundy, his last millionaire "sugar daddy"; spurned by Madson, the man he loved; and turned away by Trail, his best friend. He killed the last two, and Lee Miglin in Chicago was an excellent stand-in for Grundy. There is no question that Miglin's murder was an angry one.

The murder of Versace, coming two months after Cunanan had committed his string of murders almost one after another, is the strangest to explain. Cunanan can certainly be considered a "spree killer" in his first four murders, but the killing of Versace two months later is atypical. The gay bondage magazines Cunanan left behind in his room are evidence that his violent fantasies were not satiated by the murders. At that point, he had gestated into a serial killer perhaps with a burning hatred of gay males higher in the pecking order, more popular, more successful. As Ted Bundy once said, "Some people are just psychologically less ready for failure than others."

John Allen Muhammad and John Lee Malvo— "The Beltway Snipers"

John Allen Muhammad and John Lee Malvo were arrested for the Washington, D.C., beltway sniper killings, charged with at least ten shooting deaths in October 2002. Needless to say, forty-one-year-old Muhammad, who became a surrogate father to the seventeen-year-old Malvo, appears to have been the dominant half of the team.

John Allen Williams, who changed his surname to Muhammad in 2001, grew up in East Baton Rouge, Louisiana. His mother died when he was three and his father appears to have been absent—Muhammad was raised by his grandfather and elderly aunt. His relatives remember him as a happy kid. He was a star football player in high school.

After graduation in 1978, Muhammad enlisted in the Louisiana National Guard and married his high school sweetheart. They had a son. His fellow guardsmen remember Muhammad as an outgoing and friendly person, frequently bringing his son around to show him off.

In 1982 the first signs of trouble began to appear. He was fined and demoted one rank for failing to appear for duty; in 1983, he was fined again for striking an officer. In 1985 Muhammad converted to Islam, divorced his wife, and left the national guard to join the army. He moved to Fort Lewis, Washington, with his new girlfriend, whom he married in 1988; they had three children. His first wife, meanwhile, recalled that the divorce was bitter and that Muhammad attempted to control her and their son's life in a heavy-handed way. In 1995, Muhammad was accused of failing to return his son to his first wife after a scheduled visit.

From 1990 to 1992 Muhammad served overseas and participated in Operation Desert Storm clearing mines and bulldozing holes through Iraqi defense lines. During his military service, Muhammad achieved an "expert" marksman's grade—the highest shooting qualification in the Army.

Shortly after Muhammad's arrest, *Newsweek* magazine interviewed his former sergeant in the gulf, Kip Berentson, who stated that Muhammad was "trouble from day one."[132] Berentson said that somebody threw a thermite grenade, setting on fire the tent he was sleeping in with another sixteen men. Berentson stated that he immediately reported Muhammad as the most likely suspect and claims that the Army's Criminal Investigation Division led Muhammad away in handcuffs. Muhammad's military records, however, make no mention of the incident; in fact, they apparently indicate that he had a distinguished record in the gulf.

In February 1994, Muhammad left the army and attempted to open a karate school, but the effort failed. He attempted several other business enterprises, but all failed. In 1999 his second wife filed for divorce, and in

Gilles de Rais (1404–1440): The original "Bluebeard" believed to have murdered as many as eight hundred children in France. He confessed, "I caused their bodies to be cruelly opened and took delight in viewing their interior organs."
(Criminal History Archive)

Countess Elizabeth Báthory (1560–1615): This sadistic Transylvanian aristocrat is one of the few known female sexual serial killers. She is said to have murdered 650 young women in a ten-year period.
(Criminal History Archive)

On December 2, 1979, Richard Cottingham killed two women in this nondescript Times Square neighborhood hotel. He decapitated them and amputated their hands, then set fire to their corpses. The author briefly encountered him in the hotel's lobby as Cottingham was leaving the scene. *(Photo by author)*

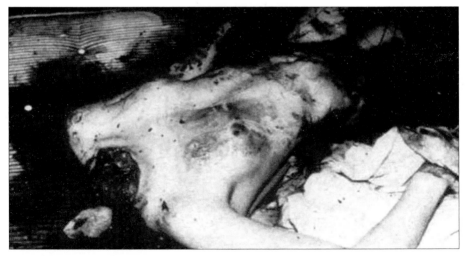

One of the Times Square torso victims found by the New York City Fire Department on the morning of December 2, 1979. *(Criminal History Archive/New York City Fire Department)*

POLICE COMMISSIONER'S
CIRCULAR No. 1
FEBRUARY. 1980

POLICE DEPARTMENT
CITY OF NEW YORK

PLEASE POST IN A
CONSPICUOUS PLACE

WANTED

INFORMATION REQUESTED HOMICIDE INVESTIGATION

DEEDEH GOODARZI

Color of coat is black.

Clothing worn by victim #2.

THE ABOVE PHOTOGRAPH IS OF DEEDEH GOODARZI, ALSO KNOWN AS JACQUELINE THOMAS, JACKIE THOMAS, SABRINA, AND CRYSTAL ROBERTS. GOODARZI IS ONE OF TWO VICTIMS OF A DOUBLE HOMICIDE WHICH OCCURED DURING THE EARLY MORNING HOURS OF DECEMBER 2nd 1979, AT THE ██████ ████████ HOTEL, ██ WEST 42nd STREET, MANHATTAN, N.Y., ROOM #417. BOTH VICTIMS HAD THEIR HEADS AND HANDS AMPUTATED. THE 10th PRECINCT DETECTIVE UNIT IS ENDEAVORING TO IDENTIFY THE SECOND FEMALE VICTIM WHOSE DESCRIPTION AND CLOTHING ARE AS FOLLOWS:

DESCRIPTION: Female, White, 16-22 years of age, between 5'1" to 5'4" tall, weighing about 100 to 110 lbs. The clothing of this victim, pictured above, are, a black full length cloth coat, a pair of "bon jour" blue jeans, size 7/8, a pair of black patent leather boots, size 8 and a burgundy colored mohair sweater, size 38.

PERSONS HAVING INFORMATION REGARDING THE SUBJECT OF THIS PHOTOGRAPH OR THE UNIDENTIFIED FEMALE, DESCRIBED ABOVE, SHOULD FORTHWITH NOTIFY THE 10th PRECINCT DETECTIVE UNIT, TELEPHONE 741-8245, 741-8225, 741-8229 OR 477-7448. CASE #1565/66, COMPLAINT Nos. 7615/27, DETECTIVE MICHAEL CLARK ASSIGNED.

ROBERT J. McGUIRE, Police Commissioner

Deedeh Goodarzi, twenty-three years old: one of the decapitated victims in the hotel. The other victim remains unidentified to this day. Their heads and hands were never located. The NYPD launched an intensive but futile hunt for the "Times Square Ripper."
(Criminal History Archive/New York Police Department)

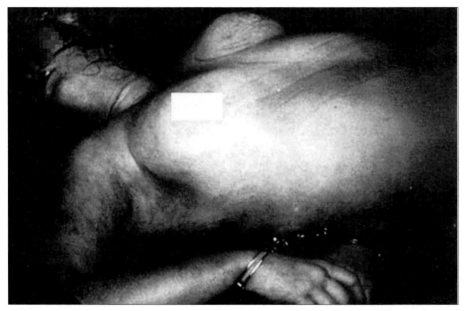

A nineteen-year-old victim found by housekeeping staff stuffed under a bed in a Hasbrouck Heights motel room in May 1980. Three weeks later the killer would lure another victim to the very same motel! None of the staff recognized him at check-in.

(Criminal History Archive/Bergen County Sheriff's Office)

Richard Francis Cottingham on trial: invisible monster whom no one remembered or noticed, including the author, whom he walked past carrying two human heads. In the end he would be convicted of five murders, including the three "torso" killings in New York. (The Record, *Hackensack, NJ)*

Typical wound patterns in a *picquerist*-type homicide. The female victim was found floating in a river in the 1950s. The killer expresses his sexuality by penetrating the victim with a knife. The victim's screams, the bloodletting, the odors, all create a harmonic sexual experience for the murderer. Some killers ejaculate uncontrollably as they stab or hack at their victims. This victim's injuries are very similar to the victims of Jack the Ripper.
(Toronto City Police)

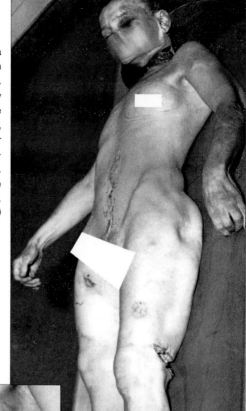

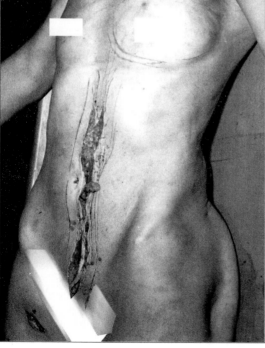

A closer view of the wounds reveal the killer's focus on the victim's genital area and breasts. Superficial wounds, so-called "hesitation cuts, are visible, indicating that the offender is not an experienced serial killer at all. Minor wounds around the breast suggest that the killer intended to amputate them but could not bring himself to commit the act. The progression of wounds from superficial to lethal reflects the killer's raging escalation during the attack. He may not kill again, but if he does, the mutilation and violence will escalate decisively.
(Toronto City Police)

Andrei Romanovich Chikatilo, the current record holder for the highest number of confirmed victims: fifty-three women, girls, and young men and boys. The author's random encounter with a second serial killer, this one in the Soviet Union in the autumn of 1991, inspired him to write this book.
(USSR Ministry of Interior)

The serial killer's murder kit: knives used by Chikatilo to kill and mutilate his victims. Chikatilo could be classified as a *picquerist*: somebody driven by a compulsion to substitute the sexual act with stabbing and slashing. Jack the Ripper was *picquerist*— one of history's oldest and deadliest sexual perversions.
(USSR Ministry of Interior)

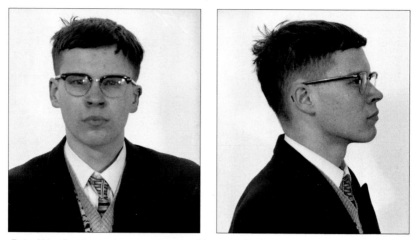

Peter Woodcock, aged seventeen, upon his arrest for the brutal serial murders of three children in Toronto, Canada, in 1956–57. *(Metropolitan Toronto Police)*

Peter Woodcock, aged nineteen, after two years of incarceration in a psychiatric facility.
(Ontario Solicitor General)

Peter Woodcock aged fifty-one, after thirty-four years of treatment. This photo was taken on the day he received his first day pass from a psychiatric facility and promptly murdered his fourth victim.
(Ontario Provincial Police/Ottawa Sun)

Peter Woodcock's first victim: September 1956, a seven-year-old male found on the grounds of a fair. The victim was strangled and suffocated by having his face pushed into the earth. At first the murder appeared not to have been sexually motivated, however, police discovered that the victim had been undressed and redressed by the killer. Note the doll-like state of the victim's clothing and the neatly buttoned jacket. The killer defecated near the victim's feet.

(Metropolitan Toronto Police)

The serial killer's signature: a compulsive sprinkling of ten coins next to the victim's body, an act unnecessary to the commission of the actual offense. *(Metropolitan Toronto Police)*

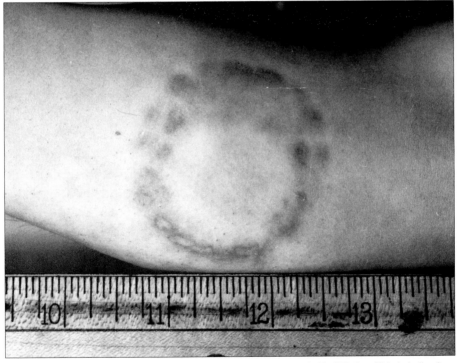

The killer's bite found beneath the victim's clothing on the bottom half of his leg. This is indicative of a highly enraged and sadistic killer who could potentially escalate to more extensive mutilation or cannibalistic rituals in future homicides. *(Metropolitan Toronto Police)*

The second victim: October 1956, a nine-year-old boy found in an industrial-port area. The victim was strangled. Again, the victim was undressed and then redressed before the killer fled the scene on his bicycle, but did not show any signs of overt sexual assault. *(Metropolitan Toronto Police)*

The signature: ten paper clips compulsively deposited next to the victim's body.
(Metropolitan Toronto Police)

The third victim: January 1957, a four-year-old girl found beneath a bridge. The serial killer not only escalated the violence of his attack by inserting a branch into his victim and battering her with a rock, but also changed his choice of sex of the victim and left her in a state of undress.
(Metropolitan Toronto Police)

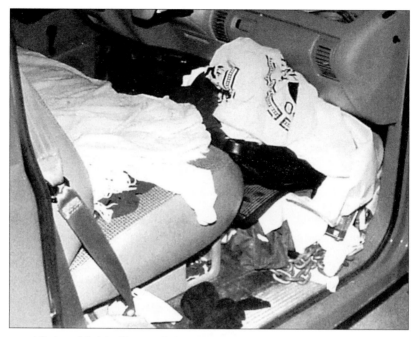

The spree killer's mobile lair: After murdering the owner of this truck, Andrew Cunanan frequently slept and traveled in it for six weeks until he shot fashion designer Gianni Versace in Miami. This is the state the vehicle was found in by police a few blocks away from the murder scene. *(Criminal History Archive/Miami Beach Police Department)*

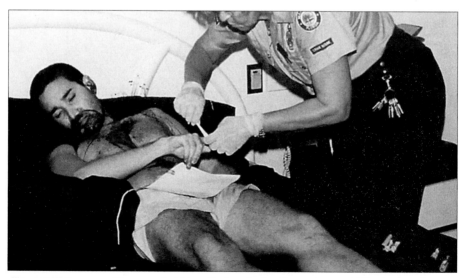

The end of the spree: Cunanan shot himself when the boathouse he was hiding in was about to be searched. *(Criminal History Archive/Miami Beach Police Department)*

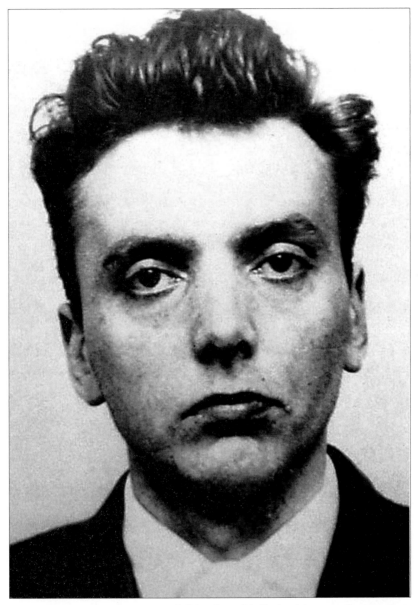

Ian Brady, one of the Moors murderers. Still imprisoned in England, he recently wrote that serial murder, "not only represents the rite of confirmation, a revelational leap of lack of faith in humanity, but also the onset of addiction to hedonistic nihilism." *(Criminal History Archive/U.K. Home Office)*

CLOCKWISE: Herbert Mullin, thirteen victims; Edmund Kemper, ten victims; Angelo Buono, one of the Hillside Stranglers; John Wayne Gacy, thirty-three victims. *(Criminal History Archive/Various Police Agencies)* Gary Ridgway, the Green River Killer, forty-eight victims. *(King County Sheriff's Office, WA)*

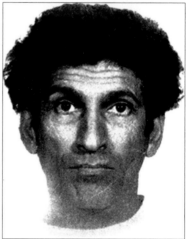

response Muhammad became highly threatening. In March 2000, she was granted a restraining order against Muhammad. Ten days later Muhammad snatched their three children and vanished. During that period he traveled to Antigua, where it is believed he met the teenage John Lee Malvo and his mother, both Jamaican nationals. Malvo's former teachers and relatives in Jamaica remember the boy as clever, sweet-natured, friendly, and obedient. "Obedient" was the most often recalled characteristic. Never a hint of trouble, always respectful, and friendly. One of his friends recalled, "He was fun to be around. He always tried to create an atmosphere of love. He always wanted to entertain, make you laugh."[133]

Malvo was also remembered as being small for his age and occasionally bullied for it. Malvo was often left in the care of his relatives or other guardians by his absent mother. His guardians, teachers, and relatives appeared very fond of Malvo and expressed concern when his mother shunted him back and forth from her custody to that of others. Eventually his mother took Malvo away to Antigua, where Muhammad encountered them.

In the summer of 2001, Muhammad returned to Washington and changed his legal name from Williams to Muhammad. Around the same time, Malvo and his mother illegally slipped into Florida in August 2001. It is still unclear what transpired, but in the summer of 2001 the police, with the help of Isa Nichols, a business consultant who had known both Muhammad and his wife, recovered the children Muhammad had abducted.

By October 2001, Malvo had joined Muhammad in Bellingham, Washington, calling him his father. The two were sleeping on bunks in a shelter for the homeless. Witnesses recall Malvo calling Muhammad "Dad" and "Sir." Muhammad submitted the boy to some kind of training program consisting of jogging in the early mornings, working out, and adhering to strict Islamic dietary rules. Although an illegal immigrant, Malvo was put into a high school in Bellingham briefly, where students recall that the boy was well versed in the history and military technology of the Vietnam and Gulf wars.

The pair hung out at a coffee shop where Muhammad began to pay inordinate attention to a guitar player and her son. Claiming to be a record producer, he invited her to come with him to New York. She recalls, however, having a "bad feeling" about him; Muhammad seemed overly interested in her son and his half-black ethnicity.

In December, Malvo's mother arrived in Bellingham seeking her son. The police inquiry into his whereabouts resulted in Malvo's being detained briefly for immigration violations. Pending a hearing, he was released and continued to live with Muhammad while his mother vanished—probably on the run from immigration authorities.

In February 2002, Muhammad was arrested for shoplifting food worth $27 from a grocery store. That same month, twenty-one-year-old Keenya Cook, who lived with her aunt Isa Nichols, the woman who had helped police recover the children Muhammad abducted, opened her front door and was killed by a shot to her face. Police have not solved the murder, but the possible implications are obvious.

In April, Muhammad visited a former army buddy, showed him two rifles and a silencer, and apparently ranted about how much damage those weapons, if silenced, could do. Muhammad was coming apart, and somehow the process involved the loss of his children and his attempts to substitute them with surrogates.

In June 2002, Muhammad took Malvo to his childhood hometown in Louisiana, where he visited his cousins. They recall that Muhammad was uncharacteristically haggard, dirty, and sullen, while Malvo appeared fearful and withdrawn. Muhammad showed his cousin his rifle and ammunition and claimed to be on some kind of secret mission for Special Forces. He contacted his first wife in Louisiana and then turned north toward the Washington, D.C., area, where his second wife had recently moved with their three sons.

The movements of Muhammad and Malvo between June and September 2002 are very obscure. We know that on September 10, Muhammad purchased the blue Caprice automobile that would be modified as a mobile sniper's nest. Muhammad and the vehicle were seen in the vicinity of his second wife's residence in Maryland. On September 21, two women were ambushed and shot outside a liquor store in Montgomery, Alabama. One of the victims died. Although the details are still unclear, police have some kind of forensic evidence that links the crime to Muhammad and Malvo.

From October 1 to October 22, the world was transfixed by a series of sniper shootings in the Washington, D.C.–Maryland area. All took place near the extensive freeway system and paralyzed daily life in the region. Outdoor school activities were suspended, and every shooting broke into television programming as soon as it occurred. Some kind of communication demanding a $10 million ransom to cease killing was received from the snipers, and a tarot card was reported to have been left at one of the scenes. Ten victims in all were killed until apparently the snipers, in a phone call, linked themselves to the Montgomery, Alabama, shooting, from which their identity via fingerprints was surfaced. Within hours of the release of a description of the wanted men, they were apprehended asleep in their vehicle.

Muhammad and Malvo faced judge and jury in separate trials in the autumn of 2003. It appears that Muhammad might have acted as the "spotter" while the younger Malvo actually committed eight of the ten shootings—the prosecution never presented any evidence clearly indicating that Muhammad was the trigger man in any of the murders. Muhammad, nevertheless, was found guilty in November, with the jury recommending the death sentence. The teenage Malvo's defense, in the meantime, is that he was "brainwashed" by the older Muhammad.

The motive behind the shooting spree remains unclear. According to Malvo's defense attorney, the shootings were part of a secret plan by Muhammad to murder his ex-wife, Mildred, and regain custody of his children. The plan, unknown to Malvo, was to shoot Mildred and make it seem to be only one of the many sniper murders. The prosecution contends that the shootings were intended to extort a $10 million ransom with which Muhammad intended to establish a utopian commune in Canada for youngsters from around the world.

During his questioning by police, Malvo was asked, "Were you the trigger man in all of them?"

"Basically, yeah."

"Basically means, in most but not all?"

"In all of them."

When asked what the objective of the murders was, Malvo replied, "It's a plan. You stick to it. You don't deviate. You don't change it."

At his trial in November, his sixth-grade teacher testified that Malvo was "very dependable, hardworking. Whenever he was given a task, he'd do it to the end."

His aunt, with whom he lived once, also testified, "He was very obedient. When I set down rules, he would obey them."

Malvo was convicted in December and the jury recommended the youth be given a life sentence.

Whatever the motives, Muhammad and Malvo fit the newly emerging profile of the spree serial killer. Unlike the typical spree killer, they did not unleash their destruction oblivious to their own safety or escape. Instead they killed selectively and evaded the danger of arrest. Muhammad and Malvo were highly organized, carefully selecting sites that offered them quick access to the highway system for escape and customizing their vehicle as a sniper's nest. But unlike traditional serial killers, they did not return to a normal life between their kills. They moved in a state of killing frenzy from murder to murder.

It will probably be found that Muhammad was the leading actor in these crimes and their timing reflected events in his life. Like Cunanan, Muhammad attempted to sustain a traditional life and career but somehow for some reason he failed. He was unable to cope with the failure and "snapped" into a raging homicidal campaign that took the lives of anywhere from ten to twelve innocent victims. In both cases, the homicidal snap followed a series of lesser breaks from the norms of society. Cunanan was dealing drugs; Muhammad was insubordinate in the military, abducted his children, and threatened his ex-wife. From a family man with a job in the military to a father with a bed in a homeless shelter whose children had been taken away, Muhammad was unable to cope with the failures of his life without blaming somebody or taking some kind of spectacularly lethal revenge. Cunanan's decline mirrored a similar pattern.

What probably made Cunanan and Muhammad serial spree killers as opposed to mass killers is the absence of serious mental illness and the intact remnants of their intelligence, ego, and capability. Both Cunanan and Muhammad were relatively competent, proud, goal-oriented individuals, and they carried that competence with them into their killing sprees.

None of these criteria and categories are necessarily immutable. Every few years a serial killer appears on the scene whose sick fantasies and imagination defy the previously defined parameters and criteria. One only needs to remember that when Renwick Williams was prosecuted in 1790 as London "Monster" for slashing women's clothing, his crime was described as "a scene that is so new in the annals of humanity, a scene so inexplicable, so unnatural, that one might have regarded it, out of respect for human nature, as impossible." The annals of humanity, unfortunately, have come a long way since then, and probably still have a distance to go: Nothing is impossible!

FIVE

THE QUESTION OF MADNESS:

Inside Their Heads

*The biggest mistake in trying to figure out why these people are this way
is that we try to analyze them through our own standard of behavior.
They don't think the way you or I think. We're not sure why—but the point is they don't.*
—JIM WRIGHT, FBI Behavioral Sciences Unit

When we remember that we are all mad, the mysteries disappear and life stands explained.
—MARK TWAIN

Few would disagree that Herbert Mullin, who thought he was saving California from the great earthquake by killing people, and Ed Gein, who was making chairs out of human skin, were entirely insane when they committed their acts. The question becomes more difficult with somebody like law student Ted Bundy, who killed twenty women while at the same time working as a suicide prevention counselor, or John Wayne Gacy, who escorted the first lady and then went home to sleep over thirty-three trussed-up corpses under his house. On one hand their crimes seem "insane," yet on the other hand, Bundy and Gacy knew exactly what they were doing. How insane were they?

The Insanity Plea

Part of the problem is that there is no precise definition of insanity—doctors define insanity differently from courts of law. The insanity plea has existed in English jurisprudence since the reign of Henry III (1216–1272), when the king could commute a death sentence of an insane criminal if it was demonstrated that irrational behavior was not unusual for the person in the past. In such cases, the prisoner would often end up being confined in a monastery. In the next century the plea was moved into the regular appeals process, no longer requiring the king's authority. In 1581 legal authorities were arguing what a test of insanity should consist of in law, settling upon "knowledge of good and evil" as the test.[134]

In 1843, English jurisprudence developed the concept of insanity as a defense against charges of murder. A mentally ill man named Daniel M'Naghten came to believe that he was personally being threatened by Prime Minister Sir Robert Peel and mistakenly shot and killed Peel's private secretary. He was acquitted on the grounds of insanity in what is known to this day as the *M'Naghten rule*. It is used in many Western countries today, including the United States, to define insanity in the courts. It states that to establish a successful defense on the ground of insanity:

> It must be clearly proved that, at the time of the committing of the act, the party accused was laboring under such a defect of reason, from disease of the mind, as not to know the nature and quality of the act he was doing; or, if he did know it, that he did not know he was doing what was wrong.[135]

In other words, to claim insanity, a defendant needs to prove that he could not distinguish between right and wrong, or that he was not aware of what he was doing, *because of* mental illness.

In 1887, U.S. judges expanded the test for an insanity plea. They felt that while the M'Naghten rule excused those who could not tell right from wrong, it did not excuse those who knew they were doing wrong but could not resist the impulse to do so because of mental incapacity. Ruling in *State of Alabama v. Parsons,* the judges stated:

> If, by reason of duress of such mental disease, he had so far lost the *power to choose* between the right and wrong, and to avoid doing the act in question, as that his free agency was at the time destroyed.[136]

In 1954, American courts further broadened the ground for a plea of insanity in *Durham v. United States:* "An accused is not criminally responsible if his unlawful act was the product of mental disease or mental defect."[137]

This broad decision was codified by the acceptance of American courts in 1962 of a test proposed by the American Law Institute:

> A person is not responsible for criminal conduct if at the time of such conduct as a result of mental disease or defect he lacks substantial capacity either to appreciate the criminality [wrongfulness] of his conduct or to conform his conduct to the requirements of law. The terms "mental disease or defect" do not include an abnormality manifested only by repeated criminal or otherwise anti social conduct.[138]

Between 1955 and 1984, every trial where this defense was used required the conflicting testimony of psychiatrists who frequently disagreed on an exact definition of "mental incapacity" and its effect on an "irresistible impulse" of a defendant. Defense lawyers for serial killers who were lucid, cleverly concealed their crimes, and functioned in their daily lives argued that they were not guilty by reason of insanity—that they could not resist the impulse to kill, even though they knew it was wrong, because they were sick.

This broad definition of legal insanity came crashing down between Dan White's so-called "Twinkie Defense"* in the murder of San Francisco mayor George Moscone and supervisor Harvey Milk in 1978 and John Hinckley's acquittal by reason of insanity for his attempt to gun down President Ronald Reagan. In October 1984 Congress passed the Insanity Defense Reform Act, which returned the insanity pleas in federal courts closer to the original M'Naghten definition and set a model for state courts as well:

> At the time of the commission of the acts constituting the offense, the defendant, as a result of a severe mental disease or defect, was unable to appreciate the nature and quality or the wrongfulness of his acts. Mental disease or defect does not otherwise constitute a defense.

---

* It's a myth that White's defense argued that his consumption of Twinkies and other junk food triggered a homicidal depression. They actually argued that his eating habits were a *symptom of* depression, which diminished his capacity to tell right from wrong.

The inability to resist an impulse to kill, for whatever reason, is no longer a viable defense for a serial killer. Most serial killers do not fit the legal definition of insanity, especially the organized ones. They search for and stalk their victims, they arrive with weapons and restraints prepared, they take their time killing, and they destroy the evidence afterward, demonstrating a full knowledge of the consequences of their crime. They elude detection and therefore are obviously aware of the wrongfulness of their act.

This was clearly hammered home with the trial of Jeffrey Dahmer in 1992, who was charged in Milwaukee, Wisconsin, with the murders of fifteen men and boys. He kept some of their body parts in his fridge, occasionally eating them. He constructed altars from their skulls while reducing the remains of their corpses in drums of acid stored in his bedroom. He attempted to transform several of his still-living victims into sex zombies by drilling through their skulls and injecting their brains with battery acid. One would think, if that's not crazy, then what the hell is? And that is precisely the argument his attorney attempted to present. It did not work.

So what is wrong with these guys? Obviously something makes them different from the rest of us. Describing them as merely evil seems too simplistic and unscientific—after all, what is "evil" exactly? Psychologists over the last decade have been desperately attempting to evolve clinical definitions and explanations for the deeds and personalities of serial killers.

Psychotics and Psychopaths

The two concepts most often associated with serial killers by the public, press, law enforcement, and academia are *psychotic* and *psychopath*. The two terms have very different meanings.

A psychotic is someone who has *psychosis*, a debilitating organic mental illness, still not entirely understood, that can result in delusions, hallucinations, and radical changes of behavior. Individuals with this disorder are rarely violent, and very few serial killers are diagnosed as psychotic. In a study of 2,000 people arrested for murder between 1964 and 1973, only 1 percent were found to be psychotic.[139] The psychotic's incapacitating disconnection with reality rarely makes him a good candidate for a long career as a serial killer. Psychotics who display violence most often direct it at themselves.

On the other hand, serial killers are most often diagnosed as *psychopaths,* or another closely related term, *sociopath.* A psychopath is profoundly different from a psychotic. The psychopathic state is not so much a mental illness as a *behavioral or personality disorder.* One forensic psychiatrist described it as follows:

> A morality that is not operating by any recognized or accepted moral code, but operating entirely according to expediency to what one feels like doing at the moment or that which will give the individual the most gratification or pleasure.[140]

Psychologist S. K. Henderson described psychopaths in his 1939 text as follows:

> The term psychopathic state is the name we apply to those individuals who conform to a certain intellectual standard, sometimes high, sometimes approaching the realm of defect but yet not amounting to it, who throughout their lives, or from a comparatively early age, have exhibited disorders of conduct of an antisocial or asocial nature, usually of a recurrent or episodic type, where, in many instances, have proved difficult to influence by methods of social, penal, and medical care and treatment and for whom we have no adequate provision of a preventive or curative nature. The inadequacy or deviation or failure to adjust to ordinary social life is not a mere willfulness or badness which can be threatened or thrashed out of the individual so involved, but constitutes a true illness for which we have no specific explanation.[141]

Psychologists theorize that psychopaths have a diminished capacity to experience fear and anxiety, which are the roots to the normal development of a conscience. Psychopaths are often very charismatic and very able at manipulating people. They are highly talented in feigning emotions while inside feeling nothing. They have no remorse for their victims and have highly developed psychological defense mechanisms such as rationalization ("She should have known better than to hitchhike"), projection ("She was a heartless manipulating slut"), and disassociation ("I don't remember killing her"). They have a very weak realization of self and compensate for that with grandiosity and an inflated notion of entitlement—meaning that they feel that they are special and "entitled" to act above the law or morality. Most notably, psychopaths lack any sense of empathy with the feelings of others.

A psychiatric manual lists some of the primary characteristics of the psychopath, many if not all of which can be found in a serial killer: glibness and superficial charm; grandiosity; continuous need for stimulation; pathological lying; conning and manipulative behavior; lack of remorse or guilt; shallow affect; callous lack of empathy; parasitic lifestyle; poor behavioral controls; promiscuity; early behavior problems; lack of realistic long-term goals; impulsivity; irresponsibility; failure to accept responsibility for actions; many short-term relationships; juvenile delinquency; revocation of conditional release; and criminal versatility.[142]

While not all psychopaths are violent, they are prone to violence more than average. It is estimated that 20 to 30 percent of prison populations consist of psychopaths.[143] But the same might be said for the populations of corporate CEOs, performing artists, and certainly for politicians. Being a psychopath alone does not make one a serial killer.

The official psychiatric term for a psychopath is *antisocial personality disorder*. The diagnostic criteria for this disorder, as described by the standard *Diagnostic and Statistical Manual of Mental Disorders,* 4th edition (*DSM-IV*), are as follows:

A. There is a pervasive pattern of disregard for and violation of the rights of others occurring since age 15 years, as indicated by at least three (or more) of the following:

1. failure to conform to social norms with respect to lawful behaviors as indicated by repreatedly performing acts that are grounds for arrest
2. deceitfulness, as indicated by repeated lying, use of aliases, or conning others for personal profit or pleasure
3. impulsivity or failure to plan ahead
4. irritability and aggressiveness, as indicated by repeated physical fights and assaults

5. reckless disregard for the safety of self or others
6. consistent irresponsibility, as indicated by repeated failure to sustain consistent work behavior or honor financial obligations
7. lack of remorse, as indicated by indifference to or rationalizing having hurt, mistreated, or stolen from another

B. Individual is at least age 18 years.

C. There is evidence of Conduct Disorder with onset before age 15 years.

D. The occurrence of antisocial behavior is not exclusively during the course of a Schizophrenic or Manic Episode.

E. Evidence of conduct disorder onset before age fifteen.[144]

BIOSOCIAL INTERACTION

Generally speaking, violent psychopaths emerge out of a combination of personal social conditions and biological and genetic factors. Brain injuries can cause a psychopathic behavioral pattern; many serial killers have a record of head injuries when they were children or recent injuries prior to their beginning to kill. But this is not the *cause* of their murderous behavior—other behavioral problems are already present. Healthy people who sustain head injuries do not become killers.

Psychopaths also show abnormal balances of chemicals currently linked to depression and compulsive behavior: monoamine oxidase (MAO) and serotonin. They show cortical underarousal, high CSF free testosterone, and EEG abnormalities.[145] A high level of urine kryptopyrrole and an extra Y chromosome have also been suspected as factors in the violent behavior of psychopaths.[146]

There is evidence that some type of congenital genetic abnormalities resulting in brain damage may be common to many serial killers. Nineteenth-century criminology tended to promote the idea of a genetic criminal type. This idea has been swept away in the twentieth century by environmental theories. Now criminology is beginning to steer a line somewhere in between the two approaches.

Forensic psychologist Joel Norris listed twenty-three types of physical characteristics of which three or more would indicate congenital genetic disorders and which he frequently found in serial killers he studied. Some of these characters included malformed ears; curved fifth finger; larger than normal gap between first and second toes; fine or electric wire hair that will not comb down; bulbous fingertips; and a speckled tongue with either smooth or rough spots.[147]

The prevailing theory is that there is a delicate balance between a chaotic or abusive childhood and biochemical factors that can trigger murderous psychopathic behavior. Healthy social factors can prevent a biochemically unstable individual from committing criminal acts; healthy biochemistry can protect a person with a turbulent childhood from growing up to be a killer. Violent offenders emerge when both elements are out of balance. This theory goes a long way to explain why some children with difficult childhoods do not become serial killers and not everyone with a head injury behaves criminally.

CAN PSYCHOPATHS BE TREATED AND CURED?

The problem with psychopaths is that the disorder is highly elusive— it is not a disease that can been directly traced to a single chemical, viral, or organic agent; it is a mysterious behavioral disorder whose history is buried deep in the offender's psychology, environment, and biochemistry. It is likely that a cure for cancer will be found before psychopaths can be routinely treated and cured. Numerous serial killers, after committing their first murders and being sent to psychiatric facilities or receiving psychiatric treatment in prison, were deemed "cured" and committed more escalated series of murders after their release. Edmund Kemper, for example, murdered his grandparents at age fifteen and was released after five years to murder seven women, including his mother. (See his case study later in this chapter.) Arthur Shawcross murdered two children in Watertown, New York; served fourteen years with treatment; and then was released in April 1987. By 1990 he had murdered eleven women in the Rochester area and was captured having lunch over a corpse he had dumped several days earlier. Richard Biegenwald was released after serving seventeen years for murder and went on to kill another seven victims before being sent back to prison.

Most often, however, psychopaths cure themselves as they age. Starting from age twenty-one, approximately 2 percent of all psychopaths go into remission every year.[148] The older the psychopath becomes, the more likely that he will become adjusted to society—especially in his midforties.

This may account for the relatively young average age of serial killers (midtwenties) and for why some serial killers vanish without being captured or identified.

Successful treatment of psychopaths, however, is so rare that articles trumpet them in psychiatric journals with a grandeur akin to the discovery of a new planet. The *International Journal of Offender Therapy and Comparative Criminology* in 1999 described a "Marcel" who raped six children and, while in a psychiatric facility, raped an adult male. After undergoing therapy, Marcel has apparently been living a normal life for the last twenty years.[149] In 2003, in the same journal, an article described a "Mr. X" who sought out treatment for his fantasies of becoming a serial killer. The article states, however, that Mr. X, while having some similar traits of serial killers, did not show any signs of being a psychopath when tested. The Ohio psychiatrists who treated Mr. X concluded, "This lack of psychopathy may have led him to treatment rather than to carrying out the planned homicides."[150]

Peter Woodcock (David Michael Krueger)— Thirty-Five Years of Therapy

I have read a lot of case histories in researching this book, but few compare to the story of my own hometown serial killer, Peter Woodcock in Toronto. "Crazier than a shithouse rat" may not be a highly scientific term, but it's the only one that comes to mind. Few have heard of Peter Woodcock, who committed his first series of crimes in 1956–1957 and escapes mention in all serial killer encyclopedias and lists (which makes me wonder how many other "hometown" serial killers around the world are not catalogued by researchers).

Woodcock was born March 5, 1939, in Toronto, Canada. It is unclear whether his young mother, Wanita Woodcock, was a seventeen-year-old factory worker or a nineteen-year-old prostitute—the record is conflicted. An adoption was arranged after his mother was allowed to keep him for a month to breast-feed him. Adoption agency records report that already in that first month, Peter showed feeding problems and cried constantly.[151]

As an infant he was shunted around numerous foster homes, unable to bond with any of his foster parents. In his first year he cried constantly and slept and ate little. After his first birthday he became terrified of anybody approaching him. He learned to talk but his speech was incoherent, described as strange whining animal noises. He had problems with at least one of the foster placements at around age two—he was treated in an emergency hospital with an injured neck as a result of a beating at the hands of one foster parent.

Peter was finally placed in a stable home when he was three. His new foster parents—Frank and Susan Maynard—were an upper-middle-class couple who had a son ten years older than Peter. Susan Maynard is said to have been a forceful woman with an exaggerated sense of propriety who became very attached to the weird child who had difficulty walking and still screamed when anyone came near.

By age five Peter had stopped screaming at the approach of strangers but remained a weird and lonely child. Other children in the neighborhood refused to play with him and he became a target for bullies. Between ages seven and twelve, Woodcock was treated extensively for emotional problems in Toronto's renowned Hospital for Sick Children.

His primary problem was a tendency to wander away from home great distances, sometimes staying away several nights. After one search, he was found cowering in some bushes and explained that he was hiding from other children. He killed the family's pet canary, blaming it on the dog. He tore down window blinds, hacked up his socks, cut his clothing, smashed the radio, and carved crude symbols into the dining room table. He also developed a strange walk in which he would swing his arms forward on the same side he would step forward.

Woodcock says that when he was seven or eight, his mother underwent a transformation after being pushed down a railway station staircase in an attempted purse snatching. After that, he says, she would beat him with a beaded rod.

Peter lived in a vivid fantasy world full of obsessions. One of his primary obsessions was Toronto's streetcar system and he compulsively rode and tracked the various routes. Decades later, while he was incarcerated in a psychiatric hospital and much of Toronto's streetcar system had been changed or dismantled, Woodcock could still recall from memory the various routes and their schedules.

Peter was sent to a nearby private school, but the weird child did not do very well there. He made no friends, participated in no games, and remained isolated from other children.

By age eleven, Peter was an angry little boy. A Children's Aid Society report written when Woodcock was eleven years old describes him as follows:

> Slight in build, neat in appearance, eye bright, and wide open, worried facial expression, sometimes screwing up of eyes, walks briskly and erect, moves rapidly, darts ahead, interested and questioning constantly in conversation . . .
>
> He attributes his wandering to feeling so nervous that he just has to get away. In some ways, Peter has little capacity for self-control. He appears to act out almost everything he thinks and demonstrates excessive affection for his foster mother. Although he verbalizes his resentment for other children, he has never been known to physically attack another child . . .
>
> Peter apparently has no friends. He plays occasionally with younger children, managing the play. When with children his own age, he is boastful and expresses determinedly ideas which are unacceptable and misunderstood.

At one point, when the social worker was walking with Woodcock at Toronto's annual fair—the Exhibition—little Peter muttered, "I wish a bomb would fall on the Exhibition and kill all the children."

Peter Woodcock was sent to a special school for emotionally disturbed children in Kingston, Ontario, a small town two hours east of Toronto. There, according to Woodcock, he began to act out on strong sexual urges with other children. He says that he had consensual intercourse with a twelve-year-old girl when he was thirteen. When Peter turned fifteen, he was discharged from the school and returned to live with his foster parents. He was reenrolled at the private school, where he remained isolated from the other children.

When Woodcock was sixteen he was sent to a public high school where kids from the neighborhood instantly recognized him and severely tormented him. Six weeks later he was transferred to a private high school. His teachers there remember him as a very bright student who excelled in science, history, and English and frequently scored 100 percent on his tests. While his peers shunned him, many adults liked him for his quick wit and intelligence. He was remembered as charming and able to hold his own in conversations. He was also a frequent visitor to a police station near his home, where he would chat with officers about police work.

Peter Woodcock's prize possession was a red and white Pee-Wee Herman Schwinn bicycle on which he satisfied his continuing compulsion to wander. He rode the bike to the far reaches of the city, even during the Toronto deep cold winters. He evolved a fantasy in which he led a gang of five hundred invisible boys on bikes called the Winchester Heights Gang. His foster parents were aware of that fantasy and his obsession for the public transit system and compulsion to wander. But nobody knew exactly what the seventeen-year-old Peter did on his long bike rides in the city.

Even today, Toronto is a remarkably crime-free city. With 2.5 million inhabitants it registers roughly fifty-two homicides a year—one a week on average. Back in 1956, the city's population hovered around the 1 million mark but the city averaged a mere ten homicides a year. Most murders were typically the result of domestic disputes or drunken brawls. Weird and strange unsolved homicides rarely occurred in Toronto in those days. Then on the evening of September 15, 1956, seven-year-old Wayne Mallette went out to play and failed to come home.

His body was found by the police approximately six hours later on the grounds of the Exhibition—the very same one on which Woodcock hoped a bomb would drop and kill all the children. The boy was dressed in a British schoolboy blazer, shirt, and plaid pants. It appeared that his clothing had been removed and he had then been re-dressed. The cause of death was strangulation. His face was pushed into the dirt and two bite marks were found on the body—one on the boy's calf and the other on his buttock. There was no evidence of rape. Pennies were found ritualistically scattered near the body and the killer had apparently defecated next to the victim as well. Police found faint bicycle tracks near the crime scene. Witness had recollections of a young teenage boy on a bike in the area.

Nine days after the murder, a fourteen-year-old boy, Ronald Mowatt, skipped school and vanished for four days. He was found hiding by police in a crawlspace beneath a staircase with a blanket and pillow. To police, he seemed a likely suspect, and before the night was out he had even signed a confession stating that he had killed Mallette accidentally in a scuffle. Nobody bothered to compare the bite marks to the accused boy's actual teeth, or if they did in those times before strict rules of discovery, nobody shared the information with the boy's defense counsel.

Three weeks later, nine-year-old Garry Morris was found dead in a grassy area near the city's port. The boy appeared to have been strangled into unconsciousness and beaten to death; he had died of a ruptured liver. There was a bite mark on his throat and this time paper clips seemed to have been ritualistically sprinkled near the corpse. Again, the clothing had been removed from the victim and then he had been re-dressed. Witnesses recalled the victim riding off on the front handlebars of a bike ridden by a teenage boy.

To this day there is no rational explanation why the Toronto police did not link the bite marks or the reports of the boy on a bike with the two child murders. Perhaps there was some police misbehavior behind Mowatt's confession—backtracking might have risked the careers of some senior homicide investigators. Mowatt was quickly convicted of murder in juvenile court and packed off to a reformatory to serve an indeterminate sentence.

On January 19, 1957, Carole Voyce, a four-year-old girl, was approached by a teenage boy on a bicycle while playing in front of her home and offered a ride. She was found dead later that night in a ravine under a bridge. Her clothes had been pulled off and she had been choked into unconsciousness. Her killer had stuck his fingers into her eyes, stripped off her clothes, and inserted his finger into her genitals. Death was caused by a branch pushed through her vagina. Tracks in the snow showed that the killer had attempted to leave the scene several times, but circled back to the victim again. At one point he had kicked her in the head. He was seen by witnesses biking out by a road at the bottom of the ravine.

Still refusing to link the murder to the Mallette killing, the police at least connected the Garry Morris and the Carole Voyce murders. A reward was offered and numerous witnesses came up with a description of the boy and his bike.

Peter Woodcock, in the meantime, continued visiting at the local police station, inquiring how the investigation was coming along. Forty years later Woodcock explained, "If you're going to do something, the last thing you do is break the patterns that you've set. Keep normal routines. It's only common sense that, if you're up to something, you don't draw attention to yourself . . . For me to have stepped out of character by not going into the police station would have been a grave mistake. They expected me to come in on a regular basis, just because I was one of those kids who came in on a regular basis. You don't do anything to arouse suspicion."[152]

In fact, Woodcock had been terrorizing and attacking children in Toronto for the last eleven months. In March the previous year he did, however, attract police attention. Woodcock had taken a ten-year-old girl to the ravine. Woodcock recalled:

> I did have plans to cut her up to see what she looked like inside. We got lost in the ravine in the dark and getting out seemed more important. I had a penknife with me. When you're naïve, a penknife seems enough to kill with. It was a turning point. I was already troubled with my fantasies and dreams. This ten-year-old girl, I did have plans of killing her. It didn't dawn on me that she would die. Well, I knew she would die, but that would be the extent of it. I wanted to look at the arm, see how the muscle attaches to it. This was going to be a very thorough anatomical lesson, though I don't believe I would have been able to name a third of the things I would have seen.[153]

Instead Woodcock and the girl returned home three hours late. Police had been called and came to the Maynard home, but the full extent of Woodcock's intentions remained hidden. He was scolded but not charged because no apparent harm had come to the girl. Woodcock promised his foster mother not to pick up any more children, but Woodcock says he continued to choke children into unconsciousness, strip their clothes away, and peer at their bodies. None of these crimes seem to have been reported—not a surprise in a conservatively Protestant city like Toronto of the 1950s. It was only in September when he went too far and killed his first victim, Wayne Mallette.

After the Carole Voyce murder, the two officers who had been called during the March episode quickly recalled the boy and his bike. Woodcock was arrested on the second day after the murder and quickly confessed. Revealingly he recalls, "My fear was that Mother would find out. Mother was my biggest fear. I didn't know if the police would let her at me."

Woodcock was found not guilty by reason of insanity and packed away into Ontario's criminal psychiatric system. (The prosecution insisted on keeping Ronald Mowatt, the boy convicted for Wayne Mallette's murder, incarcerated. He was not ordered released until May 1957, four months after Woodcock's arrest. The judge scolded him: "All I have to say to you is this. You of course yourself know whether your statement was true or not, if it was not true then you brought it upon yourself, all the trouble you have been in, in connection with this case, all the trouble given your parents, simply because you failed to tell the truth.")

Woodcock underwent thirty-five years of various forms of psychiatric therapy, including LSD treatments when they were popular in the 1960s. He was pumped full of other personality-breaking drugs: scopolamine, sodium amytal, methedrine, dexamyl.

He was subjected to "dyads"—a personality-breaking therapy in which inmates challenged each other's belief systems. The inmates referred to these sessions as "The Hundred-Day Hate-In." Dyads were developed in the late 1950s to early 1960s by a Harvard psychologist and former CIA interrogation and psychological warfare expert, Henry A. Murray. In the 1960s, one of Murray's volunteer personality-destruction subjects had been a young Harvard student—Ted Kaczynski, the future Unabomber.

Woodcock was not an ideal prisoner. He engaged in homosexual acts and exploited his fellow inmates, who were often less intelligent or less sane than he was. He formed an imaginary gang, the Brotherhood. He convinced inmates that he had contact with the mythical group on the outside. In order to be initiated into the gang, inmates had to perform oral sex on Woodcock and bring him gifts of cigarettes.

Somewhere along the way, *before* the Freddy Krueger movies came out, Woodcock legally changed his name to David Michael Krueger. The reason for his choice of name remains unclear, but his rejection of Woodcock had to do with the many puns being made of the name.

Despite the various infractions and problems with Woodcock, he gradually assumed a mask of stable sanity. He charmed the staff with his wit and intelligence in the same way he had charmed his schoolteachers three decades earlier. Psychiatric reports, however, consistently warned of his continued homicidal fantasies and characterized him as dangerous.

The problem was in the enormous political pressure on Ontario's prison and psychiatric systems to release inmates into the community to make way for new incoming offenders. By 1990, some thirty-five years after the murders, it was felt that the middle-aged Woodcock, or Krueger as he was now known, should be reintroduced into society—to continue holding him would be tantamount to admitting that the therapy programs were a failure.

Despite the objections of some of the psychiatric staff, Woodcock was transferred to a medium-security psychiatric facility in the town of Brockville, near Kingston, Ontario. As part of the preparation for Woodcock's release, hospital staff decided to issue him his first three-hour pass, allowing him to leave the hospital grounds, visit the town, buy a pizza, and bring it back to the facility. Woodcock, of course, would have to be escorted by somebody of his choice. Remarkably, under hospital rules, that person could be a former inmate of the facility. Woodcock nominated the recently released Bruce Hamill as his escort—a former "candidate" in Woodcock's imaginary Brotherhood. Hamill had spent several years in the facility after stabbing his elderly female neighbor to death. He was now considered "cured" and out on parole.

The details of Woodcock's and Hamill's communications prior to the day of the pass are unknown, but on July 13, 1991, Hamill arrived in Brockville carrying a pipe wrench wrapped in newspapers. He first went to a drugstore, where he purchased an over-the-counter sleeping medicine frequently abused by addicts. Then he went to a "big-box" hardware store and bought a hunting knife, hatchet, and sleeping bag. He rolled up the pipe wrench and weapons into the sleeping bag and proceeded on to the hospital, carrying the sleeping bag with him. Nobody bothered to unroll the sleeping bag and search it. Peter Woodcock met him at reception. The two then went for a stroll on the hospital grounds and selected a densely wooded area near the perimeter. They seeded the bushes with the weapons and then returned to the hospital building.

On the way back, they ran into another inmate, twenty-seven-year-old Dennis Kerr. He was another aspirant for membership in Woodcock's Brotherhood, and had been falsely promised by Woodcock a loan of five hundred dollars to buy a set of used drums. Woodcock told Kerr to meet him in the woods in an hour, and on the way into town he would give Kerr the money. Hamill and Woodcock returned to the hospital and filled out the paperwork for Woodcock's first pass in thirty-five years. Instead of leaving through the gate, they strolled off to the edge of the hospital grounds and slipped into the bushes to wait for Kerr. As they waited, Hamill quickly got high on the sleeping medication.

When Dennis Kerr arrived as instructed, Woodcock struck him in the head with the pipe wrench and continued to beat him into unconsciousness. After the first blow, Kerr apparently cried out, "What did you do that for?" Woodcock said:

> I could barely lift the thing, let alone swing it. I did manage to do it, and I got Dennis in the head. I hit him again, after he asked his little profound question, this time from the front, and he fell down, but not without a struggle. He struggled nearly the whole time. He seemed to be afraid to die.[154]

Woodcock and Hamill seized the hatchet and knife hidden in the bushes and hacked and stabbed Kerr, mutilating his body, cutting it open, and nearly severing his head. Drenched in Kerr's blood, they then stripped themselves naked and sodomized the corpse and chanted over it. This was Hamill's initiation into the Brotherhood.

Hamill soon passed out from the drug, while Woodcock stood over his naked body and gently caressed it with the blade of the knife. He decided he was too tired to kill Hamill. Putting on his bloody clothing, Woodcock then left the hospital grounds, walked to a police station about two miles away, and turned himself in.

He brought the police back to the murder site, where Hamill was found still sleeping next to the corpse. Woodcock was kept in police custody that night, and they noted that he masturbated openly until early morning of the next day—at least six times in the first ten hours of custody. He finally fell asleep, only to be roused with a bacon-and-egg breakfast. Woodcock said:

> Come the morning, I wake up, and they're serving bacon and eggs because it's Sunday. I haven't had bacon and eggs in something like five years. And I thought to myself, "Fancy this, all I had to do to get bacon and eggs was commit murder. You literally have to kill somebody if you want a good breakfast in this system."

So much for Peter Woodcock's first three hours of provisional freedom. Woodcock and Hamill were granted an insanity plea in December 1992 and sent back to where they came from—where they are once again being routinely evaluated for their suitability for release.

One really has difficulty summarizing Peter Woodcock's story without the word *evil* crossing the page. What other possible explanation can one have for the thirty-five years separating his first three murders and what was hopefully his last murder? What seems to happen is that confinement, whether in a psychiatric facility or a prison, somehow arrests the evolution of a serial killer's compulsion to kill. It doesn't cure it—just freezes it like a bacterial culture until freedom thaws it out and he begins from where he left off. This phenomenon has been noticed in several cases where killers were profiled as being younger than they actually were, their killing maturity was suspended by a prison sentence until their release, and they picked up from where they were the day they were arrested. Two years after his fourth murder, back in a maximum-security hospital, Woodcock-Krueger explained:

> I grew up here. My personality reflects the influences here, and I'm accused of having no morality, which is a fair assessment, because my morality is whatever the system allows, whatever I can get away with. In a setting like this, the people to fear are the staff, not God.[155]

Edmund Kemper—Serial Killer "Burn Out"

Perhaps one of the most studied serial killers, after Jack the Ripper and Ted Bundy, is Edmund Emil Kemper III of Santa Cruz, California. He was born in 1948 and was raised by an extremely domineering mother who often berated him in public. At age eight he was disciplined by his mother by being forced to sleep in a dark cellar for eight months, his only exit a trapdoor in the floor on which usually stood the kitchen table. When Ed was nine his father left, apparently unable to deal with his wife's domineering personality. Ed's mother constantly told him that he reminded her of his father—whom she hated.

At age ten, Ed Kemper was above average in size and his mother became obsessed with the thought that he would molest his sister. He was now sent back into the basement to sleep, locked in every night while his mother and sister slept in their bedrooms. His response was to kill the family cat by burying it alive. Afterward he cut the cat's head off and mounted it on a stick. When his sister received a doll for Christmas, Ed cut off the doll's head and hands.

When he was twelve his favorite game was "gas chamber," in which he asked his sister to tie him up and throw an imaginary switch. Ed tumbled over and writhed on the floor, pretending to be dying of gas.

One day his sister teased him that he liked his schoolteacher and wanted to kiss her. Ed replied, "If I kissed her I'd have to kill her first." He recalled that as a little boy he would sneak out of his house and, armed with his father's bayonet, go to his second-grade teacher's house and watch her through the windows. He fantasized about killing her and then making love to her corpse.

Ed was highly intelligent—his IQ was measured at 145, near-genius level. He also was abnormally tall for his age. At age thirteen he ran away from home to find his father. When he was returned he killed another family cat by cutting off the top of its skull with a machete and exposing its brains. He kept pieces of the cat in his closet until his mother found them.

Afterward his mother sent him to live with his paternal grandparents on their farm in the foothills of the California Sierras. There, like many boys living in a rural region, Ed was given a .22-caliber rifle for hunting. But when Ed began killing domestic farm animals and pets, his grandparents took the rifle away from him.

In August 1963, when Ed Kemper was fifteen, he suddenly killed both his grandparents. As his grandmother sat at the kitchen table reviewing children's stories she had written, Ed shot her in the head with the .22-caliber rifle. He fired two more shots into her back and then stabbed her repeatedly. He waited for his grandfather to come home and then shot him dead in the yard as he was coming up to the house. Afterward he phoned his mother and told her what he had done and calmly waited for the police to arrive. When asked at the time why he had committed the crimes, he replied, "I just wondered how it would feel to shoot grandma."

Kemper was confined at the Atascadero State Hospital in the criminally insane unit. There California Youth Authority psychiatrists and social workers strongly disagreed with the court psychiatrist's diagnosis. Their reports maintained that he showed "no flight of ideas, no interference with thought, no expression of delusions or hallucinations, and no evidence of bizarre thinking." He was diagnosed as having "personality trait disturbance, passive-aggressive type."

Kemper was such an endearing model prisoner and so intelligent that the staff trained him to administer psychiatric tests to other prisoners. Kemper later admitted that being able to understand how these tests functioned allowed him to manipulate his psychiatrists. Kemper also said that he learned a lot from the many sex offenders to whom he administrated tests; for example, he learned that it was important to kill witnesses after a rape. His psychiatrist meanwhile commented, "He was a very good worker and this is *not* typical of a sociopath. He really took pride in his work."

After five years, Kemper was certified no longer a danger to the public and released at age twenty-one to live with his mother. "They paroled me right back to mama," Kemper recalls. "Well, my mother and I started right in on horrendous battles, just horrible battles, violent and vicious."

His mother worked at the time as an administrator at the University of California in Santa Cruz and was a popular and helpful person at the campus. At home, however, Kemper claimed she was vicious and tormenting. Now divorced for the third time, she blamed her troubles on Ed, telling him, "because of you, my murderous son, I haven't had sex with a man for five years."[156] By now Kemper was a six-foot-nine-inch, 280-pound behemoth. His wish was to join the California Highway Patrol. His mother attempted to have his juvenile homicide record sealed so that he could join the police, but in the end he was rejected for being too big. Nonetheless, Kemper went to restaurants and bars frequented by police officers and often joined in their discussions and sat with them at the table. When he began killing, he got inside information on the course of the investigation. One police officer even gave him a police academy trainee's badge and identification card. He was so well liked and respected by the Santa Cruz police that when he telephoned to confess to killing and mutilating eight women, the police at first thought he was drunk and joking and refused to take his call seriously.

• • •

Kemper found a job with the California Highway Department and moved to a small apartment of his own. He complained that he still could not get away from his mother, that she constantly phoned him and paid him surprise visits. Kemper described using his "Atascadero learning" to "push her toward where she would be a nice motherly type and quit being such a damned manipulating, controlling beast."

During this period, Kemper made regular required visits to his probation psychiatrist. At the same time he started rehearsing for his upcoming series of kills. He is known to have picked up dozens of young women hitchhiking in the Santa Cruz area, developing a nonthreatening "gentle giant" persona. Later Kemper confessed that when he stopped in front of a female hitchhiker and she appeared unsure of getting into his car, he deliberately glanced at his watch. Kemper explained that this gesture subtly transmitted to the woman the message that he was a busy man and that she was of minor interest to him. Manipulation and control are the primary talents fueling the psychopathic serial killer.

On May 7, 1972, he struck. He picked up two college girls, Mary Anne Pesce and Anita Luchessa, hitchhiking on a freeway ramp. Knowing the area well, Kemper managed to drive around without them realizing that he had changed directions from where they wanted to go. He then stopped his car in a remote area he was familiar with from his work with the highway department. Kemper first handcuffed Pesce in the backseat of the car. He later confessed, "I was really quite struck by her personality and her looks, and there was just almost a reverence there. I think once I accidentally—this bothers me too, personally—I brushed, I think the back of my hand when I was handcuffing her, against one of her breasts, and it embarrassed me. I even said, 'whoops, I'm sorry' or something like that."[157]

Kemper then took Luchessa out of the car and locked her in the trunk. Within thirty seconds of apologizing to Pesce for accidentally brushing against her breast, he threw a plastic bag over her head and wrapped a bathrobe belt around her neck. But as he pulled on the belt, it snapped; meanwhile Pesce had bitten through the plastic bag. Kemper then drew his knife and began to stab Pesce in the back, but the blows did not seem to have any effect and she began to twist around, facing Kemper. He then stabbed her in the side and in the stomach, and Pesce twisted back the other way. He then grabbed her by the chin, pulled back her head, and slit her throat.

Kemper then went to the back of the car, opened the trunk, pulled Luchessa out, and began to stab her repeatedly in the throat, eyes, heart, and forearms. He recalled being surprised by how many heavy blows she took before losing consciousness.

Once the women were dead, he drove their corpses back to his apartment and carried them inside. In his apartment he dissected their bodies, handled their various internal organs, snapped Polaroid photographs of them, and cut their heads off. Kemper confessed, "I remember there was actually a sexual thrill. You hear that little 'pop' and pull their heads off and hold their heads up by the hair. Whipping their heads off, their body sitting there. That'd get me off!" But Kemper insisted, "There was absolutely no contact with improper areas."

Kemper said, "I would sit there looking at the heads on an overstuffed chair, tripping on them on my bed, looking at them [when] one of them somehow becomes unsettled, comes rolling down the chair, very grisly. Tumbling down the chair, rolls across the cushion and hits the rug—'bonk.' The neighbor downstairs hates my guts. I'm always making noise late at night. He gets a broom and whacks on the ceiling. 'Buddy,' I say, 'I'm sorry for that, dropped my head, sorry.' That helped bring me out of the depression. I would trip on that."

Afterward Kemper put what remained of the two women into plastic bags and buried them in the Santa Cruz hills, their torsos and limbs in one location, their hands in another, disguising the burial ground using techniques he had learned in the Boy Scouts. He kept the heads a few days longer before throwing them into a ravine. He returned to the grave where Pesce's headless body lay because, as he explained, he loved her and wanted to be near her.

Kemper said that just before he began killing, his fantasies of making love to women became dissatisfying because he came to believe he could never realize them. If he killed them, then they would not reject him as a man, he explained. He characterized his crimes as "making dolls" out of human beings.

On September 14, 1972, Kemper picked up fifteen-year-old Aiko Koo hitchhiking to a dance class in San Francisco. He took her to another remote area, choked her into unconsciousness, raped her, and then finished killing her. He placed her body in the trunk and on his way home stopped off for a beer. Emerging from the bar, Kemper said he opened the trunk of the car, "admiring my catch like a fisherman." He took the corpse back to his apartment, dissected it, had sex with it, and cut off the head.

The next day Ed Kemper had a scheduled appointment with his probation psychiatrists. In the morning before heading out to the appointment, Kemper buried Koo's body at one location and her hands at another, but kept her head. He then drove to the psychiatrists' office with the head locked in the trunk of his car. Leaving his car in the parking lot, he went in for his interview. The psychiatric report resulting from that day's visit reads:

> If I were seeing this patient without having any history available or without getting the history from him, I would think that we're dealing with a very well adjusted young man who had initiative, intelligence and who was free of any psychiatric illness . . . In effect, we are dealing with two different people when we talk of the 15 year old boy who committed the murder and of the 23 year old man we see before us now . . . It is my opinion that he has made a very excellent response to the years of treatment and rehabilitation and I would see no psychiatric reason to consider him to be of any danger to himself or to any member of society.

The second psychiatrist cheerfully added:

> He appears to have made a good recovery from such a tragic and violent split within himself. He appears to be functioning in one piece now directing his feelings towards verbalization, work, sports and not allowing neurotic buildup with himself. Since it may allow him more freedom as an adult to develop his potential, I would consider it reasonable to have a permanent expunction of his juvenile records. I am glad he had recently "expunged" his motorcycle and I would hope that he would do that ("seal it") permanently since this seemed more a threat to his life and health than any threat he is presently to anyone else.

One can only wonder what the psychiatrists' diagnoses would have been if either of them had looked into the trunk of Kemper's car that morning.

On November 29, 1972, Kemper's juvenile record was permanently sealed so that he could go on with his life. In the meantime, he had moved back home with his domineering mother.

On January 8, 1973, he picked up college student Cindy Schall. He shot her in the head and then drove back with her body to his mother's house. While his mother wasn't looking, he put Schall's body in his bedroom closet and went to sleep. In the morning when his mother went to work, he took the corpse to bed with him and had sex with it. Afterward he placed the cadaver in his mother's bathtub, drained it of blood, carved it up into pieces, bagged them in plastic, and threw them off a cliff. He kept Schall's head for several days, often having sex with it. Afterward Kemper buried her head in his mother's yard, facing up toward his mother's bedroom window. He said he did this because his mother always wanted people to "look up to her."

Santa Cruz was plagued at that time with a series of bizarre unsolved murders, and warnings had been issued to students not to accept rides from strangers. But Kemper's mother had given him a university sticker for his car so that he could easily enter the campus to pick her up from work. This sticker gave women a sense of security when he offered them a ride.

On February 5, 1973, he shot two more women and brought them back to his mother's house. He cut off one woman's head in the trunk of his car, and when his mother went to bed he carried the headless corpse to his room and slept with it in his bed. Kemper explained, "The head trip fantasies were a bit like a trophy. You know, the head is where everything is at, the brain, eyes, mouth. That's the person. I remember being told as a kid, you cut off the head and the body dies. The body is nothing after the head is cut off . . . Well, that's not quite true. With a girl, there is a lot left in the girl's body without the head. Of course, the personality is gone."[158]

On Easter weekend in 1973, Kemper finally decided to face his nemesis. At 5:15 A.M. he walked into his mother's bedroom while she slept and struck her head with a claw hammer. He then rolled her over and slit her throat. Upon killing his mother, Kemper said, he was shocked at how vulnerable and human she had been—that she had died just like his other victims. He said that before then he had always perceived his mother as fore-boding, fierce, and formidable, and whether he hated or loved her, she had always been a big influence in his life. Upon killing her, he felt relief.

Kemper then decided, "what's good for my victims was good for my mother." Kemper cut her head off and raped her headless corpse. He removed her larynx and fed it into the garbage disposal. "It seemed appropriate as much as she'd bitched and screamed and yelled at me over so many years," he later told the police. When he turned on the disposal, it jammed, throwing back up his mother's voice box. "Even when she was dead, she was still bitching at me. I couldn't get her to shut up," Kemper recalled bitterly.

Kemper then telephoned his mother's best friend, Sally Hallett, and invited her over for a "surprise" dinner party for his mother. He punched her, strangled her, and cut her head off, placing it in his bed. He then spent the night sleeping in his mother's bed.

Before Kemper drove away from his mother's house, he left a note for the police:

Appx. 5:15 A.M. Saturday. No need for her to suffer any more at the hands of this horrible "murderous Butcher." It was quick—asleep—the way I wanted it.
Not sloppy and incomplete, gents. Just a "lack of time." I got things to do!!!

Kemper began an aimless drive out of Santa Cruz, through Nevada and into Colorado. After several days of constant driving, he pulled over at a telephone booth, called the Santa Cruz police, and confessed to being the Coed Killer. It took several calls before they took him seriously and dispatched the local police in Colorado to pick him up as he quietly waited by the phone booth. Kemper recalls, "It was very late at night, I was exhausted . . . I was past exhaustion. I was just running on pure adrenaline. My body was quivering . . . and my mind was slowly just beginning to unravel. I had lost control of my body. I had experienced this in the killing of my grandparents when I was fifteen. I just completely lost control of myself. But as far as my mind went, I had realized what was going on and I couldn't stop it. In this case my body was just exhausted and my mind was starting to go. I was hallucinating. I finally had a thought. I was trying to think, 'Wow, I have got to stop this because it is getting so far out of hand. I am not going to be responsible for what happens any further'. . . and I didn't like that idea." Paradoxically, Kemper began to fear that he would begin to kill outside the parameters of his own insane logic. Kemper had enough insight into his condition to turn himself in once he killed his mother, and to later analyze his crimes with FBI Behavioral Sciences Unit researchers.

Kemper, for example, had nothing but disdain for fellow serial killer Herbert Mullin, who was killing in Santa Cruz to prevent earthquakes about the same time that Kemper was committing his murders. "He was just a cold-blooded killer . . . killing everybody he saw for no good reason," Kemper complained. But having said that, he immediately commented on the irony of his so "self-righteously talking like that, after what I've done."

Kemper and Mullin were incarcerated in the same prison block, and Kemper tormented Mullin by calling him "Herbie," a diminutive Mullin hated. "He had a habit of singing and bothering people when somebody tried to watch TV. So I threw water on him to shut him up. Then, when he was a good boy, I'd give him peanuts. Herbie liked peanuts. That was effective, because pretty soon he asked permission to sing. That's called behavior modification treatment."[159]

Asked if Kemper thought Mullin was insane, he replied, "Yes, judging from my years in Atascadero, I would say he is mentally ill."

On why Kemper stopped killing and surrendered to the police, Kemper said, "The original purpose was gone. It was starting to weigh kind of heavy. Let's say I started returning to some lucid moments where I—where I started to burn out the hate and fear . . . and the need that I had for continuing death was needless and ridiculous. It wasn't serving any physical or real or emotional purpose. It was just a pure waste of time."

Kemper concludes, "I couldn't keep on going forever . . . I really couldn't have. Emotionally, I couldn't handle it much longer. Toward the end there, I started feeling the folly of the whole damn thing, and at the point of near exhaustion, near collapse, I just said the hell with it and called it all off. Let's say . . . I wore out of it."

"I wore out of it." Kemper called the police and surrendered. It is likely that Andrew Cunanan shot himself for the same reason after killing Gianni Versace—he "wore out of it." Albert DeSalvo "grew out of it." Other serial killers who do not get caught neither surrender nor kill themselves, but simply "retire," leaving behind an unsolved mystery and a pile of corpses. The Zodiac Killer stopped killing and was never identified; the Green River Killer mysteriously ceased killing (although that did not stop police from identifying Gary Ridgway nearly twenty years later; it is believed that Ridgway in fact continued to kill, but less frequently and sporadically).

Asked what he thinks now when he sees a pretty woman, Kemper replied in probably his most often quoted remark, "One side of me says, 'Wow, what a pretty chick, I'd like to talk to her, date her.' The other side of me says, 'I wonder how her head would look like on a stick.'"*

Kemper has been eligible and applying for parole since 1980. He has been refused . . . so far.

What each of these cases demonstrates is that a psychiatric context is virtually impossible to definitively identify in cases of serial murder. Serial killers seem to come close to a psychiatric definition of psychopaths, but in the final analysis, they elude existing categories.

Forensic psychologist Stephen J. Giannangelo suggests that serial killers be given a new and separate category in the next DSM edition. He proposes the following category:

312.40 Homicidal Pattern Disorder

A. Deliberate and purposeful murder or attempt at murder of strangers on more than one occasion.

B. Tension or affective arousal at some time before the act.

C. Pleasure, gratification, or relief in commission or reflection of the acts.

---

* Kemper quotes repeatedly overlap a myriad of multiple sources, but the "head on the stick" remark has grown to mythical proportions in serial killer literature and culture. It even appears from the mouth of the homicidal protagonist in the movie *American Psycho,* based on the controversial book by Bret Easton Ellis, and may even appear in his book. (I have not read it.) Many years ago I read somewhere that Kemper made that remark to a *Cosmopolitan* magazine reporter interviewing him in the 1970s, but I have had no success in confirming this subsequently.

D.   Personality traits consistent with diagnosis of at least one Cluster B
     Personality Disorder (antisocial, borderline, histrionic, narcissistic).

E.   Understanding the illegality of actions and continuation to avoid ap-
     prehension.

F.   Murders not motivated by monetary gain, to conceal criminal activity,
     to express anger or vengeance, in response to a delusion or hallucina-
     tion, or as a result of impaired judgment (e.g., in dementia, mental re-
     tardation, substance intoxication).[160]

SIX

SERIAL KILLERS AS CHILDREN:

The Making of Monsters

I knew long before I started killing that I was going to be killing.
—ED KEMPER

Mother was my biggest fear.
—PETER WOODCOCK

From the case histories of Peter Woodcock, Edward Kemper, Kenneth Bianchi, and Jerry Brudos in previous chapters, one can see that these killers had all exhibited abnormal behavior in their childhood combined with unusual family circumstances: Woodcock, given up for adoption; Kemper, abused by a neurotic, overbearing mother; Bianchi, subjected to his mother's neurotic fears; Brudos, subjected to his mother's derision. But many people are given up for adoption, and many grow up with domineering mothers—they do not all become serial killers. Were these killers born with something that made them respond with murder to the circumstances of their childhood? For example, both Woodcock and Kemper killed their family pets at a very early age—the killer instinct was apparently there in early childhood. David Berkowitz, the Son of Sam also killed his adopted mother's pet bird. Animal cruelty along with bedwetting and acts of arson are frequently found in the behavioral history of serial killers when they were children.

Scientists and psychologists have been puzzling for decades over the mystery of serial killers and have collected a huge amount of data that is beginning to reveal certain distinct patterns. The most groundbreaking study was probably the one carried out by the FBI's Behavioral Sciences Unit in which FBI agents interviewed thirty-six sex murderers, including serial killers, about every detail of their life and crime. Since then, many other projects have attempted to confront the question of what motivates serial killers. The conclusion is that serial killers are *both* made and born.

When children born with certain predetermined factors are then subjected to certain life experiences, they are highly likely to become serial killers. But it is not a simple and predictable one-two-three step-by-step progression. Unraveling the making of a serial killer is like aligning a Rubik's Cube.

The Serial Killer As Infant

The single most common factor attributed to serial killers is the likely absence of infant bonding. From the very first weeks an infant attempts to establish contact with its mother through smiles, gestures, and crying. If its efforts are rewarded with affectionate touching and attention, a baby reaches out into the world to grasp and feed. As it grows, an infant begins to distinguish between strangers and parents and between various familiar people, and it seeks close contact with its parents in a bonding process. These early stages are crucial to the adult personality because it is believed that 50 percent of a human's "life knowledge," which forms the behavioral and personality components, is acquired in the first twelve months, and another 25 percent in the second year. The remaining 25 percent of life knowledge is acquired between age three and death. It is believed that infants who are deprived of human affection and touch can be substantially developed psychopaths by age two, lacking a normally developed range of human emotions such as sympathy, empathy, remorse, and affection.

It is questionable how much affection Peter Woodcock's birth mother would have shown him during the month she had him, knowing that he would be given up for adoption. It is therefore possible that no amount of loving care could have overcome the damage already done to Peter Woodcock before the Maynard family took him in.

Adoption is a frequent characteristic of serial killers. Kenneth Bianchi was adopted, as were David Berkowitz and Joel Rifkin, who murdered seventeen prostitutes in the New York area. Berkowitz and Rifkin interestingly enough are among the few rare cases of Jewish serial killers—although Berkowitz became a born-again Christian shortly before he began killing. Both were adopted into loving and stable families, which challenges the argument that chaotic family environment alone can create a serial killer.

The Serial Killer As the Lonely Child

One very common factor in the childhood of serial killers is their loneliness and isolation from their peers—even in cases where there is little or no maladjustment in parental histories. As children, they rarely fit in with their playmates. Henry Lucas and Albert DeSalvo were obviously isolated from other children outside their family by their living conditions, but the histories of other serial killers are frequently typical of Peter Woodcock's. By the subtle rules of childhood society, they do not fit in—something is already out of kilter in their personalities.

Both Berkowitz and Rifkin had lonely childhoods and harbored secret aggressive fantasies. Berkowitz surreptitiously crushed boxes of his grandparents' fragile matzoh and saltine crackers. His grandparents always thought the damage had happened in the store. Like Woodcock, he killed his adopted mother's pet—in this case, a bird. Berkowitz had no childhood friends. He said, "It was a mysterious force working against me. I felt bothered and tormented, 'Die Schmutz' [Yiddish for 'the dirty one']."

Rifkin was adopted by college-educated parents who were very supportive of him and sensitive to his handicap—dyslexia, a learning disability that makes it difficult to read and spell correctly. (Lee Harvey Oswald also had it.) Rifkin unfortunately was also clumsy and stuttered slightly, isolating him from his peers. He was bullied and the butt of jokes throughout his high school career, and he maintained a very lonely existence despite his place on the track team and position as yearbook photographer. When the yearbook came out, all the students who worked on it threw a party—and Joel was the only one not invited. Rifkin showed no signs of anger and frequently took the abuse in stoic silence. Later, however, he revealed that he secretly harbored fantasies of torturing and killing passive female slaves.

Rifkin made it into his first year of community college and had several girlfriends, but he appeared to them uncommunicative and unemotional. By now Rifkin was patronizing prostitutes. He brought one home to his parents' house and she subsequently robbed him. The next one he brought home, he killed. He went on to murder seventeen women until 1992, when police discovered a corpse in his pickup truck during a routine stop.

In 1998 police arrested twenty-seven-year-old Kendall Francois—a six-foot-four, 300-pound public school hall monitor nicknamed "Stinky" because of his bad personal hygiene. He was charged with the murder of eight Poughkeepsie, New York, prostitutes. They were found in plastic bags in the attic of his parents' house and under the front porch. The entire neighborhood complained about the smell, but Francois convinced his parents it was coming from dead raccoons in the attic.

Kendall was taunted throughout his childhood because of his excessive weight. When he passed by, the children taunted the overweight black youth, "How now brown cow." He is remembered by his fellow students and teachers as a "gentle giant" with limited intellectual abilities. He participated on the wrestling and football teams and attempted to adopt various identities. One high school picture shows him standing apart from the wrestling team, showing off his recently developed muscles. Another picture shows him posing in a preppy cardigan, his hand thoughtfully poised beneath his chin, a school ring prominently visible on his finger. But again, Kendall had no friends in school.

Loneliness gives these individuals time and space within which to develop, evolve, and dwell upon a fantasy life. The hostile and disempowering circumstances behind their loneliness often gives these fantasies a nasty and violent context focused on revenge and the desire for power. (See the discussion on the role of fantasy later in this chapter.)

The Serial Killer and His Mother

Feminist theoreticians deeply dislike the mother component of serial killer theory, dismissing it as just another aspect of the "blame it on mother" gynocidal aspect of the male drive to kill females. Perhaps. Nonetheless, there are remarkably many serial killers whose mothers showed tendency to be highly controlling, overbearing, or overprotective of their sons.

This supports the theory that some serial killers' behaviors are rooted in gender identification involving a boy's ability to successfully negotiate his masculine autonomy from his mother—a challenge not faced by females. When a boy cannot achieve this autonomy or when there is no solid foundation for him from which to negotiate this autonomy, a sense of rage develops in the child, and he subsequently carries the anger into adolescence and adulthood.

We saw that Kenneth Bianchi's adopted mother seemed to be hysterically concerned with Kenneth's health as a child, and that the child responded to these concerns with ailments. Peter Woodcock's foster mother is described as highly controlling and seems to have relished the challenge of her troubled foster child's behavioral problems. Upon being arrested, Woodcock feared only one thing: "My fear was that Mother would find out. Mother was my biggest fear. I didn't know if the police would let her at me." Peter Sutcliffe, the Yorkshire Ripper, is remembered as a normal child except for his strange need to constantly cling to his mother's skirt. Joseph Kallinger's mother refused to allow him to play outside, flogged him with a whip, beat him with a hammer, threatened to cut off his genitals, and selected his wife for him. Ed Gein so worshipped his mother that he preserved her bedroom as a shrine (but not her corpse, as in the Hitchcock movie *Psycho*.)

Other serial killers have had mothers who were either rejecting or blatantly abusive of them. Even in his adult life, Arthur Shawcross was obsessed with pleasing his critical mother. Just before he was arrested for killing eleven prostitutes, he had sent his mother a carefully selected expensive gift, which she kept but wrote back that he was a fool for wasting his money on stupid junk. Edmund Kemper's mother kept him locked in the basement; Jerry Brudos's mom stuck him in the back shed. One does not need a degree in psychology to understand why children like that may grow up hating females and harboring raging homicidal fantasies.

Cases of serial killers—particularly sexual killers—where the mother was characterized as loving and encouraging toward the son's independence are rare except in some cases of adopted children—or in the case of Ted Bundy, who thought he was adopted.

The father seems to play a lesser role in the formation of the serial killer. Nonetheless, abusive or offender fathers frequently become role models in the child's future.

Family Stability and History

The FBI study reveals that sexual and serial killers often came from unstable family backgrounds where infant bonding was likely to be disrupted. Only 57 percent of killers in the FBI study had both parents at birth, and 47 percent had their father leave before age twelve. A mother as the dominant parent was reported in 66 percent of the cases, and 44 percent reported having a negative relationship with their mother. A negative relationship with the father or male parental figure was reported by 72 percent of the convicted sex killers.

The history of the parents had also a great role to play in the child's future. Researchers at the Washington School of Medicine determined that biological children of parents with criminal records are four times as likely to commit criminal acts themselves as adults—even if they have been adopted by law-abiding parents! The FBI study showed that 50 percent of the offenders had parents with criminal pasts and 53 percent came from families with psychiatric histories. [161]

Gerald Gallego, Jr., for example, was nine years old when his twenty-six-year-old father, Gerald Gallego, Sr., was executed in Mississippi's gas chamber for two murders. When Gerald Jr. was thirteen he was charged with having sex with a six-year-old girl. By age thirty-two he had been married seven times and was living in California.

William Mansfield, Jr., on whose property in Florida police discovered the remains of at least six murdered women, was the son of William Mansfield, Sr., serving a thirty-year prison term for child molestation.

The FBI's research program describes one unnamed killer's background:

The offender's father shot and killed one of his own brothers when the subject was thirteen. Prior to this crime, the father had been investigated concerning acts of arson and insurance fraud. The father was tried for the murder but found not guilty by reason of insanity. He was diagnosed during the trial as suffering from paranoia. The father was also suspected in the killings of two other persons, including a trespasser on his property and a foster child who had disappeared. After the murder, the father was committed to a state mental hospital; however, two years later he escaped with the help of the subject's mother. [162]

Childhood Mental and Physical Trauma

Many serial killers had a truly traumatic childhood. In the FBI study, 42 percent of the killers reported physical abuse and 74 percent reported psychological abuse, while 35 percent reported witnessing sexual violence as children and 43 percent reported being sexually abused themselves. "Sexually stressful events" were reported by 73 percent of sex killers, and 50 percent admitted that their first rape fantasies began between ages twelve and fourteen. It should be noted that the FBI carefully structured its survey to eliminate self-pity and explanatory tendencies from the offenders surveyed: When asked, only 53 percent of the serial and sex killers felt themselves to have been treated unfairly as children, despite the higher reported rates of abuse.

Some psychiatrists explain the development of psychopathic tendencies as simply the brain's defensive mechanisms. An infant that is denied human touch and affection develops a sense of only itself—it becomes completely oblivious to others. This is necessary for the infant to survive. When that infant becomes an adult, that sense of self and disregard of others becomes defined as "psychopathology." Thus what starts in the infant's brain as a purely defensive mechanism can become a destructive trait in adulthood.

Physical trauma, particularly head injuries, is evident in the childhood histories of many serial killers. Earle Leonard Nelson was dragged under a streetcar at age ten and remained in a coma for six days; Carlton Gary, Richard Ramirez, and John Wayne Gacy were knocked unconscious by playground swings; Gary Heidnik fell out of a tree in grade school, causing an injury that prompted his classmates to call him "football head"; Bobby Joe Long fell from a pony and remained nauseated and dizzy for weeks; Max Gufler was subject to uncontrollable outbursts of rage after being struck on the head with a rock at age nine. The FBI sexual killer study showed that 29 percent of the subjects were "accident prone" in childhood.

Henry Lee Lucas

In some cases it is not that the psychopath necessarily wants to hurt somebody, but that he simply does not care whether he does so or not. Eventually the sexual act becomes interchangeable with murder. Henry Lee Lucas explained, "I get sex any way I can get it. If I have to force somebody to do it, I do. If I don't, I don't. I rape them. I've done that. I've killed animals to have sex with them. Dogs, I've killed them to have with them—always killed before I had sex. I've had sex with them while they're still alive only sometimes. Then killing became the same things as having sex."[163]

Officially, Lucas was convicted of killing "only" eleven people, mostly hitchhikers in Texas along Highway I-35. However, he claimed to have committed 360 murders across the United States, Mexico, and Canada, beginning from 1952, when he was fifteen years old, until his arrest in 1982. Police discount some of his confessions and believe that most likely he killed in the vicinity of "only" a hundred people, tops.

At one point in his history, Lucas was joined in his killing by Ottis Elwood Toole, a cannibalistic male prostitute. There was no recognizable sense or pattern to their killing. The victims were men, women, and children. They were young and they were old; they were prostitutes, businessmen, homemakers, tramps, and students. They were strangled, shot, stabbed, and battered to death. Some were raped; others were not. Some were mutilated and cannibalized while others were carefully buried. Some victims have never been identified to this day. Lucas's childhood history can serve as a manual on how to incubate a serial killer. It includes virtually every factor reported by different serial killers in one single life.

Henry Lee Lucas was born in one of America's poorest regions—Blacksburg, Virginia—in 1937. Viola Lucas, his mother, was a prostitute; his father, Anderson, was an alcoholic who had earlier in a drunken stupor fallen on some railway tracks and had both his legs amputated by a slowly moving train. He now supported himself and the family by skinning minks, selling pencils, and distilling illicit alcohol. The father taught Henry how to maintain their illegal distillery while he went off to get drunk. Henry himself was drinking hard liquor by age ten, and of his legless father he only remembers, "He hopped around on his ass all his life."

Viola insisted that both Henry and his father watch her having sex with her customers in a dirt-floor three-room cabin in which they lived. If they refused, she beat them with a club. Henry said, "I don't think any child out there should be brought up in that type of environment. In the past, I've hated it. It's just inside me hate, and I can't get away from it."

One of Lucas's earliest memories is of his mother shooting one of her customers in the leg with a shotgun after having sex and Henry being splashed with the man's blood. From then on he seemed to be fascinated by blood and its association with sex.

When Henry was thirteen, his father got drunk, crawled out into the snow, and lay there until he caught pneumonia and died.

Viola beat Henry with broom handles, sticks, pieces of timber, or anything else she found. She did not allow him to cry when she was beating him, and she constantly told him that he was born evil and would die in prison. He claims that the only thing he ever loved was a pet mule, but when his mother found out about his affection for it, she forced him to watch as she shot it dead. She then beat him for how much it was going to cost to haul the dead animal away.

One day when Henry was too slow getting wood for the stove, Viola hit him so hard with a piece of lumber that he remained unconscious for three days until he was finally taken to a hospital. Afterward he recalled frequent incidents of dizziness, blackouts, and weightless sensation. About a year later, while roughhousing with his brother, Henry was accidentally sliced with a knife across his left eye. The eye was left untreated and eventually had to be replaced with a glass eye.

Henry admitted to having sex with his half-brother and to the two of them cutting the throats of animals and performing acts of bestiality. He later said, "Sex is one of my downfalls."

On his first day of school, Viola sent Henry to class dressed as a girl, with his long hair set in curls and wearing a dress. Ironically, Ottis Toole, who would partner with Lucas in the crime spree, was also dressed as a girl in petticoats and lace by his mother. At least seven male serial killers, including Charles Manson, are known to have been dressed as girls in their childhood. Eddie Cole, who murdered thirteen victims, was dressed as "Mamma's little girl" by his mother and forced to serve drinks to her guests.[164]

One would think that serial killers exaggerate their childhood backgrounds in attempt to gain sympathy, and many do. In the case of Henry Lee Lucas, however, the details of his childhood history have been independently corroborated through various sources and witnesses, including his neighbors and former schoolteacher. Lucas was not exaggerating when he said, "They ain't got, I don't think, a human being alive that can say he had the childhood I had."

Biochemistry

There are questions as to whether there are biological factors linked to serial killing. After Henry Lee Lucas was convicted, he underwent numerous neurological tests that revealed fairly extensive brain damage. Small contusions indicated a frontal lobe injury, and there was damage to his temporal lobe and pools of spinal fluid at the base of his brain. There was an enlargement of the right and left Sylvian fissure at the expense of the surrounding brain tissue, which indicated significant loss of judgmental functions and was the result of head injuries sustained in childhood. CAT scans and nuclear magnetic resonance tests confirmed a brain abnormality consistent with an individual with diminished control over violent impulses.

Toxicology tests revealed unusually high levels of lead and cadmium in his nerve tissue, which combined with years of alcohol abuse to destroy a significant part of his cerebral capacity. Three indicators of cadmium poisoning are loss of dream recall, excessively strong body odor, and loss of sense of smell. Lucas does not remember his dreams and rode in a car through Texas heat with the head of one of his victims for more than three days, oblivious to the smell of the decaying flesh. His teacher recalls that as a child, Lucas smelled very bad.

Malnutrition can also be a significant contributor to brain damage. Viola forced Lucas and his father to scrounge for food on the streets and in garbage cans. His teacher reports that she brought him to her home to feed him hot meals, and Lucas recalls that those were the only hot meals he received in his life prior to jail.

Substance Abuse

Maternal alcohol or drug abuse also increases the chances of prenatal injury of the fetus. The FBI study indicated that 69 percent of subjects indicated a family history of alcohol abuse and 33 percent had family problems with drugs.

Other family violence can also potentially injure the unborn child. The father of Patrick Mackay in England repeatedly kicked his wife in the stomach while she was expecting the child. Mackay's father was a violent and abusive alcoholic until he died when Mackay was ten years old. The son then seems to have adopted the father's identity. He assaulted other children at his school and tortured animals. He became addicted to alcohol at an early age and became, like his father, violent under its influence. By the time he was fifteen, social workers had described Mackay as "a cold psychopathic killer."

Mackay began killing at age twenty-two in London in 1974. His victims were usually elderly women, whom he would stab or strangle in their homes and then rob. Mackay was caught when he returned to rob a sixty-four-year-old Catholic priest who had helped him two years earlier. He stabbed the priest in his home and then split his head open with an axe; however, this failed to kill the priest. Mackay then put him into a bathtub full of water and sat on the edge for an hour as the priest died. Because the police were aware of the connection between Mackay and the victim, he was apprehended within forty-eight hours and eventually charged with five murders, but suspected in a total of eleven.

In the end, what makes a serial killer still remains a mystery to psychologists. In the case of severely abused children, anyone can understand their eventual emergence as psychopathic killers. But what about David Berkowitz and Peter Woodcock? Although adopted, they seemed to have been brought up in stable and loving homes. Thousands of children are adopted and do not grow up to be serial killers. Thousands of children grow up in conditions far more desperate and abusive than Berkowitz's and Woodcock's, and they too do not become serial killers. Part of the problem is that we are no longer sure of what defines a "healthy" and "happy" family. The incidence of abuse, physical and psychological, is often hidden from public eye, and only in the last two decades has the true extent of sexual abuse within families come to the forefront.

Dr. Alice Miller, in her book *For Your Own Good,* maintains that the origins of adult violent behavior are found in a level of cruelty in the upbringing of children that is ostensibly invisible. Miller described a "poisonous pedagogy" in which children are cruelly punished while being told it is "for their own good." Such demonstrations of pain and punishment as being "good" send the wrong message to the child. Moreover, the parents' display of their "heroic" suspension of their love and feeling of tenderness for their child in order to inflict punishment upon him—"this hurts me more than it hurts you"—is another disturbing message a child can receive. While parental discipline is a common and necessary aspect of bringing up children, the fine line between abuse and constructive discipline is very murky and difficult to objectively define.

The Role of Fantasy

The agents from the FBI Behavioral Sciences Unit who were interviewing convicted serial and sex killers arrived at a different and more complex theory than the one that many psychologists were advancing. The FBI rejected the notion that serial killers murdered as a defensive-reactive response to extremely abusive experiences in their life. What troubled the FBI analysts was the fact that not all serial killers whom they were interviewing suffered severe abuse in childhood. For example, Ted Bundy, although born illegitimate, grew up in an apparently stable, lower-middle-class home with a loving mother and supportive stepfather. Where, why, and how did he develop the rage that led him to kill twenty young women?

The FBI concluded that serial murderers "programmed" or conditioned themselves in childhood to become murderers in a progressively intensifying loop of fantasies. They discovered that the most common childhood trait of serial killers, which also extended into adolescence and adulthood, was daydreaming and compulsive masturbation. As defined in the study, daydreaming is "any cognitive activity representing a shift of attention away from a task." Fantasy is defined as an elaborate thought with great preoccupation, sometimes expressed as thought, images, or feelings only, anchored in the daydreaming process.[165] In the FBI study, 82 percent of offenders reported daydreaming in their childhood. An equal 82 percent reported compulsive masturbation (probably accompanying the daydreams).[166] When the offenders reached adolescence and then adulthood, there was only a 1 percent drop in their daydreaming and compulsive masturbation.

Fantasies serve to relieve anxiety or fear, and almost everybody has them to one degree or another. A child who is abused may understandably develop aggressive fantasies in which he develops a power and means by which he can destroy his tormentor. But the trigger of these fantasies does not necessarily need to be extraordinarily abusive or violent events—relatively common events such as parental divorce, family illness, or even rejection by a friend can all give a child a sense of loss of control, anxiety, and fear, and may spark aggressive fantasies as a method of coping with the stress.

Only at this point do the other factors noted in the serial killers' childhood take effect. The child who lacks bonding and a sense of contact with others will internalize his fantasy and cloud the boundary between fantasy and reality. Living in his own private world, the child begins to repeat and elaborate on the fantasy, finding comfort in it while continually narrowing the perimeters between fantasy and reality. Of the killers interviewed in the FBI study, 71 percent reported a sense of isolation in their childhood. As they grew into adolescence, the sense of isolation apparently increased to 77 percent of subjects.[167] Such increased social isolation only encourages a reliance on fantasy as a substitute for human encounter. And as we have seen, so many serial killers were lonely and isolated children.

The individual's personality development becomes dependent on the fantasy life and its themes rather than on social interaction. The total escape and control that the child has in his fantasy world becomes addictive, especially if there are continued stresses in the child's life.

If the particular fantasy involves violence, revenge, or murder, they become part of that addiction; when they are combined with masturbation, a sexual component to the fantasy is developed. Psychologists identify this process as classical conditioning, in which "the repeated pairing of fantasized cues with orgasm results in their acquiring sexually arousing properties."[168] One serial killer who murdered young boys, John Joseph Joubert, remembers as an adolescent compulsively masturbating to fantasies of strangling and stabbing boys dressed only in their underwear. Joubert said that he could not recall whether these images brought on the masturbation or whether masturbation brought on the fantasies. Violence and sex become merged into a murderous obsession, which often is kept secret. As one unnamed killer in the FBI study said, "Nobody bothered to find out what my problem was, and nobody knew about the fantasy world."

As the individual continually refines and "improves on" his repeated fantasy, eventually it becomes a rehearsal for future action. At some point the serial killer, as an adolescent or as an adult (and occasionally even as a child), begins to take his fantasy out into the world on "test runs." This testing of the fantasy is what Ed Kemper was doing when he went to his schoolteacher's house at night armed with a knife and a fantasy of making love to her corpse. Thirteen-year-old John Joubert rode by a girl on his bicycle and jabbed a sharp pencil into her back. Monte Ralph Rissell, who raped and murdered five women by age nineteen, shot his cousin with an air gun when he was nine years old. When Ted Bundy was three years old, his fifteen-year-old aunt awoke one morning to find him secretly lifting up her bedcovers and placing three butcher knives beside her. As an adult, Bundy began sabotaging women's cars without any clear plan of what he would do if he succeeded in trapping a woman by those means.

The stage at which an individual begins to project his fantasy into the real world and involve other people in it is the fundamental difference between the fantasies that you and I as children spin out in our imaginations, tranquil or violent, and those that originate in the mind of the serial killer.

The most common testing out of murder fantasies in childhood involves the torture and killing of animals and bullying of fellow children. The FBI study indicated that 36 percent of subjects displayed cruelty to animals in their childhood, and 46 percent did so by the time they were adolescents; bullying of other children increased from 54 percent to 64 percent from childhood to adolescence.

Accompanying cruelty to animals and bullying, other behavioral traits were reported in the FBI survey as follows: stealing, 56 percent in childhood and 81 percent in adolescence; fire setting, 56 percent and 52 percent; bedwetting, 68 percent and 60 percent; nightmares, 67 percent and 68 percent; and rebelliousness, 67 percent and 84 percent.

Fire setting, cruelty to animals, and bedwetting form a behavioral triad that is most often identified with the childhood histories of serial killers. Most psychiatrists agree that the appearance of all three behaviors in a child signals a high likelihood of a future violent adult.

The commission of lesser crimes, such as breaking and entering, arson, voyeurism, and exhibitionism, is also a common trait in the histories of serial killers. Fetish theft—of women's underwear from clotheslines, or shoes during burglaries—are sometimes seen in the childhood records of serial killers. Jerry Brudos, for example, was obsessed with women's shoes, and even stole his teacher's shoes as a schoolboy. Twenty years later as an adult, he hacked off the foot of one of his victims and kept it in his freezer, slipped into one of his favorite high-heeled shoes. The Brudos case illustrates an important lesson: Ostensibly harmless or "comical" offenses, such as stealing women's shoes or underwear from a laundry, should not be dismissed without additional attention, especially if the offender is young. Such offenses may seem innocuous on the surface, but in murkier depths they can harbor homicidal roots. It is remarkable how many serial killers have records, some going back decades before they first killed, of minor sexual offenses such as window peeping or exhibitionism. While most minor sexual offenders do not go on to kill, most serial killers do begin with minor offenses. These offenses are often testing probes of fantasy into the realm of reality. If the individual escapes detection or avoids sanction for these offenses, especially at a young age, he can develop a sense of invincibility that carries him to the ultimate deadly peak of his fantasy. One murderer in the FBI study (probably Ed Kemper) easily made the connection between fantasy and homicide, explaining that "Murder is very real. It's not something you see in a movie. You have to do all the practical things of surviving."[169]

Unfortunately fantasy and reality rarely come together, and the serial killer is often frustrated in his attempts to perfectly bring his frequently dwelled-upon fantasy into actuality. When disappointed in the results of his attempt to realize his fantasy exactly as imagined, the killer murders again and again, searching to perfect his desperate attempts to consummate his ideal fantasy. In many ways, serial murder is a learning experience from beginning to end.

Some serial killers, when they actually succeed in realizing their fantasy, stop killing. Ed Kemper's deepest fantasy was to kill his mother, and when he finally did that, after killing one more woman, he turned himself in. It appears that Andrew Cunanan's fantasy was to kill a famous person, with Tom Cruise, Sylvester Stallone, and Gianni Versace on his list. Having killed Versace, and no doubt found it unsatisfying, Cunanan saw no point in continuing to pursue his fantasy and shot himself.

Other serial killers, however, once they find the key to acting out their deepest fantasy, continue murdering to repeat the fantasy—they "level out" and begin practicing a perfected ritualistic routine in their homicides, from which they try never to waver and which always leaves them wanting more. Other killers become bored with their fantasy once they have actualized it, and they escalate to more elaborate or violent fantasies in an addictive search of a more intensive "high."

The serial killer's personality is a complex cocktail of biological, environmental, and social circumstances. There is no one clear formula for the making of a serial killer. Some children in traumatic circumstances resort to humorous fantasy and become great comedians; some escape by weaving fantastic stories and grow up to be great writers; others illustrate their fantasies and become painters; others become architects, businessmen, lawyers, politicians, and generals (where in some cases they are given medals and honors for killing in numbers that far exceed any serial killer's body count, a cynic may respond). It is remarkable how many successful individuals can have as traumatic a childhood as serial killers do. But just to complicate such distinctions, one should not overlook the fact that some serial killers are ostensibly successful. John Wayne Gacy, who murdered thirty-three young males, was a construction contractor respected in his community who earned more than $100,000 a year. Ted Bundy was a university graduate and was admitted into law school. Christopher Wilder of Florida, who raped and murdered twelve women, was the owner of two construction companies, an amateur racecar driver, and a substantial contributor to the Seal Rescue Fund and Save the Whales. Richard Cottingham, the Times Square Torso Ripper, was a valued computer data specialist at Blue Cross in New York. Gary Heidnik, who kept female slaves shackled in a fetid basement pit (and upon whom the character of Buffalo Bill in *The Silence of the Lambs* was partially based), was a financial wizard who parlayed a small investment into a fortune. He owned several expensive cars, including a Rolls-Royce, and founded his own church in order to avoid paying taxes. Despite his wealth, he chose to live in North Philadelphia's ghetto in a rundown home where he kept, tortured, raped, and killed his slaves.* In each of these cases, the killers' fantasies were bigger than any achievement in their life.

The key to the making of serial killers lies in the nature of their fantasy

---

* As his defense, Heidnik claimed that the women were already there when he moved into the house.

and how they actualize it. FBI agents who interviewed convicted serial killers for their study remarked that the one thing that the murderers had difficulty talking about was their childhood fantasies. Somewhere in that dark territory lurks the killer seed. The FBI reported:

> Interviews with the murderers in our study revealed that their internal world is filled with troublesome, joyless thoughts of dominance over others. These thoughts are expressed through a wide range of actions toward others. In childhood, these include cruelty to animals, abuse of other children, destructive play patterns, disregard for others, fire setting, stealing, and destroying property. In adolescence and adulthood, the murderers' actions become more violent: assaultive behaviors, burglary, arson, abduction, rape, nonsexual murder, and finally sexual murder, involving rape, torture, mutilation, and necrophilia.[170]

Ed Kemper said, "I knew long before I started killing that I was going to be killing, that it was going to end up like that. The fantasies were too strong. They were going on for too long and were too elaborate."

SEVEN

THE SERIAL MURDERER'S FIRST KILL:

Triggers, Facilitators, Detective Magazines, Paraphilic Hard Porn, and the Bible

You just felt very good after you did it. It just happens to be satisfying, to get the source of blood . . .
—DAVID BERKOWITZ, Son of Sam

The psychic abolition of redemption.
—IAN BRADY, Moors Murderer

No murder is as critical in the career of any serial killer as the first. Without it, they would not exist. Many already have criminal records for petty crimes or serious violent offenses—some have no criminal records at all. Up until now, although they may have thought about it, they have killed nobody. But something nudges them forward to cross that final horrific line.

The previous chapter outlined how it is believed that the mind of a serial killer, through a combination of environmental factors, parenting, and biological and genetic predisposition, can be thrust into a pattern of often violent fantasies and obsessive thoughts that the serial killer has difficulties separating from reality.

At a certain point in his adolescence or adulthood, the future serial killer begins taking these fantasies out on "test runs." Once these attempts to involve others in his fantasy start, it will be only a matter of time before the first kill takes place—an important milestone in the history of any serial killer.

Serial Killers' Reminiscences on Their First Murder

Virtually all serial killers talk about how difficult their first murder was, and how much easier it all became afterward. Henry Lee Lucas remembers committing his first murder when he was fifteen years old. He snatched a seventeen-year-old girl at a bus stop, carried her up an embankment, and attempted to rape her. When she resisted, he strangled her. Her murder was solved only thirty-three years later when Lucas confessed:

> I had no intention of killing her. I don't know whether I was just being afraid somebody was going to catch me or what. That killing was my first, my worst, and the hardest to get over . . . I would go out sometimes for days, and just every time I turned around I'd see police behind me. Then I'd be always looking behind me and watching. Everywhere I'd go I have to be watching for police and be afraid they were going to stop me and pick me up. But they never did bother with me.[171]

Speaking in the third person, as he often did when being questioned about his crimes, Ted Bundy described his first attempted murder:

> He was horrified by the recognition that he'd done this, the realization that he had the capacity to do such a thing or even attempt—that's a better word—this kind of thing . . . The sobering effect of that was to . . . for some time close up the cracks again. For the first time, he sat back and swore to himself that he wouldn't do something like that again . . . or even, anything that would lead up to it.[172]

Bobby Joe Long, who raped and murdered nine women in Florida, recalls killing his first victim, a woman he picked up in a bar:

> She picked me up really, I didn't go after her. She was a whore. She manipulated men, and she wanted to manipulate me. Once I had her in the car, I tied her up and raped her. Then I strangled her and dumped her body alongside the highway. I knew what I was doing but I couldn't stop myself. I hated her. I hated her from the time she picked me up, but I didn't plan to murder her. I don't even think I planned to rape her either . . . I couldn't

believe what I'd done the next morning. I was sick, and I knew I was in real trouble.

But the feelings of shock, fear, regret, and remorse, wear off before long. Bobby Joe Long continued:

Then a few days later I met the Simms girl, and it was the same thing all over again. She was a barfly. She really picked me up, and I just turned on her in the car.[173]

David Berkowitz, the Son of Sam, recalled that after committing his first killing:

You just felt very good after you did it. It just happens to be satisfying, to get the source of blood . . . I no longer had any sympathy whatsoever for anybody. It was very strange. That's what worried me the most. I said, "Well, I just shot some girl to death and yet I don't feel." . . . They were people I had to kill. I can't stop and weep over them. You have to be strong and . . . you have to survive.[174]

David Gore, convicted of the torture, rape, and murder of six women, stated:

All of a sudden I realized that I had just done something that separated me from the human race and it was something that could never be undone. I realized that from that point on, I could never be like normal people. I must have stood there in that state for twenty minutes. I have never felt an emptiness of self like I did right then and I will never forget that feeling. It was like I crossed over into a realm I could never come back from.[175]

Albert DeSalvo, the Boston Strangler, recalled his first murder:

The feeling after I got out of that apartment was as if it never happened. I got out and downstairs, and you could of said you saw me upstairs, and as far as I was concerned, it wasn't me. I can't explain it to you any other way.

It's just so unreal . . . I was there. It was done. And yet if you talked with me an hour later, or half an hour later, it didn't mean nothing. It just didn't mean nothing.[176]

Triggers

Every serial killer has to begin with his first murder. The fantasies, the predisposition, the isolation are all in place waiting for him to act on them. What remains now to happen is the "trigger" that catapults the embryonic serial murderer out from his fantasy world into that of homicidal reality, and the "facilitator" that lubricates the process. The trigger is usually a series or combination of pressures in daily life that law enforcement officers call "stressors," which at some point drive the predisposed individual to crack and act on his fantasy. The facilitator is frequently either some stimulant that enhances the stressors, such as pornography or cocaine, or a depressant that lowers the inhibitions, such as alcohol.

Sometimes in the beginning, murder is not even a component of the fantasy. Bobby Joe Long's fantasy, for example, was rape, but in the end he turned to killing. During the acting out of the fantasy, the individual might accidentally kill, and from that point onward murder can become an active part of the future fantasy. Sometimes the killing is committed to preserve the fantasy when the victim's behavior threatens to disrupt it.

The FBI study indicated that in 59 percent of the serial and sexual homicides they surveyed, the stressor reported was a conflict with a female. Because of the often sexual component of serial murder, this should not come as a surprise. Monte Rissell, who would eventually murder five women, had already been on probation for rape before he killed anybody. He received a letter from his girlfriend, who was a year ahead of him in college, that she no longer wanted to see him. Armed with a .45-caliber handgun, he drove to her campus and saw her with her new boyfriend but did not do anything. He then drove to a parking lot and sat in his car drinking beer and smoking marijuana. At about 2:00 A.M. a woman drove into the lot and parked her car. Rissell approached her with his gun, abducted her, raped her, and killed her. He went on to kill four more women in a similar way.

Parental conflict is reported as a major stressor in 53 percent of the homicides surveyed. Ed Kemper reported that he began killing young women after a particularly bitter argument with his mother. Richard Chase, who killed, mutilated, and drank the blood of some of his six victims in Sacramento, California, in 1978, was typical of the FBI's disorganized offender profile. He too describes a parental trigger behind his first homicide:

> The first person I killed was sort of an accident. My car was broken down. I wanted to leave but I had no transmission. I had to get an apartment. Mother wouldn't let me in at Christmas. Always before she let me come in at Christmas, have dinner, and talk to her, my grandmother, and my sister. That year she wouldn't let me in and I shot from the car and killed somebody.[177]

Additional stress factors reported during the homicides surveyed were financial, 48 percent; employment problems, 39 percent; marital problems, 21 percent; legal problems, 28 percent; conflict with a male, 11 percent; physical injury, 11 percent; death of a significant person, 8 percent; and birth of a child, 8 percent. [178]

When serial killings begin and police have a potential suspect, investigators often make a careful survey of the suspect's life around the time of the first murder in an attempt to identify potential stressors: Was he fired from work, is he in the middle of a divorce, has there been a death or a birth in the family, did he break up with his girlfriend, is he failing in school? Often such events occur just before the first homicide, but stressors can also trigger subsequent killing cycles as well. The FBI study reports the timing of three homicides committed by one unnamed individual. The offender purchased a handgun as soon as he learned that his wife was pregnant, claiming he was worried that his wife might be assaulted while he was away from home. After the birth of his first child, the offender became preoccupied, slept restlessly, and complained of physical pain. He showed little interest in having sexual relations with his wife, and his relationships with other people were disrupted. Three murders were linked to the birth: The first occurred six weeks after the birth of the child; the second when his wife became pregnant with a second child; and the third on the day of the first child's birthday party.[179] At other times it is not as simple as that; the trigger could be an event or stressor that is obscure and is only meaningful to or understood by the killer.

The problem here is that by the very nature of their childhood, serial killers are most likely to lead lives full of stressful events. As children and adolescents they lack self-esteem, are isolated and maladjusted, and are therefore poorly prepared for coping with life as adults. By the very nature of their personalities and coping skills, they contribute to or instigate stressful occurrences and instability in their lives. The FBI survey indicates that only 20 percent of their subjects were steadily employed and 47 percent did not graduate from high school. Of killers in the study who served in the military, 58 percent received undesirable, dishonorable, or medical discharges, while 29 percent registered a criminal record while serving.

Facilitators

The final element in the homicidal formula that unleashes serial killers is what psychologists have labeled "facilitators"—alcohol, drugs, pornography, and so on. Alcohol's depressant effect can decrease inhibitions and suppress moral conscience and propriety. In his usual third-person discourse, Ted Bundy explained the role of alcohol in his twenty known homicides:

> I think you could make a little more sense out of much of this if you take into account the effect of alcohol. It's important. It's very important as a trigger. When this person drank a good deal, his inhibitions were significantly diminished. He would find that his urge to engage in voyeuristic behavior on trips to the bookstore would become more prevalent, more urgent. It was as though the dominant personality was sedated. On every occasion when he engaged in such behavior, he was intoxicated.[180]

The FBI study reported that in 49 percent of the homicides it analyzed, the killer was consuming alcohol prior to committing the murder. Of those killers, 30 percent reported that at the time of the crime, their drinking was significantly heavier than their usual amount.

Drug use just prior to murder was reported by 35 percent of the killers, but only 12.5 percent stated that the amount of drugs consumed was different from their typical habit. Regrettably, the FBI study did not specify precisely which types of drugs were being consumed; however, the most likely drug is marijuana, which is the drug most readily available after alcohol (and after nicotine and caffeine). Cocaine, which also acts as a stimulant and ego booster, was presumably the next most cited substance, perhaps equaled by various amphetamine-like substances, and followed by hallucinogenics such as LSD and PCP. (Crack cocaine was not a popular drug when the study was being conducted.) As far as opiates such as morphine or heroin are concerned, there seem to be no accounts of any heroin-addicted serial killers—probably because the frequently debilitating nature of heroin addiction is not conducive to the necessary long-term high performance demanded of a focused serial killer.

PORNOGRAPHY

Pornography as a facilitator is a more complex issue. Some psychologists maintain that pornography inspires fantasies, provides models for sexual behavior, and encourages individuals to perceive females as objects. They suggest that as a visual stimulant combined with masturbation, pornography mentally conditions its consumer to derive pleasure from the fantasies of various behaviors depicted in it. Others maintain the opposite— that it defuses fantasies and provides a harmless and perhaps even healthy outlet for otherwise dangerous desires.

The FBI study reports that 81 percent of offenders reported encountering pornography in their childhood, but does not specify the nature or extent of the encounter. Nor does the study detail the nature of the pornography or even offer a definition of pornography. Colin Wilson's theory on pornography and the rise of sex crime in the nineteenth century has been described in Chapter 2. Wilson, however, does not necessarily claim that the shift from "lusty" eighteenth-century pornography to the sadistic–prohibited behavior pornography of the nineteenth-century is the *cause*. That shift could have very easily reflected a change in cultural mores of the emerging urban industrial society, which contributed to the rise of sexual homicide. Nonetheless, many serial killers had extensive pornography collections, and some took sexually explicit photographs and made videos of their victims during the commission of their crime and after.

Until the mid 1990s, there existed a multimillion dollar pornographic publishing industry whose printed products ranged from straight sexual imagery to more fetishistic and sadomasochistic products. (Today it is mostly focused on video and digital products as opposed to printed matter.) Next to child pornography, the most offensive publications were magazines with titles such as *Stalked, Captured,* and *Bound and Fettered,* which took the nonexplicit detective magazine covers to their logical conclusions. They featured series of pornographic images of obviously kidnapped or stalked women, bound and gagged, often posed in settings such as abandoned barns, cellars, empty boxcars, back storerooms, or secret dungeons: a serial killer's fantasy land. These magazines were more or less sold openly, depending on state and local law, in porn stores that were found clustered in most major U.S. cities.

The Times Square neighborhood in New York City was at one time probably the mecca of porn stores: Dozens of stores on and around West 42nd Street sold thousands of discounted pornographic titles stacked vertically in bins two feet deep, arranged by themes: anal, gay, big breasts, bondage, fat and chubby, legs and nylons, toes and feet, pet and farm, diapering, amputees, senior citizens, sweet sixteen, spanking, golden showers, and so on. But in the mid-1990s, the Internet did to Times Square porn shops what decades of campaigning by neighborhood improvement associations could not—it wiped them out, replacing them with something many find more oppressive than pornography: the Walt Disney gift shops and Starbucks cafés that now monotonously reign over West 42nd Street and the rest of our suffocating planet.

Porn stores are now few, but unlike before, the product they distribute is *everywhere:* It pours out from the Internet like hot and cold water. Porn consumers can now electronically search, browse, and fine-tune to their desires. They can subscribe to Web sites featuring images to their precise taste, or browse through the Internet "discount bins" on newsgroups where pirated images are available for free—for the mere cost of an Internet account.

The range of violent imagery, much of it explicit, is now wide and flexible and available in a way it never was when the market economics of printed pornography still dictated a minimum number of mass consumers clustered into major fetish groups. Today there are Web sites that specialize in violent micro perversions: unconscious women shown explicitly date-raped ("sleepy sites"); posed dead women penetrated ("necro–dark fantasy sites"); fake crime scenes of semidressed or naked victims or simulated recordings of murders ("snuff-violence sites"); actual crime scenes of heavily mutilated victims and images of torture in Third World conflicts ("disgusting-shocking-dead sites"), rape images, of which Japan appears to be a big contributor ("rape-forced sites"), and a wide range of bondage, punishment, and torture sites. Unlike child pornography, which lurks on the Internet in hidden sites and is illegal, all of these other types of images are trafficked and promoted openly, and are available for free on newsgroups.

PARAPHILIAS

All of these various sexual predilections are known as *paraphilias*—"unusual loves," from the Greek *para*, meaning "beyond" or "outside the usual," and *philia*, the word for "love." Psychiatrists define paraphilia as a persistent need, for more than six months, for unusual objects, fetishes, rituals, or situations to achieve sexual satisfaction. Paraphilias can be severe, where the subject cannot engage in sex of any kind outside his paraphilia, or moderate, where the paraphilia enhances otherwise conventional sexual conduct. Multiple paraphilias often occur in one person, but usually one is dominant until it is replaced by another. Nobody is quite sure how paraphilias are developed, but they are linked to traumatic childhood and adolescent experiences that are reinforced or "short-circuited" to sexual drives. For example, after the World War II bombings of England, when thousands of children drilled in fear of gas attacks by the Nazis, there was a higher rate of fetish sex involving gas masks and rubber clothing among adults in England—especially in the 1950s and 1960s, when the children came of age. Paraphilias are then further reinforced by masturbation, which conditions a cognitive response in the subject to his fantasy. Often serial homicides incorporate or express various paraphilias. (See also the case study of Jerry Brudos in Chapter 4.)

The most extreme paraphilia is *erotophonophilia*—the preference for brutalizing and killing a victim as a means of sexual satisfaction. In a sense, erotophonophilia is what serial killing is. Other paraphilias in the context of serial murder include the following:

- *anthropophagy*—eating the victim's flesh or slicing off portions of it
- *colobosis*—a desire to mutilate male genitalia

- *coprolagnia*—a desire to eat feces

- *coprophilia*—a desire to see defecation or a fetish for feces

- *exhibitionism*—deliberate exposure of one's genitals to achieve a sense of power or control

- *flagellationism*—a desire to whip or beat a sexual victim

- *gerontophilia*—a desire for elderly victims

- *hematophilia/hematomania*—a desire to see or drink blood

- *kleptomania*—theft as a form of sexual expression

- *klismaphilia*—substitution of enemas for sexual intercourse

- *mazoperosis*—a desire to mutilate female breasts

- *necrophilia*—a preference for sex with corpses

- *necrophagia*—eating corpses in advanced stages of decomposition

- *necrosadism*—a desire to mutilate corpses

- *parthenophagy*—cannibalism of young girls

- *pedophilia*—sexual preference for children

- *pederasty*—a desire to sodomize male children

- *perogynia*—a desire to mutilate female genitalia

- *picquerism*—stabbing or cutting as a substitution for sex

- *pygmalianism*—a desire to have sex with dolls or mannequins

- *pyromania*—setting fires for sexual pleasure

- *pyrophilia*—a desire to watch fires for sexual pleasure

- *sadism*—infliction of pain for sexual satisfaction

- *scatophilia*—a desire to make obscene phone calls as a way of exerting control over a victim

- *scoptophilia*—voyeurism; seeking sexual pleasure by peeping through windows, an early behavioral trend found in some serial killers who graduate from voyeurism to rape to murder

- *zoophilia*—a desire for sex with animals

One can easily understand how some of these paraphilias become incorporated in acts of serial murder—especially ones like the desire for sex with dead bodies or cannibalism, which preclude a surviving victim. For other serial killers, the actual act of taking of a life is the primary fantasy driving them. For others, the need to kill is secondary.

The question remains, and nobody has come forth with a definitive answer: Does pornography promote and facilitate the acting out of violent behavior, or preempt it? As these images are now widely available in a way that printed pornography never was, and a generation of expanded viewers is consuming them, the resolution of this question of facilitation or preemption becomes urgently critical.

Television programmers still have not figured out what is right or wrong. Explicit images of real violence are censored, while beautifully photographed and elegantly choreographed violence is broadcast. Should we not show the full disgusting horror of an actual gunshot wound and instead censor the lie that violence is slow-motion beautiful and accompanied by music? Or would repeated showings of real violence only desensitize our repulsion to it?

DETECTIVE MAGAZINES

Perhaps a more prevalent facilitator in several serial murder cases was not explicit pornography, but illustrated men's adventure stories and detective magazines once sold at every supermarket and newsstand in America. Detective magazines became a subject of a detailed study in the mid-1980s, as their presence was found not in only serial homicide cases, but in cases of child molestation, rape, and autoerotic deaths. The covers of these magazines almost always featured a luridly illustrated or photographed image of a frightened, often bound female, thrown to the floor or ground, skirt hiked up or blouse torn. Bondage was depicted in 38 percent of the covers studied, and the subject bound was a woman in 100 percent of the covers. In 71 percent of the covers, the aggressor was a male who loomed over the woman and was always indistinguishable or lurking beyond the edges of the page. Sometimes the victim looked out to the reader as the source of her anguish. While no explicit violence or nudity was depicted in any of these magazines, numerous serial killers have reported being highly excited and inspired by such publications. It can be argued, perhaps, that precisely because the nudity was not explicit, it functioned as a stimulant rather than as a release of fantasy: The offender was driven to "fill in" with his own imaginative resources the remainder of the fantasy, instead of having it preempted by an explicit image.

When the study was conducted in the 1980s, unlike pornography, these magazines were readily available in corner stores, newsstands, and supermarkets. Some twenty magazines were regularly published, and four magazines alone accounted for a monthly circulation of nearly one million copies.[181]

Ted Bundy recalled a fascination for detective magazines and their images of abused females. In 1957, Harvey Glatman hired professional models, posed them gagged and bound as on the covers of detective magazines, took photographs, and then raped and killed them. He killed three victims in that manner. Ed Gein, the real-world *Psycho,* had a huge collection of *Startling Detective* magazines and confessed that he got the idea of skinning the heads of his victims and making them into masks from men's "true adventure" magazines, which during the 1950s and 1960s often featured sensationalized stories of Pacific cannibals and Nazi death camp atrocities. John Joubert, who murdered several young boys, reported that when he was eleven or twelve, he had seen detective magazines in the local grocery store and became aroused by the depiction of semidressed, frightened, and bound women on the covers. He began acquiring these magazines and masturbating to the images, eventually superimposing the fantasy of young boys over the images of the women. One should not, however, easily conclude that pornography or detective magazines *cause* homicidal fantasies. Joubert also reports that at age six or seven, at least six years *before* he saw his first detective magazine, he fantasized about strangling and eating his babysitter.

Detective magazines were not the only type of easily available magazine during the 1970s and 1980s depicting victimized females in various states of undress. There was a whole genre of monster movie magazines, often showing images of women attacked by creatures or being carried away unconscious by monsters. These magazines were especially directed at adolescent and teenage males, as were series of bubble-gum trading cards depicting wartime atrocities in lurid color. Comic books, especially pulp horror ones, were also cited as inciting youths to commit violent acts and were partially banned in the 1950s and early 1960s.

OTHER LITERATURE

Pornography, comics, and detective magazines are not the only types of literature, however, cited as inspiring serial killers in their first kill. The fifteenth-century child killer Gilles de Rais had been inflamed by Suetonius's *Lives of the Caesars,* which detailed (and probably exaggerated) some of the crimes of the Roman emperors.[182] According to Charles Lemire, a nineteenth-century biographer of the aristocrat–serial killer, de Rais showed his official reader and chamberlain, the university-educated Henriet Griart, "certain passages and invited him to read the text. It was the chronicle of the life and customs of the Roman Caesars. The book was illustrated with beautifully painted pictures showing the crimes of these pagan emperors. There one could learn how Tiberius, Caracalla and the other Caesars took special delight in the massacre of children. Listening to Griart read, Gilles's fine feline face was transformed. It took on a ferocious form and his eyes glowed. He did not hesitate to assert that he would imitate the said Caesars. That same night, he began to do so, following the lesson and the pictures of the book."

Although technically not a serial killer because he was apprehended after committing his first murder, Donald Fearn became obsessed with torturing a woman to death after he read historical accounts of a Colorado sect of Indians called the Penitentes, whose religious ceremonies involved torture and crucifixion. In April 1942, when his wife was in the hospital giving birth, Fearn kidnapped a seventeen-year-old nursing student and drove her to a remote one-room shack in the desert.* There he raped and tortured her with a pair of pliers and red-hot strands of baling wire for six hours before killing her.

---

* It's remarkable how many cases of sexual murder occur precisely when the killer's partner is giving birth to their child.

Herbert Mullin had just been reading accounts of Michaelangelo's dissections in Irving Stone's *The Agony and the Ecstasy* when he dragged Mary Guilfoyle out into the woods and cut open her abdomen, taking out her organs and inspecting them.

THE BIBLE AND SERIAL KILLING

We might be concerned with sexual pornography, but the Bible has had a leading role in many serial homicides as well. During the mid-1920s, Earle Leonard Nelson traveled the United States and Canada clutching a Bible and raping and strangling "sinful" landladies; he is known to have killed twenty-seven before he was arrested. In Stamford, Connecticut, Benjamin Franklin Miller, a preacher who focused on reforming prostitutes and drug addicts, strangled five of them with their own bras between 1967 and 1971. In Chicago, homosexual killer John Wayne Gacy, while strangling and sodomizing some of his thirty-three victims, recited the 23rd Psalm to them: "The Lord is my shepherd . . ." In Germany in 1959, when he was nineteen, Heinrich Pommerencke raped and killed four women after seeing a biblical film called *The Ten Commandments*. Pommerencke said, "I saw half-naked women dancing around the golden calf. I thought then that many women were evil and did not deserve to live. I then realized I would have to kill them."[183]

In Scotland in 1968–1969, an unknown serial killer was nicknamed "Bible John" because the sister of one of three female victims, who met him in a dance hall, remembered him quoting from the Bible and condemning adultery. All three women were strangled, had their purses stolen, and were menstruating at the time of their murders.

Gary Ridgway, the confessed murderer of forty-eight women, was an avid Bible reader, often reading it as he watched TV. Robert Yates, upon his conviction for the brutal murders of thirteen women in Spokane, addressed the jury referring to the Bible:

> Scripture says the heart is deceitful above all things and beyond cure; who can understand? Our hearts can be deceitful beyond our own understanding, and surely mine was. I couldn't rid myself of this sinful nature. Somewhere, through all this devastation, God was knocking on the door of my heart, but I wouldn't let him in. I thought to myself, how could a God love or

hear anything that was not clean. I thought I wasn't good enough to even speak to God, and if He wouldn't listen to me, then who would?

The Bible has many unfortunate passages calling for the punishment of female sexual misbehavior:

Now then, O harlot, hear the word of the Lord! Thus says the Lord God: "Because your filthiness was poured out and your nakedness uncovered in your harlotry with your lovers. . . . I will gather them from all around against you and will uncover your nakedness to them, that they may see all your nakedness and I will judge you as women who break wedlock or shed blood are judged; I will bring blood upon you in fury and jealousy . . . and they shall stone you with stones and thrust you through with their swords." (*Ezekiel 16:35–40*)

The Bible can be a potent motivator particularly to missionary type killers, desperate to find approval to kill somebody—*anybody*. In their twisted and immoral perception, it can license them to murder prostitutes, homosexuals, or "baby killing" abortion clinic doctors.

Pornography, detective magazines, alcohol or drugs, or any other kind of substance or literature, including the Bible, can become facilitators. While it is not believed that they *cause* serial killers to murder, they do facilitate their acts by lowering inhibitions, fueling or reinforcing existing fantasies, or imparting upon their acts a false rationale. Combined with stress, poor coping capabilities, and a history of isolation and low-esteem, and tempered by fantasies of revenge, sex, and violence, facilitators often are simply lubricants in a well-built killing machine.

The Second Murder

In a serial killer's history, every first murder has to be followed by another. It differentiates him from a common murderer. Probably the most chilling description of the process of a first-time serial murder and what comes next was provided recently by Ian Brady, one of the Moors Murderers.

While confined in a psychiatric facility, Brady recently wrote a controversial book titled *The Gates of Janus: Serial Killing and Its Analysis.** In it he describes a serial killer's first and second homicides:

The first killing experience will not only hold the strongest element of existential novelty and curiosity, but also the greatest element of danger and trepidation conjured by the unknown. Usually the incipient serial killer is too immersed in the psychological and legal challenges of the initial homicide, not to mention immediate logistics—the physical labour that the killing and disposal involve. He is therefore not in a condition to form a detached appreciation of the traumatic complexities bombarding his senses.

You could, in many instances, describe the experience as an effective state of shock. He is, after all, storming pell-mell the defensive social conditioning of a lifetime, as well as declaring war upon all the organized, regulatory forces of society. In extinguishing someone's life he is also committing his own, and has no time to stop and stare in the hazardous, psychological battlefield.

In another very significant sense, he is killing his long-accepted self as well as the victim, and simultaneously giving birth to a new persona, decisively cutting the umbilical connection between himself and ordinary mankind.

Having fought his former self and won, the fledgling serial killer flexes his newfound powers with more confidence. The second killing will hold all the same disadvantages, distracting elements of the first, but to a lesser degree. This allows a more objective assimilation of the experience. It also fosters an expanding sense of omnipotence, a wide-angle view of the metaphysical chessboard.

In many cases, the element of elevated aestheticism in the second murder will exert a more formative impression than the first and probably of any in the future. It not only represents the rite of confirmation, a revelational leap of lack of faith in humanity, but also the onset of addiction to hedonistic nihilism.

The psychic abolition of redemption.[184]

---

* The book is published in the U.S. by the apocalyptic alternative publisher Adam Parfrey. See: www.feralhouse.com.

While one should not overvalue the outdated sophomoric existential-ism that Brady claims imbues the squalid act of serial murder, his obser-vations are nonetheless insightful. They are hauntingly similar to David Gore's description quoted earlier: "I have never felt an emptiness of self like I did right then and I will never forget that feeling. It was like I crossed over into a realm I could never come back from." The serial killer's first murder can transform him into somebody other than who he was—a type of rebirth. But it is an illusion; in order to sustain his new identity, the se-rial killer needs to kill again and again.

Brady reveals a curious phenomenon underlying the subsequent sec-ond murder. If indeed the serial killer transforms his old self into a new one by committing his first murder, then his second murder is really only the first murder by the newly reinvented self. That perhaps might account for Brady's assertion that the second murder is the most exciting. After that, unless the killer can totally transform himself again, with each mur-der the satisfaction and excitement decline and dissipate. The murders gradually drift out of the killer's fantasy realm into that of his depressing reality from which he first sought escape. In response, some serial killers escalate their crimes to sustain the frontiers of fantasy, until the range of their fantasies become unworkable in the reality of the world in which they commit their acts and they self-destruct by behavior that leads to their arrest or by surrendering to police or confessing. Some perhaps com-mit suicide, while others simply cease killing and return to their normal lives, leaving behind a mystery forever unsolved.

EIGHT

THE KILLING TIMES:

The Method to the Madness

Though this be madness, yet there is method in't.
—WILLIAM SHAKESPEARE, *Hamlet 2.2*

Once the serial killer has killed his first victim he enters a complex circular process, akin to addiction, that leads him to kill over and over again. Very distinctive patterns emerge, depending on whether the serial killer is an organized or disorganized personality, and the killer leaves a unique personal imprint called a "signature" on each of his murders.

Each serial homicide goes through a number of dynamic phases, which at some points differ slightly between organized and disorganized killers.

Phase 1: Dissociative-Fantasy-Aura State

The dissociative state is a state of mind "beyond fantasy" in which the killer has crossed the boundaries that separate imagination from reality. This "hyper fantasy stage" is arrived at through a gradual process of withdrawal from reality through years of repeating and elaborating fantasies with specifically violent themes such as murder, rape, revenge, control, mutilation, cannibalism, and possession. During his childhood and adolescence, the future killer takes tentative exploratory journeys into this territory, which manifest themselves in acts of cruelty to animals, bullying of fellow children, setting fires, and petty crimes.

For most children, such forays into violence beyond mere fantasy result in very discouraging and unpleasant results. These consequences often serve to dissuade the child from ever acting out these fantasies again—and often clear the fantasy away completely for the remainder of the child's life. But for a small minority of children, these forays result in a certain level of stress and fear alleviation, satisfaction, and pleasure, which leave the child wanting more—especially if the child is under continual environmental stress. These fantasies are often accompanied by compulsive masturbation, which conditions a link between the fantasies and sexual urges.

These children cling to their violent fantasies into their adolescence and adulthood, and at some indeterminate point they cross the threshold where they no longer know or are aware of the difference between fantasy and reality. They are no longer cognizant that the thoughts they are having originated in fantasy: Reality and fantasy become merged and the person is said to be in the dissociative state.

The dissociative process can last anywhere from a few hours to a few months before some stressor such as those described in the previous chapter, along with facilitators, causes the person to "snap" and triggers an acting out of a violent fantasy. The stressor can be a culmination of accumulated long-term problems, such as a bad marriage, or a sudden and often minor episode, such as rudeness from a store clerk or rejection by a woman approached in a disco or bar.

Dr. Joel Norris described the dissociative process as the "aura phase," in which for the killer sounds and colors become more vivid, odors are more intense, and sometimes even his skin can become sensitive to the slightest pressure. The killer is oblivious to any outside stimuli and reacts only to invisible stimuli that he alone can experience and understand. The fantasy is now prolonged, entirely compulsive, and completely dominating the killer's every thought and action.

Nothing can inhibit the killer at this late stage, not the threat of punishment, laws, fear of death, morality, religion, mores, or taboos—all of these things become meaningless to the serial killer, as does the life of the person he is about to murder. The serial killer is almost a creature that defies the definition of a human, Dr. Norris says:

The killer is simply a biological engine driven by a primal instinct to satisfy a compelling lust. The ritual of killing has become bound up with an autonomic survival mechanism, almost as if the murderer had become a single-celled creature reacting to an overpowering chemical stimulus.[185]

Probably the most focused area of research today in forensic psychiatry is the point at which fantasy transforms into the dissociative process in the serial killer. At the early stages, some serial killers are aware of and can verbalize their transformation from fantasy to dissociative process. William Heirens, who murdered two women and a girl in Chicago, locked his clothes in a bathroom and threw away the key to resist going out to commit his crimes. But the urge became so strong that he crawled out naked on the ledge to recover his clothing. Henry Lee Lucas, on the eve of his release from prison for killing his mother, begged authorities not to let him go free because he was overwhelmed with the urge to kill. On the day he was released he immediately killed a woman and dumped her body near the prison gates.

Once the serial killer enters into the dissociative process, he moves on to the next phase.

Phase 2: Trolling-Hunting-Stalking Stage

"Trolling" is a fishing term describing the process in which a moving boat spreads out a net in an area likely to contain an abundance of fish. Joel Norris applied the term to serial killers when they begin to frequent and cruise areas where they are likely to find a victim. There is nothing random or accidental about trolling. Each serial killer has a precise "shopping list" for the type of victim he needs to satisfy his fantasy. Ted Bundy, for example, is said to have preferred young women with shoulder-length hair parted down the middle who looked like they were from upper-middle-class origins.

In his study of male serial killers, psychologist Eric Hickey determined that 40 percent of serial killers targeted females exclusively. At least 37 percent targeted both sexes, while 22 percent only chose males as their victims.[186] Michael Newton, looking at victims of serial murder, determined that 65 percent were female and 35 percent male. Of serial killers specifically targeting men, 42 percent were homosexual, while the other 58 percent represented female killers, revenge killings, hospital murders, and "thrill" murders.[187]

In profiling victims, Hickey maintains that between 11 and 13 percent of victims were at "high risk": they were hitchhiking, were prostitutes, worked alone as store clerks, were driving a taxicab, or were in a car breakdown when approached by their killer.[188] This suggests that more than two-thirds of victims were unsuspecting of any imminent threat, did not facilitate their deaths, and were essentially at the right place at the wrong time.

Sixteen percent of identified serial killer victims knew their killer as a friend, casual acquaintance, neighbor, or co-worker. Three percent were related to the killer by blood or marriage, of which 49 percent were children murdered by their father or mother; 13 percent were spouses; 10 percent were parents murdered by their child; and 28 percent were an assortment of grandparents, siblings, uncles, aunts, cousins, in-laws, nieces, and nephews. The remaining 68 percent in Hickey's study were killed by strangers.[189]

Aside from gender, serial killers use various other criteria for their selection of victims. Age is often important with some serial killers, who focus exclusively on children, teens, or elderly victims. While most serial killers murder victims of the same race, some specifically target victims of other races. Occupation can play a role beyond just that of a victim's vulnerability. Prostitutes, strippers, and other sex-industry workers might be specifically targeted for the sexual associations of their work. In the twisted mind of a serial killer, however, nurses, store clerks, waitresses, and flight attendants can also be targeted through some obscure sexualizing thought process.

Residence or lack of residence could result in a person being targeted. Street people, derelicts, alcoholics, and homeless people have been targeted as victims in several cases. Victims living in the same building have also been targeted, and killers working in the confines of neighborhoods are frequent as well. In Los Angeles, for example, one needs a street map to sort out the neighborhood serial killers: Skid Row Slasher, Skid Row Stabber, Koreatown Slasher, West Side Rapist, Orange Coast Killer, Southside Slayer . . .

Approximately one-third of serial killers are traveling murderers, another third kill in one specific place such as their home or farm, and the final third kill locally. Thus some 66 percent of all serial killers murder either at home or near their home.

When trolling, the serial killer is highly focused with all his senses directed at locating a victim. Once he identifies a suitable victim, his activities take on a frenzied intensity as he carefully stalks his victim in anticipation of murder. Like a cat that has spotted prey and has positioned itself to leap, the serial killer focuses all energy, thought, and effort on the potential victim, patiently waiting for the right instant to pounce. When they identify a victim, serial killers can sometimes wait in the shadows for days or weeks before finding just the right moment to strike. Some, when they spot a potential victim, file that information away for a later period when they are in the mood to kill.

Thirty-one percent of American serial killers in Newton's study approached their victims in a public place or quasi-public space, ranging from shopping malls to parks and highways, and sometimes they killed their victims there. One victim was murdered on the street only sixty yards away from Los Angeles Police Department headquarters. Sixteen percent of serial killers murdered in their home or apartment, luring their victims there. Ten percent invaded their victim's homes, 5 percent chose prostitutes for victims, 5 percent preyed solely on hospital patients, 3 percent killed while robbing their victims, and 1 percent targeted hitchhikers exclusively, although many reported to resorting to killing hitchhikers when their other methods did not yield results. "Lover's lanes" and couples in cars were selected as victims for 1 percent of killers, while classified advertisements and highway distress situations were exclusively used by 0.5 percent each. Combinations of various methods were used by 23 percent of serial killers, and the remaining 3 percent is unknown.[190]

Trolling can be simple or complex. Ed Kemper simply drove around looking for hitchhikers. In Rochester, New York, Arthur Shawcross murdered eleven women, nine of whom were roadside prostitutes he picked up in his van. Richard Ramirez, the Night Stalker, simply walked around until he found an unlocked door or open window. Albert DeSalvo, who killed thirteen women, knocked on apartment doors until his desired type of victim opened the door. He then gained entry by posing as a repairman sent by the management to fix some potential problem. Bobby Joe Long perused classified ads offering objects for sale or apartments for rent and called the numbers during the day. If a woman answered the phone, he surmised that any man in her life would be away at work during the day. Long then showed up at the location; if the victim was alone as he had hoped, he proceeded with his crime.

Whether a serial killer is an organized or disorganized personality often determines what kind of trolling technique he uses and what happens once the serial killer approaches his victim. Richard Ramirez was a mixed-category serial killer who did not so much seek out a specific type of victim as an opportunity to kill, be it a man, woman, or child. An unlocked door was all that Ramirez needed, and as soon as he encountered his victim, he attacked. In the case of Jerry Brudos, a saleswoman called at his home and was lured down into his cellar on an impulse. That is why victims whose bodies are found where the killer first met them are often classified by investigators as victims of disorganized personalities. Once the disorganized serial killer approaches his victim, he usually carries out a powerful "blitz" attack that is very quick, vicious, and highly violent, described by police as "overkill"—multiple stab wounds, extensive cutting and mutilation, a high number of blows to the head and body, multiple gunshots—excessively more wounds than necessary to cause death. Often the disorganized serial killer murders with his own hands, with a piece of clothing belonging to the victim, or with a crude weapon improvised or found at the site of the encounter.

When, on the other hand, the organized serial killer approaches his victim, an entirely different dynamic takes place and additional phases might occur before the murder takes place.

Phase 3: Persuasion-Seduction Stage

Whereas the disorganized killer lacks the confidence and social skills to interact with his victim and therefore attacks immediately upon contact, the organized serial killer is an entirely different creature. He will patiently lure, charm, persuade, and woo his victim into a vulnerable position where he can carry out his murder. Child murderers are known for this ability, often talking children into calmly walking away with them.

It is not enough for the organized serial killer to simply kill his victim—his fantasy requires that he carry out some complex ritual for which he needs to keep his victim alive for a period of time or needs uninterrupted control over the victim's body.

Some serial killers, particularly those preying on male victims, may not feel sufficiently secure in their physical abilities to overcome their victim and need to set them up in a vulnerable position. John Wayne Gacy, for example, used a complex trolling method in which he pretended to look for employees for his construction business. When he found a desirable young male, he lured him to an "interview" at his home, where he had his office. There he showed the victim his picture with the president's wife and in the course of conversation he would demonstrate his "handcuff trick" that he used in his shows as a volunteer clown for hospitalized sick children. Once he snapped the handcuffs into place, the young male, no matter how strong, had little chance of resisting Gacy. (As Gacy explained, the "trick" was "having the key.") In Atlanta, Wayne Williams, who was accused of murdering twenty-eight boys and youths, supposedly offered record contracts and lured them to a small recording studio he had in his home. Richard Cottingham wined and dined his victims, slipping a rape drug into their drinks.

The entire point of the wooing is to maneuver the victim into a location or position where the serial killer can gain uninterrupted physical control over him or her. Only organized serial killers are capable of this type of seductive encounter with their victims. This is probably the point at which the serial killer is the "craziest." All his energy, thoughts, and focus are on hurting the individual he has encountered, yet at the same time, all his overt actions and every nuance of his conduct must mask his intent and make his victim feel at ease and secure—an especially difficult task as the serial killer and his victim are often strangers to each other.

The more charismatic or physically attractive serial killers simply approach women in bars or clubs and seduce them. Some even form short-term relationships with their victims and kill them on a subsequent date to their first meeting. Other serial killers develop more sophisticated ruses. Christopher Wilder, suspected in the murder of twelve women, is known to have hired a model for a "pizza commercial" photo session. She consumed numerous pieces of pizza as he took photographs of her. At some point she slipped into unconsciousness—the pizza was drugged.

A disturbingly significant number of serial killers pose as police officers. This gives them a convenient pretext to approach and gain control over their victims without the necessity of putting them at ease. The FBI has noted that the serial killer's preferred color of automobile is blue because of its connotation with authority. Angelo Buono and Kenneth Bianchi, the Hillside Stranglers, posed as plainclothes police officers and "arrested" prostitutes. In North America, police departments recommend that if a driver is suspicious of a police vehicle attempting to pull her over in some remote location, she should try to signal the officer that she has seen him and drive slowly to some well-lighted and populated location before coming to a halt. While the police officer may be annoyed, no action is taken against a driver who does not immediately come to a stop but continues to *drive slowly* without attempting to evade the police car.

Harvey Glatman hired some of his victims as photo models. Harvey Carignan killed a woman who answered an employment ad he placed in a paper. Albert DeSalvo knocked on apartment doors at random. Some serial killers use a variety of methods: Ted Bundy used to wear a fake cast and ask women to help him carry something to his car, while at other times he posed as a police officer. Jerry Brudos killed a female encyclopedia saleswoman who mistakenly called at his house, lured another woman with car trouble back to his house, and then kidnapped two women from shopping centers.

Some serial killers contract others to bring victims to them. In Houston, Texas, homosexual Dean Corll had two teenage youths go out for him and find other young boys and children. He paid them $200 for every victim they lured to his house. In Florida, Fred Waterfield paid auxiliary sheriff's deputy David Allen Gore $1,000 for every teenage girl he brought him. Gore used his uniform and authority to lure female victims to their deaths. Waterfield and Gore raped and killed six women before they were apprehended.

Some serial killers take a female partner along with them; her presence when the killer approaches his victim makes the situation appear nonthreatening. Charlene Gallego, the wife of Gerald Gallego, approached victims on behalf of her husband, who would wait in the van. She even made herself appear pregnant to further instill the illusion of a nonthreatening situation. In Ontario, Canada, husband and wife Paul Bernardo and Karla Homolka raped and killed at least three young girls, including Homolka's younger sister. Despite the fact that one girl had already disappeared in the region, a fifteen-year-old student was kidnapped from in front of her school in broad daylight by the couple. They pulled up in a car beside the girl and Homolka got out of the vehicle and spread a map on the roof while asking the girl to approach and show her some directions. While the victim stood by the open car door looking at the map, she was suddenly pushed into the car and subdued. Despite the fact that there were numerous cars driving by, nobody saw anything extraordinary, except for one witness who recalled seeing somebody "struggling to put a big package on their backseat." Such male-female serial killer couples are not particularly rare.

It is important to remember that in these cases, the serial killer often weaves a complex relationship with his victim into which he inserts his ruse. Angelo Buono and Kenneth Bianchi did not simply drive up to their victim at the bus stop and offer her a ride home. One of them passed her on foot and struck up an innocent conversation at the end of which the ride home was nonchalantly offered. Ted Bundy carefully stalked a victim in the shopping plaza, making sure she was there long enough to make his story plausible.

The organized serial killer strikes up an ostensibly very innocent conversation, but its intention is to elicit the vital information necessary to lure the victim into a trap. Serial killers are often attractive, polite, charming, and well-dressed. Paul Bernardo and Karla Homolka were described as a "magazine cover perfect couple." Along with this charisma, the organized serial killer also has a sixth sense for weaknesses and is quick to zero in and exploit them. (Chapter 10 has more on what kinds of ruses a stranger with a hidden agenda may attempt when approaching you.)

Once the serial killer has succeeded in wooing the victim into a vulnerable position he moves on to the next phase—the capture.

Phase 4: The Trap and Capture

Once again, the capture stage is often undertaken only by organized serial killers to whom gaining physical control of their victims before killing them is central to their fantasy. (The disorganized serial killer often goes straight to the kill without wooing or capture.) It is at the capture that the serial killer drops his mask and reveals his intentions.

The capture can be as quick as a pair of handcuffs snapped shut on the victim's wrists. Often it is a blow to the head or a punch to the stomach, which makes it difficult for the victim to scream. Once the serial killer captures his victim, he can unleash his murderous fantasies on the helpless person at the site of the capture or somewhere else. Christopher Wilder, for example, after subduing his victim with drugs or a punch to the stomach, bound her hands and feet and covered her mouth and eyes with duct tape. He then stuffed the bound woman into a sleeping bag and checked into a motel. Throwing the sleeping bag over his shoulder like a sack of grain, he carried his victim from the car to his room, where he raped and tortured her. Afterward he suffocated his victim with a pillow and carried her body out in the same sleeping bag.

Richard Cottingham wooed prostitutes with drinks, dinner and sympathy before arranging an exchange of sex for cash. By the end of the evening the victim was relaxed and unafraid of him (or drugged). One of Cottingham's survivors recalled that at the end of an evening with him she had no second thoughts of lying down on a bed, facedown and turned away from him, for "a massage." Cottingham then suddenly leapt onto her back and snapped a pair of handcuffs on her wrists.

Once the serial killer has made the capture, he proceeds to act out his violent fantasies.

Phase 5: The Murder

The disorganized serial killer usually does not go through the persuading and capture phases. He attacks his victim where he encounters him or her—on the street, in a remote location, or at the victim's home or place of work. The victim often becomes a casualty by being at the wrong place at the wrong time—he or she was simply unlucky. The body is frequently found where the encounter took place and is almost never concealed.

The victim shows signs of a powerful and sudden "blitz" attack and is sometimes killed instantaneously. Extreme blunt force trauma to the head and lack of defensive wounds are often features of such an attack. The victim is rarely restrained or gagged.

The victim is often "depersonalized" by having his or her face covered or, more subtly, by being rolled over on the stomach. Sometimes severe facial mutilation is also a sign of depersonalization, as is mutilation of the genitals and breasts.

Rape or mutilation most often takes place after the victim has been rendered unconscious, is dying, or is dead. The disorganized serial killer is uncomfortable with any kind of interaction with the victim and prefers a passive and doll-like subject. As Kemper said of his victims, he needed to "possess them in the way I wanted to; I had to evict them from their human bodies."

Sexual acts committed on the victim often involve the insertion of foreign objects into the body's orifices (insertional necrophilia). Parts of the body, especially the buttocks and breasts, are sometimes bitten or slashed and stabbed, as are often the thighs, abdomen, and neck. Very often the killer does not complete the sexual act and semen is found on the victim's clothing or nearby. Sometimes the killer has sex with the victim's wounds. Parts of the victim's body might be cut away and missing.

Death is usually caused by strangulation, blunt force, or stabbing, and the weapon is often found at the crime scene.

The organized sexual killer is more complex in his crime. The act of killing is sexualized and death is often caused slowly. Asphyxiation is often used with the killer deliberately loosening and tightening his grip around the victim's throat, keeping him or her suspended between life and death. The killer rapes his victim before killing, and sometimes repeats the rape after death. Some killers focus on murdering their victims in the middle or at the climax of the sex act. The sex act is often complete or near complete, with semen discovered inside body orifices or in the pubic region. The sex organs might be bitten, bruised, or cut, and such injuries usually occur while the victim is alive. The victim often shows evidence of restraints. Severe mutilation, other than to disguise the victim's identity, is not a usual feature of the organized serial killer.

A subtype of the organized sexual killer is the sadistic sexual killer, for whom the torture of the victim is a more primary motivator than the actual sexual act. The sadistic killer derives his pleasure from seeing his victim in pain, and for that he needs his victim alive and conscious. Such killers have been known to keep their victims alive for as long as six weeks, and some carefully revive near-dead victims in order to prolong the torture. Torture inflicted on the victim is often very elaborate, and the killer brings with him various implements such as pliers, electrical devices, and probes. Some killers bring their victims to elaborately fitted and sound-proofed "torture chambers."

The most prevalent forms of sexual acts inflicted on the victim, in order of case frequency, are anal rape, forced fellatio, vaginal rape, and foreign-object penetration.[191] Very often victims are forced to engage in all of these acts, and they almost always occur before death.

Victims often show injuries in various stages of healing because they have been inflicted over an extended period of time. Bruising is often evident in genital areas and on the breasts, thighs, buttocks, neck, and abdomen. These areas may be slashed or mutilated, but rarely enough to cause death. Victims may be urinated on, and their stomach contents may contain evidence indicating that they were forced to ingest urine or feces.

Most commonly, death is caused by ligature strangulation, manual strangulation, hanging, or suffocation. Less frequently, because death occurs faster, the cause is gunshot wounds, cutting, stabbing wounds, or blunt force.

The sadistic sexual killer is usually the most organized of all. His vehicle is often specially outfitted for capturing victims and, as already noted, he may maintain a secluded torture facility outfitted with elaborate devices.

The organized killer often works with gloves and disguises and takes care not to leave any evidence behind. The body is frequently taken to another location and carefully hidden. Often he has special "burial grounds" prepared in advance and arrives equipped with a shovel.

The preceding descriptions are not fixed formulas—they are what *usually* occurs. Some killers are a mix of organized and disorganized personalities, and sometimes circumstances such as an unexpected interruption can cause an organized killer to leave behind a disorganized scene, while teams of killers, if composed of two different personalities, can also leave a mixed crime scene.

The FBI study determined that in 56 percent of cases, the victims were raped before death and 33 percent were tortured.[192] It appears that disorganized, organized, and sadistic-organized personalities represent roughly a third each of serial killers.

It should also be noted that several categories of serial killers do not easily fit any of these descriptions. These are solo female serial killers, such as mothers or babysitters who kill children in their care, nurses who kill patients, wives who kill multiple husbands, and at least one case of a prostitute who compulsively killed clients. Male nurses and doctors who kill multiple patients also do not easily fall into the previously described categories and are believed to function under the rules of a different dynamic. Finally, serial cult murders, of which there are several cases, also operate under a different set of circumstances.

Phase 6: The Totem-Trophy-Memory Stage

Many serial killers, during or after the murder, perform a ritual that most often consists of taking souvenirs or trophies of the crime. This is an essential feature, because the roots of the crime lie in the foggy dissociative process where the perimeters of reality and fantasy become blurry. The taking and keeping of souvenirs is essential for the serial killer to somehow create, and maintain the bridge between his dreamed desires and the reality of acting out his fantasy. Without the souvenir, some serial killers may not even be sure that they had acted upon their fantasy. Others use the souvenir to perpetuate the pleasure and excitement they sparked during the murder.

In addition to taking souvenirs, the disorganized killer may also pose the corpse, sometimes in an obscene position. Occasionally the posing is more ritualistic; in Los Angeles the killer of derelicts in the street poured a circle of salt around the body and took their shoes off, neatly leaving them at the feet of the victim, pointing toward the body. The body may be dumped in a place of significance to taunt authorities, such as in front of a No Dumping sign or, as Henry Lee Lucas did, near the gates of a prison. Lester Suff left murdered drug-addict prostitutes near Dumpsters, their arms turned outward to display their needle track marks. Parts of the corpse, such as genitals, the head, or limbs, may be cut away and kept by the killer. These may be later eaten by the killer or kept preserved in jars and even shown to subsequent victims. Bloodied clothing may be kept by the disorganized personality because usually no attempt is made to destroy evidence.

The organized killer is more likely to take photographs or videos of the victim both before and after killing. He may also take minor personal belongings, such as an item of clothing, jewelry, or a driver's license, as a trophy of his crime. Because the organized personality attempts to cover his tracks, he may carefully hide such items. Others may give the souvenirs as gifts to their girlfriends, wives, or daughters. Some keep elaborate scrapbooks of newspaper clippings or write detailed diaries. The FBI study reports that in 27 percent of the homicides it studied, souvenirs were kept.[193]

Some serial killers make videotapes of their victims. Although for decades there have been rumors of so-called snuff films that purport to show actual murders, so far all the videotapes recovered by police from serial killers stop short of showing the actual killing. They do, however, show horrendous scenes of torture and rape. Such tapes were recently shown at a trial of serial killers Paul Bernardo and Karla Homolka in Toronto, Canada, and of Charles Ng in California, and were rare glimpses into the chamber of horrors of a sadistic sexual murderer.

In crime fiction there is a popular notion that the criminal returns to the scene of his crime. It is absolutely true. The FBI study determined that in 27 percent of the homicides it surveyed, the killer returned to the crime scene. When the murderers were asked why, 26 percent replied that they returned to relive the fantasy; 19 percent to check into the progress of the crime; 9 percent to kill another victim; and 6 percent to have sex with the corpse. One returned fourteen hours after the murder and cut off the victim's breasts; another returned several weeks later to involve the corpse in sexual activities.[194] Arthur Shawcross was identified and captured when a police helicopter spotted him eating a bag lunch near the decaying body of one of his victims. The return to the crime scene is a vital aspect of the totem phase.

The FBI also discovered another remarkable aspect of the totem phase: In 20 percent of the homicides it studied, the killer participated to some degree in the police investigation of the crime.[195] In cases of children going missing, the killer is often among the volunteers looking for the missing child. Sometimes the killer presents himself as a witness or, as in the cases of Ed Kemper and Peter Woodcock, he goes to the police station or bars and coffee shops frequented by police officers and engages them in conversation about the case. It is a rule of thumb for police to usually investigate first the person who reports finding the body.

There are several reasons for the killer's involvement in the investigation, beyond the desire to know how far the investigation has progressed. First, it gives the killer an opportunity to prolong the excitement and pleasure that the murder sparked; second, it gives him a sense of superiority and control over the authorities around him who are attempting to solve the mystery—he knows something they do not.

Phase 7: Post-Homicidal Depression

When questioned, serial killers give different accounts of their satisfaction after the crime. Some go into a long and deep sleep; some speak of a sense of "renewal," whereas others speak of guilt, remorse, and fear. This state may last for hours or for weeks and months, but at some point the serial killer once again begins slipping back into the dissociative state. Obviously, the problem is that all of the factors that originally contributed to the killer's homicidal fantasies have not been alleviated by the homicide. Even worse, the commission of the killings can in some cases contribute additional stressors in the killer's psychopathology—making him kill more frequently and more brutally.

Ted Bundy, speaking in the third person as always, described the post-crime state of mind:

He did everything he should have done. He didn't go out at night and when he was drinking he stayed around friends. For a period of months, the enormity of what he did stuck with him. He watched his behavior, and reinforced the desire to overcome what he had begun to perceive were some problems that were probably more severe than he would have liked to believe they were.

It was the deceptive fashion, you might say, in which that psychopathology withdrew into this dormant stage that led the individual to the erroneous belief that he "got it out of himself," and this wasn't going to happen again . . .

But slowly, the pressures, tensions, dissatisfaction which, in the very early stages, fueled this thing had an effect. Yet it was more self-sustaining and didn't need as much tension or as much disharmony externally as it did before . . .

It took six months or so until he was back thinking of alternative means of engaging in similar activity, but not something that would likely result in apprehension or failure of one sort or another . . .

[After committing another crime] he was seized with the same kind of disgust and repulsion and fear and wonder at why he was allowing himself to attempt such extraordinary violence. But the significance of this particular occasion was that while he stayed off the streets and vowed he'd never do it again and recognized the horror of what he had done and certainly was frightened by what he saw happening, it took him only three months to get over it. In the next incident, he was over it in a month.[196]

Ted Bundy was an intelligent, thinking serial killer with a college degree in psychology and a precise awareness of what he was doing, yet he continued to murder repeatedly despite his inhibitions and struggle to confront the compulsion to kill. On the other hand, Kenneth Bianchi was more typically representative of the serial killer's mentality in his explanation:

We got on the freeway. I fucked her and killed her. We dumped her body off and that was it. Nothin' to it.[197]

PART THREE

FIGHTING MONSTERS

NINE

THE ART AND SCIENCE OF CRIMINAL PROFILING:

How They Get It Right and When They Don't

If you want to understand the artist, look at his work.
—JOHN DOUGLAS, former head of the FBI's Behavioral Sciences Investigative Support Unit

In a macabre way, looking at the changing face of a serial killer is like looking at the changing face of America . . .
—ROBERT D. KEPPEL, criminal investigator

Profiling and the FBI Behavioral Sciences Unit

In 1991, the Jodie Foster movie *The Silence of the Lambs,* based on the Thomas Harris bestseller, claimed that the FBI had a center nestled deep in a forested region near Washington D.C., where specially trained FBI agents ensconced in underground chambers did nothing but think about and analyze hundreds of unsolved murder files and gruesome crime scene photographs from every part of the United States. The movie proposed that they attempt to enter the minds of unidentified killers to produce a profile—a hypothetical description of a suspect based on his psychology. That is precisely what the FBI does in real life—at Quantico, Virginia, about thirty miles outside the capital.

Quantico is a fortified U.S. Marine Corps base where the FBI training academy is located. The Behavioral Sciences Unit (BSU)* is based at the

---

* Although still often referred to as the BSU, it was actually later renamed as Behavioral Sciences Services (BSS), and the profiling section was renamed as the Investigative Support Unit. (One FBI agent said, "They wanted to take the B.S. out of profiling.")

training facility and was originally established to train agents how to negotiate with and predict the behavior of hostage takers. It was in the BSU that the FBI's system of analysis of serial killers and rapists was first developed in the late 1970s, primarily by FBI agents Robert K. Ressler, John Douglas, and Roy Hazelwood.

At Quantico, buried beneath the ground in a bomb shelter once built for postnuclear intelligence operations, the National Center for the Analysis of Violent Crime (NCAVC) is housed. FBI agents specialized in profiling offenders, known as *criminal investigative analysts,* study crime data from suspected serial homicides, kidnappings, terrorist acts, and other serious and violent offenses.

In most serial homicides, FBI agents do not actively participate in the investigation, secure evidence, or pursue the suspect—that is the responsibility of the local police agency. Nor is the FBI called in if serial homicides occur in different jurisdictions—that is a myth. The FBI analysts act in an advisory capacity, only at the request of a local police department that submits a standard, thirteen-page Violent Criminal Apprehension Program (VICAP) analysis report to the FBI. The data from the VICAP report is fed into a computer known as Profiler, and the output of the computer is then elaborated on by the analysts in the form of a profile before being sent back to the local police department. Although generically called profiling, the technical term is *criminal investigative analysis* (CIA).

FBI analysts sometimes travel to the scene of a crime or assign one of a team of specially trained local FBI agents, known as *field profile coordinators,* to work at the scene. The average FBI agent is fairly well educated—a university degree is required of recruits. The agents at NCAVC often hold postgraduate degrees in various social sciences—they are highly trained, highly experienced, and highly educated. They claim to be formidable "mind hunters" and "monster fighters."

A Brief History of Profiling

The NCAVC is a relatively new program, formally established by order of President Reagan in June 1984. In the wake of the serial killer "epidemic" described earlier, it took twenty-seven years to develop and implement the

NCAVC from the time that an LAPD homicide detective named Pierce Brooks first thought of it.

Aside from fictional investigative profilers such as Arthur Conan Doyle's Sherlock Holmes or C. Auguste Dupin in Edgar Allan Poe's "The Murders in the Rue Morgue," the use of psychological profiling of unidentified criminals is a relatively new technique. It was probably first used to profile one of history's most notorious criminals, Adolf Hitler. During World War II, the OSS—the precursor of the CIA—commissioned psychiatrist W. C. Langer to construct a psychodynamic personality profile of Hitler with the purpose of anticipating decisions that Hitler might make under certain circumstances. Langer's profile turned out to be relatively accurate, down to his prediction of Hitler's suicide at the end of the war.[198]

PROFILING THE MAD BOMBER OF NEW YORK: 1956

Starting from 1940, for sixteen years, New York City was plagued by a series of bomb explosions in public places. Some thirty bombs had been planted, although not all had exploded. In 1956, the bombings began to escalate—the police were worried that it was only a matter of time before somebody would be killed. The individual was now leaving bombs inside movie theater seats, which he slashed open with a knife from underneath and stuffed the device inside.

From letters that the "Mad Bomber" left behind and sent to newspapers, it was obvious that he was a disgruntled former employee of Con Edison, New York's electric power company—but there were records for thousands of such former employees and the police did not know where to begin their search. It was at this point that the New York City police turned for help to psychiatrist and New York State Assistant Commissioner for Mental Hygiene Dr. James A. Brussel.

After reviewing the police files, Brussel told the astonished police officers, "He's symmetrically built. Perpendicular and girth development in good ratio. Neither fat nor skinny." From the notes and the behavior, Brussels had concluded that the Mad Bomber was suffering from paranoia—an obvious deduction. From there, however, Brussels turned to his knowledge of Ernst Kretschmer's study of some 10,000 patients in mental hospitals. Kretschmer found that 85 percent of the paranoiacs had what he described as an "athletic" body type. Thus Brussel concluded that if the Mad Bomber was a paranoiac, then indeed the chances were 17 in 20 that his build was symmetrical. (A recent study of serial killers, who are not all paranoiacs, concluded that 68 percent had height and weight in good proportion to one another.)[199]

As paranoia develops slowly and usually erupts in full force when the subject is near thirty-five years old, Brussel concluded that the Mad Bomber, after sixteen years of activity, must be now be middle-aged.

From the Mad Bomber's neatly printed and orderly letters, Brussel deduced that he was a very neat and "proper" man. He was probably an excellent employee, always on time and always performing the best work. From the workmanship on the bombs, Brussel concluded that he was trained as an electrician or pipe fitter. He was probably always neatly dressed and clean-shaven, and was not involved in any disciplinary infractions at work. If he had been dismissed from work, Brussel concluded, it would be for medical reasons and not for work performance or disciplinary problems.

The language of his letters showed a fairly well-educated man but either foreign born or somebody who lived among foreign-born people—there was a certain European stiffness to his writing and a lack of American slang and colloquialisms. It was as if the letters were written first in a foreign language and then translated into English. Brussel felt that because of his choice of both a knife (to slash the movie seats) and a bomb, the Mad Bomber was probably a Slav, and by his regularity, probably a Roman Catholic—very likely Polish. His letters were posted from either New York or Westchester County. He was too smart, Brussel felt, to post letters from where he lived—he likely posted them on his way to New York from somewhere else nearby. Plotting a line from New York through Westchester County, Brussels arrived at Bridgeport, Connecticut, where he knew there was a large Polish community.

Looking at the hand-printed letters, Brussel saw that every letter was perfectly formed, as expected of a paranoiac who would make every effort to avoid any appearance of a flaw, except for one letter—the W—which was formed like a double U; to Brussel it symbolized a pair of female breasts. Brussel was troubled by this sloppy anomaly in the Mad Bomber's otherwise neatly printed alphabet. Brussel was also struck by the Mad Bomber's use of a knife to slash the movie theater seats, also a crude and sloppy action uncharacteristic of his ordered and neat personality. Brussel attributed sexual motives to the two factors and suggested that the Mad Bomber's mother was probably dead and he lived either alone or with an older female relative; he was a loner, had no friends, and was single—but not a homosexual.

Finally, Brussel proposed that the Mad Bomber would be dressed conservatively and would avoid newer-style clothing. He told the police that when they arrested the Mad Bomber, he would probably be wearing a double-breasted suit and it would be buttoned.[200]

Armed with this information, the police again began to review the Con Edison company files for ex-employees who were skilled, were living in Connecticut with Polish-sounding names, might be in middle age, and were dismissed for medical reasons.

That's how the name of George Metesky cropped up, a generator wiper who was involved in an accident at an electrical plant in 1931. Metesky filed for disability payments but doctors could find nothing wrong with him. He stopped coming to work and was dropped from the payroll. He filed for worker's compensation in 1934, claiming that the accident gave him tuberculosis. After being turned down, he spent three years writing bitter letters to Con Edison. In 1937 he stopped writing, and in 1940 the first bomb exploded.

Metesky's work record indicated that before the accident, he was an excellent employee—meticulous and punctual. He was a Roman Catholic and lived in Waterbury, Connecticut, in a house with his two older sisters. He was unmarried and both his parents were dead. He was known in the neighborhood as Mr. Think, because sometimes when he was greeted he would not respond, appearing to be in deep thought. Otherwise, he was considered an inoffensive loner. When the police questioned him, he quickly confessed that he was the Mad Bomber. When arrested, he was wearing a blue double-breasted suit—buttoned. Metesky was hospitalized in a psychiatric facility.

Following the Metesky case, police began to use the services of psychiatrists more often to assist them in their investigations. The problem, however, was that each psychiatrist based his profiles on his own knowledge and experience, and when the police pooled together several psychiatrists to assist them on the Boston Strangler case, they all came up with radically different profiles. There was no systematic approach to profiling other than that of each individual psychiatrist.

PIERCE BROOKS AND LINKING CASES

Former LAPD homicide detective Pierce Brooks is considered the modern pioneer of VICAP crime data collection and case linking. In 1957, Brooks, a former naval officer and blimp pilot, became convinced that two separate homicides in the Los Angeles area might have been committed by the same individual. Surmising that if one killer had murdered two victims, he might have killed three or more as well, Brooks spent weeks thumbing through old crime files and newspaper reports at the public library. Brooks realized that he needed a computerized database of unsolved homicide descriptions, a fairly astute idea in a time when most people were unfamiliar with computers and what they can do.

Brooks proposed that every police department in California have a computer terminal linked with a central mainframe that stored data on every unsolved homicide. Every department would have access to data on homicides in other jurisdictions. Aside from the fact that most of Brooks's superiors didn't know what a computer was, back in 1957 computers were huge elephants costing millions of dollars. Nobody took his proposal seriously. Brooks put the idea aside and went on with his career to become the head of the Los Angeles homicide unit, and later a chief of police in Oregon and Colorado during the 1960s and 1970s.

By the late 1970s, Robert Ressler, an FBI instructor in hostage negotiation at the BSU in Quantico, was beginning to feel restless. Realizing that taking a systematized approach and understanding of the psychology of hostage takers was vital to police responses, Ressler came to believe that the same applied to what was then called "stranger killings"— murders where the victim and perpetrator did not know each other. These very difficult-to-solve murders were on a dramatic rise in the 1970s. On his own time, Ressler and an associate from the BSU, agent John Douglas, began to interview convicted killers, asking them why *they* thought they had killed. When the FBI hierarchy heard about Ressler and Douglas's visits to various prisons, they quickly put a stop to them, informing the agents that "social work" was not the FBI's objective. Fortunately, it was not long before the old-style FBI leadership retired, and Ressler began to lobby for a research program into the minds of multiple killers.

Ressler and Douglas managed to reactivate the interview program and systemize the data that emerged from the encounters. Two important textbooks emerged out of those interviews, authored by Ressler and Douglas along with Ann Burgess, a professor of psychiatric nursing. These books are now considered the bibles of crime analysis: *Sexual Homicide: Patterns and Motives* and the *Crime Classification Manual*. At the same time, Douglas and Ressler began to train other FBI agents in the techniques of profiling an unknown subject—an "Unsub" in BSU terminology.

For Ressler and Douglas, however, the problem remained as to how to collect, analyze, and distribute the data on various unsolved homicides throughout the United States. While exploring the possibility of a U.S. Justice Department research grant, Ressler learned that Pierce Brooks had retired from active police work and had just received a small grant of $35,000 to revive and update his original 1957 proposal of an unsolved homicide computer data network. Brooks was now based at Sam Houston University in Texas, and Ressler went down to see him. The following year, Brooks and the FBI joined forces and got a $1 million research grant to design a data collection, analysis, and distribution system that became known as VICAP. While FBI profilers began working in the field around 1979, VICAP and profiling research and analysis was formalized in the NCAVC only in 1984. It had taken twenty-seven years for Brooks to see his idea transformed into reality.

COINING AND DEFINING THE TERM *SERIAL KILLER*

While the thing itself has been around a lot longer, the expressions *serial killer* and *serial murder* came into popular use only in the mid-1980s. Prior to that, the terms *mass murderer, lust murderer, chain murders, stranger killing,* and *recreational* or *thrill killing* were used. Recently the term *sequential predation* has been gaining currency in academic literature. Nobody has precisely defined what the term *serial killer* means. The definitions of serial killers and serial murder vary from expert to expert and include the following:

- Someone who murders at least three persons in more than a thirty-day period.[201]

- At least two fantasy-driven compulsive murders committed at different times and at different locations where there is no relationship between the perpetrator and victim and no material gain, with victims having characteristics in common.[202]

- Two or more separate murders when an individual, acting alone or with another, commits multiple homicides over a period of time, with time breaks between each murder event.[203]

- Premeditated murder of three or more victims committed over time, in separate incidents, in a civilian context, with the murder activity being chosen by the offender.[204]

- Someone who over time commits at least ten homicides. The homicides are violent and brutal, but they are also ritualistic—they take on their own meaning for the serial murderer.[205]

- Someone who murders two or more victims, with an emotional cooling-off period between the homicides.[206]

The term *serial killer* might have been coined by Robert Ressler, who says that he felt the term *stranger killings* was inappropriate because not all victims of serial killers were strangers. Ressler says he was lecturing in England in 1974 at Bramshill, the British police academy, where he heard the description of some crimes as being in series—a series of rapes, arsons, burglaries, or murders. Ressler says that the description reminded him of the movie industry term for short episodic films shown on Saturday afternoons during the 1930s and 1940s: *serial adventures*. Each week, juvenile matinee audiences were lured back to movie theaters, week after week, by an inconclusive ending in each episode—a so-called "cliffhanger." Ressler recalled that no episode had a satisfactory conclusion, and every time one ended, it increased rather than decreased the tension in the audience. Likewise, Ressler felt, serial killers increase their tension and desire after every murder to commit a more perfect murder—one that is closer to their fantasy. Rather than being satisfied when they murder, serial killers are instead agitated toward repeating their killing in an often-unending cycle. That, Ressler maintains, was a very appropriate description of the multiple homicides that he was dealing with and is the history behind the term *serial killer.*[207] (Some dispute Ressler, claiming that others used the term earlier. Michael Newton says author John Brophy used the term in 1966 in his book *The Meaning of Murder*.[208] Ann Rule credits Pierce Brooks with coining the term *serial killer*.[209] But in the text of Rule's 1980 seminal book on Ted Bundy, *The Stranger Beside Me,* which introduced the current concept of a serial killer, the term itself never appears. Bundy is still described as a "mass murderer." It does seem, however, that Ressler at least introduced it into popular usage in the law enforcement community, even if others might have used the term previously.)

The FBI System of Profiling: Crime Scene Analysis

Today a local police department in the United States or Canada can fill out a VICAP form and submit it to the NCAVC for analysis of a series of unsolved murders, people missing under suspicious circumstances, or unidentified bodies. The VICAP data is then entered into the Profiler computer system. It is an artificially intelligent system, meaning that the computer program has been taught to reason like a human being. Of course, all artificial intelligence systems are limited by the number of rules by which the computer reasons. These rules, which were identified through years of interviews with serial killers and studies of homicide case data, are expressed as lines of instructions using "if-then" operators—for example, "*if* the victim is tied with duct tape, *then* the offender might be an organized personality; *if* the offender is an organized personality, *then* souvenirs of the murder might have been taken." These lines of reasoning refer to each other and can be assembled in millions of different combinations by the computer, as would a trained human mind when reasoning out a problem. In 1990, Profiler was operating under 270 rules; however, every time the NCAVC research arm learns something new about the behavior of serial offenders, the information is programmed into Profiler in the form of a new line.

Profiler is not a substitute for human analysts—it is a tool. Its output is always analyzed and reviewed by a human profiler. Profiler is used to statistically pinpoint human conclusions. Sometimes Profiler and the human analyst disagree, and the data are reviewed—perhaps a mistaken piece of data was entered into the computer, or perhaps the human analyst forgot something in his or her assessment. Human error in the analysis can be identified, because unlike humans, a computer never forgets.

The FBI system of criminal profiling, called criminal investigative analysis (CIA), is essentially a six-step process. Step One, *profiling inputs,* involves gathering as much of the following data as possible: a complete investigative report, crime scene photographs, information on the neighborhood or area, the medical examiner's report, a map of the victim's movements before death, and background on the victim.

In Step Two, *constructing decision process models,* the basic nature of the homicide is established: whether the killing was a serial or single murder; whether the homicide was the primary objective of the offender or the result of another crime; whether the victim was a high-risk victim (prostitute or hitchhiker, for example) or low-risk, such as a middle-class married female. Other factors in building the model include whether the victim was killed at the scene or elsewhere and the nature of the location where the homicide might have taken place.

Step Three, the *crime assessment,* is the stage at which the FBI profiler decides whether the crime scene has the characteristics of an organized or disorganized offender, or a mix of both. This organized/disorganized dichotomy is both controversial in current debates on the effectiveness of criminal profiling (discussed later) and unique to the FBI system of profiling. It is primarily based on the already mentioned study of thirty-six sexual murderers conducted in the early 1980s. Factors such as whether the victim's body was positioned, whether sexual acts were performed before or after death, insertion of foreign objects into the body, vampirism, mutilation, keeping of the corpse, age of the victim, and use of weapons or restraints all statistically characterize either an organized or disorganized killer. This categorization of offenders is the heart of the FBI approach.

According to this system, organized offenders have a tendency to:

- plan their crimes carefully, giving thought to escape routes and body disposal

- carefully select and stalk their victims

- prefer strangers as victims

- engage in controlled conversation with the victim

- capture their victims, kill them, and dispose of their bodies at separate locations

- use restraints, often bringing them to the crime scene

- come prepared with weapons

- commit sexual offenses with a living victim

- attempt to extensively control the victim through manipulation or threats, and desire a show of fear from their victim

- use a vehicle

- commit their crimes far away from their residence

- study police investigative techniques

- become more proficient in the commission of their crime with time

As individuals, organized killers are likely to be of above-average intelligence, attractive, married or living with a spouse, employed, educated, skilled, orderly, cunning, and controlled. They have some degree of social grace and often talk and seduce their victim into being captured. They are more likely to appear physically attractive to their victim, and their victims are often younger. They are difficult to apprehend because they go to inordinate lengths to cover their tracks and are often forensically aware. Their family background is more stable, their father was more likely to have been gainfully employed, and they are of higher birth order, often the eldest of siblings. When they commit their crimes they are likely to be angry or depressed and under the influence of alcohol, and their offense is often triggered by some kind of personal stress such as divorce, loss of a job, or financial crisis. They are likely to follow the media reports of the crime and are prone to change jobs or leave town after the crime.

Disorganized offenders, on the other hand, are more likely to:

- commit their crime spontaneously without planning

- engage in minimal conversation with the victim

- use a weapon found at the scene or leave one there

- position the body

- perform sexual acts with the corpse

- leave the body at the scene or keep the corpse with them

- try to depersonalize the body through extensive mutilation

- not use a vehicle

The disorganized offender is likely to be of lower birth order, come from a unstable family, and have been treated with hostility by his family. Parents often have a record of sexual disorders; the offender himself is sexually inhibited and sexually ignorant and may have sexual aversions. They are more likely to be compulsive masturbators. They often live alone and are frightened or confused during the commission of their crime. They commit the crime closer to their workplace or home than organized offenders and they are likely to kill victims they know and who are older than them. They often "blitz" their victims—use massive sudden force—to overcome and capture them. They are unlikely to stalk their victims for any length of time or to talk or seduce their victims into capture. Disorganized offenders are very likely to be heterosexual, be uneducated, and leave forensic evidence behind. They are unlikely to transport their victims from where they first encountered them to another location. Stress is not a major factor in triggering their crime, but significant behavioral changes may be evident in their daily conduct.[210]

A crime scene can also be mixed when there are multiple offenders of different personality types or when the offender is immature or undergoing psychological transformation midway in his killing career.

In Step Four of the FBI system, the *criminal profile,* the profiler offers a report describing the personality and possible physical and social characteristics of the unknown offender, listing objects that might be in the possession of the suspect, and sometimes proposing strategies for identifying, apprehending, and questioning him. The report can vary in length from a mere few paragraphs to pages, depending on how much information the profiler had to analyze.

Step Five, the *investigation,* depends on whether the report is accepted by the local police department and introduced into the investigative strategy. Using the profile data, police can narrow the list of likely suspects or adopt strategies likely to lead to an arrest. If additional crimes occur or more evidence or information is discovered, the profile can be updated and expanded during this stage.

Finally, Step Six is *apprehension*. The success or failure of a profile is compared to the identity of the actual offender in custody. The results are added to the variable database and the interpretive algorithms used by profilers are tuned, with the objective of further enhancing profiling accuracy in the future.

Criminal Signatures, MO, and Staging and Posing

French criminologist Edmund Locard, in the early twentieth century, determined what is today called Locard's Principle of Exchange: "Anyone who enters the crime scene both takes something of the scene with them and leaves something of themselves behind." Locard was, of course, referring to physical evidence—fingerprints, hair, fibers, blood, soil, and so forth—but his rule also applies to methodological and psychological imprints left by the offender at the crime scene.

A criminal may leave one or both traces of the following behavioral processes: MO (*modus operandi,* or method of operation) and *signature,* the personal imprint of the offender. While every crime has an MO, not all crimes will have a signature, or at least, one immediately visible. Recognizing and differentiating signature from MO is one of the profiler's essential tasks.

The MO is what the offender *needs* to do to commit his crime—break a window, cruise the highways looking for hitchhikers, pose as a fashion photographer. It is a learned and changing behavior—the repeat offender constantly alters and refines his MO to suit circumstances and to reflect things he learns. He may learn, instead of breaking a window, to seek out an unlocked door first; instead of using rope to tie a victim, the offender may discover that it is easier to use handcuffs. At its core, the MO is dynamic and changing, because it reflects outside circumstances that affect the offender's behavior.

The signature, on the other hand, comes from within the offender and reflects a deep-rooted fantasy that he has of his crime—it is something that the perpetrator does for himself, regardless of the necessities of the crime. Police instructor Max Theil, when teaching investigators to recognize signature, says, "You should ask yourself what the offender did at that crime scene that he did *not* have to do."

The signature is always static because it emerges out of a long history of deep-rooted fantasies that the offender has evolved long before he committed his first crime. He brings those fantasies with him to the crime scene. The essential core of the signature is always the same, but its expression can be evolving and changing, and extraneous circumstances can affect the character or even presence of the signature (for example, if the offender is interrupted during the commission of the crime and escapes before being able to carry out an act his fantasy might require).

Canadian serial killer Paul Bernardo's MO, for example, changed during his career. His first victim was the teenage sister of his fiancée, Karla Homolka; he drugged her into unconsciousness with Homolka's help on Christmas Eve and then raped her while Homolka videotaped. The girl died when an acute reaction to the drug combined with alcohol caused her to vomit and she choked to death while unconscious. His second murder was a crime of opportunity—he unexpectedly encountered his teenage victim, offered her a cigarette back at his car, and then overpowered her. His third victim was carefully stalked with an accomplice, Homolka, who helped him lure a fifteen-year-old girl to the car, where she was overcome by force. These were three different MOs that reflect three different sets of circumstances. Bernardo's signature, however, remained the same: wholesome teenage girls as victims, all videotaped during their rapes, the same kind of content to his verbal interaction with the victims (called *scripting*)—"I'm the king." "Call me master." "Tell me you love me." Those are signatures emerging out of things that Bernardo needed to do for himself, rather than for the purpose of the crime.

The dismemberment of one of the victims, for example, was something that Bernardo felt was necessary to conceal his crime—it was part of his MO. It has a dynamic learning curve: Bernardo's next victim was not dismembered, because Bernardo learned that it was a disgusting task and concluded that it was not necessary. On the other hand, the dismemberment by California serial killer Edmund Kemper of his victims was solely for his own fantasy fulfillment—it had nothing to do with the necessity of hiding the bodies; it was all signature. Thus the same action, in this case dismemberment of a corpse by one offender, could be MO, while by another offender it could be signature. A vital stage of profiling involves telling the two apart.

Changes in MO are usually dynamically unpredictable and erratic; the offender may use a handgun with one victim but a knife with another. Changes are directed toward refining the ease with which the crime is committed. Changes in the signature are usually constant—they are directed toward elaborating, refining, or escalating the same core fantasy theme. Had he been able to continue killing, Bernardo probably would have kept his victims alive for longer periods of time before killing them, and would have introduced more evolved scenarios into his videotaped rape sessions. The direction an offender takes in his signature, therefore, is more predictable, and a successful profile in that area can significantly aid the police in apprehending the killer.

The profiler may also encounter deliberate alterations of the crime scene or of the victim's body position. If these alterations are for the purpose of confusing or misleading the investigators, they are part of the MO and are called *staging;* if on the other hand, the alterations are for the fantasy needs of the offender, they are called *posing.*

A victim is sometimes posed to send some kind of message to the world—a victim's body might be flung beside a No Dumping sign, or as in the case of Henry Lee Lucas, near the gates of a prison. Danny Rolling, the Gainesville Ripper left the head of one of his victims on a fireplace mantel, facing the door. Albert DeSalvo, the Boston Strangler, left his victims posed in positions exposing their genitals toward the door. The intention in both cases was to shock whoever discovered the bodies. William Lester Suff, convicted of killing thirteen women between 1988 and 1991, mostly street prostitutes in Riverside, California, left some of the bodies next to Dumpsters with their arms turned outward to expose needle track marks, clearly a message on the worth of the victims. Identifying and distinguishing staging and posing is part of the profiler's task.

FBI Profiling in Action

Later in this chapter we will see that there is a significant amount of criticism of the lack of scientific method behind the FBI's profiling. But when it works, it works well. Some of the successful profiles have resulted in spectacular arrests.

The earliest cases of profiling by FBI Behavioral Sciences Unit agents were in the late 1970s. Robert Ressler was among the first agents to take the theories of profiling developed at the BSU out of the woods at Quantico and into the field of actual crime investigation.

Richard Chase—"The Vampire Killer"

On Monday, January 23, 1978, a local police department in a small town just north of Sacramento, California, called the FBI, asking for assistance with a homicide clearly outside the range of their usual experience. David Wallin had returned home at about six in the evening and found his pregnant twenty-two-year-old wife, Terry, dead in the bedroom.

Terry Wallin had apparently been attacked in the living room of the house as she was about to take out the garbage through the front door. There were signs of struggle all the way from the door to the bedroom. Two .22-caliber shell casings were found by the door. The murder had occurred some time before 1:30 that afternoon.

Terry had been shot four times through the head. The victim's sweater, bra, and pants were pulled away from her torso, exposing her midriff. There were numerous knife wounds, but the principal wound was a cut extending from her chest to her navel. A portion of her intestines protruded through the wound while several other body organs had been taken out of the body cavity and cut. Several external body parts were missing. The killer had stabbed the victim in the left breast several times, and apparently moved and twisted the knife around. Animal feces were found stuffed in the victim's mouth. A yogurt container had been used to collect the victim's blood, and by the traces on the container, the killer had used it to drink the blood. Nothing appeared to have been stolen from the house.

Two days later, a disemboweled dog was found in the same neighborhood, shot dead by the same weapon used in the Wallin murder.

FBI agent Robert Ressler's original profiling notes were as follows:

White male, aged 25–27 years; thin, undernourished appearance. Residence will be extremely slovenly and unkempt and evidence of the crime will be found at the residence. History of mental illness, and will have been involved in the use of drugs. Will be a loner who does not associate with females, and will probably spend a great deal of time in his own home, where he lives alone. Unemployed. Possibly receives some form of disability money. If residing with anyone, it would be with his parents; however, this is unlikely. No prior military record; high school or college dropout. Probably suffering from one or more forms of paranoid psychosis.[211]

The killer was obviously a "psycho" in the full clinical sense of the word—a paranoid psychotic or paranoid schizophrenic, somebody who was not in control of himself and suffering from delusions. (George Metesky, the Mad Bomber, was diagnosed as a *paranoiac*—a mental disorder distinctly different from a *paranoid*.)*

Ressler explained the reasons behind his profile as follows. The offender was white, because the victim was white and lived in a white residential area; statistically, most sexual attacks, he believed, are intraracial—white on white, black on black. Moreover, a black person would attract attention in a predominantly white neighborhood.

The disorganized mutilation of the victim indicated paranoid schizophrenia, a disease that often begins to slowly manifest itself around age fifteen and takes about ten years to become a full-blown psychosis. Thus the offender was probably around age twenty-five. The chances of his being older and not having committed similar acts previously would be slim.

Using Kretschmer's body studies of mental patients, which psychiatrist Brussel used in his profiles, Ressler projected that the killer was thin. That would make sense, as an introverted schizophrenic would be so focused on his obsessions that he would skip meals—and would also ignore his personal appearance, not caring about neatness or cleanliness. Since nobody would want to live with an individual like that, Ressler surmised that the offender lived alone. His severe mental problems precluded him from finishing school, military service, or employment—he was probably surviving on a disability check. The fact that he was unemployed was further suggested by the time of the murder—midday on a weekday. Ressler felt

---

* The paranoiac has a behavioral disorder, a type of neurosis, sometimes called a "persecution complex." The paranoiac is often functional; he or she tends to exaggerate or distort actual events into a persecution scenario, but otherwise might be functioning normally. The paranoid, however, hallucinates his persecution complex and is totally immersed in his visions, which will be accompanied by a whole complex of other symptoms. The paranoid as a psychopath is nonfunctional, which is why it is rare for any psychopath serial killer to evade capture for any extended length of time. A sense of persecution by others is not the only symptom of the paranoiac and paranoid. A conviction that one is suffering from a disease, for example, is also a symptom of both disorders.

that the murderer probably lived somewhere near the crime scene and walked away—his mind was too disordered to drive. If the killer owned a vehicle, it would be in a state of disorder—dirty, poorly maintained, filled with trash inside. As no other crimes with similar mutilation were on record, Ressler felt that the murderer had committed his first homicide—but that there would be more to come and that the killing would escalate in intensity.

The police traced Terry Wallin's movements that Monday morning and determined that she had cashed a check at a shopping mall within walking distance to her house. Police speculated that she might have been followed from the mall.

Four days later, on a Thursday, the killer struck again less than a mile away from the Wallin murder scene. Neighbors discovered three bodies at about 12:30 in the afternoon—Evelyn Miroth, age thirty-six; her six-year-old son; and Daniel Meredith, a family friend, age fifty-two. Miroth's twenty-two-month-old nephew, whom she was babysitting, was missing as well.

The males were all shot dead, but Evelyn Miroth was even more severely mutilated than Terry Wallin. There were two crossing cuts across her abdomen, through which her intestines protruded. Her body was covered in stab wounds, some particularly aimed at her face and anal area. Rectal swabs of her anus indicated the presence of copious amounts of seminal fluid. The baby's pillow was stained in blood and a shell casing was found in the playpen. The bath was filled with bloodied water as well as brain and fecal matter. It appeared that the killer had washed the infant's body afterward. A ring of blood on the floor left by a bucket-type container suggested that blood had been collected at this scene as well. Nothing had been stolen except for Daniel Meredith's wallet. The killer had escaped in Meredith's car, but it was found abandoned a short distance away with the keys still in the ignition.

In Ressler's mind, the crime scene reinforced his first profile—Ressler stressed that the killer was severely mentally ill and was totally disorganized in his actions. Ressler felt that he had probably parked the stolen car near his house and walked home, where he lived alone. He might have been drinking blood from other sources before he began to murder, so Ressler suggested that the police begin an intense survey of the area of the two homicides, asking witnesses if they had seen an unkempt, gaunt individual with bloodstains on his clothing.

On Saturday morning, during the survey, a woman told the police that she had encountered such a person in the shopping mall near the scene of the first murder, about two hours before Terry Wallin's death. He was a former classmate from high school and she was shocked by how gaunt and unkempt he had become. His mouth was caked in a yellow crust and there were bloodstains on his shirt. He had recognized her and asked her about her boyfriend, who had died in a motorcycle accident. When she got into her car, he attempted to get in with her on the passenger side, but the door was locked and she drove away, disturbed by how sick her former schoolmate had become. He was so sick that at first she didn't recognize him and had to ask his name: Richard Chase.

The police immediately checked on Chase's address—it was less than a block away from where Meredith's car had been abandoned. When the police approached the twenty-eight-year-old Chase, he began to run and was quickly apprehended. He was carrying the .22-caliber handgun, which matched the one used in the murders, and in his back pocket was Daniel Meredith's wallet. He was also carrying a box filled with blood-soaked rags.

As Ressler had projected, Chase's truck was a mess, filled with old newspapers, empty beer cans, milk cartons, and rags. In a locked box, the police found a twelve-inch butcher knife and a pair of rubber boots caked in blood. Chase's apartment, where he lived alone, was in complete disorder, covered in dirty clothing, some of which was stained with blood. There were food blenders with blood in them, and dishes in the refrigerator with human body parts. The partially consumed body of the missing infant was not found until months later, not far from where Chase lived. Police also found numerous cat and dog collars, matching descriptions of pets reported missing in the area.

Ressler's profile had been almost correct—his only mistake was stating that Terry Wallin was the first victim; she was in fact the second. A few weeks earlier, some distance away from the other murders, Ambrose Griffin had been shot through the chest as he was taking groceries from his car. The .22-caliber bullet matched Chase's weapon. Chase had fired from his truck and immediately driven away before any witnesses appeared on the scene.

The profile that the FBI constructed of Chase was instrumental in his capture. Armed with a specific description of a killer that nobody had seen, the police were able to narrow down the search for a suspect and capture him within five days of Terry Wallin's murder.

Richard Chase's story is somewhat sad—he was born a happy and sweet child in 1950 in a middle-income home. When he was twelve, however, Chase's mother began to exhibit mental problems, accusing her husband of infidelity, poisoning her, and using drugs. In high school, Chase was an average student with a few girlfriends but no really close friends. His girlfriends remember that he attempted intercourse with them but could not sustain an erection.

At about the second year in school, his personality suddenly transformed, and he became "rebellious, defiant, and unkempt." He would have been about fifteen then, when symptoms of paranoid schizophrenia often begin to first surface. (On the other hand, "defiant and unkempt" describes an entire generation during the 1960s—the hippies.) He began to hang around with "acidheads"—kids who took a lot of LSD—and in 1965 he was arrested for possession of marijuana. Again, Ressler was correct in his profile that the killer would have a drug record. But Ressler soberly reminds us, "Many in the public saw evidence for attributing Chase's murders to the influence of drugs. I disagree. Although drugs may have contributed to Chase's slide into serious mental illness, they were not a real factor in the murders; we have found that drugs, while present in many cases, are seldom the precipitating factor in serial murders; the true causes lie much deeper and are more complex."

Chase managed to graduate from high school in 1969, but could not keep up with his studies in college or hold down a job. In 1972 he was arrested for drunk driving, and in 1973, after an incident at a party, he was charged with resisting police and carrying a concealed handgun without a license. He paid a $50 fine.

In 1976, Chase was put in a nursing hospital after he was found injecting rabbit blood into his veins. Because his parents could not afford mental treatment for their son, state conservators were appointed for Richard Chase. At the hospital, Chase was reported to be a "frightening" patient and known among the staff as Dracula. He often went out into the hospital garden and captured birds in the bushes. Afterward he bit off their heads and drank their blood. Two nurse's aides quit their jobs rather than continue working around Chase.

Chase explained to staff at the hospital that his blood was turning to powder and he needed to drink blood to stave off death. When psychiatrists suggested that Chase's problems could be controlled by drugs and that he should be released, the nursing staff at the hospital howled in protest. In 1977, Chase was released anyhow—into the custody of his mother, who had believed that her husband was trying to poison her. She rented Chase an apartment to live in.

People who had encountered Chase, who was by then twenty-seven years old, remembered that he seemed to live entirely in the past—he talked of events in high school as if they had happened yesterday. He also talked a lot about UFOs and a "Nazi crime syndicate" from high school that was still pursuing him.

In August 1977, Chase was driving near Lake Tahoe when police pulled his truck over in a routine stop. He was covered in blood and in his truck was a bucket of blood and several rifles. Police determined that the blood was bovine and let him go. In September, Chase had an argument with his mother and killed her cat. Twice in October, he bought dogs from the animal shelter for fifteen dollars each. In mid-November, he answered an ad in a local paper for puppies and managed to bargain for two puppies for the price of one. Police, meanwhile, were getting a barrage of missing pet reports in Chase's neighborhood.

On December 18, after filling out a form stating that he had never been a mental patient or a criminal, Chase purchased a .22-caliber handgun. He drove around for several days shooting at people's houses until he killed Ambrose Griffin.

On January 16, 1978, he set a garage on fire. On January 23, the day he killed Terry Wallin, he wandered through the neighborhood, entering any house where the door was unlocked. Several people called the police, but he was gone by the time they arrived. In one house that Chase entered, he defecated on a child's bed and urinated in a clothes drawer. He rambled on this way, passing through the shopping mall where he encountered his former schoolmate and eventually arrived at Terry Wallin's home.

Mumbling about UFOs following him, Chase was sentenced to death, much to Ressler's regret, who felt that Chase was truly insane and did not know the nature of the acts he was committing. The death sentence, however, reflected the community's fear that convicts like Chase might be released after being declared "cured" by psychiatrists—a fear that was well founded considering how many serial killers had records of being confined and released (such as Ed Kemper and Henry Lee Lucas). In 1980, Chase accumulated a surplus of depressants and took them all. He was found dead in his cell.

Psychotic serial killers like Chase can be both difficult and easy to capture—difficult because they strike like lightning with no rhyme or reason and are therefore highly unpredictable; easy because they make little effort to conceal their acts. They are, however, rare—only a small percentage of serial killers are truly suffering from psychosis.

Criminal profiling is not intended to "solve" a case or produce a definitive identity of the perpetrator. Profiling is a contributory tool that can filter out less likely scenarios and suspects or focus the investigation on fewer possibilities. It can be used to "trigger" witness recollections by providing a starting point. In the Chase case, when police asked witnesses specifically if they had seen an unkempt, gaunt individual, Chase's name surfaced. The witness might not have come forward with his identity had police been more general in their survey.

Wayne Williams—The Atlanta Child Murders

Probably the first high-profile case FBI analysts became involved in was the Atlanta child murders of the early 1980s. Between July 1979 and May 1981, at least twenty-eight black children and youths, mostly males, were found dumped in various locations around Atlanta. Because there was some discussion as to whether these crimes were committed by a white supremacist group, eventually the federal government and the FBI became involved in the investigation. FBI agents John Douglas and Roy Hazelwood from the BSU came down to Atlanta to assist in profiling the killer.

They thought it was unlikely that a white supremacist group was committing the murders because the bodies were partially hidden, dumped in abandoned buildings or in the backs of vacant lots. A more public display of the bodies would have served white supremacists better. Because the crimes were committed in black neighborhoods, it was likely that the offender was black. A white killer would have stood out in the neighborhood and would have been noticed. Roy Hazelwood recalls driving through a neighborhood where some of the victims disappeared: "People walking on the sidewalk stopped. People mowing their lawns stopped. People stopped talking to each other and stared at us. It was like one of those E. F. Hutton ads on television . . . I knew there was no way a white serial killer could have moved through those neighborhoods without being noticed. I knew the guy had to be black."[212] Furthermore, statistically speaking, serial killers tend to kill victims within their own race.

There were no reports of any of the victims being forcibly abducted. The profilers concluded that the serial killer was using some kind of con to lure his victims away. He was intelligent, probably from a middle-class or upper-class background, and had some kind of occupation or hobby that might have been attractive to the young victims. He was probably in his midtwenties—not too old to frighten away the victims nor too young to be credible in his con. There was little evidence of sexual contact with the victims, and therefore the profilers suggested that he was sexually inadequate and probably single. He would be a police buff, might drive a police-type vehicle and own a police-type dog like a German shepherd, and might have already interjected himself somewhere into the investigation. He would be probably following media reports of the progress of the investigation.

Not long afterward, Atlanta police received an anonymous phone call from an individual claiming to be a racist killer and warning that he would kill more black kids. The caller hung up after giving police a roadside location to search for another body. Douglas had recently witnessed hoax messages while teaching in England during the Yorkshire Ripper investigation and remembered the impediment they had created to identifying that killer. He suggested that the police set up a telephone trace and then make a big show of searching the opposite side of the road from which the caller instructed them to search. Sure enough, the caller telephoned, telling the police how stupid they were in searching the wrong side of the road. His call was traced and he was quickly arrested. Again, we see that profiling is important not only in focusing on who the perpetrator might be, but also in filtering out who is not.

Incredibly, the next victim was found on the road that police pretended to search to flush out the hoaxer. Apparently the killer was following press reports and knew that he had not dumped any body there. Now he was going to show his superiority to the police.

John Douglas wrote that in February 1981, somebody in the medical examiner's office released information that was widely carried by the media: that five victims had been linked to the same killer through hair and fiber evidence. "And something clicked with me. *He's going to start dumping bodies in the river,*" Douglas wrote in his memoirs. "We've got to start surveilling the rivers, I said."[213]

Local police and FBI agents staked out bridges for weeks over rivers in the Atlanta area, and in what has been called "The splash heard 'round the world" they identified Wayne Williams after seeing his vehicle on a bridge at 3:00 A.M. in the vicinity of the sound of a large splash. No body had been located at that moment, but a suspect was now identified. Several days later, police pulled from the river two bodies downstream from the bridge. On the basis of fiber and hair evidence and witness statements that placed the victims in Williams's company, he was charged with the two murders.

Wayne Williams was a twenty-three-year-old black man who lived with his parents, both retired schoolteachers. He was an unrealized prodigy, establishing his own small low-powered radio station when he was fourteen. Although the station's range did not extend beyond a few city blocks, he attracted a lot of press attention. He claimed to be a music producer and promoter and recruited young boys whom he promised stardom. Nothing came of his promises.

Williams monitored radio and police frequencies and sold freelance photographs of accidents to local newspapers. At one of the scenes of the child murders, Wayne Williams offered his services as a crime scene photographer. In 1976 he was charged with impersonating a police officer when his vehicle was found equipped with red and blue police lights beneath the grill and on the dashboard. He owned a German shepherd.

While he appeared genteel and harmless, FBI profilers coached the prosecution on how to get Williams to make angry outbursts in the courtroom during his cross-examination. Williams was never charged with the other child murders, but after his arrest they ceased. He was convicted of only two murders, neither of which exactly fit the pattern of the child murders. The victims were twenty-seven and twenty-one, and their cause of death was not clearly established. When state forensic evidence linking Williams to the two victims was discredited by the defense, the judge in a controversial decision allowed the introduction of fiber and hair evidence linking Williams to the other victims, even though he was not charged with their murders. Williams to this day proclaims his innocence.[214]

Looking over Wayne Williams's description, it appears that the FBI profile that Hazelwood and Douglas submitted is incredibly accurate—right down to the ownership of a vehicle fitted with police lights and the dog. But just to show how difficult it is to sort fact from fiction in true-crime history, there is a radically different account of the FBI's participation in the Atlanta child murders investigation. Robert D. Keppel, a professional investigator in more than fifty serial homicide cases and a consultant to the Atlanta child murder task force, remembers things differently upon his arrival in Atlanta in March 1980:

> We couldn't wait to hear what gems of wisdom would come from the BSU's agents, most of whom were only self-proclaimed experts in murder investigations and had never investigated one lead in an actual murder case. The FBI were the kings of follow-up but couldn't solve a crime in progress. Most homicide detectives knew this . . . The profile of the probable killer provided by the BSU mirrored the wishes of the community, that is, the killer was white.[215]

Moreover, the FBI surveillance of river bridges did not start until April 24, *after* four bodies had already been found in Atlanta-area rivers between March 30 and April 20.[216] Perhaps bureaucratic intransigence can explain why the bridge surveillance was not initiated immediately after Douglas "clicked" but only after four bodies in a row had been pulled out from the rivers. One wonders, though, why neither Hazelwood nor Douglas mention in their autobiographies the earlier BSU profile suggesting that the killer was a white individual. Or did Robert Keppel get the story all wrong? Go figure it out.

Larry Bell—Profiling the Organized Offender

In 1985, FBI profilers confronted a highly organized serial killer. On May 31, in rural South Carolina, seventeen-year-old Shari Faye Smith was kidnapped on her way home from school. She was driving, but at the gates of her home, she stopped to check the roadside mailbox. He car was found at the end of the driveway, keys in the ignition, motor still running and her purse on the seat. During the next four days, the family received numerous telephone calls from the kidnapper, who said to them, "Shari is now a part of me. Physically, mentally, emotionally, spiritually. Our souls are now one . . . Shari is protected and . . . she is a part of me now and God looks after all of us."

A handwritten letter from Shari arrived several days after her kidnapping—it was her "last will and testament" and proclaimed her love for her family. It was dated June 1, 1985, 3:10 A.M. Reading the letter, the FBI was convinced that Shari was now dead.

The family kept receiving phone calls from the killer, but the calls were always placed from pay phones and never lasted long enough for the police to arrive in time at the location. The phones were dusted for prints, but the caller never left any behind. The voice was disguised as well, using an improvised electronic device.

Speaking to Shari's sister Dawn on June 4, the killer told her how he had kidnapped and murdered Shari. He said that the whole thing had "gotten out of hand." He was reading from some kind of written script, and at one point he made an error: "Okay, 4:58 A.M.—no, I'm sorry. Hold on a minute . . . 3:10 A.M., Saturday, the first of June, she handwrote what you received . . . 4:58 A.M. Saturday, the first of June, we became one soul."

Giving Dawn precise directions, to within six feet of where Shari's body was located, the killer told her, "We're waiting. God chose us." He then hung up.

Arriving at the described location, eighteen miles away from Shari's home, the police found her body. The body was dressed and decomposition had occurred to the point where police could no longer determine how Shari had been killed or whether she had been sexually assaulted. Sticky residue from duct tape was found in Shari's hair and around her face, but the tape itself had been removed.

FBI profiler John Douglas, who assembled the profile, believed it was highly likely that Shari was the killer's first murder victim. He noted, however, that the removal of the duct tape was indicative of organized planning and that generally first-time murderers do not start out this organized. This meant that the killer was probably older and more intelligent than average. When he telephoned the family he read quickly from a script and got off the phone as soon as possible. His meticulous directions to the body indicated that he must have revisited the corpse numerous times after the murder for some kind of sexual gratification and ceased only when a "relationship" was no longer possible because of advanced decomposition. Douglas believed that the killer had had a brief failed marriage from the degree of cruelty in the mind games he played with the victim's family. He probably had a criminal record for obscene phone calls or attacks on children, but would not attack prostitutes because he was intimidated by them. He was most likely living alone or with his parents and would be in his early thirties. Because he chose a body dump site to which he could return, he was probably a local man familiar with the geography of the region. Again from his detailed instructions and highly scripted phone contact, it appeared that he was meticulous, rigid, and orderly. His car would probably be well maintained, clean, and no more than three years old. The fact that he had committed the abduction in the middle of the afternoon in a rural residential district suggested a degree of controlled sophistication. The killer was using some kind of improvised variable-speed device to disguise his voice, which probably meant he was skilled in electronics or in electric trades and aware of the risk of forensic voice identification.

Two weeks exactly after Shari was kidnapped, the offender struck again, this time kidnapping nine-year-old Debra May Helmick from the front yard of her home. Her father was in the house, ten yards away. The kidnapping took place some thirty miles away from Shari's home. Witnesses saw the man pull up in a car, speak to the girl, and then suddenly force her inside the vehicle and drive away. They attempted to follow the car but it lost them. John Douglas had little doubt that it was the same offender. Douglas ventured that he would now be displaying even more compulsive behavior. People around him might notice weight loss; he might be drinking more and not shaving regularly, and he would be eagerly talking about the murder, following television reports, and cutting newspaper clippings about the crime. He would be greatly enjoying his celebrity and sense of power over his victims and the community.

The police and the FBI felt that because he was closely following the case and was phoning Shari's family, he might be flushed out into the open. The FBI had a local newspaper publish a story of how the Smiths were having a memorial service at Shari's grave, and published pictures of Dawn putting a stuffed teddy bear at her sister's graveside. FBI agents photographed the license plates of any cars that passed by the memorial service and staked out the grave for days in the hope that the killer would attempt to take the teddy bear as a souvenir. He was too smart to take the stuffed toy bait, but obsessed enough to drive by the memorial service: When he was arrested, his license number was among the cars that the FBI had noted passing the location.

The killer continued to call Dawn, telling her where the body of the nine-year-old girl could be found: "Debra May is waiting. God forgive us all," said the killer. He warned Dawn that at some point he was going to come for her.

The FBI crime laboratory, in the meantime, had been analyzing the two-page letter that Shari had written before her murder. An Esta machine is an instrument that can identify microscopic impressions in paper made earlier by somebody writing on sheets of paper higher up in the pad. The device uncovered the traces of the first nine digits of a ten-digit telephone number—a number in Alabama. This narrowed the number down to ten possible numbers. It was a remarkable piece of luck that the number and its area code were written down, and that it was an out-of-state number, meaning that long-distance charge records would be available. The police began to look through the billing records of the ten numbers to see if any had received calls from the area around where Shari was kidnapped and murdered. One of the numbers belonged to a soldier stationed in Alabama who had received calls from a house located just fifteen miles away from where Shari had lived.

When the police arrived at the house, they found an elderly couple living there. The husband was an electrician by trade. The soldier in Alabama was their son and they frequently talked on the phone. The profile and the record of the elderly man, other than his being an electrician, made him an unlikely suspect. Moreover, when the murders had occurred, the couple had been visiting their son in Alabama. They had no idea how their son's number could have ended up on the same pad from which came the sheet of paper that Shari had written her death letter on.

The disappointed police officers were almost ready to leave when they tried one more thing. They described to the couple the profile the FBI had drawn up of the hypothetical offender—did the couple know anybody who might fit the description?

Both the man and the woman responded immediately; that was the description of Larry Gene Bell, an assistant electrician who often worked for the man. He was in his early thirties, heavyset, and divorced from his wife.

He was a very neat and meticulous worker. When they were away in Alabama, Larry house-sat for them—as a matter of fact, the man remembered, he wrote down his son's number in Alabama on Larry's pad just in case he needed to get in touch with them. When they came back from Alabama, Bell picked them up at the airport. They were surprised by his physical appearance—he was unshaved, had lost some weight, and seemed highly agitated. All he wanted to talk about was the kidnapping of the Smith girl.

A search of Bell's apartment uncovered all manner of evidence linking him to the two girls. Witnesses who had seen the little girl kidnapped identified Bell as the culprit. Bell had numerous sexual offenses on his record, from several attempted kidnappings to making obscene phone calls. In 1986, he was sentenced to death.

Once again, the profile was essential not so much for the police to identify the offender as for potential witnesses to point out a possible suspect. As elaborate and evolved as the profiling process is, in the overall picture it is only one component in many different investigative procedures applied to tracking a serial killer. These basic police procedures could be as complex as laboratory analysis or as routine as surveying a shopping center, but without them, the psychological profile has nowhere to go.

The most valuable aspect of profiling is not that it identifies who the killer is, but helps in weeding out who it is not. Frequently police already have information on a killer's identity but it is buried deep within masses of files, leads, and tips among other suspects. Profiling often helps police decide whom to look at first.

Issues and Problems with the FBI System

Many scientists challenge not only the reliability of the FBI's two categorizations (three if you include "mixed") but also whether those offender categories actually display the characteristics attributed to them. There simply have been not enough data or scientific tests to confirm the FBI's system, which was first based on interviews with only thirty-six sexual murderers, not all of whom were serial killers.

For example, the FBI asserts that organized offenders were "likely to change jobs or leave town" after committing a murder. A University of Detroit Mercy study of the data the FBI used revealed some problems with that assumption. As the FBI says, no disorganized killer in their study left town or changed jobs, but out of ninety-seven homicides by organized killers, only eleven killers left town and eight changed jobs—and presumably the eight job changers are included in the eleven who left town. This means that a profiler who suggests that an unknown killer who appears organized has changed jobs or left town would be wrong 89 percent of the time.[217]

Since their introduction some two decades ago, the FBI's profiling techniques have not been empirically substantiated by scientific testing methodology. One measure of scientific integrity is the ability of a hypothesis to survive attempts to *disprove* it—attempts to *falsify* it. This is a kind of reverse-engineering approach to scientific proof known as *hypothetico deductivism*. In his criticism of the scientific foundations of the FBI's system of profiling, criminologist Damon A. Muller gives the example of water's boiling temperature. By inductive reasoning, we assume that it is *scientifically proven* that water boils at 212°F because if we repeat this experiment thousands of times, water will always boil at that temperature.[218] But we would be wrong. If you take water to a mountaintop at a higher altitude, it boils at a lower temperature. The boiling point of water depends on more complex issues than merely temperature. If instead of attempting to prove that water always boils at 212°F, we attempted to first *disprove* it, we would quickly emerge with a truer scientific assessment of the reliability of the hypothesis. Repeating the experiment thousands of times with the same result is not necessarily conclusive scientific proof. The ability of a hypothesis to survive disproval is a more reliable measure. For something to be scientific, it must present theories that are empirically testable—not just simply repeatable by experiment.

While the process is simple for testing the behavior of water, how does one reverse-engineer human homicidal behavior—how does one falsify and test the FBI's theories of fantasy underlying homicidal behavior, for example? The problem is that the FBI has not fully explained the psychological mechanics motivating the offenders it attempts to classify. For example, the FBI has not identified the process by which a killer becomes either organized or disorganized except to suggest that acute mental disorders are more often present in the disorganized murderer. The FBI sort of says, "It works, but we don't know why it works." FBI profilers have commented that they do not care *why* offenders do what they do; they are sufficiently satisfied with the investigative value of knowing *what* they do, without worrying about the whys.

The FBI does not particularly want its profiling system to be scientifically systemized. Veteran profiler John Douglas states, "The key attribute necessary to be a good profiler is judgment—a judgment based not primarily on the analysis of facts and figures, but on instinct . . . Many, many factors come together in our evaluations, and ultimately, it comes down to the individual analyst's judgments rather than any objective scale or test."[219]

Thus, according to Douglas, the FBI profiling system is not based on any systematically scientific approach, but ultimately on a subjective hunch of the profiler. One would not tolerate this kind of approach in other police sciences such as DNA testing, fingerprint identification, and ballistics testing. But often police departments turn to the FBI for assistance when they come to an investigative dead end and find themselves in a "nothing to lose" situation. The scientific veracity of FBI profiling, therefore, remains largely unchallenged. When the profiles are correct, the FBI is praised; when the profiles are wrong, well, "no harm done."

Gradually the FBI's system of remote psychological profiling began coming under heavier scrutiny and criticism in the 1990s. On April 19, 1989, a gun turret mysteriously exploded, killing forty-seven crewmen on board the battleship USS *Iowa*. Navy investigators decided that Clayton Hartwig, one of the sailors who perished in the turret, deliberately caused the explosion. It was alleged that he was motivated by a frustrated homosexual fixation on a fellow crewman. The Navy Investigative Service (NIS) met with veteran FBI profilers John Douglas, Roy Hazelwood, and Richard Ault, asking them to conduct an *"equivocal death analysis"*—a type of psychological autopsy intended to determine a cause of death: Was the death accidental, suicide, or murder? This type of analysis works on the same principles and techniques as criminal profiling, from which it is almost indistinguishable other than that the subject is identified and often more is known about him than about an unknown killer.

John Douglas felt uncomfortable with the data the navy was providing and declined to participate in profiling Hartwig. Hazelwood and Ault plunged ahead, a decision they would come to regret. Using only the information that the NIS provided them, as was standard procedure with other investigative agencies making such requests, Hazelwood and Ault concluded that Clayton Hartwig was:

> . . . a very troubled young man who had low self-esteem and coveted power and authority he felt he could not possess. The real and perceived rejections of significant others emotionally devastated him. This combined with the inability to verbally express anger and faced with a multitude of stressors had he returned from the cruise, virtually ensured some type of reaction. In this case, in our opinion, it was a suicide. He did so in a place and manner designed to give him the recognition and respect that he felt was denied him.[220]

Unlike police agencies, however, the navy subsequently issued a statement that the *Iowa* explosion was caused by the late Clayton Hartwig, and cited the FBI profile as primary evidence. Ault and Hazelwood made matters even worse when they testified to the veracity of their profile before both Senate and House committees reviewing the navy's investigation of the explosion. John Douglas felt that Ault and Hazelwood botched the profile and worse, "We never testify to a profile. We use it as an investigative tool, and [Ault and Hazelwood] used it as tantamount to proof."[221]

After the navy released its conclusions, there were many skeptical critics of the investigation, from the Hartwig family to CBS's *60 Minutes* investigative news program. The sailor who was supposedly the subject of Hartwig's fixation asserted that he and Hartwig were the "best of friends . . . I think he loved me as a brother, but nothing sexual or anything." There were allegations asserting that the navy was scapegoating Hartwig to cover up technical problems with its battleships. The matter became of interest to Congress, and both House and Senate committees looked into the question. A House Investigations Subcommittee started to ask how the FBI profilers concluded that the sailor committed suicide without any surviving witnesses or physical evidence. On December 21, 1989, Hazelwood and Ault were called to testify before the committee about their profile and the methods and practices of the BSU. It was not going to be a good day for the two FBI agents.

In opening the questioning that day, one of the congressmen stated, "Given the serious defects in the Navy investigation that we have uncovered in our previous hearing today's testimony becomes even more crucial to the Navy's case against Hartwig. If the psychological assessment compiled by the FBI is flawed, then exactly what is left with which to support its conclusions?" It was obviously the intention of the subcommittee to question the navy investigation by discrediting the BSU's profile.[222]

Hazelwood and Ault arrogantly insisted to the incredulous congressmen that their profile was always definitive; they did not qualify it on scales of probability. They either committed to a position or said they did not know. Their profile "could be used or discarded or discounted. That is simply our opinion."

Representative Les Aspin of Wisconsin asked, "You do not configure it as your job to put in qualifiers. The world is full of qualifiers, and you come down yes or no."

"Yes, sir," replied Ault.

Another congressman asked whether the interviews on which the FBI profilers based their analysis were bias-controlled. Hazelwood and Ault rejected that as a technique in academic research. They were criminal investigators, not researchers, they explained. When it was mentioned that one expert in forensic psychology questioned the validity of some of the witness interviews submitted to the FBI profilers because they were not conducted by clinicians experienced in interviewing people under stress, Ault snapped back, "First of all, I certainly appreciate that wonderful academic approach to a practical problem. It is typical of what we find when we see people who have not had the experience of investigating either crime scenes, victims, criminals, and so forth in active, ongoing investigations. Second, in the real world, you just can't work that way with the NIS. So, we have to take the information as we get it."[223]

Testifying before a Senate committee, Ault was asked if there was "any hard evidence, any evidence that would support the idea that Hartwig actually carried out this act"; he replied, "No, Sir, this opinion that we submitted is based on a half scientific, half art form."

After Hazelwood and Ault concluded their testimony, a panel of clinical psychologists and a psychiatrist tore the FBI profiling program apart like a pack of wild dogs: "The FBI report which has been discussed substantially here this morning is incorrect as to form, as I understand what psychologists are able to do . . . flawed in terms of failing to present in a candid fashion the limits of the science . . . "

In its March 1990 report, the House committee was scathing in its dismissal of the BSU's techniques:

> Unfortunately, if there was a single major fault in this investigation, it was the FBI system for producing the Equivocal Death Analysis. These documents, most commonly generated after orthodox police investigations have reached no conclusions, are invariably unequivocal in reaching a conclusion. The analysis contains no comment on probabilities, no qualifications and no statement of the limitations of a posthumous analysis in which the subject cannot be interviewed . . .
>
> Just as the FBI psychological analysis was key to the Navy investigation, so it was to the subcommittee inquiry. As a result, the subcommittee, using the professional services of the American Psychological Association, sought the opinions of 11 independent clinical licensed psychologists and one psychiatrist. Additionally, the subcommittee consulted independently with a psychiatrist and a psychologist who had some previous knowledge of this case. Ten of the 14 experts consulted considered the FBI analysis invalid. And even those who believed the analysis to be somewhat credible were critical of procedures, methodology, and the lack of a statement of the limitations of a retrospective analysis of this nature.
>
> The FBI psychological analysis procedures are of doubtful professionalism. The false air of certainty generated by the FBI analysis was probably the single major factor inducing the Navy to single out Clayton Hartwig as the likely guilty party . . . The procedures the FBI used in preparing the Equivocal Death Analysis were inadequate and unprofessional . . . The FBI agents' Equivocal Death Analysis was invalidated by ten of fourteen professional psychologists and psychiatrists, and heavily criticized even by those professionals who found the Hartwig possibility plausible . . . The FBI should review its procedures and revise its Equivocal Death Analysis format to address probabilities and make clear to consumers of such reports their limitations and speculative nature.[224]

Some press coverage took glee in portraying the BSU as unprofessional quacks. *New York Daily News* columnist Lars-Erik Nelson wrote, "Deep within the FBI there exists a unit of people who—without ever talking to you or anyone who knows you—are prepared to go into court and testify that you are a homicidal maniac." He concluded with the hope that "any defense lawyer, any judge, any jury would laugh this kind of quack evidence out of court." The *Washington Post* editorialized, "Long-distance personality analyses by experts who have never met the subject are almost always ludicrous. But when the subject is dead, cannot defend himself and is found to be guilty of a horrendous crime, opinions like this are deserving of contempt."

It was revealed by the FBI's own testimony that they had used Equivocal Death Analysis in more than fifty cases but obtained "satisfactory results" in only three.[225] The failures of profiling in general were dredged up. In Los Angeles in the mid-1970s a panel of psychologists drew up a profile of the "Skid Row Slasher"—a serial killer preying on homeless people. The day after they issued a description of a tall, emaciated white male with stringy blond shoulder-length hair with latent homosexual tendencies and possibly some congenital defects, the real Skid Row Slasher dropped his wallet replete with ID near the scene of his latest attack. Vaughn Greenwood was a chubby, short-haired black man of medium height. Despite the evolution of the FBI's profiling system since the Skid Row Slasher days, (a profile for which it was not responsible), the tendency since *Iowa* has been to question the real effectiveness of the FBI as Sherlock Holmes–like analysts.

Hollywood came to the rescue just in the nick of time. The February 1991 release of *The Silence of the Lambs* could not have occurred at a better moment for the besieged FBI profilers. The huge box-office and critical success of the Jodie Foster movie quickly refocused the news media toward positive promotional stories on the FBI's Behavioral Sciences Unit. FBI agents Clarice Starling (Jodie Foster) and Jack Crawford (a character synthesized from Douglas, Ressler, and Hazelwood, portrayed by Scott Glenn) introduced the public to Quantico's world of profilers, unsubs, and organized and disorganized offenders. Perversely, the suave serial killer Hannibal "the Cannibal" Lecter, portrayed by Anthony Hopkins, grew to even greater cult status, and by 2000 he would headline the sequel, *Hannibal*. Matchbook covers and small classified ads in detective magazines offered diplomas in "criminal profiling." TV shows such as *Profiler, Millennium,* and *CSI* ranged in their portrayals of profilers from scientists to magicians with psychic powers.

The controversy over the lack of scientific method, however, has not died out. If profiling is more an art than a science, it means that the accuracy of the profile depends on the talent of the individual profiler. That becomes problematic because to accept the analysis of one profiler is to sometimes reject the talents of another—the process becomes highly antagonistic and career-threatening among profilers. Moreover, the lack of applied scientific method can lead investigators outside the profiling specialty to conclude that their analysis is as valid as or better than a profiler's. As Representative Frank McCloskey put it during the *Iowa* hearings, "It would seem to me that in many ways politicians, teachers, or people in the insurance business would have similar outstanding psychological skills. I don't know that that certifies them to make some of these judgments."

The dependence on individual profiler talent is not conducive to the investigative cooperation that complex multijurisdictional cases often require. For example, the profile used by the Unabomb task force to investigate a series of bombings for which Ted Kaczynski would be eventually charged suggested that the serial killer was in his midthirties to early forties, perhaps with some college education but most likely a skilled blue-collar worker. FBI profiler Bill Tafoya dissented, suggesting that the killer probably had a graduate degree, perhaps even a Ph.D., in a "hard" science—something like electrical engineering or mathematics—and would be in his early fifties. Tafoya claims that tremendous pressure was put on him to "get with the program" and amend his profile to one consistent with the task force's then current investigative strategy focused on blue-collar aircraft workers around age forty.[226] When Kaczynski was arrested he was fifty-three years old and held a Ph.D. in mathematics, as Tafoya's profile suggested.

Most recently, profiling has again come under question, over the speculations offered on the Beltway Snipers who terrorized the Washington, D.C., region in the autumn of 2002. Although it is unclear what the official FBI profile on the sniper was, former FBI profilers and private profiling consultants almost unanimously ventured that the sniper was an organized white loner, in his mid- to late thirties, killing for the "thrill" of it and not for political or ideological motives. Instead police ended up arresting two black suspects: forty-one-year-old John Allen Muhammad and seventeen-year-old John Lee Malvo, whose motives are still unclear. Despite the fact that several witnesses described "dark-skinned" suspects and an earlier witness reported two "Hispanic" men, police continued to focus on what is known as "RWG"—regular white guys. One Beltway Sniper task force officer responded to the witness reports, "Anybody could put makeup on . . . we don't want anyone to give up on the fact that it could be a white guy."[227]

Former FBI counterintelligence agent I. C. Smith explained, "First you start with the statistic that 80 to 90 percent of all (serial) shooters are white guys. Then you back out the guys happily married. That leaves the introspective loner types." This is exactly the primary weakness of profiling: its basis in statistical probability. Indeed, the majority of snipers in the past have been white antisocial male thrill killers. But a profile collapses the moment an offender does not conform to the statistical norm. Since numerically serial snipers are still a relatively rare phenomenon, there is a high probability of a profile being invalidated by the appearance of a single anomaly. Criminologist Robert Keppler commented, "In a macabre way, looking at the changing face of a serial killer is like looking at the changing face of America . . . Because serial offenders exist at the margins of society, and not in the mainstream, even though they can camouflage themselves in the mainstream of their victim pool, it is at the margins where one sometimes has to look to find the truth about what is taking place in society."[228] While this might be less of a critical issue in a dead-end investigation, in a rapidly unfolding case like that of the Beltway snipers, an inaccurate profile could have misguided investigative efforts and jeopardized lives.

Researchers are only now beginning to explore the scientific veracity of criminal profiling. This is difficult, because most practicing profilers have refused to cooperate in controlled tests of their profiling abilities, no doubt fearing for their personal and professional credibility should they score unfavorably. Two recent studies on profiling, while not necessarily putting profiling itself under question, looked into the question of what kind of practitioners were most accurate in their profiles.

The first test, the results of which were reported in 2000, compared the profiling skills of a group of professional profilers (those known to have been retained by police departments to submit profiles), a group of psychologists with no training in forensic or criminal psychology, police officers with five or more years of experience, psychics, and sophomore science and economics students.[229] The drawbacks of this study were that the group of profilers were not law enforcement officers, the way FBI profilers are, and that only five profilers volunteered to participate in the test. The other groups consisted of twenty to thirty-five volunteers each.

Each participant was given the same investigative file of a closed case for which the offender's identity and pathology were known to the researchers, and asked to assemble profiles describing the offender's physical characteristics, cognitive processes, offense behaviors, and social history and habits. They were then scored on how accurate their profile was compared to what the researchers knew about the actual offender.

The psychics scored at the bottom of the scale. The profilers scored at the top for most accuracy. The psychologists with no criminal training followed them. In some categories, such as offense behaviors and physical characteristics, the psychologists actually scored marginally better than the profilers. Notwithstanding the fact that only five profilers were participating in the test, it did indicate that professional profilers did best at what they say they do best—criminal profiling. That psychological insight was a primary factor in the accuracy of this type of profiling was confirmed by the fact that psychologists scored second best. What was surprising, however, were the results from the other groups. In terms of accuracy, students, then police, and finally psychics followed the profilers and psychologists. That untrained science and economics students scored better than police was troubling, because FBI profilers are law enforcement officers first, and profilers second. Moreover, the FBI stresses that the primary qualification of their profilers is a long career as a criminal investigator prior to subsequent training as a profiler-analyst.

In 2002, the same team of researchers tackled the issue of the effect of investigative experience on profiler accuracy. This time they gathered six groups: thirty-one senior detectives with a minimum of ten years investigative experience; twelve seasoned homicide detectives; nineteen trainee detectives, all with a minimum of ten years of general police duties; fifty police academy recruits with less than six weeks' training; fifty police academy recruits with less than three weeks' training; and thirty-one sophomore chemistry students. Each participant was given a similar task as in the previous test.[230]

The results were astonishing: Sophomore chemistry students outperformed all the police groups across the board. Among the police groups, police recruits scored higher than experienced homicide detectives and outperformed the other police groups on some of the questions. These results contradict the FBI's assertions that investigative experience is the highest qualification that successful profilers can bring to the job.

The researchers suggest that paradoxically, the more experience an investigator has, the more that experience gets in the way of interpreting data for the purposes of profiling. Investigators, they propose, develop over the years a set of commonsense "heuristics"—impressions about criminals and crime that are based not necessarily on fact but on subjective experience and perceptions. Thus college students and police recruits with no such prejudicial experience produced more accurate profiles. The other factor that might be taken into account is the educational requirements of senior police officers at the time when they were originally recruited, which may account for their poorer performance in comparison to current police recruits. Formal education, it seems, is most valuable for effective profiling, instead of long police investigative experience. In that context, it should be noted that many FBI profilers hold MAs and Ph.D.s in behavioral sciences, which may account more for the BSU's effectiveness than their investigative experience.

In the end, however, before jumping to conclusions, one needs to remember that these tests presented only one case for profiling, and the nature of that particular case could perhaps favor the performance of one group over another. Nonetheless, we can see that if profiling is based on statistical probability, the more experienced investigators are, the more likely they are going to base their profiles on their perception of probability, as was the case with the Beltway Sniper.

Other Profiling Systems: Diagnostic Evaluation and Investigative Psychology

The FBI's crime scene analysis approach is not the only kind of behavioral profiling system. There is also diagnostic evaluation (DE), an adaptation of largely Freudian psychotherapeutic theory to crime analysis that depends on the diagnostic conclusions of the individual profiler. This was what Dr. James Brussel was practicing in his profile of the Mad Bomber in the 1950s. DE is highly individualistic from practitioner to practitioner and not used often now as an investigative tool.

There is also investigative psychology (IP), used often by profilers in England, which is based on a collection of theories founded on the premise that a crime can be analyzed as an interpersonal transaction in which criminals are performing actions in a social context between themselves and their victims. IP was developed by David Cantor, an environmental psychologist, and first applied to the investigation of serial killer and rapist John Duffy, dubbed "The Railway Rapist" in London in 1986.

Cantor structured four broad approaches to creating an IP profile:

1. *Interpersonal coherence:* Actions performed by criminals make sense with the criminals' own psychology. Victims, for example, are selected for reasons important only to the offender.

2. *Significance of time and place:* Crime scenes are chosen for reasons relevant to the personality of the offender and his residence and place of work. Certain personalities prefer a familiar ground in which to commit their offense, while for others it is irrelevant.

3. *Criminal career:* Criminals, while they may escalate their crimes, do not change a basic way they commit their crimes throughout their career.

4. *Forensic awareness:* A criminal's awareness of evidence and attempts to destroy it indicates experience and extent of prior record.

It is obvious that IP is similar to the FBI's criminal investigative analysis in many ways. The primary difference is the FBI's dualistic categorization of offenders as organized or disorganized.

GEOGRAPHIC PROFILING

Criminal investigative analysis and psychological profiling are not the only types of profiling available to analyze the patterns of a serial killer. The most recent studies in England are proposing a very simple so-called *circle hypothesis,* which suggests that serial offenders live within a circle whose diameter is equal to the distance between the offender's two farthest offenses. On the average, this equals an area of approximately ten square miles. Various studies confirmed this hypothesis: Eighty-seven percent of forty-five serial rapists in the south of England resided in this range; 82 percent of serial arsonists and 70 percent of serial rapists studied in Australia; and 86 percent of 126 U.S. serial killers as well.[231]

The most recent advances in computer-driven geographic profiling of serial offenders has been made in Canada, where a radically new dimension has been added to profiling systems. A system called Orion, developed by former Vancouver police constable D. Kim Rossmo, operates on the principle of geoforensic profiling. What makes this system extraordinary is that it goes beyond identifying a hypothetical personality of the suspect—it ferrets out where the suspect lives and even his possible identity.

Kim Rossmo was fascinated by accounts of a particular type of rural crime that has been plaguing India since 500 B.C., called a *dacoity*. A dacoity is when a gang of five or more members of one village raids and robs another village. The dacoity is always committed at night and always when the moon is new, because with little electrical lighting in rural India, the new phase of the moon provided almost complete cover of darkness for the raiding party.

The Indian police developed a systematized geographic profiling system for capturing dacoity gangs. The police calculates the speed at which a person could travel on foot cross-country and plot a distance radius. Because farmers working in the fields at dawn would observe any strangers moving through their territory, the police knew that the gang had to get into the territory of their own village before dawn. Thus the probable village from where the gang came was quickly identified. As dacoity gangs followed a tradition by which they would not attack a member of their own caste, the police, once they identified the village, could further narrow down suspects by caste. From that point on, standard police investigative techniques could focus on the narrowed list of suspects.

Rossmo also listened to stories of his fellow officers who pursued suspects with dogs. They told him that suspects almost always did the same thing when attempting to flee on foot: Right-handed suspects, when turning, tended to turn left; when encountering obstacles, they moved to the right; when throwing away incriminating evidence, they threw to their right; and when hiding in large buildings, they kept to outside walls.

Rossmo studied cases in which geoforensic profiling was attempted. When Angelo Buono and Kenneth Bianchi were dumping bodies on hillsides in Los Angeles, the LAPD measured the distances between each site and then, using a computer, plotted circles on a map. The center of each circle represented victim availability; the circumference represented capacity; while the radius represented ability. Vectors drawn from the various sites narrowed down an area of about three square miles, which the Los Angeles Police then saturated with uniformed officers in an attempt to frighten off the serial killers. Later, when Buono and Bianchi were apprehended, it turned out that Angelo Buono's residence and upholstery shop, where some of the victims were raped and murdered, was near the center of the plotted zone.

Rossmo's Orion system takes into account not only geographical factors, but traffic flow factors, urban zoning, census data, and offender personality profiles to emerge with a highly probable offender location. Although Orion does not work with all types of personalities, it is highly effective with nontraveling serial offenders—rapists, bank robbers, child molesters, and killers who live in the same territory where they commit their crimes and do not change residences.

Orion mathematically plots zones that an offender is likely to strike in, known as *jeopardies*, taking into account that most criminals tend not to strike too close to their own home but not too inconveniently far away either. From the jeopardies, depending on the personality of the criminal as profiled, Orion begins to calculate his or her probable place of residence by measuring "decay" from each crime site—where a convenient crime site becomes too close to a possible residence of an offender. To be practical, the system needs several crime scenes to triangulate an accurate rate of decay—which is precisely why it is so powerful a tool with serial offenders. Orion becomes more than 90 percent accurate with six or more crime locations entered into the system.

When Orion went online in Vancouver, it quickly proved itself in catching a child molester who was attacking children in different parts of the city. The police had a vehicle description, but little else. After determining the traffic patterns at the times of the attacks, Orion plotted jeopardies, eliminating industrial, commercial, and other nonresidential areas. Based on census data and reflecting the probable socioeconomic background of the offender as identified by psychological profiling, Orion calculated a list of postal codes, in order of probability, where the offender likely resided. These postal codes were then filtered through motor vehicle registration and driver's license files to match to the suspect vehicle described. A very short list of suspects was identified and subsequently investigated by standard police procedure, quickly leading to the arrest of the child molester.

As powerful and as automated as all these systems are, Profiler and Orion are no better than the information fed into them. The geographical targeting done by Orion depends on the quality of the psychological profile of the suspect, as different profile types behave differently in geographical space. Likewise, Profiler's ability to analyze data is only as good as the artificial intelligence rules written for it by human programmers. Furthermore, if police on the scene do not recognize, note, and identify certain crime scene characteristics, there is nothing to input into Profiler. Finally, the output of these computer systems only provides high probability rates—it still remains up to human officers to interpret the data and fit them into their investigations in an effective manner.

Profiling still remains very much a human activity, because while a computer might process information faster than a human, the depth and flexibility of human thinking power exceeds that of the computer—including the mind of the offender. The criminal imagination is creative in ways that often can escape the strictly defined rules of a computer's artificial intelligence—only the human mind can keep up. Profiling is as much an intuitive art, unapproachable by a computer, as it is a precise science.

TEN

SURVIVING A SERIAL KILLER:

Escaping the Monster's Clutch

Take it from one who knows: It pays to be paranoid.
—DANNY ROLLING (The Gainesville Ripper)

People should learn to see and so avoid all danger. Just as a wise man keeps away from mad dogs, one should not make friends with evil men.
—BUDDHA

The information in this chapter is based on FBI interviews with serial offenders and their victims who survived. *This not a "how-to" guide to survival*—as much as there might be similarities between serial killers and their behaviors, in the end, each one is an individual capable of exhibiting entirely new and unknown characteristics. The information here is presented with the purpose of identifying some of the options available and the risks involved with each. They are not foolproof measures and if you choose any of them, *you do so at your own risk*.

Avoiding the Serial Killer

You might *already* be a survivor of a serial killer, without even knowing it. You may have sat near one in a movie theater or in a restaurant; you might have passed one in the street or parked your car next to one. One might have approached you—do you remember any odd requests from a stranger to help him carry a package to his car or look for a lost puppy? Some man whose attentions you turned away in a bar? A nice couple who offered you a ride in their car—they looked fine but somehow there was something not quite right, and you turned them down? Maybe you are alive simply because you chatted with a friend a minute longer instead of walking off alone, or because somebody else, whom you do not even recall, arrived in the parking lot as you were getting into your car. Maybe you are a heterosexual male who was invited home by a homosexual, and you turned him down; maybe you are gay, and turned down an invitation from a guy you just didn't quite like for some inexplicable reason. The serial killer begins setting you up for death when he engages you in some kind of innocent contact—whether he gets to finish the job is often up to you.

Serial killers are frequently mobile, and the chances of passing one in the street or having casual contact with one might be not all that astronomical. I bumped into two that I know of. Your own deeds and actions, however, can dramatically increase those chances. The FBI categorizes serial killer victims as "high risk" or "low risk," and often that category can depend on your behavior and simple choices you make.

From the descriptions of how serial killers select their victims, we see that various factors stack up together to determine risk. Some factors are not under the control of a victim, such as age or race, while others are.

Thus, based on the FBI survey of serial killers and their victims, we can say that being white in the United States immediately increases your risk: Ninety-two percent of victims were white (although recently there has been an increase in black serial killers and black victims). Being female (82 percent), unmarried (80 percent), and between ages fifteen and twenty-eight (73 percent) all put you at higher risk.[232]

Beyond that, "victim facilitation" can then propel you into an even higher risk category. Factors such as residence in a bad neighborhood; activity as a prostitute; sex-industry employment; hitchhiking or a habit of picking up hitchhikers; employment at night; and employment serving casual customers, such as a convenience store clerk or waitress, all increase the statistical probability that you could come to the attention of a serial killer. (Checking into a cheap hotel in a bad neighborhood . . .) These "high facilitators" are evident in 11 to 13 percent of victims of serial killers.[233] That means, however, that the remaining balance of serial killer victims were simply victims of chance—they were in the wrong place at the wrong time.

It should be noted that not being alone has at best a marginal effect on your safety: Thirty-seven percent of victims, or more than a third, had a companion with them when they were killed.[234] The presence of a companion could have even increased a false sense of security, contributing to their death. A child or a teen accompanied by one other is only marginally safer. Big groups—five and up, unmanageable by even a team of two serial killers—are safer, unless the offender can separate a victim from the group.

Trust Your Intuition

One very important lesson that comes forth from reviewing accounts of people who were approached by serial killers but disengaged from them is *never underestimate your instincts or your intuition.* Numerous accounts are given by women who for no explicable reason, other than an intuitive "bad feeling" or "women's intuition," refused to walk into a serial killer's trap. In reality, female intuition or male "gut feeling" is not a sixth sense. You have probably perceived something concrete that spells out danger, but your brain has not caught up with your perception—you do not know yet what it is you have seen to have analyzed it logically. That is intuition.

Remember the woman whom Ted Bundy approached on campus wearing a cast and asking to help carry his books to his car? She reported that as she approached his Volkswagen, she noticed that the front passenger seat was missing. For some reason that she could not explain, she suddenly felt afraid and she placed the books on the hood of the car and hurried off, feeling embarrassed by her "irrational" anxiety. It probably saved her life because Bundy had precisely removed the passenger seat to more easily transport his victims, but she had not logically figured that out.

If something does not feel right, then it probably is not. Never ignore such feelings; do not be embarrassed to act "irrationally" in front of a stranger or be afraid of appearing to be rude. Better rude than dead.

Never Get into the Car

The bottom line is, once they get into the car, few victims return alive. Nineteen-year-old Carol DaRonch was in a shopping mall when a neatly dressed Ted Bundy politely approached her, told her he was a police detective, and asked her for her car's license number. He then informed her that he and his partner, who presumably was somewhere nearby, were investigating a number of break-ins into cars that had just occurred in the parking lot—would she mind accompanying him back to her car to see if anything had been stolen?

After "inspecting" her car, Bundy managed to persuade her to get into his Volkswagen to drive to the police station and "file a report." She was annoyed, because nothing had been stolen and moreover she became suspicious about a policeman driving a Volkswagen. Brought up in a Mormon community to be polite and respectful of authority, DaRonch had the boldness to ask Bundy to show her some identification, but not enough to *demand* a good look at it when he merely flashed a wallet with a small gold badge in it. Despite her misgivings, the aura of authority that Bundy projected overcame her good sense. She got into the Volkswagen and they began to drive. Bundy told her to fasten her seat belt, but at this point she smelled alcohol on his breath and refused. Along the way Bundy suddenly brought the car to a stop at a deserted spot and attempted to handcuff her. She struggled and Bundy accidentally snapped both cuffs on the same hand. She managed to roll out of the car while Bundy attempted to hit her on the head with a crowbar or tire iron. Kicking, screaming, and blocking the blows of the weapon from striking her head, she luckily managed to escape from Bundy. Years later, she testified at his murder trial as the only survivor of an attack by Bundy.

A study of serial homicides indicated that in 78 percent of the cases, the killer used a vehicle directly or indirectly in the murder, and that 50 percent of the serial killers who did use a vehicle used it to offer their victims a ride.[235] In Canada, fourteen-year-old Leslie Mahaffy, locked out of her house by her parents as punishment for coming home late, encountered handsome and charming Paul Bernardo passing by her home in the middle of the night. After chatting for a few minutes, she asked him for a cigarette and he told her he had some in his car parked down the street. She was doomed the moment she sat down in the passenger seat to smoke it and continue talking with him, even while cautiously leaving the car door open and her legs dangling out on the curb. At one point Leslie turned toward the open door to blow some smoke out. At that instant Bernardo snapped the trap shut: He placed a knife against her throat and told her to lift her legs into the car. Bernardo pushed her into the rear seat, blindfolded her, and threw a blanket over her. He then calmly drove forty miles back to his house, where he and his wife, Karla Homolka, raped and murdered her. I repeat: *Do not get into the car!* (And don't lock your children out of the house no matter how late they come home.)

Also do not be fooled by the presence of a baby seat or children's toys in the vehicle—or even the children themselves. Gary Ridgway, the Green River Killer, once returned to a body dump site to have sex with the corpse of one of his victims while his son slept in the vehicle.

Dealing with Strangers and Recognizing Warning Signs of Duplicity

According to Gavin de Becker, a threat prediction expert who quotes the saying of Buddha with which this chapter opens, there are behavioral indicators of potential violence in some people.[236] When a stranger approaches you with ulterior motives, there can be underlying warning signs of duplicity. Learn to recognize the signs that there might be more to the contact than what appears on the surface. These signs include the following:

- *Feigned weakness:* The stranger makes a big deal of letting you know that he might be physically weaker than you. "Please help me carry this to my car. Ever since my back injury I can hardly move." He is wearing a cast or walking with a cane. That's how Ted Bundy trapped some of his victims.

- *Too much information:* The stranger gives you too much unnecessary and detailed information: "My sister has a sweater just like that. She was living in California but she moved home last year. Her boyfriend gave it to her for Christmas, but afterward they broke up . . ." When somebody is telling a lie, even if it sounds credible to you, he has less confidence in what he says; thus he tends to fill in more details than necessary to bolster it. This revelation of details also makes a stranger appear more familiar to you than he really is.

- *The unrequested promise:* "Just one drink and then I will take you home, *I promise.*" You never asked him to promise you anything.

Sudden offers of unsolicited promises can be a sign of an underlying agenda.

- *Friendly authority:* The stranger projects some kind of nonthreatening authority: "I'm the park ranger here. I guess you didn't see the signs; this part of the park is closed. I'll escort you/drive you out of here." "I'm a police officer. You shouldn't be walking alone here; we are on the lookout for a serial killer in this neighborhood. Get in and I'll drive you out of here." You want to cooperate in the fear of turning the authority to an unfriendly mode. This is a tough one too, because some serial killers come tricked out with police identification and police-like vehicles. Insist that he call a uniformed backup if you have not done anything wrong and you are being "arrested."

- *Challenging your ego:* The stranger labels you in a subtly critical way, hoping that you will be challenged to prove them wrong. "You're probably not strong enough to help me lift this box into the back of my van." "You're not scared of me, are you?"

- *Teaming:* Often a manipulative stranger tries to "team up" with you. You and he suddenly become a "we"—"I hate drinking alone, I know a great place *we* can go to up the road." "I'm going there too, *we* can get there in my car." This is an attempt to somehow bond with you or quickly establish a familiarity—"we are in the same boat."

- *Feminine referencing:* The stranger projects an image of himself in relationships with other females or children, therefore reassuring you that he is not interested in you and is harmless. "I'm supposed to pick up my wife from the campus—do you know where the night classes are held? Jump in, I'll give you a lift and you can show me." "My daughter wants a sweater just like that, and I've been looking for it everywhere. Where did you get it? Can you show me if I give you a ride?" References to children or pets also projects a friendly and harmless image: children's toys in the car or the presence of a baby seat.

- *Imposed obligation:* A stranger imposes his help on you, and thus you feel an obligation to him. That obligation can then be manipulated into placing you into a vulnerable position. "Let me help you carry that to your car" can lead to "Can you give me a lift to the corner?" You come out of your home and find your tire flat. "Let me change that flat tire for you" can be followed up by "May I come inside to wash my hands?" But maybe he was the one who punctured the tire in the first place. Having accepted his help, you would feel bad to refuse a simple request like that.

- *An appeal to a vulnerable third party:* "Help me find my lost puppy before it gets away too far." "I need to drop off this medicine to an elderly person but you can't park there. Can you just come and sit in my car while I run up for five minutes?" "My little girl is missing—can you help me search for her?"

- *Never taking no for an answer*—A classic. No matter how many times you say, "That's okay, I don't need your help," the stranger insists on helping you. If you give some weak excuse or sound unsure, he will persist. Do not be afraid to be blunt and rude: "I said, NO! Go away. I do not want your help."

So many victims later say, "But he was so nice." Niceness is not the same as being nice. Niceness can be a deadly manipulative tool. A charming smile can mask the most evil intentions.

Thus, one's first line of defense is not risking attracting or exposing oneself to a predator in the first place. The second line of defense is "brushing off" or ignoring unanticipated, suspicious, or unwanted attention. It might make you appear unfriendly, but it may also save your life. If something does not quite feel right, do not think about it: Politely, quickly, and calmly extract yourself from the situation. Be firm but polite if you can— you do not want to unnecessarily spark anger or a sense of discourteous rejection in a potential serial killer. But in the final analysis, if the stranger does not accept a firm and polite "no" for an answer, tell him loudly to leave you alone. If the man is decent in the first place, while your rudeness might offend him, it will not turn him into a violent offender. If on the other hand he meant you harm, he might understand that you will not be an easy target—he might move on. Do not be embarrassed about appearing capricious or unfriendly if pressed—better that, than police sampling seminal fluids from your cold rectum the next morning.

Desperate Measures

If, however, you are unfortunate enough to find yourself among the 75 percent of victims who simply had the bad luck of being targeted by a serial killer at random and were not able to evade or disengage from him, there are still things you can do. The point we are describing now is where the serial killer refuses to be brushed off by you, and moves beyond the stage of casual contact. By words, demeanor, showing a weapon, or actions, he confronts you and indicates that he is ready to use force if you do not comply with his demands—getting into his car, taking your clothes off, closing your eyes, being quiet, turning around, putting your hands behind your back, engaging in sex with him—whatever the demand might be. If you are unable to run away to safety, what can you do?

Of the serial killers studied by the FBI, 7.5 percent of their victims survived—not encouraging, but nonetheless a sliver of good news. The FBI then tried to pursue what it was in the victim's behavior that resulted in their survival. The question is whether to resist the attacker. The FBI asked the serial killers, how did they perceive the behavior of their victims? In the *opinion of the serial killers,* 28 percent of all of their victims acquiesced or offered no resistance, 31 percent attempted to negotiate verbally, 7 percent verbally refused to obey the killer, 10 percent screamed, 5 percent attempted to escape, and 19 percent tried to fight back.

The serial killers reported that in the face of resistance from their victims, 34 percent had no reaction, 15 percent threatened the victim verbally, 25 percent escalated the level of their aggression, and 25 percent became outright violent. Thus in more than two-thirds of the cases, the killer countered resistance from the victim, and in half of the cases they countered it with increased force. In summary, resistance sparks force or increased levels of force.[237]

It should be pointed out, however, that of the victims in the survey who, in their killers' opinions acquiesced to demands, *all were murdered* without exception. Of the twenty-eight victims who offered physical resistance in the form of screaming, running, or fighting, three survived. Thus except for a slight marginal advantage in resistance, the bad news is that *both* resistance and acquiescence often equally result in death.

Of course, you do not know you are facing a serial killer who is intent on killing you (unless he tells you). Sometimes the serial killer himself is unsure whether his intention is to kill you. The primary threat is rape or physical confinement—one hopes that by evading that, one will consequently escape being murdered later.

The FBI study on sexual and serial homicides refers to a study of 108 convicted serial rapists and their 389 victims. The data collected from this study is very valuable, as serial homicide is mostly a sexual crime and often begins or ends with a rape. Rape had occurred in 98 percent of the serial homicides studied by the FBI: 56 percent before the victim's death and 42 percent after death. The study identified four types of rapists; some experts are now urging that these types be applied to serial killer classification systems:

1. *Power-reassurance (or compensatory rapist):* This type of rapist often has a rape fantasy that his victim actually likes it and will fall in love with him as the result of the rape. He may attempt foreplay and to make a date with his victim afterward. Rape results from sexual arousal and loss of self-control. The rapist is called compensatory because of his terminal sense of inadequacy, which leads him to believe that no "normal" woman would want to have sex with him, unless he compensates it with rape. The rape is a highly sexual act and the offender often has a history of sexual behavior such as voyeurism, excessive masturbation, and exhibitionism. He will do what the victim *allows* him to do.

2. *Power-assertive (or exploitative rapist):* The sexual component is less important here, and the rape is more of an expression of aggression in which the rapist needs to build his own fragile ego and sense of inadequacy by humiliating his victims, dominating them, and having them submit to him.

3. *Anger-retaliatory (or displaced rapist):* The sexual attack is an expression of anger and rage. The victim often serves as a stand-in for the rapist's real object of hate. The behavior can vary from simple

rape to highly elaborate acts of murder and mutilation. Edmund Kemper might be described as a displaced rapist, because he killed eight victims before finally killing the person he actually wanted to—his mother. Most displaced personalities, however, do not get an opportunity to kill the subject of their deep hate, and thus continue killing "innocent" victims.

4. *Anger-excitation (or sadistic rapist):* The sexual act is an expression of aggression fused with sexual desire. In a cycle, sexual arousal gives rise to aggressive desire, which in turn further arouses the rapist. Sometimes the attack begins as a consensual seduction, but then escalates in intense and violent sexual aggression. The rapist often focuses his attack on parts of the victim's body such as the breasts, anus, buttocks, mouth, and genitals. Paul Bernardo was an example of the sadistic personality.

The rape study determined that different types of rapists will respond in different ways to victim behavior—a particular mode of behavior will be more effective in escaping harm from one type of personality than with another and vice versa—with some rapists a behavior can escalate an attack. The following are some of the options that the FBI recommends.

Escape

Escape remains the best and safest of all measures, but we are presuming in this chapter that it is now too late for this option. Nevertheless, if escape does look possible further down the line, you should take into consideration several things. First, to where are you escaping? If you are in a remote area and there is no place or people to run to, escape could be futile. Second, are you unencumbered? If your legs are tied or tangled in clothing, you will not get very far. What is the age and athletic shape of your attacker, in comparison to yourself—can you outrun your assailant?

What type of weapon are you being threatened with? You can outrun a knife or a club, but the situation is different with firearms. There are several things to take into consideration if you are threatened by a firearm. Unlike what we see on television shows, in reality a target becomes rapidly and progressively difficult to hit with a handgun after a distance of about fifteen to twenty feet, especially if the target is moving quickly and weaving. In *Marine: A Guided Tour of a Marine Expeditionary Unit,* Tom Clancy writes about the newly issued state-of-the-art Beretta M9/M92F handgun: "Even with trained shooters like policemen, pistol shooting is, in a word, hideous. Forget what you see on television or in the movies. Accurate pistol fire from beyond about five yards is almost unheard of. For example, in the last twenty years there are painfully few recorded instances of New York City policemen hitting anything beyond twenty-five feet/eight meters with a pistol."

If the assailant has a revolver, a type of handgun that has a revolving drum in the center, the chances are that he will be able to fire only six shots before having to reload—something that often takes at least five seconds at minimum to do. Although it is a little much to ask, perhaps, having the presence of mind to count shots while escaping can help give you that extra burst of straight running power once six shots have been fired. The risk, however, is that some .38-caliber revolvers have only five shots, while some .22-caliber revolvers have eight and nine shots. Furthermore, a device called a speedloader can shorten the reload time. It is, however, a favorably calculated risk that a revolver will be a six-shot weapon. Also, the shorter the barrel, the shorter the weapon's effective range.

The difficulty of hitting distant targets applies to automatic (semiautomatic) handguns as well—it is not as easy as shown on TV. Automatics are squarelike weapons with no revolving drum in the center. As these weapons come in great varieties of capacities from seven to seventeen shots, counting shots will be of little help, unless you are intimately familiar with the specifications of the particular weapon you are threatened with, and even so, the rapid rate of fire that a pistol can unleash may make counting accurately impossible. (Nor can you be sure that the weapon was loaded to maximum capacity in the first place.)

Outrunning an assailant armed with a rifle is virtually impossible, unless the assailant is truly a bad shot—something that the victim is unlikely to know until it is too late. On the other hand, an attacker is often as nervous as you are, and possibly under the influence of drugs or alcohol. This could significantly reduce his shooting skills.

To attempt to outrun an assailant armed with a firearm is a very dangerous and highly risky proposition, but not entirely impossible. It is a calculated risk that one may need to attempt under certain circumstances, bearing in mind the various factors described previously.

Finally, one word of caution about escape: In the case of sadistic personalities, running may actually arouse the assailant and lead to an escalation of violence. However, the chances of surviving an attack by a sadistic personality are minimal anyway, so escape is always an option that you should constantly be alert to.

In any case, you should always be ready for escape, while pursuing any one of the following strategies when escape is not immediately an option:

VERBAL CONFRONTATIONAL RESISTANCE

Verbal resistance should be the *first* action that you take when confronted by an assailant where there are no immediate means to escape. Immediately, yell and shout at the assailant: "Leave me alone! Go away! Help! Police!"

Do not scream. Screaming from the throat can be mistaken for play and also projects fear to the assailant. Instead shout and yell from your diaphragm, which can also prepare you for taking a blow without having the wind knocked out of you and projects a forceful stance to the assailant.

You want to convey to the attacker a clear and succinct message that you are not going to be an easy target. The serial killer sometimes begins his approach without having yet decided whether to use physical force. The decision to use force will be inevitable at some point in his attack, but by forcing the assailant to consider the decision earlier than he is ready to commit to it, you may defuse the attack. Sometimes an attack is preceded by a cat-and-mouse-like dynamic between the assailant and victim—the assailant may need reassurance that he will overcome and capture his victim or that his victim will behave in a submissive and fearful manner. Bold, verbal indications that the capture may not be easy may shake the confidence of some assailants.

PHYSICAL CONFRONTATIONAL RESISTANCE

Physical resistance encompasses both moderate responses, such as struggling, punching, kicking, and pushing away, and violent responses, such as blows to the face, eyes, groin, and throat, intended to seriously injure or kill the assailant. The use of such defenses depends on the size and strength of the victim, the presence of weapons, location, and so on. Such measures should be undertaken quickly, powerfully, and decisively and should be immediately followed by escape. Do not hold back. Do not hesitate. Surprise is a key element. Do not wait around and see what effect, if any, your attack had on the assailant. Run. Run. Run. You are not trying to win. *Escape is your objective.*

The downside, however, is that the victim should anticipate that physical resistance will be met with increased force by the assailant. Studies are conflicted on the precise effect of resistance on the injury of victims. One study found that of seriously injured rape victims, only 41 percent were injured after they resisted. The other 59 percent received their injuries *without* resisting.[238] Other studies show that certain types of rapists (power-reassurance, anger-retaliatory, anger-excitation) tended to injure victims who resisted more severely, while victim injury was unaffected by resistance to power-assertive rapists.[239]

Another study noted that serial offenders tended to be of two types: *increasers,* those who had a tendency to increase their level of violence as their career progressed, and *non-increasers,* those who did not. The two types showed different response patterns. Response patterns also varied whether rapists were in the early, middle, or late stages of their careers and by their types. This study found that victim resistance was related not to the amount of force used, but to the amount of time the offender spent with the victim. Assaults on resisting victims lasted two to three times longer than on passive victims. This was not only because of the time necessary to overcome resistance, but also because of the additional pleasure derived by certain types of offenders from the victim's resistance.[240]

VERBAL NONCONFRONTATIONAL DISSUASION

In many cases, serial killers "depersonalize" their victims—they are substitutes for other people or props in their fantasies. Ted Bundy stated that he avoided getting into any extended conversations with his victims because that might remind him of their personal characteristics. The FBI suggests that talking is probably *the most effective and promising way* to defuse a violent situation.

Tell the rapist that perhaps you and he could go for a beer first, suggests the FBI. This is not as stupid as it sounds. Any kind of unanticipated reaction can stall the rapist and give the victim time to set the stage for an escape. Focus on personalizing yourself in the assailant's perception: "I am a total stranger. Why do you want to hurt me? I have never done anything to hurt you. What if I were somebody you cared about? How would you feel about that?" Keep the dialogue in the present tense, the FBI suggests—serial killers rarely think too far into the future. *Do not* use lines like, "You will end up in jail if you do this," for you might only remind the assailant of the necessity of killing you as a potential witness— even if he has come to like you. Above all, *do not* use the popular feminist appeal, "What if I were your mother, sister, or daughter?" The assailant might be precisely fantasizing that he is raping and killing his mother, sister, or daughter when he is attacking you. Such statements as "I have VD" or "I am pregnant" should also be avoided, as they may reinforce the assailant's fantasy that you are somehow "bad" and deserving of rape and death.

There are numerous accounts of serial killers who somehow sympathized with their victims upon learning something about them. Monte Rissell, who killed five women, upon learning that one of his victims had a father dying from cancer, let her go free because his own father had died from cancer. Bobby Joe Long, who killed at least ten women, felt sorry for a young woman he had kidnapped when she confided that she had been abused as a child, and let her go free. Christopher Wilder sent one of his kidnapped victims home on an airplane. It should be noted, however, that in *all* of these cases, the surviving victims were raped nonetheless.

Arthur Shawcross killed eleven prostitutes in the Rochester area, but he recalls sparing the life of one:

> You know, I had her by the throat and you know I mean she was fighting me and she was telling me, "Please, I'm on medication." She says, "I know *you're* on medication." And when she said that, I came out of what I was doing . . . and I sat down in the driver's seat and I just hold my hands like this, trembling, and started crying. "What the hell am I doing?" . . . It just shocked me. I just pulled away and said, "What the fuck am I doing?" You know? Then we talked for a while. Then she asked me could I take her home. I said all right.[241]

Making some kind of personal connection with the serial killer is similar to a tactic used by serial killers themselves to lure victims (teaming); transforming "you and him" into "us" can work with some types.

Unfortunately, there are far more accounts of serial killers feeling sympathy for their victims *after* they have killed them. Sympathy is often expressed by the assailant's killing his victim quickly and painlessly or, as in the case of Edmund Kemper, visiting the site where the body is dumped with remorse in his heart. Albert DeSalvo chose not to pose one of his victims to whom he took a liking, but only after raping and strangling her first.

When the assailant is in the heat of his attack, dissuasive dialogue, however, will generally not work. The more intelligent assailant is unlikely to leave you alive, even if he likes you, because he knows that you are a witness.

PHYSICAL DISSUASION

You can push away, twist, wrestle, evade, kick, and use various means of moderate force to keep the attacker at bay. This of course, depends on your own strength and stamina, but you may eventually wear the attacker down or convince him that you are not going to be an easy submissive victim. The downside to this tactic is that your resistance will actually excite a certain type of offender into escalating his attack.

Another type of physical dissuasion could be faked fainting, choking, seizures, or mental illness or other sickness, or actual physical responses such as crying, vomiting, or loss of bowel and bladder control. All of these reactions could turn off a potential rapist—but on the other hand, in the cases of a sadistic or displaced-anger rapist, they may actually escalate the attack. The FBI suggests that these are too idiosyncratic in their results and not reliable.

ACQUIESCENCE

The acquiescent victim tells the assailant, "Don't hurt me and I'll do what you want." This may defuse the violence in the short term and buy the victim time to stage an escape. It is recommended by the FBI as the *last* resort, because in the end it does little to guarantee your survival. Moreover, acquiescence can also trigger increased violence in some types of offenders. Monte Rissell proceeded to rape at gunpoint a prostitute, who was not particularly afraid of sex with strangers. In her attempt to defuse the violent aspect of the rape, she attempted to be as co-operative as possible. In response, Rissell killed her. He later explained, "She asked which way I wanted it. It's like this bitch is trying to control things." Richard Cottingham's last victim assured him that he did not need to handcuff her to have sex—but sex was not what his attack was about. He proceeded to rape and torture her for several hours.

One mission-type serial killer profiled by Ronald Holmes felt it was his mission to rid the world of prostitutes. He confessed that at least on a dozen occasions he confronted women with a pistol and demanded that they "permit" him to rape them. He said that he released unharmed those women who responded that he would have to kill her before she would allow him to rape her. Three victims, however, had acquiesced to the rape in fear of being killed; he raped and murdered them because they "proved" to him by their acquiescence that they were prostitutes.[242]

Negotiated acquiescence can be worse. Remember the rehabilitation counseling student Beverly Samans, whom Albert DeSalvo attacked. (See Chapter 2.) She acquiesced to being fondled as long as he promised not to rape her. Instead, her attempts to set the terms of the encounter reminded DeSalvo of his wife, and he became particularly enraged at Samans's attempts to "control him." He stabbed her twenty-two times, the only victim the Boston Strangler killed with such rage.

On the other hand, one of the victims of Chris Wilder, held prisoner in a motel room, acquiesced until she had a chance to dash into the bathroom and begin screaming desperately for her life. (Wilder raped and murdered twelve women in 1984, and embarked on a cross-country killing spree when his first killings were uncovered.) The bottom line is that acquiescence alone is rarely going to save your life; acquiescence *as a prelude to escape,* however, is worth considering.

We see that the prognosis is not good—survival in the hands of a serial killer is at best a marginal and highly idiosyncratic process. What may save your life with one type of personality may condemn you to death with another. Obviously, it is not a viable proposal for a victim, at the moment of attack, to attempt to sort out which of the four personality profiles applies to the assailant. Thus the FBI has defined a sort of flow chart of recommended approaches, based on what logically and statistically gives the victim a marginal increase in the chances for survival.

The FBI operates on the presumption that violence begets increased aggression from the assailant, and therefore recommends that the first response is *not to be violent*. For this reason, the FBI recommends that victims first assert themselves through verbal resistance.

If verbal resistance has no effect, than the victim has a choice of two strategies. If the offender is armed, then verbal dissuasion is recommended. Attempt to engage the offender in conversation and steer him away from attacking.

If the offender has no weapon but persists in his aggressive actions toward the victim, then moderate physical resistance is recommended immediately. This, the FBI suggests, could be effective with compensatory rapists, and sometimes with exploitative rapists. If however, this response brings on increased anger and aggression from the attacker, the victim should immediately cease resisting. If the assailant ceases his aggression at this point and is willing to enter into conversation, it is likely that he is an exploitative personality, and the victim should attempt to verbally manipulate him in that case.

If the strategy fails, and the attacker continues to escalate his aggression, then the victim needs to make a difficult decision between acquiescence and violent resistance. Physical dissuasion, such as pretending to faint or crying and vomiting, is not recommended, as it is unlikely that the attacker cares particularly about the physical well-being of his victim, and may actually become excited by visible physical reactions to his attack.

Summing It Up

In summary, the first response should always be to escape. The second response should be verbal confrontational resistance. If the attacker persists, there is no weapon present, and he is not excessively violent, then the victim should offer physical dissuasion. If the attacker is a compensatory personality, he will likely flee at this point. If however, the attacker continues with the same level of aggression, the victim should begin talking in an attempt to engage the assailant in a conversation. The conversation should be in the present and focused on talking the assailant down from his state of rage. The intent is to redirect the assailant's fantasy by personalizing oneself to the attacker. However, if the assailant pays no attention to the victim's attempts to engage him in conversation and continues his aggression without escalating the level of violence, then he is most likely an exploitative personality. The victim should then continue attempts to engage him in conversation *if* there is no means to escape or opportunity to critically injure the attacker.

If, however, there is a clear escalation in aggression, the victim will need to attempt to distinguish between personalities. If the primary objective of the attacker appears to be to humiliate or demean the victim either verbally or physically, then the assailant is likely a displaced-anger personality. In that case, the victim should continue trying to verbally communicate to the attacker that she has not abused him and make a show of care and concern for the assailant—"It sounds to me like somebody really did something bad to you. But it can't be me, because we've never met." Challenging the fantasy is essential: "How do you know that I'm a bitch? You've never met me before. We're strangers. I could be a really nice person."

If, however, instead of a demeaning and humiliating approach, the rapist is making eroticized and bizarre demands, then he is likely a sadistic personality. This is the most dangerous personality, and no amount of verbal engagement will shake him from his goal. In this case, the victim should attempt anything possible to escape, including the use of lethal force if possible.

Obviously, the victim will not always have an opportunity to think about what is happening and respond with a schedule of strategies. However, there are sufficient case examples of victims and assailants engaging in drawn-out dialogues and escalating dynamics of violence to warrant some thought to the possibility that an informed victim might favorably increase her chances of survival with a well-thought-out response.

The following actions are suggested to enhance your survival:

1. Never get into the car!

2. Flee.

If unable to flee:

3. Use firm *verbal confrontational resistance*—firmly tell the attacker to leave you alone.

If that does not work:

4. Use *moderate physical dissuasion*—twist, kick, push, and punch to attempt to wear the attacker down.

If that fails:

5. Use *verbal dissuasion*—attempt to engage the attacker in conversation, talk him down from his rage, challenge his fantasy. Attempt to set a stage for an escape—invite him for a drink in a more populated area.

If that fails:

6. Use *violent resistance*—attack your assailant's eyes, throat, genitals, and face. Strike him with any convenient object nearby, such as a rock or club. Punch him, kick him, stick your fingers in his eyes, bite his nose off. Fight for your life, because at this point you have nothing left to lose.

Currently many college campuses in North America host Rape Aggression Defense (R.A.D.) Systems training sessions. These two-day courses offer some elementary practical advice and training practice in techniques to defend yourself if confronted by a rapist. (See: http://www.rad-systems.com to locate a session near you.)

Finally, here are some words of advice from someone who ought to know: Danny Rolling, the Gainesville Ripper, who in 1990 descended on the Florida college town and, invading the homes of students, raped, killed, and horribly mutilated six victims. (The seventh Gainesville victim was a victim's boyfriend who was stabbed to death as he fought Rolling.) These are a serial killer's security tips:

1. Park your car in the light.

2. Buy yourself a .38-caliber revolver. Get a permit to carry it on your person, and put it in your handbag where it's easy to get to.

3. Buy some Mace on a keychain and have it ready when you get out of your car.

4. If your bedroom window doesn't have a screen, get one and nail it to the windowsill.

5. Place a bunch of empty bottles in the windows.

6. Get some curtains.

7. Buy a deadbolt and put it on your bedroom door so you can lock yourself in.

8. Sleep with your .38-caliber revolver under your pillow. It won't go off by accident.*

9. If someone bothers you, don't ever let an attacker get control. Fight for your life. Scream as loud as you can! Spray Mace in his face. Kick him in the balls. Scratch at his eyes.

10. Pull your .38-caliber and blow him away!

Take it from one who knows: It pays to be paranoid.[243]

---

* Experts are divided on the safety of sleeping with a loaded handgun under a pillow. There is always the risk that one can unintentionally grip and discharge the weapon while asleep or that children find the weapon if it is not securely put away every morning.

Acknowledgments

I owe a lifetime of thanks to my mom, Svetlana. Thanks to my dad, Boris, who was a big reader of almost every kind of book and shared them all with me, but smoked too much to make it through life long enough to read this one.

Thanks to filmmaker Guiseppe Asaro and Kathy Foy, in whose home in Los Angeles I began working on this book; and a big thanks to my in-laws, Lidy and Aronne Zinato and his sister Jone—*the zia*—in whose home in Carpenedo-Venice, Italy, I finished it. Their support of and belief in me through hard lean times I will always remember.

Thanks to Sergio Pastrello of Professional Video in Martellago-Venice, my crazy comrade in travels through the Italian television business, and to my friends in Toronto— Flavio Belli, Tom Dungey, Paul Eichgrun, Shannon Griffiths, Doug James, Peter Lynch, Dave Walker, and Tony Wannamaker—all of whom kept me sane, advised, amused, or employed in their various means and ways these last few years. My cousins Lucy, Boris, and John Zawadzki—and Leo—were always behind me.

A special thanks to Sarah Christie, who over a period of several years diligently restored and copied for me photographs from the archives of the Toronto Police Service, some of which appear in this book. Thanks to Eddie at Dencan Books in the Junction in Toronto, who kept me supplied with true-crime classics. I thank Jack Webster, former Toronto police homicide squad chief and recently retired force historian, for his relentless help and advice in guiding me through the historical records of the Toronto Police Service and for his own observations on the nature of the criminal mind and homicide. And thanks to some great schoolteachers: Dina Fayerman, Rochelle Carr, and the late Murray Hirsch, who taught me how to read and ask.

And a real big thanks to my agent, Deidre Knight, who made this happen, and my editor, Ginjer Buchanan at Penguin Group USA, who went for it.

Above all, Quantel and Alisa—Q & A—who have made life worth living and a whole lot of fun too. It's been a trip!

Endnotes

1. Rod Leith, *The Prostitute Murders: The People vs. Richard Cottingham*, Secaucus, N.J.: Lyle Stuart, 1983, pp. 17–18.
2. Peter Conradi, *The Red Ripper*, London: Virgin, 1992.
3. Robert F. Kennedy, "Eradicating Free Enterprise in Organized Crime," in *The Pursuit of Justice*, New York: Harper and Row, 1964.
4. Robert D. Keppel with William J. Birnes, *The Riverman: Ted Bundy and I Hunt for the Green River Killer*, New York: Pocket Books, 1995, pp. 424, 443.
5. Eric W. Hickey, *Serial Murderers and Their Victims*, 3rd ed., Belmont, Calif.: Wadsworth/Thomson Learning, 2002, p. 132.
6. Ibid., p. 133; see also Philip Jenkins, "African-Americans and Serial Homicide," *American Journal of Criminal Justice*, 17(2), 1993, pp. 47–60.
7. Hickey, *Serial Murderers*, p. 35.
8. Ibid., p. 213.
9. Ibid., p. 247.
10. Gene Johnson, "Green River Killer May Contribute Little to Serial Killer Studies," Associated Press, November 9, 2003.
11. Mike Archbold, *King Country Journal*, 8 November 2003 http://www.kingcounty journal.com/sited/story/html/14840.
12. Robert K. Ressler, Ann W. Burgess, and John E. Douglas, *Sexual Homicide: Patterns and Motives*, Lexington, Mass.: Lexington Books, 1988, p. 2.
13. U.S. Department of Justice, *Crime in the United States*, press release, Washington, D.C.: FBI National Press Office, October 13, 1996.
14. Mark Riedel, "Counting Stranger Homicides," *Homicide Studies*, 2(2), May 1998, pp. 206–219.
15. Federal Bureau of Investigation, *Uniform Crime Report 2001*, Washington, D.C.: U.S. Government Printing Office, 2002.
16. *Uniform Crime Report 2001*.
17. Peter Wyden, *The Hired Killers*, New York: Bantam Books, 1963, p. 4.
18. Michael Newton, *Serial Slaughter: What's behind America's Murder Epidemic?*, Port Townsend, Wash.: Loompanics, 1992, p. 6.

19. Stephen J. Giannangelo, *The Psychopathology of Serial Murder,* London: Praeger, 1996, p. 5.

20. Newton, *Serial Slaughter,* p. 5.

21. Federal Bureau of Investigation, *Preliminary Uniform Crime Report 2002,* Washington, D.C.: U.S. Government Printing Office, June 16, 2003.

22. Newton, *Serial Slaughter,* p. 5.

23. Hickey, *Serial Murderers,* p. 132.

24. Newton, *Serial Slaughter,* p. 4.

25. "Texas woman might be serial killer victim," San Antonio Express-News http://news.mysanantonio.com/story.cfm?xla=saen&xlb=180&xlc=1131955, February 21, 2004.

26. Allan Dowd, "New Remains Found at Accused Canada Killer's Farm," *Reuters* January 27, 2004; "B.C. missing women investigation cost $70M," *Canadian Press,* February 21, 2004; and "Canadian Police Confirm Finding Remains of Nine More Vancouver Women at Pig Farm," *Associated Press,* January 27, 2004.

27. Ressler et al., *Sexual Homicide,* pp. x–xi.

28. Philip Jenkins, *Using Murder: The Social Construction of Serial Homicide,* New York: Aldine de Gruyter, 1994, pp. 58–59.

29. John Gill, "Missing Children: How Politics Helped Start the Scandal," FatherMag.com, 2000 http://www.fathermag.com/006/missing-children/abduction_2.shtml.

30. Michael Fumento, Hudson Institute, *American Outlook,* Spring 2002 http://www.fumento.com/exploit.html.

31. John Gill, *op cit.,* http://www.fathermag.com/006/missing-children/abduction_3.shtml.

32. John Gill, *op cit.,* http://www.fathermag.com/006/missing-children/abduction_3.shtml.

33. Ronald M. Holmes and James De Burger, *Serial Murder,* Newbury Park, Calif.: Sage, 1988, pp. 19–20.

34. Michael Newton, *The Encyclopedia of Serial Killers,* New York: Facts on File, 2000.

35. Hickey, *Serial Murderers,* p. 242.

36. J. Best, "Missing Children: Misleading Statistics," *Public Interest,* 92, 1988, p. 92.

37. Kenneth Chew, Richard McCleary, Maricres Lew, and Johnson Wang, "The Epidemiology of Child Homicide in California, 1981 through 1990," *Homicide Studies,* 3(2), May 1999, pp. 151–169.

38. David Finkelhor, Gerald Hotaling, and Andrea Sedlak, "The Abduction of Children by Strangers and Non-Family Members: Estimating the Incidence Using Multiple Methods," *Journal of Interpersonal Violence,* 7(2), June 1992, pp. 226–243.

39. Jenkins, *Using Murder,* pp. 26–27.

40. Ibid., p. 28.

41. Newton, *Serial Slaughter,* p. 2.

42. Ibid., pp. 2–3.

43. Internet Crime Archives, "Serial Killer Hit List—Part 1," http://www.mayhem.net/Crime/serial.html.

44. Internet Crime Archives, "Killers on the Run," http://www.mayhem.net/Crime/killersatlarge.html.

45. "SA Police Nab Two Alleged Serial Killers," *The Namibian,* http://www.namibian.com.na/Netstories/2000/July/Africa/008E23B9B0.html, July 6, 2000.

46. Steven A. Egger, *The Killers among Us: An Examination of Serial Murder and Its Investigation,* Upper Saddle River, N.J.: Prentice-Hall, 1998, pp. 74–75.

47. Ibid., p. 74.

48. Ibid., p. 75.

49. Mark Seltzer, *Serial Killers: Death and Life in America's Wound Culture,* New York: Routledge, 1998, p. 1.

50. Angus McLaren, *A Prescription for Murder: The Victorian Serial Killings of Dr. Thomas Neill Cream,* Chicago: University of Chicago Press, 1993.

51. Paul Plass, *The Game of Death in Ancient Rome: Arena Sport and Political Suicide,* Madison: University of Wisconsin Press, 1995.

52. Seneca, *De Clementia,* 1.25.1.

53. Roland Auguet, *Cruelty and Civilization: The Roman Games,* London: Routledge, 1972, p. 67.

54. Seneca, *De Clementia,* 2.4.

55. Brian Meehan, "Son of Cain or Son of Sam: The Monster as Serial Killer in *Beowulf,*" *Connecticut Review,* Connecticut State University, Fall 1994.

56. George Bataille, *The Trial of Gilles de Rais,* Los Angeles: AMOK, 1991, p. 14.

57. National Archives of France, *Inquest by Commissioners of the Duke of Brittany, September 18–October 8, 1440.* Call Number: 1 AP 585, originally from the Archive de la Trémoille.

58. National Archives of France, Statement of Guillaume Hilairet and his wife Jeanne Hilairet, September 28–30, 1440.

59. National Archives of France, Statement of Andre Barbe, September 28–30, 1440.

60. Original manuscript of the quoted ecclesiatical trial is in the Archives de la Loire-Atlantique. G. 189. There are later copies in Latin, Ms. 17663; in French, Ms. 21395, Bibliothèque National, Paris. The original for the civil trial, Manuscrit du precès civil. A copy made in 1530 can be found in Archives communales de Thouars. There are numerous modern copies in the Bibliothèque National, the Bibliothèque de l'Arsenal, and the Bibliothèque de Nantes.

61. Peter Haining, *Sweeney Todd: The Real Story of the Demon Barber of Fleet Street,* London: Robson Books, 2002, p. 10–11.

62. Pierre De Lancre, *Description of the Inconstancy of Evil Angels,* Paris, 1612, cited in Raymond Rudorff, *Monsters: Studies in Ferocity,* London: Neville Spearman, 1968, p. 135.

63. Cited in Jan Bondeson, *The London Monster: A Sanguinary Tale,* London: Free Association Books, 2000, p. 92.

64. Lombroso Goltdammer's *Archiv,* p. 13, cited in Richard von Krafft-Ebing, *Psychopathia Sexualis.* Translated by Charles Gilbert Chaddock, Philadelphia: F. A. Davis Company, 1894, p. 67.

65. Lombroso, in Krafft-Ebing, *op cit.*

66. Ibid., p. 378.

67. See Gary Colville and Patrick Lucano, *Jack the Ripper: His Life and Crimes in Popular Entertainment,* London: McFarland, 1999; L. Perry Curtis, Jr., *Jack the Ripper and The London Press,* New Haven, Conn.: Yale University Press, 2001.

68. Dr. Thomas Bond, *Report,* November 10, 1888. Metropolitan Police File 3/140, folio 220–223, London.

69. Klaus Theweleit, *Male Fantasies,* Minneapolis: University of Minnesota Press, 1987, p. 196.

70. Colin Wilson, *A Criminal History of Mankind,* New York: Carroll & Graff, 1990.

71. Michel Foucault, *Madness and Civilization,* trans. R. Howard, New York: Pantheon, 1965, p. 210.

72. Ressler et al., *Sexual Homicide,* p. 24.

73. Theodor Lessing, *"Aussenseiter der Gesellschaft—Verbrechen der Gegenwart,"* Berlin: Verlag Die Schmmiede, 1925. Reprinted as *Haarmann: Die Geschichte eines Werwolfs,* Müchen: Roger & Bernhard, 1973, pp. 112–114.

74. James A. Brussel, *Casebook of a Crime Psychiatrist,* New York: Dell, 1968, p. 178.

75. Elliott Leyton, *Hunting Humans: The Rise of the Modern Multiple Murderer,* Toronto: McClelland-Bantam, 1987, p. 136.

76. George W. Rae, *Confessions of the Boston Strangler,* New York: Pyramid, 1967, p. 48.

77. Earl James, *Catching Serial Killers,* Lansing, Mich: International Forensic Services, 1991, p. 235.

78. Rae, *Confessions,* p. 46.

79. James, *Catching Serial Killers,* p. 164.

80. Leyton, *Hunting Humans,* p. 138.

81. Jim Hogshire, *You Are Going to Prison,* Port Townsend, Wash.: Loompanics, 1994, p. 77.

82. Brussel, *Casebook,* pp. 161–166.

83. Rae, *Confessions,* p. 22.

84. Newton, *Serial Slaughter,* p. 126.

85. John E. Douglas, Ann W. Burgess, Allen G. Burgess, and Robert K. Ressler, *Crime Classification Manual,* New York: Lexington Books, 1992, pp. 17–18.

86. Stephen G. Michaud and Hugh Aynesworth, *The Only Living Witness: A True Account of Homicidal Insanity,* New York: New American Library, 1983, p. 55.

87. Myra MacPherson, "The Roots of Evil," *Vanity Fair,* May 1989.

88. Ann Rule, *The Stranger Beside Me,* New York: New American Library, 1980, p. 8.

89. Michaud and Aynesworth, *The Only Living Witness,* p. 48.

90. Ann Rule, *The Stranger Beside Me,* pp. 25–26.

91. Ibid., pp. 31–32.

92. Michaud and Aynesworth, *The Only Living Witness,* p. 74.

93. Ibid., pp. 125–126.

94. Keppel, *The Riverman,* pp. 34–35.

95. Michaud and Aynesworth, *The Only Living Witness,* p. 310.

96. Ibid.

97. Philip Carlo, *The Night Stalker: The Life and Crimes of Richard Ramirez,* New York: Pinnacle Books, 1997, p. 172.

98. Ronald M. Holmes and Stephen T. Holmes, *Serial Murder,* 2nd ed., Newbury Park, Calif.: Sage, 1998, pp. 42–44.

99. Robert K. Ressler and Tom Shachtman, *Whoever Fights Monsters,* New York: St. Martin's Press, 1992, p. 148.

100. Clark Howard, *Zebra,* New York: Berkley Books, 1990, pp. 17–18.

101. Ibid., p. 18.

102. See Rich Harris, Associated Press, Chairman of the Unabom Committee of Media Organizations, letter to "Fellow Journalist," September 23, 1997.

103. Unabom Trial Media Group, *General Guidelines for Credentials,* 1997, cited in Alston Chase, *Harvard and the Unabomber: The Education of an American Terrorist,* New York: Norton, 2003, p. 388 n.

104. Chase, *Harvard and the Unabomber,* p. 125.

105. Henry David Thoreau, *Walden,* New York: Signet Classic, 1999, p. 261.

106. Chase, *Harvard and the Unabomber,* p. 263.

107. Timothy Leary, *Flashbacks,* New York: Putnam, 1983, p. 37.

108. See H. A. Murray "Studies of Stressful Interpersonal Disputations," *American Psychologist,* 18(1), January 1963.

109. Chase, *Harvard and the Unabomber,* p. 266.

110. See Mark Bourrie, *By Reason of Insanity: The David Michael Krueger Story,* Toronto: Hounslow Press, 1997.

111. Ann Rule, *Lust Killer,* (updated edition), New York: New American Library/Signet, 1988, p. 133.

112. Ibid., p. 134.

113. Ibid., p. 137.

114. Ibid., p. 143.

115. Ibid., p. 145.

116. Ibid., p. 150.

117. Brent E. Turvey, "The Impressions of a Man: An Objective Forensic Guideline to Profiling Violent Serial Sex Offenders," http://www.corpus-delicti.com/impress.html, March 1995.

118. http://www.algora.com/Ashes.htm.

119. Tim Cahill, *Buried Dreams: Inside the Mind of a Serial Killer,* New York: Bantam Books, 1986, p. 6.

120. Robert D. Keppel and William J. Birnes, *The Psychology of Serial Killer Investigations,* New York: Academic Press, 2003, p. 132.

121. Ibid., pp. 144–167.

122. Ibid., p. 435.

123. Don Lasseter and Dana Holliday, *Zodiac of Death,* New York: Berkley Books, 1999.

124. Michael Kelleher and C. L. Kelleher, *Murder Most Rare: The Female Serial Killer,* New York: Dell, 1998. p. 9.

125. R. A. Wesheit, "Female Homicide Offenders: Trends over Time in an Institutionalized Population," *Justice Quarterly,* 1(4), 1984, p. 478.

126. Hickey, *Serial Murderers,* p. 217.

127. Wesheit, "Female Homicide Offenders," p. 478.

128. Michael Kelleher and C. L. Kelleher, *Murder Most Rare,* p. 29.

129. Steven J. Boros and Larry C. Brubaker, "Munchausen Syndrome by Proxy: Case Accounts," *FBI Law Enforcement Bulletin,* June 1992.

130. Kathryn A. Hanon, "Munchausen Syndrome by Proxy," *FBI Law Enforcement Bulletin,* December 1991.

131. http://www.crimelibrary.com/notorious_murders/mass/cunanan/world_3.html?sect=8.

132. *Newsweek,* November 4, 2002, pg. 26.

133. Rosie DiManno, "Sniper Suspect Remembered as Clever, 'Obedient' Child," *Toronto Star,* November 26, 2003, p. 2.

134. J. Richard Ciccone, "Murder, Insanity, and Medical Expert Witnesses," *Archives of Neurology,* 49(6), 1992, p. 608.

135. *Queen v. M'Naghten,* 8 Eng. Rep. 718, 722 (H.L. 1843).

136. *State of Alabama v. Parsons,* 81 Ala. at 597, 2 So. at 866–867.

137. *Durham v. United States,* 214 F.2 at 874–875.

138. Model Penal Code § 4.01 (Proposed Official Draft 1962).

139. Hickey, *Serial Murderers,* p. 63.

140. John Godwin, *Murder USA: The Ways We Kill Each Other,* New York: Ballantine, 1979, p. 300.

141. S. K. Henderson, *Psychopathic States,* New York: Norton, 1939, p. 19.

142. R. Hare, *Manual for the Revised Psychopathy Checklist,* Toronto: Multi-Health Systems, 1991.

143. Hickey, *Serial Murderers,* p. 77.

144. American Psychiatric Association, *Diagnostic and Statistical Manual of Mental Disorders: Quick Reference Guide,* 4th ed., American Psychiatric Association, Washington, D.C.: 1994, pp. 649–650.

145. See W. H. J. Martens, "Marcel: A Case Study of a Violent Sexual Psychopath in Remission," *International Journal of Offender Therapy and Comparative Criminology,* 43(3), 1999, p. 392.

146. Jack Olson, *The Misbegotten Son,* New York: Island Books, 1993, pp. 546–547.

147. Joel Norris, *Serial Killers,* New York: Anchor Books, 1989, pp. 246–247.

148. H. H. Goldman, *Review of General Psychiatry,* London: Prentice-Hall International, 1992, p. 290.

149. Martens, "Marcel."

150. A. Reisner, M. McGee, and S. Noffsinger, "The Inpatient Treatment and Evaluation of a Self-Professed Budding Serial Killer," *International Journal of Offender Therapy and Comparative Criminology,* 47(1), 2003, pp. 58–70.

151. Bourrie, *By Reason of Insanity.*

152. Ibid., p. 58.

153. Ibid., p. 45.

154. Ibid., p. 26.

155. Ibid., p. 25.

156. Giannangelo, *Psychopathology,* p. 75.

157. Margaret Cheney, *The Co-Ed Killer,* New York: Walker, 1976, p. 90.

158. Donald T. Lunde, *Murder and Madness,* New York: W. W. Norton, 1979, p. 199.

159. Donald West, *Sacrifice Unto Me,* New York: Pyramid, 1974, p. 166.

160. Giannangelo, *Psychopathology,* p. 98.

161. Ressler et al., *Sexual Homicide,* pp. 16–19.

162. Ibid., pp. 17–18.

163. Dr. Joel Norris, *Henry Lee Lucas,* New York: Zebra Books, 1991, p. 42.

164. Newton, *Serial Slaughter,* p. 15.

165. Ressler et al., *Sexual Homicide,* p. 34.

166. Ibid., p. 29.

167. Ibid.

168. Giannangelo, *Psychopathology,* pp. 32–33.

169. Quoted in *FBI Law Enforcement Bulletin,* August 1985.

170. Ressler et al., *Sexual Homicide,* p. 74.

171. Norris, *Serial Killers,* p. 112.

172. Newton, *Serial Slaughter,* p. 78.

173. Norris, *Serial Killers,* p. 148.

174. Leyton, *Hunting Humans,* p. 196.

175. Jennifer Furio, *The Serial Killer Letters,* Philadelphia: Charles Press, 1998, p. 213.

176. Earl James, *Catching Serial Killers,* International Forensic Services, Lansing, MI: 1991, p. 164.

177. Ressler and Shachtman, *Whoever Fights Monsters,* p. 17.

178. Ressler et al, *Sexual Homicide,* pp. 46–47.

179. Ibid., p. 48.

180. Michaud and Aynesworth, *The Only Living Witness,* p. 107.

181. P. E. Dietz, B. Harry, R. R. Hazelwood, "Detective Magazines: Pornography for the Sexual Sadist?" *Journal of Forensic Sciences,* 31 (1), January 1986, pp. 197-211.

182. Leonard Wolf, *Bluebeard: The Life and Crimes of Gilles de Rais,* New York: Potter, 1980, pp. 162–163.

183. Colin Wilson and Donald Seaman, *The Serial Killers,* London: Virgin, 1994, p. 184.

184. Ian Brady, *The Gates of Janus: Serial Killing and Its Analysis,* Los Angeles: Feral House, 2001, pp. 87–88.

185. Norris, *Serial Killers,* p. 24.

186. Hickey, *Serial Murderers,* p. 149.

187. Newton, *Serial Slaughter,* p. 63.

188. Hickey, *Serial Murderers,* p. 255.

189. Newton, *Serial Slaughter,* p. 64.

190. Ibid., pp. 70–73.

191. Douglas et al., *Crime Classification Manual,* p. 138.

192. Ressler et al., *Sexual Homicide,* p. 54–55.

193. Ibid., p. 63.

194. Ibid., p. 62–63.

195. Ibid., p. 64.

196. Michaud and Aynesworth, *The Only Living Witness,* pp. 109–110.

197. Ted Schwarz, *The Hillside Strangler: A Murderer's Mind,* New York: Signet, 1982, p. 180.

198. Steven A. Egger, "Psychological Profiling: Past, Present, and Future," *Journal of Contemporary Criminal Justice,* 15(3), August 1999, pp. 242–261.

199. James, *Catching Serial Killers,* p. 291.

200. James A. Brussel, *Casebook of a Crime Psychiatrist,* New York: Dell, 1968.

201. R. Holmes and S. Holmes, *Murder in America,* Thousand Oaks, Calif.: Sage, 1994.

202. S. A. Egger, "A Working Definition of Serial Murder and the Reductions of Linkage Blindness," *Journal of Police Science and Administration,* 12, 1984, p. 348–357.

203. V. Gerbeth, *Practical Homicide Investigations,* Boca Raton, Fla.: CRC Press, 1996.

204. B. T. Keeney and K. Heide, "Gender Differences in Serial Murderers," *Journal of Interpersonal Violence,* 9(3), September 1994, p. 383–398.

205. Helen Morrison, *Mind of a Killer,* CD, Chicago: Kozel Multimedia, 1995–1998.

206. Deborah Schurman-Kauflin, *The New Predator: Women Who Kill,* New York: Algora, 2000.

207. Ressler and Shachtman, *Whoever Fights Monsters,* p. 32–33.

208. Newton, *Encyclopedia,* p. 205.

209. Ann Rule, forward to *Signature Killers,* by Robert D. Keppel, New York: Pocket Books, 1997, p. xv.

210. Robert K. Ressler, Ann W. Burgess, John E. Douglas, Carol R. Hartman, and Ralph B. D'Agostino, "Sexual Killers and Their Victims: Identifying Patterns through Crime Scene Analysis," *Journal of Interpersonal Violence,* 1(3), September 1986, p. 288–308.

211. Ressler and Shachtman, *Whoever Fights Monsters,* p. 3.

212. Roy Hazelwood with Stephen G. Michaud, *The Evil That Men Do,* New York: St. Martin's Press, 1998, p. 93.

213. John Douglas and Mark Olshaker, *Mindhunter: Inside the FBI's Elite Serial Crime Unit,* New York: Scribner, 1995, p. 211–212.

214. There is a plausible argument for Williams's innocence; see Chet Dettlinger with Jeff Prugh, *The List,* Atlanta: Philmay Enterprises, 1983.

215. Keppel, *The Riverman,* pp. 114–115.

216. Bernard Headley, *The Atlanta Youth Murders and the Politics of Race,* Carbondale: Southern Illinois University Press, 1998, p.120.

217. Robert J. Homat and Daniel B. Kennedy, "Psychological Aspects of Crime Scene Profiling: Validity Research," *Criminal Justice and Behavior,* 25(3), September 1998, p. 334.

218. Damon Muller, "Criminal Profiling: Real Science or Just Wishful Thinking?," *Homicide Studies,* 4(3), August 2000, p. 234–264.

219. John Douglas and Mark Olshaker, *Journey into Darkness,* New York: Scribner, 1997, p. 17.

220. Quoted in Richard L. Schwoebel, *Explosion aboard the* Iowa, Annapolis, Md.: Naval Institute Press, 1999, p. 254.

221. Charles C. Thompson II, *A Glimpse of Hell: The Explosion on the USS* Iowa *and Its Cover-Up,* New York: Norton, 1999, p. 247.

222. H. Paul Jeffers, *Who Killed Precious,* New York: Pharos Books, 1991, p. 181.

223. House of Representatives, *Review of Navy Investigation of U.S.S.* Iowa *Explosion,*

joint hearings before the Investigations Subcommittee and the Defense Policy Panel of the Committee on Armed Services, December 12, 13, and 21, 1989.

224. House of Representatives, *U.S.S. Iowa Tragedy: An Investigative Failure,* report of the Investigations Subcommittee and Defense Policy Panel of the Committee on Armed Services, March 5, 1990.

225. Thompson, *A Glimpse of Hell,* p. 246.

226. Gordon Witkins, "Did the FBI Ignore the 'Tafoya Profile'?," *U.S. News & World Report,* November 17, 1997.

227. Paul Sperry, "Cops 'Wasted Time' Hunting White Guy," http://worldnetdaily.com/news/article.asp?ARTICLE_10=29422 October 25, 2002.

228. Robert D. Keppel and William J. Birnes, *The Psychology of Serial Killer Investigations,* New York: Academic Press, 2003, pp. 214–215.

229. Richard Kocsis, Harvey Irwin, Andrew Hayes, and Ronald Nunn, "Expertise in Psychological Profiling: A Comparative Assessment," *Journal of Interpersonal Violence,* 15(3), March 2000, p. 311–331.

230. Richard Kocsis, "Investigative Experience and Accuracy in Psychological Profiling of a Violent Crime," *Journal of Interpersonal Violence,* 17(8), August 2002, p. 811–823.

231. David Canter, Toby Coffey, Malcolm Huntley, and Christopher Missen, "Predicting Serial Killers' Home Base Using a Decision Support System," *Journal of Quantitative Criminology,* 16(4), 2000, pp. 457–458.

232. Ressler et al., *Sexual Homicide,* p. 200.

233. Hickey, *Serial Murderers,* p. 255.

234. Ressler et al., *Sexual Homicide,* p. 200.

235. James, *Catching Serial Killers,* p. 297.

236. Gavin de Becker, *The Gift of Fear,* New York: Dell, 1997.

237. Ressler et al., *Sexual Homicide.*

238. V. Quinsey and D. Upfold, "Rape Completion and Victim Injury as a Function of Female Resistance Strategy," *Canadian Journal of Behavioral Science,* 17, 1985, pp. 40–50.

239. R. Prentky, A. Burgess, and D. Carter, "Victim Responses by Rapist Type: An Empirical and Clinical Analysis," *Journal of Interpersonal Violence,* 1, 1986, pp. 73–98.

240. Robert Hazelwood, Roland Reboussin, and Janet I. Warren, "Serial Rape: Correlates of Increased Aggression and the Relationship of Offender Pleasure to Victim Resistance," *Journal of Interpersonal Violence,* 4(1), March 1989, pp. 65–78.

241. Jack Olson, *The Misbegotten Son: A Serial Killer and His Victims,* New York: Island Books, 1993, p. 508.

242. Ronald M. Holmes and Stephen T. Holmes, (1998), p. 82–83.

243. Danny Rolling and Sondra London, *The Making of a Serial Killer,* Portland, Ore.: Feral House, 1996, p. 191.

Selected Sources

Books

American Psychiatric Association, *Diagnostic and Statistical Manual of Mental Disorders, Quick Reference Guide* (4th ed.), American Psychiatric Association, Washington, D.C.: 1994.

Auguet, Roland. *Cruelty and Civilization: The Roman Games,* London: Routledge, 1972.

Battaile, George. *The Trial of Gille de Rais,* Los Angeles: AMOK, 1991.

Becker, Gavin de. *The Gift of Fear,* New York: Dell Books, 1997.

Bondeson, Jan. *The London Monster: A Sanguinary Tale,* London: Free Association Books, 2000.

Bourrie, Mark. *By Reason of Insanity: The David Michael Krueger Story,* Toronto: Hounslow, 1997.

Brady, Ian. *The Gates of Janus,* Los Angeles: Feral House, 2001.

Brussel, James A., M.D. *Casebook of a Crime Psychiatrist,* New York: Dell, 1968.

Cahill, Tim. *Buried Dreams: Inside the Mind of a Serial Killer,* New York: Bantam, 1986.

Carlo, Philip. *The Night Stalker: The Life and Crimes of Richard Ramirez,* New York: Pinnacle Books, 1997.

Chase, Alston. *Harvard and the Unabomber: The Education of an American Terrorist,* New York: W.W. Norton & Co, 2003.

Colville, Gary & Lucano, Patrick. *Jack the Ripper: His Life and Crimes in Popular Entertainment,* London: McFarland, 1999.

Conradi, Peter. *The Red Ripper,* London: Virgin Publishing, 1992.

Curtis, L. Perry Jr., *Jack the Ripper & The London Press,* New Haven: Yale University Press, 2001.

De Lancre, Pierre. *Description of the Inconstancy of Evil Angels,* Paris, 1612.

Dettlinger, Chet., with Prugh, Jeff. *The List,* Atlanta: Philmay Enterprises, 1983.

Douglas, John E., Burgess, Ann W., Burgess, Allen G., and Ressler, Robert K. *Crime Classification Manual,* New York: Lexington Books, 1992.

Egger, Steven A. *The Killers Among Us: An Examination of Serial Murder and its Investigation,* New Jersey: Prentice-Hall, 1998.

Foucault, Michel. *Madness and Civilization,* tr. R. Howard, New York: Pantheon, 1965.

Furio, Jennifer. *The Serial Killer Letters,* Philadelphia: Charles Press, 1998.

Gerbeth, V. *Practical Homicide Investigations,* Boca Raton, FL: CRC Press, 1996.

Giannangelo, Stephen J. *The Psychopathology of Serial Murder,* London: Praeger, 1996.

Godwin, John. *Murder USA: The Ways We Kill Each Other,* New York: Ballantine, 1979.

Goldman, H. H. *Review of General Psychiatry,* London: Prentice Hall International, 1992.

Haining, Peter. *Sweeney Todd: The Real Story of the Demon Barber of Fleet Street,* London: Robson Books, 2002.

Hare, R. *Manual for the revised psychopathy checklist,* Toronto: Multi-Health Systems, 1991.

Hazelwood, Roy, with Michaud, Stephen G. *The Evil That Men Do,* New York: St. Martin's Press, 1998.

Headley, Bernard. *The Atlanta Youth Murders and the Politics of Race,* Carbondale and Edwardsville: Southern Illinois University Press, 1998.

Henderson, S. K. *Psychopathic States,* New York: Norton, 1939.

Hickey, Eric W. *Serial Murders and Their Victims,* (Third Edition) Belmont, CA: Wadsworth/Thomson Learning, 2002.

Holmes, Ronald M. & De Burger, James. *Serial Murder,* Newbury Park, CA: Sage Publications, 1988.

Holmes, Ronald M. & Holmes, Stephen T. *Serial Murder,* (Second Edition), Newbury Park, CA: Sage Publications, 1998.

Holmes, R. & Holmes, S. *Murder in America,* Thousand Oaks, CA: Sage Publications, 1994.

Hogshire, Jim. *You Are Going to Prison,* Port Townsend, WA: Loompanics Unlimited, 1994.

Howard, Clark. *Zebra,* New York: Berkley Books, 1990.

James, Earl. *Catching Serial Killers,* Lansing, MI: International Forensic Services, 1991.

Jeffers, H. Paul. *Who Killed Precious,* New York: Pharos Books, 1991.

Jenkins, Philip. *Using Murder: The Social Construction of Serial Homicide,* New York: Aldine de Gruyter, 1994.

Kelleher, Michael and Kelleher, C. L. *Murder Most Rare,* New York: Dell Books, 1998.

Kennedy, Robert. *The Pursuit of Justice*, pt. 3, "Eradicating Free Enterprise in Organized Crime" (1964).

Keppel, Robert D., with Birnes, William J. *The Riverman: Ted Bundy and I Hunt for the Green River Killer,* New York: Pocket Books, 1995.

Keppel, Robert D. *Signature Killers,* New York: Pocket Books, 1997.

Krafft-Ebing, Richard von. *Psychopathia Sexualis*, authorized translation by Charles Gilbert Chaddock, PA: F.A. Davis Company, 1894.

Lasseter, Don and Holliday, Dana. *Zodiac of Death,* New York: Berkley Books, 1999.

Leary, Timothy. *Flashbacks,* New York: Putnam, 1983.

Leith, Rod. *The Prostitute Murders: The People vs. Richard Cottingham,* Secaucus, NJ: Lyle Stuart, 1983.

Lessing, Theodor. *Aussenseiter der Gesellschaft—Verbrechen der Gegenwart,* Berlin: Verlag Die Schmmiede, 1925. Reprinted as *Haarmann: Die Geschichte eines Werwolfs,* München: Roger & Bernhard, 1973.

Leyton, Elliott, *Hunting Humans: The Rise of the Modern Multiple Murderer,* Toronto: McLelland-Bantam, 1987.

McLaren, Angus. *A Perscription for Murder: The Victorian Serial Killings of Dr. Thomas Neill Cream,* Chicago: University of Chicago Press, 1993.

Michaud, Stephen G., and Aynesworth, Hugh. *The Only Living Witness: A True Account of Homicidal Insanity,* New York: New American Library, 1983.

Newton, Michael. *Serial Slaughter: What's Behind America's Murder Epidemic?*, Port Townsend, WA: Loompanics, 1992.

———. *The Encyclopedia of Serial Killers*, New York: Facts on File, 2000.

Norris, Joel. *Serial Killers*, New York: Doubleday (Anchor Books), 1989.

Olson, Jack. *The Misbegotten Son: A Serial Killer and His Victims*, New York: Island Books, 1993.

Plass, Paul. *The Game of Death in Ancient Rome: Arena Sport and Political Suicide*, Madison, WI: University of Wisconsin Press, 1995.

Rae, George W. *Confessions of the Boston Strangler*, New York: Pyramid, 1967.

Ressler, Robert K., Burgess, Ann W., Douglas, John E. *Sexual Homicide: Patterns and Motives*, Lexington, MA: Lexington Books, 1988.

Ressler, Robert K. and Shachtman, Tom. *Whoever Fights Monsters*, New York: St. Martin's Paperbacks, 1992.

Rolling, Danny, and London, Sondra. *The Making of a Serial Killer*, Portland, OR: Feral House, 1996.

Rudorff, Raymond. *Monsters: Studies in Ferocity*, London: Neville Spearman, 1968.

Rule, Ann (writing as Andy Stack) in *Lust Killer*, New York: Signet, 1983.

Rule, Ann. *The Stranger Beside Me*, New York: New American Library, 1980.

Schurman-Kauflin, Deborah. *The New Predator: Women Who Kill*, New York: Algora, 2000.

Seltzer, Mark. *Serial Killers: Death and Life in America's Wound Culture*, New York–London: Routledge, 1998.

Seneca. *De Clementia*.

Schwarz, Ted. *The Hillside Strangler: A Murderer's Mind*, New York: Signet, 1982.

Schwoebel, Richard L. *Explosion Aboard the Iowa*, Annapolis, Maryland: Naval Institute Press, 1999.

Theweleit, Klaus. *Male Fantasies*, Minneapolis: University of Minnesota Press, 1987.

Thompson, Charles C. *A Glimpse of Hell: The Explosion on the USS Iowa and Its Cover-up*, New York: W.W. Norton, 1999.

Thoreau, Henry David. *Walden*, New York: Signet Classic, 1999.

Wilson, Colin. *A Criminal History of Mankind*, New York: Carroll & Graff, 1990.

Wilson, Colin & Seaman, Donald. *The Serial Killers*, London: Virgin Publishing, 1994.

Wolf, Leonard. *Bluebeard: The Life and Crimes of Gilles de Rais*, New York: Clarkson N. Potter, 1980.

Wyden, Peter. *The Hired Killers*, New York: Bantam Books, 1963.

Academic Journals, Articles, Websites, Primary and Other Sources

American Law Institute, *Model Penal Code* § 4.01 (Propose Official Draft, 1962).

Archbold, Mike. *King Country Journal*, 8 November 2003. http:www.kingcountyjournal.com/sited/story/html/148405.

Best, J. "Missing children: Misleading Statistics," *The Public Interest*, No. 92, 1988.

Bond, Dr. Thomas. *Report*, 10 November 1888, Metropolitan Police File 3/140, *folio 220–223*, London.

Boros, Steven J. M.D., and Brubaker, Larry C. "Munchausen Syndrome by Proxy: Case Accounts," *FBI Law Enforcement Bulletin*, Washington, D.C.: June, 1992.

Canter, David, et al. "Predicting Serial Killers' Home Base Using a Decision Support System," *Journal of Quantitative Criminology*, Vol. 16, Nov. 4, 2000.

Chew, Kenneth, et al. "The Epidemiology of Child Homicide in California 1981–1990," *Homicide Studies*, Vol. 3 No. 2, May 1990.

Ciccone, J. Richard. *Murder, Insanity, and Medical Expert Witnesses*, 49 American Medical Association's Archives Neurology 608, 1992.

Crime Archives: http:www.mayhem.net.

Daniel M'Naghten's Case, 8 Eng. Rep. 718, 722 (H.L. 1843).

Dietz, P. E., Harry, B., Hazelwood, R. R. "Detective Magazines: Pornography for the Sexual Sadist?" *Journal of Forensic Sciences*, JFSCA, Vol. 31, No. 1, January 1986.

DiManno, Rosie. "Sniper Suspect Remembered as Clever, 'Obedient' Child," *Toronto Star*, Nov. 26, 2003.

Egger, Steven A. "Psychological Profiling: Past, Present, and Future," *Journal of Contemporary Criminal Justice*, Vol. 15 No. 3, August 1999.

———. "A Working Definition of Serial Murder and the Reductions of Linkage Blindness," *Journal of Police Science and Administration*, 12: 348–57. 1984.

Finkelhor, David, et al. "The Abduction of Children by Strangers and Nonfamily Members: Estimating the Incidence Using Multiple Methods," *Journal of Interpersonal Violence*, Vol. 7 No. 2, June 1992.

Fumento, Michael. Hudson Institute, *American Outlook*, Spring 2002. http:www. fumento.com/exploit.html.

FBI, *Preliminary Uniform Crime Report 2002*, June 16, 2003

FBI, *Uniform Crime Report 2001*, Washington, D.C.

Gill, John. "Missing Children: How Politics Helped Start the Scandal," FatherMag.com, 2000. http:www.fathermag.com/006/missing-children/abduction_2.shtml.

Hanon, Kathryn A. "Munchausen's Syndrome by Proxy" *FBI Law Enforcement Bulletin*, Washington, D.C.: December 1991.

Hazelwood, Robert, Reboussin, Roland, and Warren, Janet I. "Serial Rape: Correlates of Increased Aggression and the Relationship of Offender Pleasure to Victim Resistance," *Journal of Interpersonal Violence*, Vol. 4, No. 1, March 1989.

Homat, Robert J. & Kennedy, Daniel B. "Psychological Aspects of Crime Scene Profiling: Validity Research," *Criminal Justice and Behavior*, Vol. 25, No. 3, September 1998.

Inquest by Commissioners of the Duke of Brittany, September 18–October 8, 1440, National Archives of France, Call Number: 1 AP 585, originally from the Archive de la Trémoille.

Jenkins, Philip. "African-Americans and Serial Homicide," *American Journal of Criminal Justice*, 17(2), 1993.

Johnson, Gene. "Green River Killer May Contribute Little to Serial Killer Studies," The Associated Press, Nov. 9, 2003.

Keeney, B.T. & Heide, K. "Gender Differences in Serial Murderers," *Journal of Interpersonal Violence*, Vol. 9 No. 3, September 1994.

Keppel, Robert D. & Walter, Richard. "Profiling Killers: A Revised Classification Model for Understanding Sexual Murder," *International Journal of Offender Therapy and Comparative Criminology*, Vol. 43 No. 4, 1999.

Kocsis, Richard, et al. "Expertise in Psychological Profiling: A Comparative Assessment," *Journal of Interpersonal Violence,* Vol. 15, No. 3, March 2000.

———. "Investigative Experience and Accuracy in Psychological Profiling of a Violent Crime," *Journal of Interpersonal Violence,* Vol. 17 No. 8, August 2002.

MacPherson, Myra. "The Roots of Evil," *Vanity Fair,* May 1989.

Martens, W.H.J. "Marcel: A Case Study of a Violent Sexual Psychopath in Remission," *International Journal of Offender Therapy and Comparative Criminology,* 43(3) 1999.

Meehan, Brian. "Son of Cain or Son of Sam. The Monster As Serial Killer in *Beowulf,*" *Connecticut Review Fall 1994,* Connecticut State University.

Morrison, Dr. Helen. Forensic Psychiatrist, Evaluation Center, Chicago, *Mind of a Killer CD,* Kozel Multimedia, 1995–1998.

Muller, Damon. "Criminal Profiling: Real Science or Just Wishful Thinking?," *Homicide Studies,* Vol. 4 No. 3, August 2000.

Murray, H. A. "Studies of Stressful Interpersonal Disputations," *American Psychologist,* Vol. 18, No. 1, January 1963.

Prentky, R., Burgess, A. & Carter, D. "Victim Responses by Rapist Type: An Empirical and Clinical Analysis," *Journal of Interpersonal Violence, 1,* 1986.

Quinsey, V. & Upfold, D. "Rape Completion and Victim Injury As a Function of Female Resistance Strategy," *Canadian Journal of Behavioral Science, 17,* 1985.

Riedel, Mark. "Counting Stranger Homicides," *Homicide Studies,* Vol. 2, No. 2, May 1998.

Reisner, Andrew, et al. "The Inpatient Treatment and Evaluation of a Self-Professed Budding Serial Killer," *International Journal of Offender Therapy and Comparative Criminology,* 47(1) 2003.

Ressler, Robert K., et al, "Sexual Killers and Their Victims: Identifying Patterns Through Crime Scene Analysis," *Journal of Interpersonal Violence,* Vol. 1 No. 3, September 1986.

Sperry, Paul. "D.C. Sniper Terror," *WorldNetDaily.com,* Oct. 25, 2002.

Turvey, Brent E. MS. *The Impressions of a Man: An Objective Forensic Guideline to Profiling Violent Serial Sex Offenders,* http:www.corpus-delicti.com/impress.html, Nov. 9, 1997.

U.S. Department of Justice, Press Release, *Crime in the United States,* FBI National Press Office, Washington, D.C. : Oct. 13, 1996.

U.S. House of Representatives, *Review of Navy Investigation of U.S.S.* Iowa *Explosion,* Joint Hearings before the Investigations Subcommittee and the Defense Policy Panel of the Committee on Armed Services, Dec. 12, 13, and 21, 1989.

U.S. House of Representatives, *U.S.S.* Iowa *Tragedy: An Investigative Failure.* Report of the Investigations Subcommittee and Defense Policy Panel of the Committee on Armed Services, March 5, 1990.

Wesheit, R. A. "Female Homicide Offenders: Trends Over Time In An Institutionalized Population," *Justice Quarterly,* Vol. 1, No. 4, 1984.

Witkins, Gordon. "Did the FBI Ignore the 'Tafoya Profile'?," *U.S. News & World Report,* Nov. 17, 1997.

Index